O9-ABH-018

GRACE LIBRARY CARLOW COLLEGE
PITTSBURGH PA 15213

MEASURING CORPORATE ENVIRONMENTAL PERFORMANCE

Best Practices for Costing and Managing an Effective Environmental Strategy

Marc J. Epstein, Ph.D.
Graduate School of Business
Stanford University

HD
30.255
E67
1996

A research study carried out on behalf of
The IMA Foundation for Applied Research, Inc.
Research Affiliate of the Institute of Management Accountants
Montvale, New Jersey

IRWIN
Professional Publishing®

Chicago • London • Singapore

CATALOGUED

Recycled/Recyclable
Printed on paper that contains
at least 50% recycled fiber

Co-published with
The IMA Foundation for Applied Research, Inc.
10 Paragon Drive
Montvale, NJ 07645-1760
(800) 638-4427

The IMA Foundation for Applied Research, Inc. (FAR) is the research affiliate of the Institute of Management Accountants. The mission of the Foundation is to develop and disseminate timely management accounting research findings that can be applied to current and emerging business issues.

Edited by Claire Barth, senior editor, FAR

IMA Publication No. 236-95301
© The IMA Foundation for Applied Research, Inc., 1996
All rights reserved. No part of this publication may be reproduced, stored in a retrieval system, or transmitted, in any form or by any means, electronic, mechanical, photocopying, recording, or otherwise, without the prior written permission of the publisher.

This publication is designed to provide accurate and authoritative information in regard to the subject matter covered. It is sold with the understanding that neither the author nor the publisher is engaged in rendering legal, accounting, or other professional service. If legal advice or other expert assistance is required, the services of a competent professional person should be sought.

From a Declaration of Principles jointly adopted by a Committee of the American Bar Association and a Committee of Publishers.

Irwin Professional Book Team

Executive editor: *Amy Hollands Gaber*
Marketing manager: *Brian Hayes*
Production supervisor: *Lara Feinberg*
Senior desktop production supervisor: *Andrea Rosenberg*
Manager, direct marketing: *Rebecca S. Gordon*
Project editor: *Christina Thornton-Villagomez*
Senior designer: *Heidi J. Baughman*
Compositor: *ZGraphics, Ltd.*
Typeface: *11/13 Times Roman*
Printer: *Quebecor Book Group*

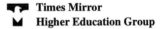 **Times Mirror**
Higher Education Group

Library of Congress Cataloging-in-Publication Data

Epstein, Marc J.
   Measuring corporate environmental performance : best practices for
costing and managing an effective environmental strategy / Marc J.
Epstein.
     p   cm.
   Includes index.
   ISBN 0–7863–0230–5
   1. Industrial management—Environmental aspects. 2. Strategic
planning—Environmental aspects—Cost effectiveness. I. Title.
HD30.255.E67   1996
658.4'08—dc20   95–20807

Printed in the United States of America
  2 3 4 5 6 7 8 9 0 Q 2 1 0 9 8 7 6

Foreword

Corporate practice in the environmental area is at a crossroads. After decades of contention among environmentalists, regulators, and companies, a fundamental rethinking of the relationship between the environment and industry is underway. Many still hold the view that environmental improvement and company (and industry) competitiveness represent a zero sum game. Some environmentalists, for example, believe that the earth and its biodiversity must be protected at any cost. Conversely, some in business—instinctively opposed to any form of government regulation as wasteful and ineffective—seek to thwart environmental regulation at every turn and even dismantle it. Who has the upper hand in this struggle depends on the political party in power, the state of the economy, and the latest scandal.

A new view is emerging, however, which frames the issue in a very different way. Instead of seeing environmental improvement and company competitiveness as an inevitable tradeoff, this new view seeks to reconcile them. While protecting the earth is essential, the new view does not resort to emotional appeals about saving the planet as its driving motivation. Instead, environmental improvement is seen as the process of reducing waste, improving the efficiency with which a company uses inputs, and, ultimately, raising the productivity with which companies and hence society use natural resources.

In this emerging view, innovation takes center stage. Reacting to environmental regulation gives way to rethinking company activities so as to anticipate or be unaffected by regulations. The company's task, in the new view, is not simply to employ armies of lawyers and regulatory affairs professionals to ensure compliance but to embed the opportunity cost of environmental impacts into the strategy development and operational improvement process.

There is still a good deal of skepticism about and resistance to the new view. Accustomed to lengthy and frustrating struggles with regulators about compliance, companies have a difficult time seeing environmental improvement as anything more than a tradeoff with "normal" operations.

Among the most prominent barriers to the new thinking, however, is an information gap. Most companies lack information about the direct costs of dealing with obvious discharges, much less a comprehensive understanding of all their environmental impacts and the opportunity cost of poorly utilizing company resources.

In this book, Marc Epstein makes an important contribution to closing this information gap. Based on an array of fascinating case studies, Epstein shows us best practices in measuring and controlling environmental performance in some of the world's great companies. He provides specific, practical, and actionable tools for understanding environmental costs, evaluating environmentally related capital investments, and measuring environmental performance.

All companies face a choice. They can continue to struggle to eliminate or relax environmental regulations, and can continue to view good environmental performance as a cost. Alternatively, companies can seek competitive advantage in cost and quality from innovative solutions to minimizing or eliminating environmental impacts. Epstein's book provides some of the important tools to make this transition.

This book, along with others, promises to hasten the time when thinking and company practice in the area of the environment will be transformed. If more companies (and environmentalists) can embrace the paradigm of innovation, and design measurement and control systems accordingly, then progress in improving our environment will be far more rapid and the cost to the economy will be minimized or even eliminated altogether.

Michael E. Porter
Harvard Business School

Perspectives

A CEO'S PERSPECTIVE

In 1989, when I became chairman and CEO of DuPont, the first major speech that I gave was in London. In my remarks there, I said that CEO stood not only for "chief executive officer," but also for "chief environmental officer." I challenged DuPont and the others in the industry to focus on "corporate environmentalism," which I defined as "an attitude and performance commitment that place corporate environmental stewardship fully in line with public desires and expectations." That meant going beyond regulations and reducing the environmental impact of our products and processes voluntarily.

We have made much progress since that time, and last year we took an important next step in our corporate Commitment to Safety, Health, and the Environment. We stated that our goal is zero not only for injuries, illnesses, and incidents but also for emissions and waste.

The commitment to a "zero" standard is a logical extension of corporate environmentalism. It is not just an environmental objective, it is a business objective. It is a way to ensure that we consider environmental objectives in everything we do. Concern for the environment has become part of the concept, design, and implementation of every project. Our business success now depends on it.

The environmental integration discussed in this book is what DuPont and many other companies around the world are already practicing. We are striving to integrate environmental information into decision making. We design processes, products, and packaging with environmental values and objectives in mind. We anticipate environmental trends to find the most cost-effective solutions to regulatory requirements, pollution prevention, and source reduction. We no longer view the environment and business as two different topics, let alone competing topics.

That understanding is necessary if we in business hope to make significant contributions to sustainable development. At DuPont we have concluded that substantial development will not occur from the top down. We believe that sustainable development has to be generated one household, one manufacturing plant, one community at a time. If we can take care of local problems, many of the big environmental problems we face will take care of themselves.

But we can't continue to do the same things the same way and expect different results. To sustain our communities, we have to see the local community as an ecology in which the natural and human communities are in relationship. At DuPont we call this "local sustainability." The ideal we are striving for is to have our plant sites operate in harmony with the community. In a figurative sense, we are moving toward a "boundary-less" plant where information, understanding, concerns, and people flow freely between the plant and its surroundings.

We are also convinced that long-term environmental protection will only take place in the context of economic growth and competitiveness. Economic competitiveness is part of local sustainability. A community has to be competitive educationally, economically, and in other ways, to attract investment that provides jobs and income. Economic growth, environmental protection, and educational systems must be addressed together as part of a vision of sustainability.

Achieving and maintaining an acceptable standard of living for all the world's people will require a high and continuously rising level of industrial productivity. It has become clear, however, that the future belongs to those companies that see environmental protection as an integral and valued condition for global growth and success.

E. S. Woolard, Jr.
Chairman and CEO
E.I. du Pont de Nemours & Company

A REGULATOR'S PERSPECTIVE

The past few years have encompassed an important shift in the environmental priority and sophistication of many large corporations. There are many reasons why a number of companies have begun to take the environment very seriously, reorganizing functional responsibilities, engaging the most senior executives in environmental oversight, elevating decision making about environmental commitments, spending substantial amounts of money to go well beyond compliance with laws, and redesigning whole systems of resource use and production. Liabilities both criminal and civil, the fear of exposure as an obstructionist polluter, concern to attract environmentally conscious engineers and scientists, a sense of responsibility to neighbors and customers, all of these are involved. But fundamentally, a transformation of public values has occurred and no one is immune. Edwin Artzt, former chairman of Procter & Gamble, made this clear to me during my time at EPA a few years ago when he proudly displayed a selection of his company's new green consumer products—highly absorbent compostable diapers, energy-conserving detergent concentrates, recyclable plastic containers—and then observed, "All these things we're doing, we're not doing them for you or because laws make us do them. Our customers are demanding that we do them!"

And so we are. Consumer products companies were first to get the message. Manufacturers, however, particularly in the chemical industry, have also gotten it. The stunning success of U.S. EPA's voluntary toxic reduction program, 33/50, through which industry has reduced its releases of 17 high priority toxic substances by 50 percent in five years, has confirmed that there is environmental statesmanship in American industry. Half of the nationwide 1988 levels of releases of such toxics as cadmium, cyanide, mercury, benzene, and lead, some 700 million pounds worth, all legal releases under the law, are no more. Other achievements of responsible, committed companies are also notable: DuPont's commitment to phase out manufacture of chlorofluorocarbons a year earlier than required and to discontinue deep-well injections of acids, Monsanto's reduction of 90 percent of its air toxics, 3M's development of a new heat transfer process to substitute for methyl chloride, an ozone depleter.

We have reached the point where, for major companies, the pertinent questions concern how to organize environmental responsibilities, where to concentrate capital expenditures for maximum environmental benefit, how to develop substitutes for persistent bioaccumulative chemicals, how to ensure not just clean manufacture but also safe disposal, how to redesign processes to come as close as possible to zero pollution, and increasingly, how to make money from clean products. The chairman of one company with a large number of unresolved Superfund sites was able, a few years ago, to commit on liability levels and remedy selection on a good proportion of them in one highly productive six-month period. I asked him what had occurred to break the logjam. "I took the matter away from the lawyers," he said, "and I gave it to the plant managers and engineers." The response mode changed from minimizing legal and financial exposure to practical technical problem solving in the shortest possible time. 3M Company developed its breakthrough in adhesive manufacture by requiring that any budgeting outlay involving continued reliance on ozone depleting chemicals, and any research project proposals to explore alternatives, be elevated to a high-level executive review group, which gave its OK to spending extra funds on a concept that paid off.

From the perspective of a regulator, I should say that corporations may sometimes underestimate the value of a good reputation. I can recall a number of occasions when as EPA administrator I was moved to obtain a change in legislation or regulation because of a persuasive critique by a company with an outstanding record for environmental performance. I can also recall instances where something went wrong at a good company and regulators and enforcers gave the corporation the benefit of the doubt. What our mothers taught us about the value of a good name is still true. Once earned it is very valuable.

Marc Epstein digs into the details of corporate environmental responses. His focus is on where the environmental action now is in American corporations. The achievement of a corporate transformation involves a unifying, all-engaging set of responses not unlike what is entailed in total quality management. Commitment and clear communication of goals and objectives at the top, active enlistment of middle managers and empowerment to rethink and reinvent, openness to better ways to consult and serve the various customers, help to vendors and suppliers to upscale their performance—all of these are necessary.

The task of cleaning up America and pointing our companies to a qualitatively different and cleaner future is not finished, but it is well underway. Epstein understands and explains what's entailed. He chronicles one of the most successful of modern American economic achievements, the steady and progressive and increasingly remunerative integration of environmental goals and economic objectives.

William K. Reilly
Texas Pacific Group
Former Administrator–U.S.
Environmental Protection Agency

AN ENVIRONMENTALIST'S PERSPECTIVE

Those who spend a significant part of their lives as I do, focusing on the uphill battle of ensuring that our Earth's resources are preserved more or less intact for our descendants, often despair at how few people sustain interest in the environment as they move about in the process of their day-to-day existence. Food, shelter, and family represent urgent needs that usurp concern for trees, soil, or oceans for most of us, especially if they are not met. Tragically, many people on the planet will never meet those urgent fundamental needs. But in the developed world, where more of the population should be able to think beyond the next meal to global community tradeoffs, "enlightened self-interest" does not always translate into preserving the natural resources we all share. This is true in spite of the fact that it is the Earth that bore us and the Earth that provides the wherewithal to sustain both commercial and individual well-being.

The Coalition for Environmentally Responsible Economics (CERES), which I am privileged to help lead, has worked together for over five years believing that manufacturing and service businesses can make a difference in this struggle, and that it is short-sighted and in the long run suicidal if they do not take a leading role in the fight to ensure that our resources are not squandered. CERES members, who include investment professionals and environmental and other stakeholder groups, introduced the idea of an environmental ethic, or vision statement, in 1989, originally called the Valdez Principles and now called the CERES Principles. The Principles are intended to capture the broad brush, global issues with which commerce must concern itself. CERES encourages individual companies to adopt them and to use them to develop an environmental management system. The Principles would lose their ability to sustain effort through the ebbing and flowing of popular interest in the environment, however, if companies were not willing and able to annually report on progress to their various publics.

To ensure that we don't squander our precious ecological capital, many people in business and in non-profit environmental service have in fact become convinced that thousands of daily business decisions will have to be made in a dramatically different way than we are accustomed. The choices confronted will include the decisions from the boards of directors' long-range corporate planning to daily operational choices for the staff of both large and small business entities. Projections of costs that include environmental changes of all kinds must be developed and ways to use them perfected. Public preferences and market competition must somehow be anticipated as well as possible. All planning must be flexible to accommodate large and small ecosystem idiosyncrasies, technology and knowledge advances, and changing political environments. For businesses to become efficient and effective environmental managers, there will have to be nothing less than a revolution in thought and practice.

Since about 1970, environmental management has largely been conducted in response to regulation. Regulation generally has been promulgated in response to public outcry over practices that cause harm to the environment. Regulation and the corporate response to regulation have thus been trapped in permanent crisis management, with little private/public trust and a default to antagonism when problems must be solved. Utopian sustainable economic activity would move corporations, in Marc Epstein's words, "to be crisis prepared rather than crisis prone." In fact, crises should be minimized if corporate management can effectively foresee environmental impacts and plan to avoid the negative.

As corporate planners and operations personnel see and manage more of their environmental future, the collection of data for planning and self-management purposes will become more extensive and sophisticated. Dr. Epstein helps this cause by collecting best corporate practices and commenting on their relative effectiveness. Though there is no single corporate model in the book that encompasses all the various pieces of environmental accounting, such as incentive systems for personnel, capital budgeting planning, or the effective costing of the life-cycle impacts of products, assembled together in one place the multiple examples comprise a very complete picture of the best ecological accounting system as it exists today. This is a natural and valuable complement to the process of public reporting that CERES continues to develop with the CERES companies.

To his credit, Marc Epstein does not present these visionary, if a bit anecdotal, systems as the perfect models for the future, but presents this as a work in progress. In fact, utopia might include widespread use of intelligent ecological management systems built upon data collected that gives managers a picture of the environmental impact of all corporate activities, both global and local, combined with capital and profit planning systems that discount both internal ecological costs and external costs.

The total environmental accounting system would then culminate in a digestible, widely disseminated public information system, such as that which CERES promotes.

The adversarial climate of the past was fueled by lack of information. Environmentalists often did not understand challenges that business faces in balancing multiple interests, such as the environment, job creation, and financial survival, and business often chose to ignore the environmental consequences of its actions. Information and a complete accounting system can bring more understanding of these challenges to all sides of the debate. There is a natural tension between various competing interests, but that tension does not have to be destructive; it can be creative.

This book should serve as a good beginning or a strong foundation: a point of departure. As is clear from the examples cited, we have both the intelligence and the tools to build an exciting new management system. And, we hope, a sustainable economic future.

Joan Bavaria
President, Franklin Research
& Development Corp.
Co-Chair and CEO of CERES

A CERTIFIED MANAGEMENT ACCOUNTANT'S (CMA) PERSPECTIVE

Environmental stewardship is a critical business tool. When environmental solutions are included as an additional, complementary corporate strategy, businesses can satisfy economic and environmental goals by dealing with environmental issues effectively. Reducing waste in the delivery pipeline and in product design, usage, and disposal means eliminating costs to businesses and society. It's that simple. The challenge lies in the way we think and do.

Using intelligent technology combined with a forward form of thinking requires encouragement of desired behavior and attitudes that may not be supported by some traditional systems and protocols. More "out of box" and purposeful thinking, especially by the accounting community, will further enable innovative scientists and managers to design for the future while achieving success today. The management accountant's role has a direct impact on the success of achieving these strategic environmental objectives. Marc Epstein's research provides a comprehensive reference for the accounting community (indeed for all functions) to simplify the basic understanding of what can be a complex subject.

Businesses are beginning to incorporate the more rewarding responsibilities and skills of business consultants into accounting's traditional business monitoring activities. More emphasis is being placed on managerial accounting, correlated to the environmental paradigm shift that society and business have been making. A focus on improving managerial accounting skills and tools inevitably will enhance the results of external reporting disclosures. To accomplish this result, the accounting community needs to understand the fundamental issues, the language, and the factors involved. We also need to use the best tools for measurement, the best problem-solving methods, and the best decision models offered today and avoid becoming locked onto those tools when better ones are offered. Dr. Epstein's research and recommendations do much to provide the accounting profession the means to accelerate this process and learning.

As Dr. Epstein points out, today's best available tools and methods include standards of the International Organization for Standardization (ISO), total quality management, activity-based cost management, and life cycle cost management. Using these tools provides information, especially environmentally related information, for making the best business decisions, to assist in identifying desired behavior, and to expedite the changes needed.

To quote Bob Allen, AT&T's CEO and chief advocate of environmental stewardship, "the environment affects all of us and it will take all of us to protect it. Designing for the environment is a key in distinguishing our processes, products, and services." In our conversion to strategic environmentalism, AT&T's vision includes fully integrating life cycle environmental consequences into each of our business decisions and activities. AT&T's commitment for today and tomorrow is evident through our Design for Environment (DFE) team and a newly created Environmental Law and Compliance office. Among the DFE subteams is the Green Accounting Team, a multifunctional, globally represented team whose charter is to integrate environmental considerations into AT&T's accounting policies, practices, and tools.

As multifunctional teams across the world engage in discovering solutions, management accountants are assisting in identifying relationships across structural boundaries, learning with other team members, and getting excited about helping create a business environment that emphasizes sustainable development while achieving economic and customer-delighting goals.

Jeannie Wood, CMA
(Dayton Chapter of the Institute of
Management Accountants)
Green Accounting Team Leader
Business Planning & Analysis
 Global Manufacturing
World Headquarters, AT&T

Preface

This book is about business. It was written by a former business executive and current business professor and researcher and focuses on actions business executives must take for the sake of good business. This book is about the effective use of resources in business—capital, labor, and raw materials—and how business executives can manage these resources more effectively in a changing society.

This book is not about government policy or appropriate government regulations in the area of environmental management. It is not an attempt to make business executives into environmentalists. Rather, it is an outline of how companies can and must respond to the growing need for more effective management of available resources. It is a plan for action that leads to the consideration of the environmental impacts of company products, services, and activities and the benefits of sustainable development. It shows a way to more broadly consider the interactions of companies with their various stakeholders. Including these considerations in the decision-making process produces more efficient and effective corporations that are both more profitable and more environmentally responsible. This approach is beneficial without regard to the political party in power or the regulatory climate in existence at any particular time.

Managing resources well can benefit the environment, the community, and the corporation. Further, better management of corporate environmental performance can improve international competitiveness. But these benefits can be achieved only if environmentally related expenditures are seen properly as corporate strategic investments and if environmental responsibility and corporate environmental strategy are integrated into the corporate culture. This integration requires a commitment from executives at all levels in the organization and especially in departments of EH&S (environment, health, and safety), accounting/finance, and operations. Unless all three of these departments are committed to the corporate environmental strategy, corporate pronouncements by the chief executive are likely to remain only hollow mission statements.

The need to integrate environmental impacts into management decision making is not driven by environmental activists, current social trends, or public relations. It is driven by the fact that environmental costs are a very large and rapidly growing corporate expense. These costs can be contained only by the development of information systems that measure, monitor, and report environmental costs and benefits.

Corporations were caught unprepared to alter their approach to environmental management. Decisions related to environmental impacts had been reactive to environmental regulations rather than proactive to environmental planning. Corporate expenditures for pollution prevention and pollution control equipment were guided by views of current and future compliance requirements rather than by any thinking about possible benefits that might help produce a positive return on investment for the company. But with the significant increase in the scope of those costs, corporate executives saw they needed to view environmental management in a more strategic way. EH&S executives realized that better information and better techniques would help them make more informed choices among capital improvements, process improvements, and product improvements. Should they minimize capital investments to meet current environmental regulations, or should they increase capital investments for improved equipment that might be better suited to meet possible future requirements?

Executives needed help in understanding which past, present, and future environmental costs should be included in product costs. They had to manage the growing environmental staff and costs and discover incentives that would motivate employees throughout the organization to act in environmentally responsible ways. They wanted help from the corporation's management accountants but found that the accounting community had just started to address these issues.

This study has been directed to provide answers to this problem. It was gratifying to observe the rapid changes in corporate environmental practices even during the time that this project was being conducted. With the rapidly growing interest in these issues, substantial developments and improvements are occurring continually.

But this book is also about the environment. On the 25th anniversary of Earth Day it may be that environmentalists, regulators, and business executives are finally coming together to solve problems that are fundamental to our society. They are beginning to recognize that sustainable development is in the interests of all constituents and is necessary for both business and the environment to thrive. I am pleased that Michael Porter agreed to write the Foreword and that Ed Woolard, Joan Bavaria, and Bill Reilly provided their perspectives. At the core of this work is the idea that all constituents' interests must be considered. This book recognizes that the ultimate goal is concurrent engineering, which integrates environmental considerations into all design decisions. Its multifunctional approach demands that accounting, legal, operations, engineering, and others consider the environmental and financial impacts of a company's products, services, and activities. It requires the examination of the impacts through the entire product life cycle.

Companies need to view environmental impacts as opportunities to improve business performance and create environmental assets (goodwill). They should view efforts to reduce environmental impacts in the context of continuous improvement and use this book to help benchmark their performance. It is hoped that this research will help companies move in the direction of corporate sustainable development, which in the long run will help reduce corporate environmental impacts and costs and increase long-term corporate profitability.

Marc J. Epstein
Stanford, California

Publisher's Notes

The environmental movement is no longer considered a fad. Consumers are more responsive to environmental concerns when they buy, use, and recycle products. Corporations are recognizing that reducing environmental impacts will benefit the community and their long-term profitability. Environmental protection has become big business.

Corporations need to develop environmental strategies to remain competitive:

- They need to learn how to measure, report, and manage environmental impacts.
- They need to find better ways to measure past, present, and future environmental costs and benefits.
- They need specific guidance on how to implement a corporate environmental policy.

Dr. Marc Epstein of the Graduate School of Business at Stanford University undertook a study to discover how corporations are dealing with environmental impacts. His field research included reviews of the internal and public documents of more than 100 leading corporations and visits to more than 30 of them. The resulting research study gives details of state-of-the-art and best-in-class corporate environmental measurement and reporting. It describes innovative approaches some companies have used in implementing a corporate environmental policy.

Guidance in the preparation of this report was generously provided by the Project Committee of The IMA Foundation for Applied Research, Inc. (FAR):

Paul P. Danesi, Jr.
Project Chair
Texas Instruments
Attleboro, Massachusetts

Robert J. Melby
Defense Contract Audit Agency
Smyrna, Georgia

Anthony A. Varricchio, CMA
Dexter Nonwovens
Windsor Locks, Connecticut

Kenneth Merchant
University of Southern California
Los Angeles, California

David Vogel
Consultant
Wilmington, Delaware

The Foundation is the research affiliate of the Institute of Management Accountants. The mission of the Foundation is to develop and disseminate timely management accounting research findings that can be applied to current and emerging business issues.

FAR's environmental research project is expected to lead also to the issuance of multifaceted guidance for the management accountant. As this publication goes to press, IMA's Management Accounting Committee (MAC) has under consideration draft documents dealing with *Implementing Corporate Environmental Strategies* and *Tools and Techniques for Environmental Accounting*. A successor to the Management Accounting Practices Committee, MAC is IMA's senior technical committee charged with responsibility for approving authoritative management accounting guidance.

This report reflects the views of the researcher and not necessarily those of the Foundation, the IMA, or the Project Committee.

Julian M. Freedman, CMA, CPA, CPIM
Director of Research
The IMA Foundation for Applied Research, Inc.

Acknowledgments

This project began as a study that was to examine the implementation of environmental accounting in three companies. It expanded into a comprehensive look at the state of the art and best practices of corporate environmental management through the examination of documents from more than 100 companies and interviews or field visits to more than 30.

A project of this scope could not have been completed without the help of many individuals and companies. To them I offer my deepest appreciation. Though the list of people who provided guidance and support numbers in the hundreds, I would like to single out a few who provided extensive support.

Archie Dunham, Paul Tebo, and Dale Martin at the DuPont Company, Martin Smith at Niagara Mohawk Power, and Tom Hellman at Bristol-Myers Squibb, in addition to giving me access to company personnel and records, provided significant insight into the way they think about environmental management issues. Ladd Greeno at Arthur D. Little and Tom White at Arthur Andersen, LLP, provided substantial insight as to the frameworks their firms are using with clients to improve the quality of environmental management. At each company that provided information for this research, many executives and staff personnel from areas as diverse as accounting, operations, legal, engineering, finance, and environment, health, and safety gave of their precious time to aid in this project by providing internal company documents and access to personnel and processes.

Special thanks goes to The IMA Foundation for Applied Research, Inc. (FAR) and IMA's Director of Research Julian M. Freedman, without whose support this research project could not have been accomplished. The FAR Project Committee, chaired by Paul Danesi at Texas Instruments, made numerous constructive comments on the various drafts of the manuscript. Claire Barth, senior editor at IMA, improved the manuscript immeasurably with her skillful editing. Of course, any errors remain with the author. It is FAR's concern for management accounting research that will improve the quality of accounting, management, and operations to benefit business and society.

Special thanks to my colleagues at the Harvard Business School and Stanford Business School, especially Bob Kaplan, Bill Bruns, and Krishna Palepu at Harvard and Srikant Datar at Stanford. They have given me inspiration, a more complete understanding of the general manager's perspective, better comprehension of the challenges, methods, and benefits of field-based research, and significant insights on management accounting and its role in improving corporate environmental management practices.

Dr. Stephen A. Book, a long-time friend and trusted research colleague, has guided me as to appropriate statistical methods and aided me in finding the appropriate research approaches to properly answer the various questions that engaged me throughout my career.

A special thank you goes to Michael Porter, Ed Woolard, Joan Bavaria, and Bill Reilly for providing their perspectives on this important subject. Their comments reflect a growing consensus that increased corporate concern for reducing the environmental impacts of corporate products, services, and activities and striving for sustainable development will improve both the environment and long-term corporate profitability. This book attempts to provide the guidance to corporations to aid them in those efforts.

Finally, I thank three women who have been important to all aspects of my life: Joanne, Deborah, and Judith. Joanne has provided research assistance and all three have provided emotional support, affection, and joy for more than 25 years. It is to Joanne, Deborah, and Judith that this book is dedicated.

About the Author

Marc J. Epstein is at present visiting professor in the Graduate School of Business at Stanford University. Dr. Epstein received his Ph.D. from the University of Oregon. Most recently he has taught at Harvard Business School and previously was Joseph Kerzner Professor of Accounting at Yeshiva University and a professor at UCLA, USC, and California State University.

In 1973, Dr. Epstein was director of social measurement services at Abt Associates, Inc., the first company to produce a corporate social audit. Since that time he has conducted numerous projects and written two books related to corporate social and environmental performance.

Dr. Epstein has had a continuing relationship with the IMA over a long period of time. He was coauthor of *Corporate Social Performance: The Measurement of Product and Service Contributions*, published by the NAA (as the IMA was then called) in 1977. He has written a number of articles for *Management Accounting*. Most recently he wrote an exposure draft for a Management Accounting Guideline, "Implementing Corporate Environmental Strategies," for the Society of Management Accountants of Canada (SMAC). This draft, based on his book, is expected to become an IMA Statement on Management Accounting (SMA).

Dr. Epstein is the author of more than 50 professional papers and a dozen books and is currently editor-in-chief of *Advances in Management Accounting*. He also has written articles for popular press, including *The New York Times*, and has lectured extensively to various audiences on financial and environmental management topics. He has had broad industry experience and has been a consultant to business and government for more than 20 years.

Executive Summary

MOTIVATION FOR THE STUDY

In the 25 years since the first Earth Day, the environmental movement has matured. It no longer is considered a fad, of interest only to students and avid environmentalists. Instead, governments, corporations, and individuals finally are recognizing the benefits of environmental sensitivity, and environmental progress is occurring. Consumers are more responsive to environmental concerns in their purchasing, use, and recycling decisions. Corporations are recognizing the benefits to the community and to their long-term corporate profitability of reducing environmental impacts. Green consciousness has increased partly because of an increased concern for the fragility of the environment and partly because of increased regulation and regulatory enforcement. Environmental protection also has become big business, with estimates of the size of the global business in pollution control and remediation equipment in the hundreds of billions of dollars. Environmental protection and economic growth have become closely aligned, both in the growth of the environmental technologies business and the movement to redesign processes to reduce environmental impacts, improve production efficiency, and reduce costs.

The rapid growth of corporate environmental expenditures also has dramatically changed the landscape of environmentalism in corporations. Most major corporations are spending in the tens of millions of dollars annually on environmental costs, with the larger ones spending in the hundreds of millions and some spending more than $1 billion per year. Environmental, Health, and Safety departments in corporations (which will be referred to as EH&S throughout the book regardless of any particular corporate label) have grown substantially in both size and importance, and the significance of their decisions has increased dramatically.

Corporations must make choices among capital improvements, process improvements, and product improvements. They must decide about various capital expenditures, considering changing environmental regulations, changing technology, and the changing cost of technology. EH&S departments are attempting to develop the financial and analytical skills to evaluate these alternatives. They are determining the technologies available elsewhere in their organizations that can be transferred to EH&S.

Both the accounting and environmental areas are concerned about how to measure, report, and manage environmental impacts. Standard measurement techniques, reporting formats, and audit protocols do not exist for corporate environmental performance. As companies have been trying to improve their management of environmental impacts, they have found they need better systems for integrating the measurement of these impacts into the various organizational systems—product costing, capital investments, performance evaluations, and product design. They need better ways to measure past, present, and future environmental costs and benefits.

This book is intended to provide specific guidance to corporate executives on approaches to implementing a corporate environmental policy. It relies on field research that reviewed internal and public documents of more than 100 leading corporations and interviews and visits to more than 30. The study included an investigation of both the state of the art and the best in class of corporate environmental measurement and reporting along with academic approaches to the development of applicable models. This extensive investigation involved more than two years of extensive reviews and visits.

SCORING CORPORATE ENVIRONMENTAL PERFORMANCE

The project began as an attempt to document the practices of corporations that had complete systems for effectively identifying, measuring, monitoring, reporting, and managing environmental impacts. Though I discovered no companies that at present have such a comprehensive system, many do have a wide diversity of corporate practices that constitute important building blocks of such a system (see Exhibit ES–1). At the lowest level, some companies have not developed any environmental policy or strategy or even any systematic way of thinking about or managing their environmental impacts. In many cases, this lack of corporate environmental sensitivity is evidence of companies that:

EXHIBIT ES–1
Corporate Environmental Performance Scorecard

TEN COMPONENTS OF CORPORATE ENVIRONMENTAL INTEGRATION		MEASURES OF ENVIRONMENTAL LEADERSHIP
1. Development of a corporate environmental strategy	CORPORATE ENVIRONMENTAL LEADER	1.0 Implementation of corporate environmental strategy Significant integration of corporate environmental impacts into management decisions Moving toward sustainable development
2. Integrating environmental concerns into product design systems		
3. Systems for identifying, organizing, and managing environmental impacts		2.0 Significant progress in at least five components and at least modest progress in two others
4. Information systems for internal reporting		3.0 Significant progress in at least three or four components and modest progress in at least two others
5. Internal environmental auditing systems		
		4.0 Modest progress in at least three or four components and some progress in at least two others
6. External environmental reporting and external environmental audits		
		5.0 Development of environmental goals Beginnings of an action plan Some progress in at least one or two components
7. Costing systems		
8. Capital budgeting systems		
9. Integrating environmental impacts into performance evaluation systems		6.0 Development of approach to environmental problems but with compliance orientation Minimal sensitivity to corporate environmental impacts
10. Implementing a corporate environmental strategy		
	CORPORATE ENVIRONMENTAL LAGGARD	7.0 No recognition of environmental impacts and minimal compliance with regulations Continuous violations of regulations

- Are crisis prone rather than crisis prepared;
- Produce environmental impacts that have substantial future environmental consequences involving increased costs, increased community concerns, and damaged reputation;

- Decrease current and future corporate profitability through decreased revenues and increased costs.

Negative environmental impacts have tarnished the reputations of many of these corporate environmental laggards. The poor public perception of the companies, along with financial analysts' concerns about pending environmental liabilities, has caused their stock prices to be lower and cost of capital to be higher than for comparable, more environmentally responsible companies.

In the middle of this scale are companies that have recognized environmental problems, developed a corporate mission statement, and made progress toward defining a policy that confronts the problems. These companies have developed partial systems to deal with environmental problems and may have transferred technologies from other parts of their companies to use in the growing environmental arena. They may have set up environmental systems for improved costing, capital budgeting, performance evaluations, product design, or recycling but likely have not developed an integrated program. They probably have not linked the environmental information related to waste and toxicity to the essential financial and operational decisions made on a daily basis.

At the highest level are corporate environmental leaders that have fully integrated environmental information into the management decision-making process. This integration involves identifying, measuring, reporting, monitoring, and managing environmental impacts. The impacts include both costs and benefits and managing them effectively requires tracking present environmental impacts and estimating future ones. Reporting environmental impacts has two parts: internal reporting for improved management decisions and external reporting for better accountability to the various stakeholders of the firm. Adequate external reporting allows owners and potential investors to do more accurate analysis and make more informed decisions.

In my research, I have seen no company that has achieved the highest level, but I have seen numerous companies that are making serious efforts to develop and implement environmental strategies. These companies recognize the competitive advantages they can gain by examining capital improvements, process improvements, and product improvements. They see the current advantages in the reuse and recycling of materials. They also recognize the benefits of integrating the likely future impact of the ultimate responsibility for post-consumer waste, along with other likely future environmental costs, into current product costing and product pricing decisions. Even when the integration is not complete, identifying and analyzing the future costs and benefits of projects and products and performing a life cycle assessment have proved extremely beneficial in reducing future environmental costs and rethinking general corporate strategies in addition to a particular environmental strategy.

The corporate environmental performance score measured in Exhibit ES–1 and repeated as Exhibit 11–1, is more a predictor of future environmental performance than a measure of past performance. (The measures are described more fully in Exhibit 11–2.) When managers and analysts evaluate the systems being developed and already in organizations they can assess both environmental and fiscal responsibility and indicators of future environmental liabilities. These 10 components and systems correspond directly to the material covered in detail in Chapters 2 to 11 of this book. These 10 chapters summarize both the state of the art and best corporate practices in each of these areas. Chapter 11 lists and discusses the 15 steps to Environmental Strategy Implementation. It provides guidance to companies trying to improve their environmental management systems. It also serves as a summary of the key steps discussed in the book.

CONCLUSIONS FROM THE FIELD RESEARCH

Key findings of both the state of the art and the best practices are summarized in Exhibit 11–3 and discussed briefly below. These findings and suggestions for improvement are referred to throughout the book and summarized and discussed in more detail in Chapter 11.

Five or 10 years ago, most corporations did not seriously consider their environmental liabilities in either internal decision making or external reporting. The rapid increase in environmental costs now has caused companies to begin to integrate these considerations into management decisions at all levels. Though this study documents that measuring and reporting corporate environmental performance is still in its infancy, significant developments are occurring. Companies are beginning to recognize that they need to be proactive rather than reactive and that a planning orientation rather than a compliance orientation pays off in both reduced environmental impacts and increased long-term corporate profitability. They are beginning to see the power of using an approach such as life cycle assessment (LCA) to broadly identify the impacts of products from cradle to grave. (In the area of environmental issues this expression could be "cradle to cradle"—the idea that when a product reaches the end of its life cycle, it is "reborn" in a new form through recycling.) Even the LCA approach typically does not go far enough because it often is used only for identifying impacts and not for measuring those impacts for use in important financial decisions, including capital investment decisions.

Financial tools are available to improve decisions throughout organizations. They can measure the impacts for a more useful life cycle assessment. What is needed, however, is more cooperation between EH&S personnel and legal, accounting, and operations managers. Management accountants must begin to provide the information managers need to make better internal decisions on these continually rising environmental costs. In some cases all it requires is learning techniques already used in other parts of the corporation. In most cases, it requires better information on the total environmental costs and what causes those costs—most companies know neither the total of their environmental costs nor which products cause those costs. Many companies continue to undercost products because they have no system for accurately accumulating environmental costs. In other cases, cost and benefit estimation techniques need to be adapted for a specific corporate use. Improved corporate environmental management does result from better use of existing models. Many corporations can save hundreds of millions of dollars of corporate costs and also reduce environmental impacts.

Sustainable development is being adopted as a core value in an increasing number of corporations. Further, CEOs generally have recognized the strong likelihood that in the next decade their corporations will be held responsible for post-consumer waste through some concept such as "product take-back," which will require companies to be responsible for the ultimate reuse, recycling, or disposal of the products they produce. There are significant corporate developments in integrating environmental impacts into management decisions. Companies that have made a start need to continue to maintain their leadership position because leadership in this arena brings competitive advantages, and many of the laggards are beginning to make progress.

DESIGN OF THE STUDY

In 1992, the Institute of Management Accountants decided that corporate accountants needed additional guidance to understand the methods that might prove useful in measuring and reporting corporate environmental performance. The IMA sponsored this study to identify the state of the art and best practices in the development of measuring and reporting systems for the internal management of corporate environmental impacts. The study describes current practices and opportunities and prescribes additional available frameworks.

The research study involved six phases. First, an extensive literature review examined previous research and corporate studies in the areas of environmental accounting and related fields. The studies included recycling and waste reduction programs, environmental management, strategy, accounting, engineering, and so forth.

Second, accounting and environmental regulations were analyzed. Appendix A includes a summary of that review. Prior surveys of environmental reporting were also analyzed; the results are reported in the relevant chapters.

The third phase consisted of obtaining and examining annual reports, environmental reports, and other internal and external documents from well over 100 corporations to determine environmental impact identification, measurement, reporting, monitoring, and management practices.

Fourth, from the literature reviews and the analysis of company documents companies were selected that appeared to be best in class in at least one area of environmental management. I then conducted phone interviews and field visits at more than 30 companies. In most instances, company personnel interviewed by phone or in person included both senior executives and middle managers in operations, accounting, legal, and EH&S. In most of the field visits, senior corporate executives, often the CEO or COO, were part of the interview schedule.

The literature review, the review of company documents, and the interviews and field visits provided the data for the fifth phase. In it, the information was summarized, analyzed, and evaluated to produce the state-of-the-art and best-practice information that is the core of this study. The results of this field research are organized by subject and discussed extensively in Chapters 2 to 11.

The sixth and final phase, growing out of the extensive field research, involved establishing frameworks that can guide companies. The frameworks provide ways to think about developing and implementing environmental management strategies. They give techniques that can be used to improve analysis and decisions in areas such as product costing and capital investments.

The primary focus of this book is on how companies are integrating environmental impacts into management decisions and on how accountants can improve that process. It describes better ways to integrate available techniques into measurement and reporting systems that relate to areas such as product costing, product pricing, capital investments, and performance evaluations. It is hoped that this guidance will lead to increased institutionalization of environmental accounting, a broadened role for management accountants inside the firm, and improvement in the implementation of corporate environmental strategy, which will lead to better business decisions.

The extensive research completed for this book convinces me that the development of a sound environmental strategy and its effective implementation are critical for business success and that better management of environmental impacts does produce lower environmental costs and higher corporate profits.

ORGANIZATION OF THE RESEARCH REPORT

This book contains the results of a comprehensive study of the state of the art and best practices in the integration of corporate environmental impacts into management decisions. Chapter 1 presents background on environmental issues, both historical and legal, and describes the research in more detail. Chapters 2 to 11 provide in-depth information about the 10 components of corporate environmental integration.

Chapter 11 also gives a detailed description of the corporate environmental scorecard and guidance on how to implement a corporate environmental strategy. It provides a framework for implementing an environmental strategy, comments on observed critical variables for success of an implementation, gives concluding observations, and comments on the direction of corporate environmental management and the measurement and reporting of corporate environmental performance.

The book includes three appendices. Appendix A reviews both the environmental regulations and the financial reporting regulations that guide environmental disclosures and influence environmental performance. Appendix B provides some background on the corporate social audit, cost-benefit analysis, and environmental accounting. Appendix C lists companies cited in this book (the general index gives the pages where descriptions of their company practices are located). Finally, a glossary of acronyms used in the book and an extensive bibliography of related materials appear at the end of the book.

A CHANGING LANDSCAPE

The corporate landscape is changing. Dow Chemical Chairman Frank Popoff has said that "there is a need to assume responsibility for one's product even after it has left the plant." In a 1991 McKinsey survey of senior executives worldwide, more than 80 percent agreed with that statement (Winsemius and Hahn, 1992, 249). In the research described in this study, almost every senior executive acknowledged that responsibility.

Many of the companies thought to be among the nation's worst polluters are now among the most progressive and most environmentally sensitive companies in America. They still have environmental problems, but many are seriously attempting to clean up their previous messes. They are designing products and processes to minimize future environmental impacts and corporate costs. Though their current environmental liabilities still may be high, they are reducing future environmental liabilities through improved integration of environmental impact considerations into management decisions. These corporations may be among the most environmentally responsible and the most profitable in the long term.

Corporations have been undercosting and overcosting products and alternatives based on inadequate information regarding the costs and benefits of corporate environmental impacts. Improper costing and capital investment decisions have cost industry billions of dollars. This book provides examples of current corporate activities, processes, and techniques that improve environmental management. It is hoped that these examples will be an impetus for other companies to better manage their environmental costs as a way both to reduce environmental impacts and to improve corporate profits.

Contents

Foreword   *iii*

Perspectives   *v*

Preface   *xv*

Publisher's Notes   *xix*

Acknowledgments   *xxi*

About the Author   *xxiii*

Executive Summary   *xxv*

Motivation for the Study xxv
Scoring Corporate Environmental Performance xxvi
Conclusions from the Field Research xxix
Design of the Study xxx
Organization of the Research Report xxxii
A Changing Landscape xxxiii

Chapter One
INTRODUCTION   1

The Failure of Social Accounting and the Genesis of
    Environmental Reporting 2
Corporate Environmental Performance and the Law 5
The Tone at the Top 7
The Goal of Sustainable Development 7
Design of the Study 8
Organization of the Research Report 11

Chapter Two
THE IMPORTANCE OF A CORPORATE
ENVIRONMENTAL STRATEGY AND HOW
TO DEVELOP IT   13

The Role of Environmental Strategy in International
    Competitiveness 13

International Regulations and Multinational Corporations 15
The Role of Government Partnerships 17
Specific Partnership Programs 20
The Notion of Sustainable Development 22
The Development of a Corporate Environmental Strategy 25
Role of Corporate Mission Statement in Clarifying
    Corporate Commitment 27
Summary 28

Chapter Three
MINIMIZING ENVIRONMENTAL IMPACTS   31
Recycling and the Take-Back Principle 32
Life Cycle Assessments and Life Cycle Cost Assessments 34
Reducing Waste Through Product and Process Redesign 43
Reducing Waste Through Operations and Purchasing 46
Summary 48

Chapter Four
SYSTEMS FOR IDENTIFYING, ORGANIZING, AND
MANAGING CORPORATE ENVIRONMENTAL
IMPACTS   50
An Introduction to Environmental Strategy
    Implementation 50
Organizational Structure 53
Centralized vs. Decentralized EH&S Management 59
The Challenge of Organizing Across International
    Boundaries 60
Other Organizational Issues 62
Total Stakeholder Analysis 62
Tools and Frameworks for Analysis 66
Balanced Scorecard 72
Summary 74

Chapter Five
INTERNAL REPORTING INFORMATION
SYSTEMS   75
Waste Management Information Systems 76
The Development of One Environmental Accounting
    and Reporting System 78

Other Environmental Information Systems 83
Management Accounting Systems and Financial
    Reporting Systems 84
Is a Link Necessary or Desirable? 86
Summary 87

Chapter Six
INTERNAL ENVIRONMENTAL AUDITING
SYSTEMS   88
What Is Environmental Auditing? 88
Types of Environmental Audits 89
Internal Environmental Audit Departments 92
The Importance of the Self-Audit 92
Assurance Letters 93
The Role of Environmental Auditing in Business
    Acquisitions and Divestments 93
Environmental Auditing Practices and Programs 96
Eco-Auditing 99
Broader Corporate Environmental Internal Audits 100
Lack of Standards in Environmental Auditing 102
Summary 104

Chapter Seven
EXTERNAL REPORTING SYSTEMS AND
ENVIRONMENTAL AUDITS   106
The Variety of Environmental Disclosures in Corporate
    Annual Reports and Corporate Environmental Reports 107
Moving Toward a Standard Environmental Report 120
Preparation of the External Environmental Report and the
    Role of EH&S Professionals in the Accrual Process 129
External Audits of Environmental Reports 134
The Coordination of External Audit, Internal Audit,
    and Self-Audit Procedures 140
Summary 143

Chapter Eight
COSTING SYSTEMS   145
Costing Systems 145
The Costs to Include in Product Costs 146

Identifying and Tracking Environmental Costs 149
Additional Issues Related to Costing 153
Life Cycle Costing 154
Cost Management 156
Full-Cost Accounting 158
Environmental Externalities 162
Summary 163

Chapter Nine
CAPITAL BUDGETING SYSTEMS   164

The Capital Expenditure Approval Process 165
One Company's Corporate Environmental
    Planning Process 169
The Need to Expand the Analysis for Environmental
    Capital Investments 172
Cost Assessment Methods 174
Option Assessments, Option Screening, and
    Scenario Forecasting 180
Monetizing Environmental Externalities 190
Contingent Valuation 192
Risk Assessment 193
Option Pricing Theory 195
Other Issues in Capital Budgeting Under Uncertainty 195
How to Estimate Future Liability Fuzzily or Statistically 196
Summary 197

Chapter Ten
PERFORMANCE EVALUATION SYSTEMS   212

Evaluating Corporations, Strategic Business Units,
    and Facilities 213
Incentives for Individual Environmental Responsibility 216
Other Examples of the Integration of Environmental
    Responsibility into Performance Evaluations 226
Striving for Environmental Responsibility in a
    Global Enterprise 227
The Use of Company Environmental Awards
    for Employees 229
The Use of Internal Waste and Environmental Taxes 230
Summary 230

Chapter Eleven
IMPLEMENTING A CORPORATE ENVIRONMENTAL STRATEGY   232
Scoring Corporate Environmental Performance 234
Some Surprises from the Field Research 238
Fifteen Steps to Environmental Strategy Implementation 243
Additional Guidelines for Managers and
    Management Accountants 245
Concluding Remarks 248

Appendix A
THE REGULATIONS THAT GOVERN ENVIRONMENTAL REPORTING   251
Environmental Regulations 252
The Process of Assessing Liability Under CERCLA 255
Accounting Regulations 256
Surveys and Studies of External Financial Reporting of
    Environmental Liabilities 262
Summary 264

Appendix B
A BRIEF REVIEW OF THE SOCIAL AUDIT, ENVIRONMENTAL ACCOUNTING, AND COST-BENEFIT ANALYSIS   267
Social Responsibility and the Social Audit—
    the Development of Frameworks and Models 267
Social Accounting and the Social Audit—
    Company Implementations 270
Environmental Economics and Cost-Benefit Analysis 271
Previous Studies by the Institute of Management
    Accountants 276
Further Thoughts on the Failure of Social Accounting 278

Appendix C
COMPANIES CITED   279

Glossary of Acronyms   285

Bibliography   289

Index   305

Chapter One

Introduction

The downward spiral of poverty and environmental degradation is a waste of opportunities and of resources. What is needed now is a new era of economic growth—growth that is forceful and at the same time socially and environmentally sustainable. Unless we are able to translate our words into a language that can reach the hearts and minds of people young and old, we shall not be able to undertake the extensive social changes needed to correct the course of development.

Gro Harlem Brundtland, *Prime Minister of Norway*
Chairman—United Nations World Commission
on Environment and Development

Though government decision makers certainly understand the consequences of environmental degradation, they also need to understand the importance of economic growth and balanced policies focused on sustainable development. But business leaders, who make so many of the important decisions as to the allocation of resources in our society, also need to understand the environmental impacts of corporate activities. Numerous discussions with business leaders have convinced me that many of them do sincerely want to reduce the environmental impacts of their company's activities. They want to act responsibly while being sensitive to the needs of various constituents—employees, customers, suppliers, shareholders, and the community. They want to establish and implement a sensible corporate environmental strategy but have had little guidance as to frameworks and methods for doing it.

To respond effectively to environmental concerns, business leaders need a way to think about environmental impacts and how to incorporate those impacts into the decision-making process. They need to translate the concerns into familiar language commonly used in business. In

EXHIBIT 1–1
Corporate Environmental Concerns

- How can companies better manage rapidly increasing corporate environmental costs?
- What are the state of the art and best practices in identifying, measuring, reporting, monitoring, and managing corporate environmental impacts?
- How can companies better measure and report environmental impacts for better decisions?
- How can companies institutionalize environmental responsibility?
- How can companies improve the implementation of a corporate environmental strategy for improved business decisions?
- What techniques can be used to better integrate environmental impacts into business decisions related to product costing, product pricing, product design, capital investments, and performance evaluations?
- Can better planning and the use of these techniques reduce corporate environmental impacts and thereby improve both the environment and long-term corporate profitability?

Brundtland's terms, it is the only way in which the changes can be undertaken. Environmental performance must be translated into the language of dollars within the framework of accounting. Managers need to be able to measure and report corporate environmental impacts and integrate those impacts into decisions on product costing, product pricing, capital investments, product design, and performance evaluations.

Corporate executives are developing and implementing environmental strategies. Exhibit 1–1 summarizes some of their environmental concerns that are addressed in this book.

Until recently, we have had very little information on how corporations have approached these issues and how their approach could be improved. This study was developed to address those problems.

THE FAILURE OF SOCIAL ACCOUNTING AND THE GENESIS OF ENVIRONMENTAL REPORTING

In the 1960s, corporations started to reevaluate their roles and responsibilities in society. Societal concerns at that time related to business ethics, equal employment opportunities, workplace safety, and numerous other social issues. In 1970, with the celebration of its first Earth Day, the United States began to concern itself with issues surrounding environmental degradation. Researchers, academics, and a few business leaders began to write about corporate social accounting and corporate social responsibility. Abt Associates, Inc., a leading consultant in the corporate social audit, was the first company to include an external social audit in its annual report. Numerous others followed with various analyses of social, economic, and environmental impacts and various disclosures on their corporate social performance.

Corporate social accounting did not survive the 1970s in good health. It had been used too extensively as a public relations tool and not extensively enough as a way to make fundamental changes in corporate culture. Though its use for external reporting certainly improved both corporate accountability and communications with the various stakeholders of modern corporations, more permanent changes could be achieved only by incorporating social accounting into the internal accounting systems of these organizations. Then and only then could a system be developed that would integrate social concerns into the corporate decision-making process and communicate the results to the various corporate stakeholders by means of a well-developed external reporting system. Neither the executives nor their accountants, however, were interested in a significant, permanent change in corporate culture and the implementation of corporate social accounting.

Growing environmental concerns have prompted new approaches to managing social and environmental impacts. These approaches have brought environmental issues into the central strategic planning of major corporations. Executives have started to view environmental expenditures as critical investments for corporate success rather than as regulatory compliance expenditures. Environmental regulations have grown very large very fast, however, and corporations generally were unprepared to deal with them. Stricter environmental regulations, even stricter enforcement, and the possibility of individual and corporate criminal prosecution for violations of environmental laws have forced corporations to see environmental sensitivity as a more critical component of corporate strategy.

The focus switched to effective implementation in industry to improve environmental management and reduce corporate environmental costs; it was only secondarily on external reporting. This focus on improving the management of social and environmental impacts also was prompted by increased societal concerns for the fragility of the environment.

Further, disclosure rules by the Financial Accounting Standards Board (FASB) and the Securities & Exchange Commission (SEC) have compelled corporations to disclose certain contingent liabilities and accrue these liabilities for likely future payments for environmental cleanups. The size of these potential liabilities has grown tremendously— total corporate liabilities for environmental cleanup in the United States due to Superfund have been estimated at more than $1 trillion.

One of the most extensive analyses of environmental costs was completed in 1991. It examined costs related to Superfund program sites listed on the National Priorities List (NPL), the Resource Conservation and Recovery Act (RCRA) corrective action program, the underground storage tanks (UST) program, federal facility cleanups, and state-required and private voluntary cleanups (Russell et al., 1991, 16). The analysis concluded that over the next 30 years the cost to clean up hazardous waste sites in the United States will be $752 billion.

Financial analysts are concerned that they cannot evaluate a company's financial condition effectively if they are not aware of these potential environmental liabilities. The FASB and the SEC are reviewing whether current regulations are adequate and whether the enforcement of those regulations is sufficient to provide adequate disclosure of environmental liabilities for external users to evaluate the financial condition of the firm. In addition, an increasing number of companies now recognize that poor environmental performance may affect their reputation—and thus their business revenues, stock price, and cost of capital. They also acknowledge that benefits accrue to companies that voluntarily disclose their corporate environmental performance in both annual reports and environmental reports. All these elements have caused a significant increase in both internal and external environmental reporting and its integration into the decision-making process.

Internal reporting makes sense only if it leads to improved environmental and business decisions. External reporting makes sense only if it reports the actual corporate environmental performance and environmental programs. External reports that lack an underlying corporate substance are identified quickly as transparent.

Finally, and perhaps most important, corporate executives now recognize that environmental considerations are critical components of many managerial decisions. These considerations need to be integrated into management strategy, its implementation, and the measurement of its success. Companies need to integrate environmental impacts and costs into performance evaluation, product design, product costing and pricing, and capital investment decisions, which in turn must be merged into the financial reporting and management accounting systems. Corporate executives need an approach that will help them implement corporate strategy. They should recognize that there is not necessarily a trade-off between environmental responsibility and corporate profitability. Long-term profitability indeed may depend on integrating environmental considerations into corporate decisions.

CORPORATE ENVIRONMENTAL PERFORMANCE AND THE LAW

The attention to issues of corporate environmental management certainly has been increased by legislation and enforcement of related civil and criminal liabilities. Civil and administrative penalties can be imposed when a company is found in violation of various environmental laws. Typically, an administrative order is issued requiring corrective action. Penalties also can be imposed. The company can consent to the order, negotiating its terms, or can contest the order. Penalties can reach $25,000 per day for each violation.

Further, the federal environmental laws also provide for criminal liability for many of the same offenses subject to civil liability. Criminal sanctions tend to apply to a narrower range of violations but can be significantly more severe than civil penalties. The U.S. Sentencing Commission was established in 1984 to bring uniformity to the sentencing of persons convicted of federal offenses. In December 1993 an Advisory Group on Environmental Sanctions proposed a new set of guidelines to the U.S. Sentencing Commission for sentencing "organizations" convicted of environmental offenses. To date those guidelines have not been adopted (U.S. Sentencing Commission, 1993).

A significant change has occurred in the criminal prosecution of the environmental laws, whereby officers, directors, and employees now are being prosecuted in addition to the corporations that employ them. Regulators believe that because corporations can only be assessed fines, a successful deterrent for environmental violations is the threat of prison terms for the responsible corporate employees.

Indeed, one of the most noticeable changes I observed during this two-year research project was managers' dramatically rising concern for the potential personal liability of environmental violations. Increased civil and criminal environmental liabilities have caused companies to develop organizational systems that aim to avoid regulatory noncompliance through carefully performed "compliance audits."

Company activities and programs designed to improve environmental responsibility certainly create significant benefits for both the corporation and the environment, in improved decision making, reduced costs, improved competitiveness, and focused strategic management. Numerous companies also report that better environmental management systems provide a "seat at the table" with environmentalists and regulators who are instrumental in determining government environmental policy. These companies report many examples of court cases and hearings in which judges and juries have lessened sentences and fines because of sincere company efforts to improve environmental management systems.

This book contains significant evidence that improved environmental management and the integration of environmental impacts into management decisions bring strategic advantages. Companies discussed increasingly have noted the additional benefits of improved corporate environmental performance in regulatory hearings and civil and criminal cases.

The legal process has had other effects on environmental protection. A recent study concluded that 88 percent of the money paid out between 1986 and 1989 by insurers for Superfund claims went to pay for legal and administrative costs, while only 12 percent was used for actual site cleanups (Acton and Dixon, 1992). It generally has been agreed that too much of the money paid for environmental costs in our society by both business and government is spent on regulation, enforcement, and various other legal and transaction costs and not enough on the actual cleanup.

Regulatory changes clearly are necessary to change the incentives to clean up environmental problems and prevent future environmental costs. Government policy that encourages source reduction through pollution prevention benefits the environment and corporate profits more than regulations that result in the inefficient use of corporate and government funds. Most parties agree that current regulations and practices related to Superfund particularly and to many other environmental regulations generally encourage neither the proper management of environmental impacts nor the proper allocation of corporate or government funds. Though substantial effort was expended to reconcile differences in positions among industry, insurance companies, environmentalists, and regulators over Superfund liability, by early 1995 no revised legislation had been passed.

THE TONE AT THE TOP

When the World Commission on Environment and Development headed by Prime Minister Brundtland issued its report in 1987, the report was widely acclaimed as one of the most important documents of the decade. The Commission, established by the United Nations, set out to investigate problems related to the environment and economic development and to propose realistic solutions balancing the desire for environmental protection with the need for economic development and prosperity. One of the most important proposals, which applies to countries and corporations alike, is that sustainable development can occur only if organizational leaders do more than just set a "tone at the top." Organizations need to have concrete methods for implementing policies for both economic development and environmental protection.

Setting the tone at the top through goals and mission statements is important, however. "The single greatest factor that will differentiate the nineties from the eighties is the importance of environmental issues…" (K. Grahame Walker, chairman and chief executive officer, The Dexter Corporation). Walker is head of a major supplier of specialty materials, the oldest company on the New York Stock Exchange. His statement recognizes the importance of the environmental issue and setting the tone at the top. Dexter has a notable set of published environmental principles. More important is the way the company integrates this tone at the top and these principles into a corporate environmental strategy and into the corporate culture.

THE GOAL OF SUSTAINABLE DEVELOPMENT

At the 1992 Earth Summit in Rio de Janeiro more than 100 nations pledged to move toward implementing the concept of sustainable development at the local level. Sustainable development generally has been defined as development that meets the needs of the present without compromising the ability of future generations to meet their own needs. But what does it mean for corporate planning?

After endorsing the principles of the Coalition for Environmentally Responsible Economies (CERES), which commit companies to a code of environmental conduct, Sun Company acknowledged: "We run a business, and this is a business decision. We believe that the future belongs to those companies that see environmental protection as a valued condition for economic growth."

ABB, the well-known, global power-generation company, has committed itself to sustainability in its mission statement. It defines sustainable development as "economic and social policies designed to meet the needs of those living today without compromising the ability of future people to meet their needs."

One of the first state government attempts at sustainable development is a plan by the state of Virginia, described in *Blueprint for Sustainable Development in Virginia.* It provides ways in which Virginia can simultaneously attain economic prosperity, environmental protection, and community building.

Another company that has committed itself to sustainable development is Ciba-Geigy.

> To engage effectively in environmental protection and safety, a company must have a solid financial basis. At first glance, economy and ecology (or profitability, environmental protection and safety) may appear to be contradictory. But not if we think in terms of longer time scales. Recent clean-up projects have shown it can be far more expensive to clean a polluted body of water or improve an old, poorly conceived landfill than to apply precautionary measures to prevent problems in advance. Most conflicts between goals, therefore, are of a short-term nature... Active and competent environmental protection is just as important to Ciba's survival as the conventional pillars of research, production and marketing... We are committed to striking a balance between our economic, social and environmental responsibilities to ensure the prosperity of our enterprise into the twenty-first century (Ciba-Geigy Limited, 1993).

DESIGN OF THE STUDY

In 1992, the Institute of Management Accountants decided that corporate accountants needed additional guidance to understand the methods that might prove useful in measuring and reporting corporate environmental performance. The IMA sponsored this study to identify the state of the art and best practices in the development of measuring and reporting systems for the internal management of corporate environmental impacts. The study describes current practices and opportunities and prescribes additional available frameworks. Following its suggestions will help senior corporate managers and their finance, accounting, EH&S, and

EXHIBIT 1–2
The Study Design

Phase 1
Carry out literature review of academic and corporate studies in areas including accounting, environmental management, engineering, and strategy.

Phase 2
Review accounting and environmental regulations.

Phase 3
Review internal and external documents from more than 100 corporations, including corporate annual reports and corporate environmental reports.

Phase 4
From literature review and analysis of company documents, select best in class companies in one area of environmental management.

Carry out phone interviews and field visits with more than 30 companies, including visits with EH&S, accounting, legal, operations, and senior corporate executives

Phase 5
Summarize and analyze data.
Describe state of the art.
Describe best practices.

Phase 6
Develop frameworks for development and implementation of environmental strategy.
Develop techniques for analysis and implementation.

---

operations staff to improve corporate environmental performance dramatically.

The research study included a wide variety of companies: publicly held and privately held; large and small; in widely diverse industries; regional, national, and multinational; and with large and small environmental impacts. It involved six phases (see Exhibit 1–2). First, an extensive literature review examined previous research and corporate studies in the areas of environmental accounting and related fields. Some of that research is reported in Chapter 1 while other relevant work is cited in the chapters appropriate to the specific focus of the work. The studies included recycling and waste reduction programs, environmental management, strategy, accounting, engineering, and so forth.

Second, I analyzed accounting and environmental regulations. Appendix A includes a summary of that review. I also analyzed prior surveys of environmental reporting; the results are reported in the relevant chapters.

Third, I obtained and examined annual reports, environmental reports, and other internal and external documents from well over 100 corporations to determine environmental impact identification, measurement, reporting, monitoring, and management practices.

Fourth, from the literature reviews and the analysis of company documents companies were selected that appeared to be best in class in at least one area of environmental management. I then conducted phone interviews and field visits at more than 30 companies. In most instances, company personnel interviewed by phone or in person included both senior executives and middle managers in operations, accounting, legal, and EH&S. In most of the field visits, senior corporate executives, often the CEO or COO, were part of the interview schedule, so it was possible to obtain a thorough understanding of the company's progress and difficulties in the environmental management area.

The literature review, the review of company documents, and the interviews and field visits provided the data for the fifth phase. In it, the information was summarized, analyzed, and evaluated to produce the state of the art and best practices that are the core of this study. The results of this field research are organized by subject and discussed extensively in Chapters 2 to 11.

The sixth and final phase, growing out of the extensive field research, involved establishing frameworks that can guide companies. The frameworks provide ways to think about developing and implementing environmental management strategies. They give techniques that can be used to improve analysis and decisions in areas such as product costing and capital investments. They should improve environmental planning and reduce environmental impacts and company costs.

This book reviews both the regulations and practices related to external reporting of environmental contingent liabilities, environmental practices, and environmental audits. Its primary focus, however, is on how companies are integrating environmental impacts into management decisions and on how accountants can improve that process. The book describes better ways to integrate available techniques into measurement and reporting systems that relate to areas such as product costing, product pricing, capital investments, and performance evaluations. It is hoped that this guidance will lead to:

- Increased institutionalization of environmental accounting;
- A broadened role for management accountants inside the firm in measuring and reporting internal environmental impacts;

- Improvement in the implementation of corporate environmental strategy, which will lead to better business decisions.

The extensive research completed for this book convinces me that the development of a sound environmental strategy and its effective implementation are critical for business success and that better management of environmental impacts does produce lower environmental costs and higher corporate profits.

ORGANIZATION OF THE RESEARCH REPORT

This book contains the results of a comprehensive study into the state of the art and best practices in the integration of corporate environmental impacts into management decisions. This chapter provides background on environmental issues, both historical and legal, and describes the research in more detail. Chapters 2 to 11 provide in-depth information about the 10 components of corporate environmental integration. In each chapter the reader will find a description of state-of-the-art corporate environmental practice, the best corporate practices, and some prescribed approaches to improving corporate environmental performance.

Finally, the book concludes with a more detailed description of the corporate environmental scorecard and guidance on how to implement a corporate environmental strategy. It provides a framework for implementing an environmental strategy, comments on observed critical variables for success of an implementation, gives concluding observations, and comments on the direction of corporate environmental management and the measurement and reporting of corporate environmental performance.

The book includes three appendices. Appendix A reviews both the environmental regulations and the financial reporting regulations that guide environmental disclosures and influence environmental performance. References to those regulations are made throughout the book, and Appendix A provides information about their substance.

Appendix B provides some background on the corporate social audit, cost-benefit analysis, and environmental accounting. It will interest many readers because it provides perspective on the precedents of some of the current work in measuring corporate environmental impacts.

Appendix C lists companies cited in this book (the general index gives the pages where descriptions of their company practices are located).

Many companies will find this information useful for benchmarking their corporate environmental performance. Finally, a glossary of acronyms used in the book and an extensive bibliography of related materials appear at the end of the book. Students and researchers should find the appendices and bibliography of particular interest.

The study deals throughout with the concerns raised in Exhibit 1–1. Exhibit 4–1 in Chapter 4 details portions of the Environmental Strategy Implementation, providing approaches and solutions to the issues related to measuring and reporting corporate environmental performance. In Chapter 11, these solutions are integrated in the fifteen Steps to Environmental Strategy Implementation and the corporate environmental scorecard.

Corporations have been undercosting and overcosting products and alternatives based on inadequate information regarding the costs and benefits of corporate environmental impacts. Improper costing and capital investment decisions have cost industry billions of dollars. This book provides examples of current corporate activities, processes, and techniques that improve environmental management. It is hoped that these examples will be an impetus for other companies to better manage their environmental costs as a way both to reduce environmental impacts and to improve corporate profits.

Chapter Two

The Importance of a Corporate Environmental Strategy and How to Develop It

B efore beginning a discussion of how to implement an environmental strategy, we must examine the importance of such a strategy and how companies can approach its development. What are the issues and interdependencies of corporate environmental strategy, competitiveness, international trade, and regulation?

Numerous studies, reviewed in this chapter, indicate that the benefits of environmental innovations often far exceed the costs. The following chapters describe how companies can more broadly identify, measure, and manage environmental costs and benefits to reduce environmental impacts and improve corporate profits. The final chapter presents a framework that can aid companies in choosing among product improvements, process improvements, and capital improvements and in identifying and measuring the total costs and benefits of environmental activities.

THE ROLE OF ENVIRONMENTAL STRATEGY IN INTERNATIONAL COMPETITIVENESS

In a widely respected series of books on competition and a paper and essay on the relationship of the environment to competition, Michael Porter has described a framework useful for thinking about the role of government in environmental regulation. In this section, we explore Porter's work, his work with Claas van der Linde, and the work of others on environmental strategy, environmental regulation, and international competitiveness. "Government policy contributes to competitiveness if it encourages innovation...and undermines competitiveness if it retards innovation or undermines the intensity of competition" (Porter and van der Linde, 1994, 9).

Which description is most appropriate for present U.S. environmental policies? One of Porter and van der Linde's central arguments (1994, 1) is that the entire environment-competitiveness debate has been framed incorrectly and that the "policy makers, businesses, and environmentalists have unnecessarily driven up costs and slowed progress on environmental issues." Instead of framing the issue as a trade-off between environmental regulation and competitiveness and then being concerned about how the trade-off can be relaxed, Porter and van der Linde argue that the goal should be eliminating the trade-off.

They contend that competition is dynamic rather than static. "Firms can respond to environmental regulation, or even anticipate it, with innovation. Properly designed environmental standards can thus trigger innovation that at least partially offsets the costs of complying with them." These innovation offsets can lower the net cost of pollution abatement and remediation while at the same time providing companies with an absolute competitive advantage over firms in foreign countries not subject to similar environmental regulations. The net cost of the abatement is the difference between the social costs and the social benefits. Private industry bears many of these social costs, so it should have some flexibility in how it addresses the problems. Innovation offsets can range from better products to improved product yield. Porter and van der Linde argue that strict environmental regulations will cause companies to seek innovative solutions to minimize their cost of compliance while improving their products.

The opportunity for innovation must be maximized by allowing industry to take part in choosing the most effective solutions to environmental problems. Further, environmental regulations should foster continuous improvement and the regulations should leave little uncertainty about the regulation itself (Porter and van der Linde, 1994, 30).

Porter has argued that U.S. environmental policy does not make American industry less competitive in the international marketplace. He points out that Germany and Japan have tough environmental laws, yet they continue to increase their GNP growth rates and rates of productivity. What is needed in the United States is regulation that focuses on pollution prevention rather than only on pollution control. "[S]tandards must be sensitive to the costs involved" (Porter, 1991).

Jaffe et al (1994) also have concluded that environmental regulation may not have a negative impact on international competitiveness. While not in favor of increased regulation, the authors argue that it may be a positive influence, causing business to become more efficient and competitive. More competition may cause business to examine production processes more closely and seek to improve them. Total quality environmental management (TQEM) may result in increased profitability and increased environmental responsibility, including a general improvement in production quality, production efficiency, and environmental standards.

In a widely quoted study, Professor Stephen Meyer (1992, 42) refutes the hypothesis that strong environmental policies inhibit economic growth and development, stifle employment, and reduce competitiveness. He shows that there may even be a positive relationship between environmental regulation and economic performance. He further states that the desire to avoid the expected high costs of waste disposal and pollution abatement can fuel process and product innovations. These innovations in turn improve productivity, raise input-output efficiencies, and bring substantial cost savings.

INTERNATIONAL REGULATIONS AND MULTINATIONAL CORPORATIONS

The Business Council for Sustainable Development (BCSD), established by Dr. Stephan Schmidheiny, comprises 48 chief executive officers from around the world. The Council's vision of how to achieve sustainable development, documented in *Changing Course* (Schmidheiny, 1992), calls for a partnership between business and government. They argue that sustainable development makes good business sense and if businesses are allowed to operate in open and competitive markets they will make the commitment and the capital investments to achieve this goal. Schmidheiny and the BCSD view free trade as having an important role in progress toward sustainable development.

Recent discussions and passage of the General Agreement on Tariffs and Trade (GATT) and the North American Free Trade Agreement (NAFTA) should aid both free trade and the environment. GATT began in 1948 as a series of multilateral agreements among nations, with the most recent in 1994. Its primary goal has been to encourage the liberalization of international trade and to foster economic and social growth. Some executives are concerned that it will open U.S. markets to a flood of low-priced imports and that the agreements do not address environmental issues. Others argue that open trade:

- Contributes to sustainable development by increasing economic growth;
- Facilitates the adoption of needed environmental protection by providing access to environmentally advanced goods and technologies;
- Minimizes waste through trade in recovered material for recycling. (Gavin, 1991, 78)

NAFTA also is expected to promote more free trade among the nations. A side accord to NAFTA establishes a commission and procedures for resolving disputes about environmental matters. It attempts to create a level playing field among the United States, Mexico, and Canada by standardizing certain environmental regulations.

The Montreal Protocol is an international agreement that calls for the phasing out of chlorofluorocarbons (CFCs). The signatories to the original agreement in September 1987 committed to reducing by one-half their consumption of five CFC compounds, by 1988. In 1989 DuPont decided that it would support a ban of CFC use by the end of the century. This move influenced the decision of the United States and the European Community (EC), in June 1990, to agree to end the use of CFCs by the year 2000.

The EC also has been striving for sustainable development and an environmental policy that prevents pollution and assesses liability. It has established an environmental policy based on the general principles in the Maastricht Treaty on European Union. The Fifth Environmental Action Programme, proposed in 1992, marked a radical departure from previous EC environmental policy. It recognized the need to integrate environmental considerations into all other policy areas and brought the goal of sustainable development to the top of the political agenda (European Community *Environment Guide*, 1994, 4).

Many transnational companies "anticipate that environmental standards will become normalized worldwide within the next 15 years" (Robinson et al., 1994, 56). This expectation may be among the reasons that multinational corporations usually go beyond compliance with local environmental regulations if they are below U.S. standards and the best available technology. Ciba-Geigy, for example, like most large multinational companies has the same environmental policies throughout its worldwide organization, even though local environmental standards often are lower than Ciba's standards. These lower standards in less-developed countries have been an important element of the discussions surrounding international environmental regulations relating to international trade.

A more important factor in international differences is the age of manufacturing facilities. Most corporate executives interviewed in this study mentioned that their new facilities, wherever located, use the latest technology in production and environmental controls and are designed to reduce the production of waste. Problems do remain at older facilities. As companies respond to incentives to produce more products abroad under NAFTA, new production facilities likely will exceed the environmental performance at many of their older U.S. facilities. Environmental problems are often more difficult to resolve in decades-old facilities that use outdated technology and where a total reconstruction of the plant is not commercially feasible.

As an example, Ciba-Geigy recently pioneered a waste water treatment technology in Indonesia before introducing it in the United Kingdom or the United States. In spite of this age difference among facilities, the most compelling long-term environmental challenge for most corporations is, as Ciba executive Hans Kindler says, "building environmental responsibility into the management process, moving away from end-of-pipe installations towards integrated solutions, and gaining competitive advantage by developing environmentally compatible products and processes."

THE ROLE OF GOVERNMENT PARTNERSHIPS

Many corporate leaders advocate more government partnerships and incentives to provide environmental leadership and innovation, rather than the government's current command and control approach. DuPont's chairman, Ed Woolard, has said, "Congress can legislate, environmentalists can agitate, but only industry can innovate."

Dow Chemical CEO Frank Popoff has stated:

Competitive advantage must not be gained through noncompliance or minimum compliance. Some companies try to reduce cost this way. But it is deadly. Sooner or later mandates will come into place to prevent such an approach, and put the company—or the whole industry—at an enormous competitive disadvantage. Success truly belongs, I believe, to those companies that not only comply with environmental standards, whether mandated or self-imposed, but do it more efficiently and effectively than others...I believe such companies will always have a competitive advantage over those that do not comply—and especially those that actively avoid complying by moving operations to another country where environmental regulations are less stringent (Avila and Whitehead, 1993, 55).

There is limited evidence that some federal and state government agencies are becoming more flexible and willing to consider innovative solutions to environmental problems. The views of academics and business leaders cited above recognize the contrast between the focus on minimizing compliance costs, including pollution control, and the innovation offsets that include pollution prevention and source reduction. These innovation offsets easily can exceed the costs of compliance if total costs and benefits are identified and measured properly. Avoiding the production of waste so that no money needs to be spent cleaning it up often is accomplished through a combination of capital improvements, process improvements, and product improvements.

Supreme Court Justice Stephen Breyer recently has written about the excesses of environmental regulation. He states that the smaller the risks at issue, the more likely that the costs of regulation will be excessive. He argues that government should develop a more rational approach, setting priorities and making trade-offs among regulatory programs. One example of these excesses Breyer cites is a ban on asbestos products that has cost approximately $200 to $300 million to save seven or eight lives over the past 13 years (Breyer, 1993, 61).

Attempts to improve the measurement of environmental impacts are being made at both a national and a corporate level. The Commerce Department is beginning to report a "green GDP" as a first step toward determining the impact of economic growth on the environment. The first report, issued in mid-1994, examined whether the economy is using up natural resources faster than it is finding new resources or alternative resources. Much more progress needs to be accomplished in this area, but this report is a notable first step. Jaffe et al., (1994) have further argued that "in an era of increasing reliance on incentive-based and other performance-based environmental regulations, accurate accounting for pollution control will become an even more pronounced problem."

The studies cited above examined the role of governmental regulation and the development of governmental environmental strategies. Corporations need to understand the governmental strategies and changing regulations, but they must develop their corporate strategy and their corporate environmental strategy to improve their own competitiveness and profitability. While managers monitor the changes in regulations, they can develop corporate strategies and policies that reduce environmental impacts and improve corporate profitability, in part through innovation offsets. Developing an environmental strategy and integrating it into total corporate strategy to improve the management of institutions generally (on a macro-level) and individual corporations specifically (on a micro level) is better for the U.S. environment, society, and economy. Given current regulatory constraints, corporations must begin to make significant progress in this area and deal effectively with changing economic and environmental conditions.

This book does not advocate any particular national environmental policy (except more cooperation and understanding between government and industry). Rather, it attempts to describe how corporations can develop and implement an environmental strategy to effectively organize and deal with the environmental realities in U.S. society. Environmental improvements need not be feared or avoided because they do not need to hurt international competitiveness. They might even force a closer examination of production processes and produce improved product designs, production quality, and production efficiency and yields, along with environmental improvements. These improvements, in turn, often result in better products, increased environmental responsibility, and increased profitability.

For many people, sustainable development is the goal for global environmental survival, national economic prosperity, and sound corporate growth. But both environmentalists and corporate executives often are frustrated with what appears to be the lack of flexibility of both regulations and regulators in dealing effectively with the challenges of balancing sound economic and environmental policies.

The EPA's Green Lights Program and 33/50 Program are examples of attempts by government to work with industry to develop sensible solutions to environmental problems. Various other attempts at partnerships (between corporations and environmental organizations, the corporation's suppliers, and government) also have been developed. For example, the New York State Department of Environmental Conservation secured approval from the Environmental Protection Agency (EPA) to develop solutions to some environmental problems at Bristol-Myers Squibb.[1] "This partnership will improve the efficiency of environmental protection and have a positive impact on industry's competitiveness and survival, leading to a strong economic recovery for the state."[2] Tom Hellman, vice president of EH&S at Bristol-Myers Squibb, agrees that New York is trying to balance economic growth and environmental protection and that these partnerships have important implications for sustainable development. They allow companies to integrate environmental considerations into the formulation of overall business strategy. Continued development is an integral part of the entire concept of sustainable development that sometimes is overlooked by both environmental activists and regulators.

If lines of communication are opened and the concepts of command and control and media-specific solutions are broadened, corporations and governments may find they share goals for economic growth and environmental protection and can find viable solutions that provide maximum benefit to the corporation and society. This discovery likely also will promote the kind of analysis that more broadly identifies benefits and costs, measures them, and reports them for both internal and external decision making. The DuPont 80/20 analysis (see page 173) suggests that sustainable development can be advanced best by more carefully analyzing benefits and costs. Discussions related to the balancing of economic growth and environmental protection are necessary at the highest levels of government. Further, a directed effort at developing joint corporate-government solutions aimed at sustainable development likely would prove very fruitful. The recognition of trade-offs and the development of partnerships may be among those solutions.

SPECIFIC PARTNERSHIP PROGRAMS

EPA's 33/50 Program

A vast number of U.S. companies signed on to the voluntary EPA 33/50 pollution prevention program. The program challenged companies to reduce the release or off-site transfer of emissions of 17 chemical

---

1. This discussion draws heavily on Rappaport, 1993.

2. "Multi-media Pollution Prevention," *Pollution Prevention Bulletin*, New York State Department of Environmental Conservation, Spring 1993, as quoted in Rappaport, 1993.

substances targeted by the Superfund Amendment and Reauthorization Act (SARA). The goal was a 33 percent reduction by the end of 1992 and 50 percent by the end of 1995. Amoco was among the companies joining. It met the 1992 deadline and currently is making additional changes to achieve 90 percent reduction by 1995. Rockwell International also participated in the 33/50 program. The company reported that by 1992 use of 13 of the 17 listed chemicals already had declined past the 50 percent reduction goal for 1995. Many companies disclose their progress in the reduction of 33/50 releases in their external environmental reports.

EPA's Green Lights Program

To further the partnership concept between business and government for pollution prevention, the EPA in 1991 established the Green Lights program. Green Lights is aimed at reducing the amount of electrical energy used, to reduce both pollution and energy costs. The EPA assists corporations, schools, state and local governments, lighting manufacturers, electric utilities, and many other groups to reduce the amount of electrical energy they use by providing grants and help in designing and implementing the reduction programs.

Green Lights encourages the use of energy-efficient lighting when it is profitable and improves lighting quality. Through this initiative, more than 1,500 major corporations already have agreed to reduce emissions of greenhouse gases and help curb acid rain and smog by voluntarily upgrading their lighting systems. Many companies have reported that through this program they already have reduced the use of energy by 30 percent to 40 percent. Programs such as this are designed to prevent pollution while helping organizations save on operating costs.

Other Initiatives and Programs

The EPA recently has acknowledged that its ability to combat pollution has fallen short of its goals. The agency now believes that part of the problem may lie in its focus on specific pollutants rather than on broader issues. Historically, the EPA has focused on specific problems such as the elimination of DDT or the cancerous effects of asbestos. It often has developed policies only in response to emergencies, rather than dealing with an overall environmental policy for the country. The Common Sense Initiative, proposed by the EPA in 1994, seeks to analyze the overall environmental impacts of entire industries and the range of emission problems they pose, with the notion of trying to determine the best approaches to address specific problems. This initiative also proposes bringing environmentalists and industry together to work on common environmental issues.

Another example of a government partnership with industry that seems to be working is a joint-venture project of Northern Telecom Ltd. and others with SEDUE, the Mexican Department of Urban Development and Ecology. Northern Telecom volunteered to share its own experience by managing a three-year cooperative training and demonstration program for Mexican industry aimed at eliminating CFC 113. The project illustrates that solvent elimination processes used by a large multinational can be transferred beneficially to companies using similar processes in developing countries (Marcil, 1992, 198).

Among the newest partnership programs between the EPA and business are the supplemental environmental projects (SEPs). SEPs are offered to violators of environmental laws as alternatives to paying fines. A company can mitigate part of its fine by doing something akin to environmental public service. Examples of acceptable SEPs are programs to reduce or prevent pollution, restore the environment, or improve and promote the general public's awareness of environmental issues. The EPA must approve the program, and it cannot benefit the company economically (Grant Thornton, 1994, 1).

In another example of government/corporate partnership, Amoco participated in a study with the EPA and the Commonwealth of Virginia at Amoco's refinery in Yorktown, Virginia. Over a three-year period, the company conducted tests to identify sources of pollution. It measured emission levels, determined the most cost-effective ways to reduce or eliminate the pollutants, and analyzed each method for its feasibility. Joint business/government partnerships often are more effective in determining methods for pollution reduction than either government or business acting alone.

THE NOTION OF SUSTAINABLE DEVELOPMENT

Sustainable development requires progress that meets the needs of the present without compromising the ability of future generations to meet their own needs. The bottom line is to find the least costly way to reduce the amount of pollution (Makower, 1993).

Stephan Schmidheiny and the BCSD have prescribed their notion of global sustainable development from a business perspective. "An increasing number of corporate leaders are convinced that it makes good business sense to secure the future of their corporations by integrating the principles of sustainable development into all their operations..." (Schmidheiny, 1992, 84). These leaders believe that no long-term economic growth can take place unless it is environmentally sustainable. The consensus is that this notion of sustainable development is suitable for both nations and corporations.

Another view of sustainable development for business requires corporations to operate in a different framework. Suggested actions include:

a) use renewable resources in preference to non-renewables

b) use technologies that are environmentally harmonious, ecologically stable and skill enhancing

c) design complete systems in order to minimize waste

d) reduce as much as possible the consumption of scarce resources by designing long life products that are easily repairable and can be recycled

e) maximize the use of all the services that are not energy- or material-intensive but which contribute to the quality of life. (Davis, 1991, 38).

The E.B. Eddy Group's EH&S report centers around sustainable development. While many companies are concerned primarily about complying with environmental regulations, E.B. Eddy's environmental performance is driven by sustainable development. In its mission statement the company states:

Sustainable development is not a question of choice between growth and the environment, it is the establishment of a decision-making process which integrates the efficient conversion of resources with concern for long-term environmental consequences.

This excellence is more than product quality. It also refers to quality of process and, most importantly, quality of people. The combination of quality process, people and products will make sustainable development a reality and will be a market for opportunity for the company.

Schmidheiny has argued that the cornerstone of sustainable development is a system of open, competitive markets in which prices reflect the costs of environmental as well as other resources. But the markets have failed to integrate environmental costs into economic decisions. These costs—externalities—are spread throughout society and are external to business operations. The most important correction necessary in current market systems is to factor these externalities into the cost of doing business. Schmidheiny states that there are three basic ways to move business to internalize environmental costs: governmental regulation, business or industry self-regulation, and economic instruments (i.e., pollution taxes, trading pollution rights). His view is that competitive advantage and increased profitability are among the reasons to strive for sustainable development and that environmentalism is good for business (Schmidheiny, 1992). Chapter 8 of this book discusses the prospects for including external environmental costs in corporate decision.

Cairncross (1992) supports environmental policies that place the burden on the "polluters" and not on society. She argues that government and business need to act in partnership to promote economic growth while minimizing environmental impacts.

General Motors, a member of the President's Council on Sustainable Development, has acknowledged in its 1994 Public Interest Report that it agrees with the principles that:

- A healthy economy and a healthy environment go hand in hand;
- America must lead the way in promoting economic growth and environmental preservation at home and abroad;
- We must move beyond the false choices and unnecessary antagonisms of the past to create the partnerships needed to ensure sustainable development.

Thus, there is increasingly widespread agreement about the notion of sustainable development. Companies have come to recognize that a balance between economics and environmental sensitivity is required of business. Further, they recognize that they can achieve competitive advantages through a conscientious examination of processes and products—that a reduction in environmental impacts often leads to increased long-term corporate profitability through higher production yields and improved product quality. Integrating environmental impacts into management decisions often requires balancing economics and the environment—the core of sustainable development. It also often demonstrates the significant financial advantages that can be achieved through innovation in process and product designs motivated by environmental concerns.

THE DEVELOPMENT OF A CORPORATE ENVIRONMENTAL STRATEGY

Lent and Wells conducted a survey of 41 mostly Fortune 200 firms. The survey indicated that environmental management is "becoming central to corporate strategy and is being managed as an arena of competition rather than as a compliance driven function" (Lent and Wells, 1992, 379). The authors argue that this change is being driven by three important new developments:

- Customers are buying more products that they can identify as having positive environmental attributes;
- The threat of ozone depletion and the response by business to eliminate CFCs brought environmental management into the mainstream of business;
- Total quality management and pollution prevention are a good fit in that they seek to prevent defects and pollution before they occur.

Professor Scott Barrett views part of the relationship between business and environmental regulators as a game of strategy. "Business can play an instrumental role in environmental protection by employing strategy to create competitive advantage, and government can use strategy to protect the environment more effectively than the standard theory permits" (Barrett, 1992, 203).

Substantial competitive advantages can be achieved through improved environmental performance. They often are reflected in improved product quality, improved production yields, and improved profitability, the result of redesigned processes and products. There is also substantial support for balancing economic and environmental concerns in industry by adopting the principle of sustainable development. Companies have come to recognize that their own future depends on balancing these concerns and that reduced environmental impacts and the institutionalization of corporate environmental responsibility can lead to improved operations and profitability.

One recent change affecting the analysis of environmental projects is the significant decline in energy prices. Low energy prices have made it more difficult for many companies to justify substantial investments in energy conservation, as the social and financial benefits may not outweigh the significant financial costs. This decision process depends in part on an analysis of the total costs and benefits through a Total Stakeholder Analysis, as discussed in Chapter 4. If present energy costs and prices adequately reflected the full costs of energy production, including the environmental costs, investments in capital and process improvements of energy producers would be justified more easily. It is critical that all companies in the energy production industries include these full costs in their development of corporate strategy and the calculation of product costs for the future sustainability of both the environment and the companies. Current energy prices and a company's estimate of future energy prices may have an enormous impact on the calculation of the benefits of environmental improvements and also on the development of both general corporate strategy and corporate environmental strategy.

Understanding the importance of environmental improvement must lead to the development and implementation of a corporate environmental strategy that can be used to set corporate policies, change corporate culture, and integrate environmental impacts in managerial decisions at all levels, in all facilities, and at all geographic locations of the organization. This strategy must initiate corporate environmental policies that can adapt to changing environmental regulations and changing technologies and can integrate forecasts of likely changes into management planning processes and environmental management decisions. It must produce a company that is proactive rather than reactive and that focuses on environmental planning rather than on environmental compliance. It must push the company to change the design of products and processes to eliminate waste, reduce environmental impacts, and make investments likely to improve long-term corporate profitability.

The process begins with the development of a strategy that has the commitment of senior company officers and will be implemented. Having the CEO and other senior corporate officers set the tone at the top is critical but not sufficient. A corporate environmental mission statement usually is adopted to convey the corporate commitment throughout the organization. Then corporate environmental strategies must be developed that can move the corporation to be more environmentally responsible. Such a move must be seen as a core corporate value, central to company operations, rather than as a reaction to current governmental regulations. The implementation must continue through:

- Broad-based institutional support for the company strategy;
- Development of an EH&S organizational structure;

- Environmental policies;
- Personnel who support a desire for increased environmental responsibility and a change in corporate culture.

The development of an environmental strategy is important for small companies and large companies alike, in high-impact and low-impact industries. It must become an important part of the corporate performance appraisal system that evaluates the performance of the corporation, its divisions and facilities, and its employees.

ROLE OF CORPORATE MISSION STATEMENT IN CLARIFYING CORPORATE COMMITMENT

The president's letter to the shareholders in corporate annual reports usually conveys the goals, missions, and strategy of the company. In the 1992 Annual Report of Pacific Gas & Electric, the president's letter describes a strategy for the future linked directly to cleaning up and protecting the environment. The president and chairman indicate that, in anticipation of the 1992 Energy Policy Act, which promotes energy efficiency and the use of renewable resources, the company began developing a new business strategy. The strategy emphasizes meeting growth in electricity demand through improved customer energy efficiency and renewables. "Efficiency is the most cost effective way to meet our customers' growing electric needs, and also maximizes the benefits to the environment." The company is seeking to expand its natural gas system for its customers, which also improves the environment by promoting "clean" energy sources. One of the company's stated goals—to improve the quality of the environment—has been added to its mission statement.

An example of this strategy can be seen in the company's customer energy efficiency (CEE) programs. PG&E believes that "by using energy wisely, Californians can save money and improve air quality and PG&E can meet future electric demands without building major new power plants. CEE is expected to reduce PG&E customer energy bills by more than $2 billion by the year 2000..."

The result of the development of a corporate environmental strategy within a company is a mission statement in the annual report or the EH&S report. The mission statement represents the goals the company will strive to achieve and the commitments it has made to its various constituents— employees, shareholders, customers, and the public. Often the statement is but a few paragraphs. In DuPont's case it is a detailed statement and commitment personally signed and agreed to by the 30 most senior officers of the company. The DuPont statement has been revised several times, most recently in July 1994. It is specific in its goals, including zero emissions and zero waste (see Exhibit 2–1).

Another example of a mission statement is Eastman Kodak's Health, Safety, and Environment Guiding Principles, shown in Exhibit 2–2. This statement emanates from the company's Vision of Environmental Responsibility:

> To be among the world's best companies in protecting the health and safety of our people, communities, and customers, and the quality of our environment. Our products, services and facilities, as well as the business opportunities that we pursue, reflect the fact that environmental responsibility is a fundamental Kodak value.

Eastman Kodak has established a Public Policy Committee of the Board of Directors and a Management Committee on Environmental Responsibility to set the overall direction for EH&S. It also has EH&S coordinating committees to administer policy at the group and unit levels. These committees are vehicles to help the company carry out the policies established in its corporate mission statement.

SUMMARY

It is with a strong mission statement and a tone at the top set by the CEO that corporate environmental sensitivity gets started. Executives must recognize that the development of a strong corporate environmental strategy and environmental policies are critical to changing corporate culture and reducing environmental impacts. Managers should be proactive and plan a strategy to be more environmentally responsible and increase corporate profitability.

Following changing government regulations is not the answer. The competitive advantages that can be gained through environmental planning place companies ahead of mere compliance with regulations. Environmental responsibility must be seen as a core corporate value. The development of a support system through policies and an appropriate organizational structure is critical. In the balance of this book we examine how companies can identify, measure, and integrate environmental impacts into a corporate strategy and into all relevant management decisions to reduce those impacts and increase profitability.

EXHIBIT 2–1
The DuPont Commitment (Safety, Health and the Environment)

The DuPont Commitment
Safety, Health and the Environment

We affirm to all our stakeholders, including our employees, customers, shareholders and the public, that we will conduct our business with respect and care for the environment. We will implement those strategies that build successful businesses and achieve the greatest benefit for all our stakeholders without compromising the ability of future generations to meet their needs.

We will continuously improve our practices in light of advances in technology and new understandings in safety, health and environmental science. We will make consistent, measurable progress in implementing this Commitment throughout our worldwide operations. DuPont supports the chemical industry's Responsible Care* and the oil industry's Strategies for Today's Environmental Partnership as key programs to achieve this Commitment.

Highest Standards of Performance, Business Excellence

We will adhere to the highest standards for the safe operation of facilities and the protection of our environment, our employees, our customers and the people of the communities in which we do business.

We will strengthen our businesses by making safety, health and environmental issues an integral part of all business activities and by continuously striving to align our businesses with public expectations.

Goal of Zero Injuries, Illnesses and Incidents

We believe that all injuries and occupational illnesses, as well as safety and environmental incidents, are preventable, and our goal for all of them is zero. We will promote off-the-job safety for our employees.

We will assess the environmental impact of each facility we propose to construct and will design, build, operate and maintain all our facilities and transportation equipment so they are safe and acceptable to local communities and protect the environment.

We will be prepared for emergencies and will provide leadership to assist our local communities to improve their emergency preparedness.

Goal of Zero Waste and Emissions

We will drive toward zero waste generation at the source. Materials will be reused and recycled to minimize the need for treatment or disposal and to conserve resources. Where waste is generated, it will be handled and disposed of safely and responsibly.

We will drive toward zero emissions, giving priority to those that may present the greatest potential risk to health or the environment.

Where past practices have created conditions that require correction, we will responsibly correct them.

Conservation of Energy and Natural Resources, Habitat Enhancement

We will excel in the efficient use of coal, oil, natural gas, water, minerals and other natural resources.

We will manage our land to enhance habitats for wildlife.

Continuously Improving Processes, Practices and Products

We will extract, make, use, handle, package, transport and dispose of our materials safely and in an environmentally responsible manner.

We will continuously analyze and improve our practices, processes and products to reduce their risk and impact throughout the product life cycle. We will develop new products and processes that have increasing margins of safety for both human health and the environment.

We will work with our suppliers, carriers, distributors and customers to achieve similar product stewardship, and we will provide information and assistance to support their efforts to do so.

Open and Public Discussion, Influence on Public Policy

We will promote open discussion with our stakeholders about the materials we make, use and transport and the impacts of our activities on their safety, health and environments.

We will build alliances with governments, policy makers, businesses and advocacy groups to develop sound policies, laws, regulations and practices that improve safety, health and the environment.

Management and Employee Commitment, Accountability

The Board of Directors, including the Chief Executive Officer, will be informed about pertinent safety, health and environmental issues and will ensure that policies are in place and actions taken to achieve this Commitment.

Compliance with this Commitment and applicable laws is the responsibility of every employee and contractor acting on our behalf and a condition of their employment or contract. Management in each business is responsible to educate, train and motivate employees to understand and comply with this Commitment and applicable laws.

We will deploy our resources, including research, development and capital, to meet this Commitment and will do so in a manner that strengthens our businesses.

We will measure and regularly report to the public our global progress in meeting this Commitment.

* Replaces November 1971 Policy
  July 1994

EXHIBIT 2–2

Eastman Kodak (Health, Safety, and Environment Guiding Principles)

Health, Safety and Environment Guiding Principles

Guiding Principle 1: *To extend knowledge by conducting or supporting research on the health, safety, and environmental effects of our products, processes and waste materials.*

Guiding Principle 2: *To operate our plants and facilities in a manner that protects the environment and the health and safety of our employees and the public, and is efficient in the use of natural resources and energy.*

Guiding Principle 3: *To make health, safety, and environmental considerations a priority in our planning for all existing and new products and processes.*

Guiding Principle 4: *To develop, produce, and market products and materials that can be manufactured, transported, used, and disposed of safely and in a way that poses no undue environmental impact.*

Guiding Principle 5: *To counsel customers on the safe use, transportation, storage, and disposal of our products and, for those services we provide, to provide them safely.*

Guiding Principle 6: *To participate with governments and others in creating responsible laws, regulations and standards to safeguard the community, workplace, and environment and in applying environmentally sound management practices and technologies.*

Guiding Principle 7: *To measure our environmental performance on a regular basis and provide—to officials. employees, customers, shareowners, and the public—appropriate and timely information on health, safety or environmental hazards, initiatives, and recommended protective and preventive measures.*

Guiding Principle 8: *To recognize and respond to community concerns about our operations and to work with others to resolve problems created by handling and disposal of hazardous substances.*

Guiding Principle 9: *To encourage employees to apply off the job the same principles for health, safety and the environment that are applied at work.*

Reprinted courtesy Eastman Kodak Company.

Chapter Three

Minimizing Environmental Impacts

The 3Rs of environmental management are:

- Reduce: generate less waste;
- Reuse: reuse that which retains its usefulness;
- Recycle: send for recycling that which cannot be reused.

The goal is to eliminate the production of all waste through improved product and process design. This goal means eliminating the waste within the manufacturing facility and the post-consumer waste after the product is used. It is only after a thorough analysis of the 3Rs that disposal should be considered.

In 1986, Dow Chemical developed its waste management program, Waste Reduction Always Pays (WRAP), to emphasize its focus on continually seeking out ways to reduce waste. This program benefits the environment significantly and also has led to savings in fuel, raw material, and environmental control costs. It has increased productivity and improved product quality.

It is with concepts such as these in mind that the take-back principle was established and life cycle assessments and life cycle cost assessments were introduced. The senior executives I talked with agreed overwhelmingly that they expect U.S. companies to be required, within the next decade, to take responsibility for the reuse, recycling, or ultimate disposal of the products they produce. Whether this trend begins in Europe or elsewhere, it is likely that various government regulations and competitive pressures will force companies worldwide to consider disposal costs related to post-consumer waste in their various management decisions including costing, capital budgeting, and product design.

RECYCLING AND THE TAKE-BACK PRINCIPLE

One approach governments are using to reduce and prevent pollution is to require manufacturers to "take back" their products at the end of their useful life. The companies must be concerned with the ultimate disposal of their products including post-consumer waste. This approach will encourage manufacturers to be more environmentally sensitive to the components of their products and to apply that sensitivity throughout the supply chain. The German government, for example, is expected to become the first to require most manufacturers to take back and recycle their products once their service life ends. BMW already has set up recycling plants in Germany and in the United States. BMW owners can exchange their cars for a $500 voucher toward the purchase of a new or dealer-certified used BMW (Protzman, 1993).

Germany also has strict regulations that hold the manufacturers of consumer goods responsible for the recycling of packaging. In a recent court ruling, it was held that cities and towns have the right to impose taxes on disposable containers such as cans, paper plates, plastic cups, and silverware. Under local regulations, two McDonald's franchises were charged the equivalent of 30 cents for each paper plate they used to encourage take-back and recycling. McDonald's of Germany now is considering whether to close some of these German outlets because of these taxes, while other municipalities are considering similar taxes (Kinzer, 1994). Certainly pressure is increasing for the reduction, reuse, recycling, and take-back of products throughout the world.

This approach places the responsibility for product disposal on the manufacturers in the hope that they will design their products so as to facilitate recycling and disposal. This product-oriented environmental strategy already has begun in Europe and Japan. "In 1990, Japan enacted the Law for Promotion of Utilization of Recyclable Resources, a far reaching new statute that mandates national requirements for the take back of a variety of products, including televisions, refrigerators, and other appliances" (Hayes, 1993).

There are numerous other examples of companies participating in programs that focus on the ultimate disposition of their products and the drive to reduce waste. In 1990, the Unocal Corporation began a program to buy pre-1971 automobiles for $700. This program is believed to have reduced pollution emissions in the Los Angeles area by 12.8 million pounds. Unocal has continued to offer this scrappage program as an effective way to reduce emissions (Hahn, 1992). Through its product take-back programs in Europe, IBM has recycled or reused 82% of the 12,000 metric tons of computers returned to IBM. Parts and components of these returned machines are tested, refurbished, and then recycled. Those parts not recyclable are disposed of properly.

Many companies indeed are concerned that if they do not become more environmentally sensitive, they will not be able to sell their products in various countries, including most of Europe, because of various European Community initiatives along with emerging requirements of the International Organization for Standardization (ISO). Whether these programs are voluntary or regulatory, growing public pressure is causing governments, corporations, and individual consumers to be concerned with the environmental impacts and the reuse, recycling, and ultimate disposition of the products they buy.

In the last few years consumer interest in recycling has increased dramatically in addition to the increased concern for product take-back. At Browning-Ferris Industries, Inc., the number of households served by recycling programs increased from 40,000 in 1988 to 4.4 million in 1994.

Weyerhaeuser has made a profitable business out of recycling waste-paper. The first year in which Americans recovered more paper for recycling than was put into landfills was 1993. Weyerhaeuser collected 1.8 million tons of office paper, corrugated packaging, and newsprint to supply fiber to its own mills as well as domestic and overseas customers. By 1995 the company expects to increase that amount to 3 million tons.

The Eastman Kodak Company is among a few companies that produces a single-use recyclable camera. Its product, the FunSaver, must be returned to the photo finisher to get color prints. Kodak pays a handling fee to the photo finisher for each returned camera and also pays the shipping costs. Since the inception of this program in 1990, more than 25 million cameras have been recycled and diverted from waste streams and landfills. More than 85% of each camera is recycled or reused, and many do not require disassembly. The best estimates are that only 50% of the single-use cameras are being recycled, and Kodak is looking into ways to raise that return percentage to 60% by increasing the incentive to photo finishers and starting other incentive programs.

Another area that has focused substantial efforts on product recycling has been the manufacturing and servicing of copiers. Xerox's new copiers and printers are designed with customer-replaceable copy cartridges that are to be returned and remanufactured. This focus on design for the environment is part of an Environmental Leadership Program that emphasizes asset management to minimize the total environmental impact during the product life cycle, including the post-consumer waste. It also is sensitive to the bottom line, however. The mission statement contains as an objective the "profitable utilization of unserviceable parts and equipment consistent with environmental goals," although "environmental health and safety concerns take priority over economic considerations." The goal is that by 1997 all products will be brought back to the factory, and new designs will have a 0% disposal rate. Ideally these waste-free products would be produced in a waste-free factory. The current goal requires reducing both the number of components and the amount of materials used. For example, in the copier industry as in many other industries including the automobile industry, the number of different plastics used is being reduced substantially, permitting easier recycling of materials.

Examining the financial trade-offs and the environmental impacts of various design options early in the product design development identifies the potential for reducing the total product life cycle costs. To promote the copier cartridge recycling program, customers are offered financial incentives for returns. The product costs and product pricing policy reflect incentives for returns and the benefits to Xerox of reusable products. For other manufacturers, pushing concern for environmental impacts to the product design stage reduces both environmental and company costs. In many cases, a focus on take-back not only forces a change in the process and product design but often encourages the consideration of full cost accounting discussed in Chapter 8. A recognition of the ultimate cost of responsibility for disposal of post-consumer waste should cause manufacturers to ensure that they do not undercost and underprice their products because of inadequate information regarding the environmental cost component of product costs.

LIFE CYCLE ASSESSMENTS AND LIFE CYCLE COST ASSESSMENTS

One approach to the consideration of the total impacts of products on various stakeholders is through life cycle assessments. "Life Cycle Assessment (LCA) is a design discipline used to minimize the environmental impacts of products, technologies, materials, processes, industrial systems, activities, or services" (*SETAC News*, 1993, 1). The Society of Environmental Toxicology and Chemistry (SETAC), founded in 1979, is made up of professionals from academia, business, and government interested in promoting the use of multidisciplinary approaches to examining the impacts of chemicals and technology on the environment. In 1990, SETAC established an LCA Advisory Group to advance the science, practice, and application of LCA so as to reduce the resource consumption and environmental burdens associated with products, packaging, processes, or activities.

The Business Council for Sustainable Development (BCSD) is developing material on accounting for internal environmental costs to delineate their principles more explicitly. The BCSD distinguishes among life cycle analysis, life cycle assessment, and life cycle cost analysis. It defines life cycle analysis as a "system-oriented approach which estimates the environmental effects and energy and resource usage associated with a product, process or operation throughout its chain of commerce." Life cycle assessment is an extension of life cycle analysis and is viewed "as a holistic, three-stage methodology:

"(1) Inventory, which identifies and quantifies the environmental energy and resources impacts of a product or activity across its life cycles.

"(2) Impact, which assesses potential environmental problems of concerns identified in the inventory stage.

"(3) Improvement, which evaluates opportunities to effect reduction in environmental releases and resource use.

"Life cycle cost analysis adds a monetary component to life cycle analysis. It assigns a cost to each impact quantified in the life cycle analysis, and sums these costs to estimate the net environmental costs of a product or process" (BCSD, 1993, 13).

The Department of Defense (DOD) has been using life cycle costing in its acquisition of defense weapons systems. "Under Title 10 of the U.S. Code, the Secretary of Defense may not approve entry of a major defense acquisition program either into engineering and manufacturing development or into production without considering a life cycle cost estimate from a source independent of the sponsoring component" (Anderberg, 1994, 5). Anderberg proposes that regulations regarding the "acquisition life cycle include a disposal phase on the same plane as the development, production, and operations and support phases." In fiscal year 1994, the DOD budgeted $5.7 billion for environmental issues, primarily cleanup, remediation, and compliance. Much of the cleanup and remediation fund may be traced to the disposal of weapon systems. The Cost Analysis Improvement Group within the DOD is responsible for the life cycle cost estimates included in the package of information on which defense system purchasing decisions are made. The Group now will begin to consider environmental costs and impacts, using an LCA approach. It is to "treat the impact of the system on the environment in the same sense as the impact of the environment on the system."

Life cycle costing is a method of cradle-to-grave product accounting first used for defense procurement in the mid-1960s and adapted in the last few years to analyze environmental problems. Life cycle costing attaches a monetary measure to every effect of a product and projects likely future costs, much like cash flow analysis. Then it compares two or more product or packaging alternatives based on its projections (Kleiner, 1991, 40).

Though life cycle assessment, life cycle analysis, life cycle costing, and life cycle cost analysis are terms that all have been used in this general area, in this study we have used LCA to refer to a life cycle assessment in its most comprehensive form. We have used it as part of an Environmental Strategy Implementation (ESI) that includes identifying and measuring past, current, and future impacts of a product from "cradle to cradle" (an expression that implies "from inception to second beginning"). ESI also includes environmental and other impacts, both costs and benefits, and looks at impacts on the company and all of its stakeholders. It uses a Total Stakeholder Analysis (TSA) as a basis for the identification and various accounting, economic, and social science measurements for its costing. Impacts are identified and measured except when measurement is considered undesirable. Physical measures are used only when monetized measures are deemed inappropriate.

Ciba-Geigy has begun using life cycle assessments to aid in project selection and as an input to the product design process. The company has developed a computer program that simulates the environmental impact of various product and process changes. It uses LCA to make product packaging choices and to compare the energy requirements for the production of various materials.

Dow Chemical has been developing its LCA methodology and has completed pilot programs in the chemical and plastics businesses with full implementation expected in 1995.

EXHIBIT 3–1
Bristol-Myers Squibb (Environment 2000—Product Life Cycle)

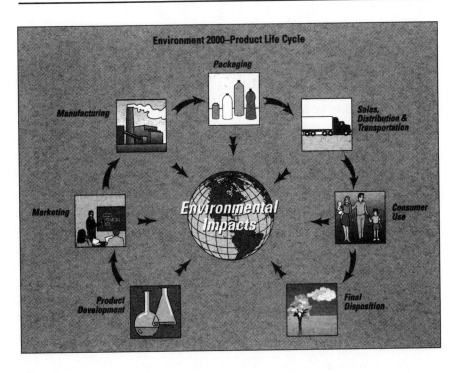

In 1992, Bristol-Myers Squibb embarked on a company-wide pollution prevention program called Environment 2000 (see Exhibit 3–1), based on integrating product life cycle management into the core of its businesses and thereby integrating environmental protection into all decisions of the company. EH&S Vice President Thomas M. Hellman has stated that "understanding the relationship between environmental quality and product design provides an opportunity to achieve competitive advantage in the marketplace."

Using a framework developed by external consultants—Environmental Resources Management, Inc. (ERM)—Bristol-Myers Squibb has developed a protocol for use throughout the company to help in identifying EH&S issues at each stage of a product's life cycle. This approach drives the consideration of impacts throughout all parts of the company so that all employees can easily see the part they play in reducing environmental impacts.

In many cases measures of the environmental impacts must be developed so that the effects can be evaluated better. Among the tasks suggested in the Bristol-Myers Squibb initiative are:

- Designation of a pollution prevention coordinator;
- Establishment of pollution prevention teams and identification of targets for pollution prevention activities;
- Identification of the environmental impacts;
- Measurement of the impacts;
- Identification of the opportunities to reduce the impacts.

Then the technical, regulatory, and economic feasibility must be examined and goals for improvement must be established and implemented. The cycle is completed through an evaluation of performance, reports to management, and the feedback loop that leads to a reassessment of options and striving for continuous improvement.

Why is the program called Environment 2000? It is in partial recognition of the difficulty in changing a corporate culture. Bristol-Myers has recognized that it will take until the year 2000 to get all the programs implemented and the changes in place. Business units now integrate product life cycle goals in their five-year strategic plans, and product life cycle reviews are being completed on a regular basis. In the company's 1993 Report on Environmental Progress, EH&S Vice President Thomas Hellman stated that "during a product life cycle review, employees from marketing, R&D, manufacturing, packaging, finance, and other functional areas work together to inventory the environmental impacts of our products and processes. For existing products, the life cycle review helps us identify where we can make improvements. For new products under development, product life cycle helps us to prevent the use of materials and practices that may be detrimental to the environment."

The review aids the company in evaluating the potential risks and opportunities related to a product. It is the type of analysis that proactive companies increasingly are using to understand the costs and benefits of various actions and to improve management decisions. With increased information on the likely future impacts of company products on the environment, companies are better able to forecast profits and determine whether current actions can increase benefits or reduce costs to the environment and the company. The objective, approach, and benefits of the Bristol-Myers Squibb product life cycle are stated in Exhibit 3–2.

EXHIBIT 3–2
Bristol-Myers Squibb (Pollution Prevention Throughout the
Product Life Cycle

**Pollution Prevention Throughout
the Product Life Cycle**

Objective:
To systematically identify
opportunities to prevent pollution
and gain competitive advantage

Approach:
To highlight how employees from
many functional areas can prevent
pollution that is generated throughout
a product's life cycle (e.g., product
design, manufacture, distribution, sales,
consumer use, and ultimate fate) and
thereby reduce the environmental impact
of our businesses' activities.

Benefits:
• Reducing environmental liabilities;
• Increasing cost-effectiveness of
  complying with environmental
  regulations;
• Developing safer and more
  environmentally sound products;
• Minimizing waste of energy
  and raw materials;
• Differentiating products
  from the competition; and
• Being recognized as a good
  environmental citizen.

One of the first product life cycles completed by Bristol-Myers Squibb was for Ban Roll-On. Through a process that identifies the environmental impacts associated with the "formulation, manufacture, packaging, distribution, use, and ultimate fate," the product life cycle team identified more than 20 potential action items for improving Ban Roll-On. Changes were made and savings realized from this process. By downsizing the package to a snug-fit carton, the company realized a savings of 600 tons of recycled paperboard and 55 percent shelf space, which translates into pollution prevention and cost reduction.

Bristol-Myers Squibb also has been a leader in recycling and waste reduction. This process of improved product life cycle management has reduced environmental impacts in many ways:

- Reformulating products so that chemicals can be replaced by water as solvents;
- Using closed-loop technologies to capture and reuse manufacturing chemicals;
- Extracting oil from metal manufacturing scrap before sending it to a salvage company;
- Making extensive recycling efforts and various waste minimization efforts;
- Redesigning products to minimize packaging or making certain packaging is made of recycled or recyclable materials.

It is through both process and product improvements such as these that sustainable development can be achieved and that the resulting environmental improvements can benefit both the environment and the bottom line.

Managers at The Body Shop believe they have a moral obligation to achieve sustainable development, and LCA is an important process in achieving that goal. LCAs have been initiated separately for 50 ingredients used in Body Shop products. The company produced its first environmental audit in 1992. To ensure due environmental diligence in its supply chain, the company has set up a program of product stewardship that takes a life cycle approach to the sourcing, manufacture, and use of products. The program has four elements:

- Risk assessment of raw materials;
- Environmental accreditation of suppliers;
- Life cycle assessment to cover the full range of potential ecological impacts associated with the sourcing of ingredients as well as the manufacture, distribution and use of products;
- Distribution of guidance notes on commodities and products used, which are available to all buyers.

EXHIBIT 3–3
Migros

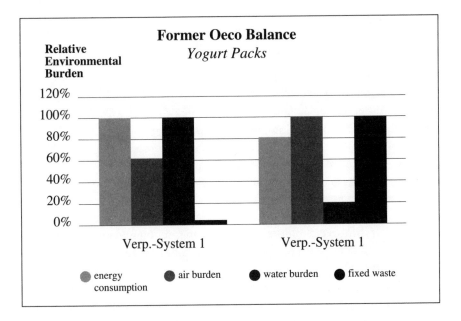

Migros, a Swiss retail trading company, developed an environmental information system and then a computer-based life cycle assessment system for its product packaging. The "Oeco Balances," as they are called, show the environmental burden of air, water, energy, and waste packaging alternatives. The totals of environmental burdens of all life phases of a packing system (packaging and logistic repacking) are considered, from the manufacture of the packing raw material to the waste disposal including transport, possible washing processes, and so on.

Exhibit 3–3 shows the Oeco Balance for two yogurt packaging alternatives according to the Oeco Balance model. Negative "eco-points" are assigned for each adverse environmental impact associated with a product from cradle to grave.

In 1987 Northern Telecom acknowledged its commitment to protect the environment and since has developed a program using life cycle assessments. "Design for Disassembly is one practice that could allow us to recycle and reuse our products and individual components most effectively. Under PLCM [product life cycle management], environmental criteria, such as recyclability, are to be incorporated into each phase of product development. Ultimately, we hope to ensure that our products have the least harmful environmental impact in all life cycle phases."

The 3M Company has developed a Life Cycles Model to anticipate product responsibility requirements encountered during the product life cycle and to provide a plan to deal with those requirements. The Life Cycles Model assists business units in developing products with an optimum balance of performance, cost, and EH&S characteristics. It is intended to encourage business units to make prudent choices in developing products and packaging that can be manufactured, distributed, used, and disposed of safely. The key phases in this model are the product concept, product design, process, distribution, use, and disposition. During each phase of the product life cycle, the model identifies and solves environmental, health, and safety problems. Then the solution is evaluated for its benefits and for any new problems it creates for each of the other life cycle phases. The ongoing problem/solution analysis systematically deals with the problems and solutions faced in each phase of the design and redesign of a product.

Life cycle assessments provide a valuable framework for identifying the total impacts of a corporation's activities, processes, and products. Too few companies have adopted these frameworks, and even fewer have applied physical and monetary measures to produce an analysis highly useful for management decisions.

Beginning in Chapter 4, we introduce the approach to Environmental Strategy Implementation that is central to this book. It provides a framework and a procedure to do the most comprehensive LCA including identifying and measuring the impacts. It proposes a Total Stakeholder Analysis to aid in identifying impacts. Measurements then are proposed to help companies measure costs and benefits to both the company and its various stakeholders. These measurements are in monetary terms whenever possible. When such measures are impractical or undesirable, the complete identification of all stakeholder impacts has been useful. It allows management to consider all impacts and all stakeholder interests in the decision-making process.

A complete Environmental Strategy Implementation allows companies to better evaluate their products through the entire value chain, from suppliers to producers to customers. It gives companies improved information to choose among various process improvements, product improvements, and capital improvements. It allows them to understand the impacts of their products on various stakeholders and to redesign products and processes to reduce those impacts.

An Environmental Strategy Implementation provides information to aid in effective planning for changes in societal and environmental trends and in environmental regulations and technology. It allows managers to understand the full impacts of products and processes on both the environment and on long-run corporate profits and provides information to reduce these impacts and increase corporate profits. The use of both LCA and ESI is likely to increase substantially in the near future.

REDUCING WASTE THROUGH PRODUCT AND PROCESS REDESIGN

The EPA's Design for the Environment Program is a voluntary program that works closely with private sector partners to incorporate environmental considerations, especially risk reduction and pollution prevention, at the front end of the design process. The existence of such a program shows that concern for post-consumer waste, recycling, reusing, and proper disposal is growing rapidly, with the copier and automotive industries among the leaders.

In 1993, for example, Ford issued design guidelines to its suppliers to improve the recyclability of its vehicles and increase the recycled material content. Nearly 80% of the content of its new cars now can be recycled. It is using many other recycled materials in its production, including 54 million recycled soft drink bottles, to produce luggage racks, reinforcement panels, and door padding. It also moved aggressively to reduce solid waste and now is recycling more than 70% of the solid waste material from its plants.

As part of the Vehicle Recycling Partnership, General Motors, Ford, and Chrysler have agreed to use the same code for labeling plastic parts weighing more than 100 grams to make these parts easier to sort and recycle. Currently GM uses in-plant scrap materials for the production of fender liners, fascias, wheel covers, and speaker grill housings for a variety of automobile models.

> Almost everything in a car can be recycled. The only question is how much are we prepared to pay and what will the consequences be for the environment. A car consists of metal (60–70%), plastics (10–15%) and rubber (5%) as well

as smaller amounts of glass, wood, paper and textiles... The role of plastics within car production is disputed. On the one hand, they save weight, which reduces fuel consumption; on the other, certain plastics are not yet economically recoverable. Consequently, in order to facilitate recycling, every plastic component is specially coded... Before the different parts are separated from each other, oil and other hazardous liquids as well as the battery, the automatic belt tensioners and the airbag are removed from the car ("With Respect for Nature," SAAB, 1992).

Motorola's chief executive officer, Gary Tooker, has emphasized that current products must be designed and manufactured so that they will have a positive impact on the environment. Like most other senior executives, Tooker believes that "product disassembly, reuse and recycle will be mandated by take-back rules expected to be in place around the world." So Motorola, in addition to an eight-hour course on environmental awareness required of all employees, is conducting an eight-hour course for its engineers on designing for the environment. It has made these courses available to its suppliers, thus driving the concerns for environmental impact reductions earlier in the supply chain and emphasizing the importance of environmental considerations in all procurement decisions.

It is the combination of many of these approaches that creates benefits for both the environment and the company. At IBM, "progress is being achieved through a number of source reduction methods, such as chemical and material substitution, process reengineering, reuse and recycling initiatives; and a host of air, water, waste and energy management programs." The company instruction on environmental impact assessment requires IBM engineers to assess the potential safety and environmental impact of products and processes during the design stage. New efforts have focused the attention of the design engineers "on all aspects of a product's life cycle, including packaging, material selection, energy efficiency and recyclability."

AT&T has employed total quality management (TQM) principles and reduced paper use in its offices by more than 25 percent in three years with savings of 6,000 tons of paper and millions of dollars. The company is recycling more than 60 percent of its waste paper and applying the design for environment approach to manufacturing so that "the design of any product will take into account the environmental impact of its entire life cycle." It has developed a Green Index that scores design characteristics of AT&T products based on environmental sensitivity. Scores are analyzed to determine how the product's environmental impacts can be reduced. AT&T has found that driving environmental considerations to the product design stage has moved the company closer to sustainability and has reduced both environmental impacts and company costs.

Outside the manufacturing sector, service companies have found numerous opportunities to reduce their environmental impact. Just as consumer products manufacturers and distributors have changed product packaging, restaurants have reduced packaging and often made other significant efforts to reduce environmental impacts. McDonald's drink trays are made from recycled newspapers, and the materials from which the company's buildings are constructed include recycled photographic film, computer casings, and recycled automobile tires. In addition to recycling efforts, the company has reduced the volume of waste produced by switching from foam packaging to paper wrapping for its sandwiches, reducing the volume of sandwich packaging by 90 percent. Companies continually find waste reduction and recycling opportunities through careful analyses of the environmental impacts. Again, we see the important benefits to both the environment and the corporate bottom line from product improvements motivated by a thorough review of the environmental impacts of the products and processes.

Herman Miller, a manufacturer of office furniture systems, has included environmental considerations in its product designs. It has an environmental quality action team that ensures environmental issues are included in business decisions. The only woods the company uses in its products come from carefully managed forests that are not depleted by their use. It also considers cradle-to-grave design by examining the use of aluminum in its products. The aluminum requires little energy to fabricate, generates few pollutants, and disassembles easily for recycling. The company has significantly reduced impacts on the environment and company costs through an $11 million energy center. The center turns scrap material into energy to heat and cool the company's 800,000-square-foot manufacturing and corporate headquarters facility. Herman Miller also has a program to recycle materials used in its factory and offices and to reduce the amount of packaging materials.

In 1967, Xerox Corporation was faced with a potential health hazard associated with the disposal of its photoreceptor drums. These drums were made from aluminum with an arsenic alloy coating and created a potential danger in disposal. To avoid this potential hazard, Xerox decided to reclaim the drums. What began as a way to avoid a potential hazard became a profitable business for Xerox. The drums were remanufactured for reuse at a fraction of the cost of a new photoreceptor drum, and the remanufacturing of parts has been expanded. Currently Xerox is reclaiming about 1,000,000 parts of equipment pieces representing a total value of $200 million (Bhushan and Mackenzie, 1994).

Many companies have achieved substantial benefits by analyzing processes and products to determine ways in which waste can be reduced and toxicity eliminated. Rockwell, for example, has been able to generate enough income from its recycling programs to offset all the costs of disposing of hazardous and nonhazardous wastes and to return $300,000 annually to the business. One of IBM's divisions has avoided 400,000 cubic feet of packaging waste through its reusable and recycled packaging, saving more than $4 million annually.

REDUCING WASTE THROUGH OPERATIONS AND PURCHASING

Another way to minimize environmental impacts is to put pressure on suppliers to reduce the negative environmental impacts of the components of the products or services they provide. By pushing these concerns throughout the supply chain, companies can reduce their environmental impacts and their environmental costs. It is also an opportunity to stimulate markets for environmentally sensitive products and materials.

McDonald's, for example, has incorporated waste reduction goals into the process of evaluating its suppliers. It encourages suppliers to be proactive in developing environmentally preferable products and packaging. All these efforts are part of McDonald's three waste reduction principles: reduce, reuse, recycle. The company is taking a "total life cycle approach to solid waste." Like many other companies, it is holding its suppliers accountable by conducting audits of supplier facilities, processes, and products for environmental impacts before beginning or continuing relationships. The company's life cycle approach and comprehensive look at its products and processes has significantly affected the volume of packaging used and the amount of waste produced. Further, costs have been reduced substantially so that the benefit to the environment and the company's profits is substantial.

McDonald's began a McRecycle USA program in 1990. It included halting the use of polystyrene clamshell and coffee cup containers in favor of clay-coated paperboard for its coffee cups and paper wrapping for its sandwiches.

As part of its program for reducing environmental impacts, The Body Shop has implemented an environmental accreditation scheme for its suppliers. This scheme grades external suppliers on predetermined criteria with a 0–5 star rating and has focused on raw materials and third-party manufacturers.

Tedd Saunders, whose family owns and operates the Boston Park Plaza Hotel, initiated various waste reduction programs into hotel operations. Among those programs were switching from paper and plasticware products in the employee cafeteria to china and glass, replacing the small plastic amenity bottles with a pump dispenser system, and replacing all the windows in the hotel with better insulated thermopane windows. The new amenity dispensers cost more than $91,000 to install but save $36,725 per year and eliminated the purchase of almost 2 million small plastic bottles. "What distinguished this program from many other green efforts was not only the desire to incorporate an environmental policy into every facet of the company but also to create an aggressive communications and education campaign for our employees, guests, and the general public" (Saunders, 1993, 67).

Many companies have found that simple changes in company processes and products bring significant savings. Recycling cardboard, tin cans, and plastic containers saves Cracker Barrel more than $100,000 annually in reduced trash hauling costs. In addition, working with its suppliers to reduce packaging, the company has dramatically reduced the amount of cardboard and plastic received that otherwise would need to be disposed of.

In 1991, Bristol-Myers Squibb adopted environmentally sensitive corporate purchasing guidelines that identify key environmental issues to be considered before any purchasing decision is made. These issues include renewable resources, process waste reduction, energy efficiency, hazard reduction, and supplier environmental stewardship. The purchasing department rates vendors on their environmental efforts through monthly reports and works with vendors to find solutions to environmental problems. The importance of environmental considerations in purchasing decisions is related explicitly to vendors. In addition, guidelines have been established for environmental evaluations of the facilities and operating practices of contract manufacturers and suppliers.

British Telecommunications (BT), while generally considered an environmentally clean company, recognizes that its operations still have an environmental impact. It is committed to environmental purchasing and requires its suppliers to make a positive contribution to the environment. The company publishes an Environmental Impact Generic Standard (GS 13) that details the environmental expectations it has for its suppliers. The company expects its suppliers to demonstrate that they minimize environmental hazards both in their own operations and in the goods and services they supply to BT. The company uses a whole-life approach to purchasing that takes into account the cradle-to-grave impact of goods and services on the environment. This standard details requirements the suppliers must meet for BT approval.

The supplier provides information to BT in response to the Generic Standard. That information is used, along with other commercially relevant data such as price, product reliability, quality, functionality, and so on, to determine who is awarded a contract. The relative weight given to any one environmental aspect varies according to the type of product being purchased and its expected environmental impact (Tuppen, 1993).

It is critical that, as part of the Total Stakeholder Analysis discussed throughout this book, companies not only examine the impact of the company and its products on its various stakeholders but also the impact of its stakeholders on various operations. We have seen numerous examples of companies that have established policies all suppliers and contractors must comply with to retain the company's business. Such companies often request permission to visit and inspect the supplier's facilities to be sure of compliance with company policies relating to the minimization of environmental impacts.

The full integration of suppliers into a Total Stakeholder Analysis requires recognizing the interrelationships through the supply chain, which are becoming more obvious. Companies affect their suppliers and through their policies can improve environmental sensitivity. Likewise, a supplier's use of recycled and recyclable materials and sensitivity to environmental impacts can significantly reduce a company's environmental impacts and financial costs. Process and product redesigns often are encouraged through careful monitoring of supplier relationships.

SUMMARY

Though many companies have increased the amount of recycled materials they are using and the number of products being recycled, much more can be done. Many companies have only begun this process, and many others have not yet transferred technologies company-wide. Decentralization of U.S. industry has, in many cases, reduced the ability to spread beneficial management practices throughout various business units and facilities. Further, companies only now are beginning to see the value of multifunctional teams that include EH&S professionals to provide input to process and product design.

By developing corporate environmental strategies and policies oriented toward environmental planning rather than compliance, companies can reduce environmental impacts substantially through process and product designs. Product quality, production yields, and profitability can be increased, and waste can be reduced or eliminated. Striving for continuous environmental improvement usually causes both environmental impacts and corporate costs to decrease. Companies are recognizing that by focusing on process and product design rather than on pollution control and cleanup, they increase profitability. But much more needs to be done.

Chapter Four

Systems for Identifying, Organizing, and Managing Corporate Environmental Impacts

F ollowing the development of a corporate environmental strategy, a company must turn quickly to the task of implementing that strategy. A system must be developed for identifying, organizing, and managing environmental impacts. This chapter begins with some of the issues involved in organizing a corporate structure to effectively manage these impacts and then proceeds to discuss a framework that aids companies in identifying environmental impacts. Finally, it examines some alternative frameworks for thinking about these impacts.

Analysis of environmental impacts also will prove useful in measuring overall corporate performance. Such measurement can be viewed as one element of the nonfinancial measures of performance that are becoming increasingly important in industry, such as corporate attempts at continuous improvement and benchmarking. This chapter describes additional results of the field investigations into the state of the art and best practices in measuring corporate environmental performance and implementing corporate environmental strategies.

AN INTRODUCTION TO ENVIRONMENTAL STRATEGY IMPLEMENTATION

As I interviewed and visited company executives, they mentioned certain issues and problems over and over. The balance of this book discusses these issues and problems and describes possible approaches and solutions (see Exhibit 4–1).

EXHIBIT 4–1

*Issues in the Measurement and Reporting of Corporate Environmental
Performance and the Execution of an Environmental Strategy
Implementation (ESI)*

Issues and Problems	Approaches and Solutions
1. How to organize the EH&S function	1. a) Need to have strong support from and access to senior corporate management. Build on strong corporate mission statement. b) Advocate environmental planning, rather than only compliance. c) Be a catalyst for linking the environmental information system to informational needs in both financial reporting system and management accounting system. d) Drive environmental information through various systems and involve legal, engineering, product design, accounting, finance, and operations to reduce environmental impacts and company costs.
2. How to identify impacts and potential environmental problems	2. Use Total Stakeholder Analysis for integration in Environmental Strategy Implementation (ESI) or life cycle assessment (LCA).
3. How to measure impacts	3. a) Need to measure fully in physical units. b) Need to measure in monetary units when possible.
4. How to report impacts within the company	4. Develop system for providing environmental impacts to relevant internal decision makers.
5. How to report impacts to external stakeholders	5. Develop strategy for disclosing environmental impacts in both corporate annual report and environmental report. *(continued)*

Many of the corporate concerns tend to center around how to broadly identify environmental costs and benefits. This identification and measurement encompass the broadest concept of life cycle assessment, which is described in this book and is being developed in numerous companies. After identifying and measuring impacts, the implementation proceeds with integration of the results into corporate information systems so that the results can be incorporated in various management deci-

EXHIBIT 4–1 *(concluded)*

Issues and Problems	Approaches and Solutions
6. How to integrate environmental costs into product costs	6. a) Track and accumulate current environmental costs related to current production. b) Use measurement of future environmental costs in product costing decisions. c) Assign current and future environmental costs related to current production to products. d) Assign current and future environmental costs related to past production to administrative costs so they do not affect costing, pricing, or performance evaluation decisions.
7. How to integrate environmental inputs into capital investment decisions	7. a) Use measurements of future environmental costs and benefits in capital investment decisions and integrate with other variables. Use standard discounted cash flow methods and standard company discount rates and methodology. b) Use risk assessments and various forecasting approaches to aid in analyzing potential changes in regulations, technologies, and the cost of technologies.
8. How to improve environmental performance	8. a) Identify impacts of alternative choices. b) Use available techniques to choose best alternatives among product improvements, process improvements, or capital improvements. c) Build into ESI or LCA model to ensure that all company personnel consider product impacts from cradle to cradle. d) Strive for continuous improvement of corporate environmental performance.
9. How to drive improved environmental performance throughout the organization	9. a) Integrate into existing performance evaluation system for all employees and teams. b) Develop environmental performance index for the measurement of facility, business unit, and corporate performance.

sions involving product costing, product pricing, product design, capital investments, and performance evaluations. The approaches suggested here currently are being introduced and used in numerous companies and can be adapted readily to companies of different sizes and complexity, in different industries, and with different environmental sensitivities.

This chapter also introduces the steps for Environmental Strategy Implementation (ESI) discussed in each of the remaining chapters and summarized in Chapter 11. These implementation steps begin with a thoughtful development of a corporate environmental strategy. The steps then move through the various systems and decisions in the organization to build a total structure for implementing corporate environmental policies, reducing corporate environmental impacts, and increasing long-term corporate profitability. These 15 steps should provide the guidance necessary to help companies improve the management of corporate environmental impacts.

ORGANIZATIONAL STRUCTURE

Corporate expenditures are rising rapidly, and improved organization and management of corporate environmental impacts have become critical. Mobil, for example, has seen its annual environmental expenditures grow to more than $1.25 billion annually, split almost evenly between capital expenditures and protection/compliance expenditures. To manage these expenditures and the environmental, health, and safety concerns of the corporation, Mobil employs more than 750 full-time environmental professionals.

The 3M Company made a commitment to environmental improvement in 1975. Its early entry into environmental management has allowed the company to develop and refine its organizational structure over 20 years. It has developed an environmental policy, identified specific objectives, and implemented standards. The organizational structure of the company reflects this commitment by incorporating its policies and objectives into the company's operation. The various operating units use corporate staff specialists and senior management for support and assistance. Exhibit 4–2 is an example of a detailed EH&S system for a large multinational corporation.

Exhibit 4–3 provides another example of an organizational structure for an environmental management system. Monsanto clearly identifies the roles of senior executives along with other officers and employees in the development of an environmental strategy (vision and policy) and the implementation of that strategy (performance measures, procedures,

EXHIBIT 4–2
3M Quality Environmental Management Organization (Environmental Policy)

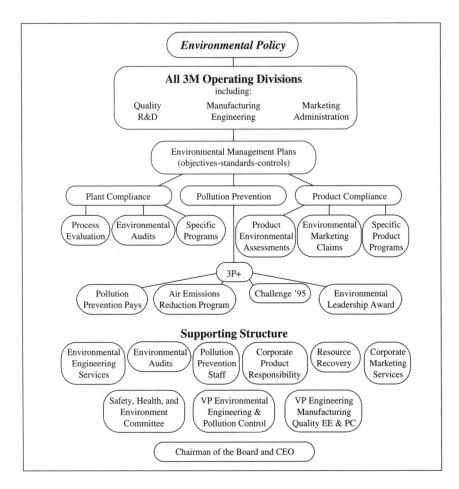

controls, and reporting). The system demonstrates an organizational structure and approach that attempt to drive environmental responsibility and sensitivity throughout the organization.

Role of the Board of Directors

The organizational structure of the EH&S function is critical to its success. Many companies have established board-level committees to assume responsibility for corporate environmental performance.

EXHIBIT 4–3

Monsanto's Environmental Management System

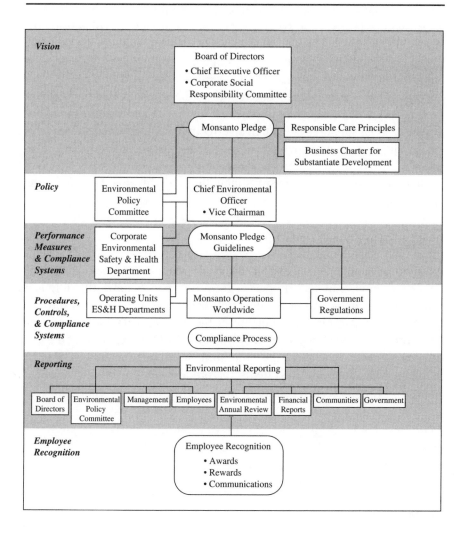

Sun Company has an executive-level EH&S Committee, chaired by the CEO. It meets monthly to review performance, policies, and strategies. In addition, the board of directors receives a monthly report on EH&S highlights.

Rockwell has a board-level Environmental and Social Responsibility Committee composed of seven nonemployee directors. The executive vice president and deputy chairman has the lead responsibility for the company's environmental programs. Reporting to him is the vice president of EH&S, who leads the team of EH&S professionals worldwide.

Browning-Ferris Industries (BFI), the large waste collection and disposal company, has set up a Council for EH&S Excellence to guide the company's activities in designing, implementing, communicating, and monitoring EH&S programs. The Council is composed of a broad cross section of BFI's management and reports to the company's senior officers.

It is only with a strong commitment from the top and a well-established organizational support system that an effective environmental strategy can be developed and implemented. That system must include effective measures of environmental performance that are reported internally for comprehensive management decisions including individual and business unit performance evaluations.

Role of the CEO

In most companies, a major effort in identifying, measuring, and reporting environmental impacts does not begin until the CEO is committed to improved environmental management. Often it is through an environmental mission statement or the development and articulation of a corporate environmental strategy that the CEO sets the tone at the top. It is then necessary to drive this commitment through the organization by implementing the various systems for product design, product costing, capital budgeting, information, and performance evaluation. This approach also provides consistency between the EH&S function and corporate goals and gives EH&S the internal credibility to promote the progress within divisions and facilities necessary for improved environmental management.

It is also critical that the lines of communication be open from EH&S executives directly to the CEO and that the CEO be involved in setting environmental management policies and making key environmental impact decisions. At Sun Company, for example, two senior management positions have environmental responsibilities—senior vice president and chief administrative officer and vice president of EH&S. Both have direct access to the CEO.

Role of the General Counsel

A decade ago it was common for the senior environmental officer also to be corporate general counsel because the focus was often on a narrow view of protecting the company's assets. The only environmental concerns were that outside pressures would cause unnecessary lawsuits from which the company needed protection. As companies have come to recognize the importance of corporate environmental performance both to society and to the company, proactive environmental management now is required to replace the protective stance previously established. Planning must replace compliance, and the chief legal officer generally should not be in charge of EH&S. EH&S departments need a proactive, planning orientation and a staff of full-time EH&S professionals.

As discussed in Chapter 7, the general counsel should not be primarily responsible for determining the accrued environmental liability but should have one input to the decision along with operations, accounting, and EH&S personnel, who likely have different perspectives of the broad environmental liabilities the company faces. These alternative views are based on broad examinations of company activities and the production of both products and waste. They also include an understanding of the likely changes in societal demands for corporate responsibility for reuse, recycling, and ultimate disposal of post-consumer waste. The EH&S professionals also generally have a better understanding of the impacts of current and pending legislation and regulations on the company and need to be involved in the analysis to determine whether process or product redesign could reduce corporate environmental liabilities.

Though some corporate EH&S departments I visited are headed ably by current or former members of the general counsel's staff, this situation is generally not ideal. The most proactive environmental programs generally were headed by professionals with an EH&S or operations background who viewed themselves in a planning and strategy function. They were attempting to integrate new environmental policies throughout the organizations and generally had strong support from and access to the CEO.

Likewise, in the accrual process, though it is true that most general counsels do understand the current state of Superfund litigation and settlements, most do not think broadly enough about disclosure responsibilities, do not understand other environmental obligations related to current corporate activities and current and pending regulations, and do not have accurate numbers related to environmental costs. No one person in the organizations that I visited typically had all that information. That is why my research has led me to conclude that an accrual committee composed of representatives of EH&S, legal, accounting, operations, and engineering departments can best determine the appropriate accruals and be an important source of suggestions for improvements in the design of the corporation's products and processes.

Role of the EH&S Vice President

Among the most important responsibilities of the senior EH&S officer is coordination and communication with management at various company business units and facilities. At Sun Company, senior business unit heads prepare quarterly updates of EH&S performance for an executive EH&S committee chaired by the CEO. The vice president of EH&S also communicates corporate EH&S performance to the same senior managers on a quarterly basis.

At many companies the senior EH&S officer is on the committee that approves major capital expenditures, facilitating the full integration of environmental considerations into major management decisions. EH&S responsibility in the capital investment decision process at companies such as DuPont, Union Carbide, and Bristol-Myers Squibb is discussed in Chapter 9.

At BFI, the divisional vice president of environmental compliance is responsible for general issues of environmental compliance including the waste approval function relating to special, nonhazardous wastes and the interpretation of regulations for various regions and divisions. But the primary responsibility for meeting EH&S requirements rests with regional and district managers and with the corporate office providing support, training, and audit functions. Violations of environmental regulations are reported through the operations managers rather than the environmental compliance department and, depending on seriousness, would be reported to the regional manager, then to the general counsel's office, and ultimately to the president. In each of the regions, environmental compliance officers monitor performance and are responsible for improving environmental performance. They report both to the regional vice president and to the EH&S vice president.

What is the typical background of EH&S vice presidents? The necessary focus on planning rather than compliance requires certain skills and orientation that normally do not suggest the appointment of someone with a legal background. Many companies also have decided not to choose someone with an environmental background. (It may be that the rapid rise in importance of environmental affairs and growth of environmental staffs has left the area with a shortage of experienced senior personnel.) My research found that many of the senior EH&S officers were promoted into this position from senior operations positions. They thus understand company operations and environmental concerns and have the credibility within the corporation to influence changes in organization, direction, processes, and products.

Role of Business Unit and Facility Staff

Operating personnel at the various company facilities are essential to the proper functioning of an environmental management system. Though strategies, policies, and procedures can be developed by a central EH&S staff, business unit and facility managers and staff must understand the importance to the company of excellent environmental performance. EH&S education and training are necessary to explain the role each employee has in the environmental audit process. The self-audit and daily monitoring of environmental impacts and waste production must be important parts of each employee's job. Managers must develop incentive systems to ensure that environmental risks are not hidden and that employees will report potential hazards and develop creative solutions to reduce environmental impacts.

CENTRALIZED VERSUS DECENTRALIZED EH&S MANAGEMENT

With the rapid growth of the EH&S function in most organizations, companies typically have found it beneficial to expand the central EH&S staff and also to install and train EH&S professionals in major facilities and business units. These persons typically have dual responsibilities to both central EH&S staff and to the facility or business unit general manager.

At Sun Company, "day-to-day environmental compliance and operational decision making are handled principally by each facility or business unit. The corporate staff acts as a partner in providing consultative services regarding compliance, program administration, development of compliance strategies, review of facility plans and consulting on long-term programs. The corporate staff is also involved in the prioritization of capital projects and related project funding." Though there are company examples of both increased centralization and increased decentralization in EH&S management, the Sun experience is fairly common.

When EH&S staffs were started initially, they tended to be part of a central corporate staff and often reported to the general counsel. As professional EH&S staffs grew, it often was deemed necessary and desirable to push primary EH&S responsibility to the business units, and many companies reduced their central staff. Now many companies have recognized that a central staff along with EH&S personnel at the facilities are both necessary. Substantial advantages can be achieved at the business unit and facility level in product and process design, operational controls, and self-audits to control and reduce waste production and other environmental impacts. But a strong central EH&S staff is necessary to provide overall strategic planning, guidance, and coordination to the environmental function. A central EH&S staff is critical to the internal audit function and to furnish overall direction for identifying, measuring, and reporting environmental impacts. It is essential for developing and applying tools for costing, capital investments, and performance evaluation and for directing the environmental strategy integration throughout the organization.

THE CHALLENGE OF ORGANIZING ACROSS INTERNATIONAL BOUNDARIES

It is certainly difficult to make decisions about the best organizational structure to provide necessary guidance and incentives for improved corporate environmental programs. The situation is usually further complicated as the businesses and the geographical diversity increase and particular business needs, local laws, and different cultures must be confronted. (See further discussions of related issues in Chapter 5 on information systems and Chapter 10 on performance evaluation systems.)

ABB, the power generation holding company, has 200,000 employees in 5,000 separate profit centers. It is structured as a matrix-style organization across business and geographic areas. The challenge is how to maintain environmental excellence and control in such a large, decentralized organization. The company is attempting to drive a global environmental strategy throughout the organization. A further challenge is how to manage for environmental compliance, focus on environmental planning, measure corporate environmental performance, and establish benchmarks for environmental success. The company has established an Environmental Advisory Board that reports to the chairman and a small central staff. In each country where the company operates, an environmental controller and an environmental control officer (in the United

States, a legal counsel and an EH&S officer) guide environmental planning and compliance activities.

Like many other companies, ABB is highly decentralized, with global environmental policies and general monitoring provided by a central office environmental compliance committee that relies on local operating companies to plan for and comply with environmental regulations and strive for the corporate mission of environmental excellence. Though the generation of cost-effective technologies for clean energy production is central to ABB businesses, the responsibility is decentralized and generally is located in the general counsel's office. This approach often can lead to more emphasis on compliance than on planning.

Large, decentralized organizations are challenged further by the common lack of an information system that collects all compliance data and eases the transference of technologies for environmental compliance across company and geographic boundaries. As a division or business unit achieves success in reducing environmental impacts, those achievements should be well distributed throughout the company. But companies only now are developing systems for accumulating compliance data and information about the costs and benefits of environmental programs. A comprehensive information system at ABB would need to include the foregoing items, along with an analysis of the future environmental costs and benefits of company capital improvements, process improvements, and product improvements so that both capital investment and product costing decisions fully include environmental impacts.

ABB has recognized that generating waste is a nonvalue-added activity and is trying to get rid of it. The company has chosen to incorporate environmental sensitivity as part of the fabric of the company rather than create one environmental segment within the company. It is trying to determine the best way to change a corporate culture and implement the new environmental strategy. The task is difficult within a global company, but through attempts discussed here and through performance evaluations (discussed in Chapter 10) the company is making progress.

Most multinational companies have established worldwide standards for environmental performance, creating benefits and bringing challenges. New facilities abroad usually are constructed with the latest environmental technologies and processes designed to minimize waste, but older facilities often still have negative environmental impacts. Reducing those impacts and complying with various local and national regulations create challenges in organization and coordination. Thus, strong business unit and facility EH&S officers, reporting to both business unit managers and a central EH&S staff, are important. Likewise, a strong central EH&S staff is important for planning, guidance, and coordination.

OTHER ORGANIZATIONAL ISSUES

As companies emphasize reducing total environmental costs, some incorrectly have focused their attention only on reducing overhead costs. Implementing an activity-based costing and management system to better analyze and manage costs may indeed reduce total overhead costs. Improved analysis of the costs and benefits of various capital investment projects also may reduce total environmental costs. Certainly analyzing the choices between capital improvements, process improvements, and product improvements will direct attention to reducing costs and production waste. But managers must be certain that their organizations focus on improving company operations to reduce environmental impact and to improve financial performance rather than on moving costs from one category to another. This issue is not primarily about costing. It is a management issue.

The focus should not be on complying with current government regulations but rather on planning to reduce environmental impacts so that companies can move toward sustainable development. Companies need to change their corporate culture to integrate environmental impacts into all aspects of corporate action. It is generally desirable for the senior EH&S officer to have direct access to both the board of directors and the CEO and not be in a legal function. Often, the legal compliance approach is detrimental to the planning necessary to move toward environmental sensitivity in corporate decision making. It has become clear that numerous benefits do accrue to companies that make capital, process, and product improvements as a result of the analysis of corporate environmental impacts. These companies usually go beyond regulatory compliance and make voluntary improvements.

We now turn to an examination of various frameworks being used to improve environmental management and implement corporate environmental strategy.

TOTAL STAKEHOLDER ANALYSIS

As discussed earlier, life cycle assessment is a general methodology that is of increasing interest to corporations. Companies recognize that identifying the impacts of their activities, products, and services from cradle to grave provides insights for various corporate decisions including capital investments and product pricing. But both the methodology and the practice need to be expanded to focus on measuring, reporting, managing, and monitoring issues of central concern. In addition, companies need a systematic way to identify the impacts not only for improved environmental management but also for an analysis that examines the total impact of a company's activities, products, and services on various stakeholders both at present and in the future. Total Stakeholder Analysis provides such a systematic analysis.

In a recent article on corporate governance, Joichi Aoi, chairman of the board of Toshiba Corporation, wrote about the important issues facing managers as they attempt to lead their companies "into a new era of technology-based competition." He argued that "corporate success will depend on management's ability to satisfy not just its investors and employees, but the entire range of interests that make up our society" (Aoi, 1994).

As we begin to focus on constituent interests that are broader than maximizing shareholder value and developing human capital, a more complete analysis of the impacts of various decisions on all corporate stakeholders is essential. One way to perform that analysis is through a Total Stakeholder Analysis. TSA requires identifying, measuring, and reporting the benefits and costs to various corporate stakeholders of the environmental impacts of products, services, processes, and other corporate activities. It further requires developing a feedback loop that ensures continuous monitoring of the impacts to observe changes and to provide for corporate adjustments to products, services, and processes. It is through this process that companies can achieve continuous environmental improvements.

Stakeholders are identified in Exhibit 4–4. They should be thought of as all individuals, groups, or organizations that have a "stake" in the activities and well-being of the corporation or its activities and impacts. In some cases, measuring useful information will be too difficult or too expensive. In those cases, merely identifying the impacts often will alert corporate officers to the effect of corporate activities on stakeholders, which previously had been ignored in corporate decision making. In some cases, useful measures will be available, and impacts can be quantified using physical measures or monetized using financial measures.

While quantified and monetized measures are best, even comparison of corporate environmental performance with preset corporate goals often

EXHIBIT 4–4
Total Stakeholder Analysis (TSA)

Identifying and Measuring the Benefits and Costs of the Corporation's Facilities, Processes, Products, and Services

1. Impact on customers
2. Impact on shareholders
3. Impact on employees
4. Impact on suppliers
5. Impact on competitors
6. Impact on local community
7. Impact on company
8. Impact on society
9. Impact on environment

---

leads to improved performance because it focuses attention on previously neglected areas. In addition, some companies compare their absolute improvements with relative improvements over time or with benchmarks in the same industry, striving for continuous improvement in environmental performance.

The Total Stakeholder Analysis is an essential ingredient in the completion of a successful Environmental Strategy Implementation. Many regulatory environmental projects have been seen to produce a negative return on investment because the costs and benefits were improperly identified and measured. Many voluntary environmental projects have been evaluated incorrectly due to an incomplete analysis of the likely impacts.

Businesses continuously perform analyses of likely consumer response to proposed products and services. Often, the time horizon before these proposed products and services are marketed is long. Analyses must be completed to determine the likely impact on the market and the company of both existing and proposed products.

Similarly, a TSA should be completed on all company activities, products, and services. If completed on all environmental projects and all other activities with an environmental impact, companies could more properly evaluate the costs and benefits of an Environmental Strategy Implementation. Through broader identification and measurement of environmental impacts, many projects will be seen to provide significant positive returns to the company and to shareholder value. It is not that these situations are all win-win. But a broader identification of social, environmental, and financial impacts does permit managers to complete an improved total project evaluation.

TSA requires examining both present and future impacts. It also requires companies to examine the likely future impact on the company of external environmental costs that may be internalized through future government regulation. Decision making can be improved through focus groups, scenario forecasting, multifunctional assessments, community surveys, and the use of various social science research methods. Some of these methods, such as contingent valuation (discussed in Chapter 9), are not accepted universally. But they do provide information useful to increase the understanding of various stakeholder and company interests in proposed environmental improvements.

Surveying Community Interests

Many companies regularly conduct community surveys to help determine their environmental impact. These surveys assess public opinion on the company's performance in such areas as air pollution, water pollution, and odors. Survey results often are communicated to stakeholders through various means including environmental annual reports. The surveys are important because they assist the company in identifying and measuring the impacts, as required by the TSA, and in improving internal management decisions.

Browning-Ferris Industries has held a stakeholder meeting to describe the company's activities in environmental management and solicited suggestions for improvement. Stakeholders included public and private sector customers, environmental and public interest group leaders, investors and investor groups, local community representatives, and regulators. As a result of this meeting, the company changed its policies and scheduled additional stakeholder meetings.

Dow Chemical has established community advisory panels in most of the communities in which it has facilities. The mission of these panels is "to provide a forum for addressing issues, concerns, and opportunities affecting Dow and the community." The panels consist of independent community leaders who make an unedited, independent, published report to the community. The forum and the report have given Dow a clearer view of how its actions are perceived and advice on how it can improve its community relations and its performance in areas of community concern.

Community advisory panels are a part of the Responsible Care Initiative of the Chemical Manufacturers Association and have become a part of the EH&S program in numerous companies. In addition to surveying community interests, many companies have well-developed programs for communicating their efforts in environmental improvement to the community, through community newsletters and more formal environmental reports. These programs are discussed more fully in Chapter 7. The broadening scope and influence of the corporation on the community has made it necessary for many companies to adapt their organizational charts to include broader items such as environmental impacts on the community and on its workers.

TOOLS AND FRAMEWORKS FOR ANALYSIS

Total Quality Environmental Management

Among the current trends in management practice is total quality management (TQM). W. Edwards Deming, an American statistician, used statistical theory to help improve production quality in plants during World War II. After the war, U.S. companies generally rejected his ideas for statistical quality control, so he went to Japan where his ideas were well received. He developed total quality management as a management approach that focuses on continuous process improvements to better meet customer needs and expectations.

The Global Environmental Management Initiative (GEMI) is a group of 28 companies dedicated to fostering environmental excellence by businesses worldwide. It was founded in 1990 with the goal of promoting environmental management and sustainable development. The group has taken the TQM principles and applied them to environmental management to provide a systematic approach and methodology for continuous improvement in environmental performance. Numerous companies have instituted a total quality environmental management (TQEM) approach to improving environmental quality, including McDonald's, Xerox, Procter & Gamble, 3M, and Eastman Kodak.

A GEMI Primer (1993) was developed to aid companies in their efforts to improve environmental management and environmental performance and to adopt TQEM. The primer relies heavily on the research and design work of the Cambridge, Massachusetts, research and consulting firm, Abt Associates. One of the systems approaches GEMI suggests is the use and implementation of the Plan Do Check Act (P-D-C-A) cycle, which aids in implementing change in the organization. Procter & Gamble adopted this P-D-C-A cycle in the mid-1980s for use in its businesses and has included it as a tool for improving environmental results. The company emphasizes that the cycle is continuous, as shown in Exhibit 4–5.

A goal of TQEM is to establish a corporate culture in which continuous improvement is the norm, so that the entire system works toward the multifaceted goal of meeting or exceeding all customers' requirements and anticipating their future needs. In this goal, "customer" is defined broadly to include all corporate stakeholders who may be affected by the environmental actions of the company. To drive down environmental costs over the long term, GEMI suggests a number of approaches to establishing a culture of continuous environmental process improvements. A second primer on cost effectiveness and business decision making was issued in 1994 (Global Environmental Management Initiative, 1994).

At BFI, the TQEM concepts have become integral, and the corporate culture indeed has changed. The motivating force and the backbone for the movement toward increased environmental responsibility is the concern for what the customer wants and needs and a recognition that the company depends on "customer-led quality." There is a focus on the driver, and the employees are empowered to deliver service. This employee involvement and commitment is essential to the company. The concern for the customer and the environment is not just part of a corporate mission statement. It has been integrated into all company activities.

In 1991 the President's Commission on Environmental Quality (PCEQ) was started in response to former President Bush's call for the "private sector to undertake, in cooperation with government, initiatives for environmental improvement" (PCEQ, 1993, vii). One of the auxiliary committees was the Quality Environmental Management Subcommittee, whose goal was to demonstrate the usefulness of TQM as a method for achieving pollution prevention. The Subcommittee also produced a TQEM model focused on continuous environmental improvement.

In 1992, Abt Associates conducted a study of 85 U.S. companies. It concluded that companies are moving from a compliance-oriented approach to a more strategic approach in their environmental management. Abt found that more companies are pursuing competitive environ-

EXHIBIT 4–5
Procter & Gamble (Total Quality Environmental Management)

---

1 Plan

- Each process, handling or equipment change is assessed by environmental experts.
- Goals have been set to reduce waste (air, water and solid) by 15% per year and per unit of production.
- Benchmarking and monitoring legal compliance are performed on a regular basis.

2 Do

- Waste (air, water and solid) is regularly measured and recorded.
- Unloading, storage and handling areas of chemicals are walled to contain any spills.
- Positive release systems are installed to check the effluent before release.
- Personnel are trained in good environmental practices.
- Emergency drills are in place.

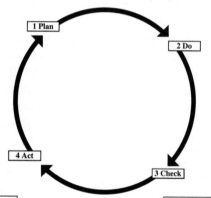

4 Act

- Policies and standards are in place.
- In each plant, an environmental programme leader is responsible for managing the improvement programme. They get the support of a central environmental group in Europe for technology development, training and auditing.
- Worldwide networks are set up to share experience and information.
- Audit recommendations are implemented within one year.

3 Check

- Statistical tools are used to monitor the environmental quality performance of processes.
- Each incident is centrally reported and studied.
- For the past ten years, formal, internal audits have been used to analyse the effectiveness of environmental management systems. They are performed annually by the plant people, and every fourth year by European staff experts. They involve an objective set of criteria and a quantitative rating system. Results are reported to European management.

mental advantage through TQEM and that the most strategic of these companies make investments in environmentally related activities with the expectation that these activities will be profitable (Hochman et al., 1993).

Environmental Self-Assessment Program

In an effort to continue progress in improved environmental management, in 1992 GEMI produced an environmental self-assessment program (ESAP) designed by Deloitte & Touche. It provides a checklist of elements of environmental management targeted at the principles of the International Chamber of Commerce's Business Charter for Sustainable Development. A self-scoring system built into the ESAP provides a numerical way for companies to assess their environmental programs in key areas linked to the International Chamber of Commerce (ICC). GEMI hopes that through careful measurement and analysis of their performance, companies will find ways to increase the quality of environmental policy, planning, implementation, and monitoring. The ESAP also helps companies to prioritize environmental improvement opportunities.

BFI has recognized that for improved measurement and reporting of corporate environmental performance, benchmarks are necessary so that the company can track performance and achieve continuous improvement. Both internal and external decision makers need to develop frameworks to evaluate their performance over time. BFI has used the ESAP to provide those benchmarks and to determine where further work is needed to improve its environmental performance. BFI also is considering an external environmental audit to supplement its internal audit program but believes that the benchmarks are necessary before the external audit is conducted. Whether through an ESAP or other approaches to measuring environmental performance, self-assessments, benchmarks, and external evaluations all aid in the goal of continuous improvement of corporate environmental performance.

Environmental Self-Assessment Matrix

The Council of Great Lakes Industries (CGLI) also has developed a TQEM primer and self-assessment matrix for improving environmental management. This self-assessment process does not attempt to determine whether a company is in compliance with current environmental regulations. Rather, it is used as a model for companies to continuously improve their environmental management. The program is based on seven matrix

EXHIBIT 4–6
Alcoa (Environmental Remediation Process Model)

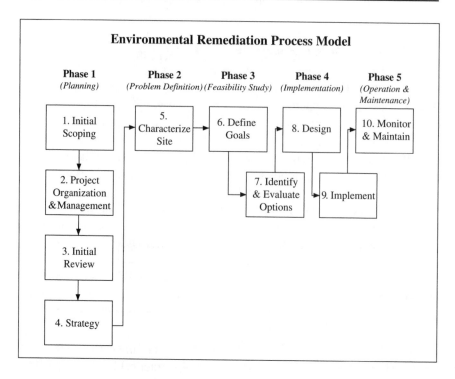

categories adapted from the Malcolm Baldrige National Quality Award competition. The categories are leadership, information and analysis, strategic planning, human resources, quality assurance of environmental performance, environmental results, and customer/shareholder satisfaction. Each category has 10 levels, from beginning to growing to maturing, and each category is weighted. The composite score determined after completion of the self-assessment provides a baseline score that companies can refer to during subsequent assessments. In addition to the matrix, the CGLI also has developed a questionnaire that parallels the elements in the matrix. It may be helpful in determining areas for environmental improvement.

Environmental Remediation Process Model

Alcoa has stated that it "believes that its financial health is directly tied to sound environmental, health and safety practices." To implement this

EXHIBIT 4–7
Alcoa (Relative Ability to Influence Remediation Cost Over Project Life)

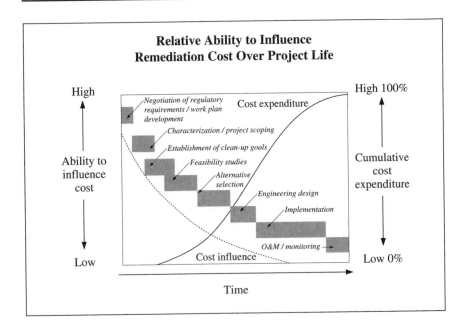

**Relative Ability to Influence
Remediation Cost Over Project Life**

approach, Alcoa established the Alcoa Remediation Team (ART) to develop procedures that ensure "to the extent practicable, that environmental remediation strategies are cost effective and appropriately protective in accord with technical, legal, regulatory, and Alcoa Policy perspectives." It developed the environmental remediation process model (ERPM) (see Exhibit 4–6) to aid environmental professionals in developing effective remediation strategies.

Exhibit 4–7 shows that to exert a significant impact on project cost, environmental remediation must be considered early in the strategic-planning process. If the remediation team waits until plans for a project are fully developed, remediation will have little effect on costs, which likely will continue to rise out of control. ART found that, while only 10 percent of project costs have been expended at the point an environmental remediation plan is adopted, more than 80 percent have been committed.

Alcoa's ERPM comprises the following steps:

- Do initial scoping;
- Plan for project organization and management;

- Do initial review;
- Plan strategy;
- Characterize site;
- Define goals;
- Identify and evaluate options;
- Design;
- Implement;
- Monitor and maintain.

The company determined that because 80 percent of the costs of remediation are committed before the project begins, its ERPM model requires involvement of strategic planning early in the process.

BALANCED SCORECARD

Like many other corporate executives, Eastman Kodak's CEO, George Fisher, has pledged his commitment to ensure that Kodak will "be among the world's best companies in protecting...the quality of our environment" and have "products, services, and facilities...reflect the fact that environmental responsibility is a fundamental [corporate] value. It is a philosophy and approach that is woven throughout the company. It is a value that impacts everything we do individually and collectively." In Chapter 10, we will examine how companies can implement an environmental strategy that takes a corporate mission statement and tries to change a corporate culture through effective use of performance evaluation systems. As discussed earlier, setting the tone at the top as Kodak has done is critical. Let us now consider how the balanced scorecard approach developed by Robert Kaplan and David Norton can be adapted to include a core value such as environmental responsibility as an overlay over the entire scorecard model.

Two recent articles (Kaplan and Norton, 1992 and 1993) proposed a balanced scorecard. It gives managers an easy-to-use tool that translates strategy into measurable variables and provides a framework to track them. Companies often do not connect various financial performance measures with nonfinancial measures of corporate performance in such areas as productivity, environmental management, and customer satisfaction. The corporate scorecard developed by Kaplan and Norton is based on a recognition that managers need both financial and operational measures to effectively manage an enterprise, and a choice between the two is not necessary. They write that "the balanced scorecard is like the dials in an airplane cockpit: it gives managers complex information at a glance." It also forces managers to recognize the impact of how the implementation of one corporate policy affects the performance of several variables simultaneously and whether "improvement in one area may have been achieved at the expense of another."

Such insight is exactly what is required of today's managers. They need to institutionalize environmental considerations into all levels of management decisions. They need to link environmental information systems with the management accounting, management control, and financial reporting systems already in place in organizations. They need to integrate them with existing cost management and capital investment decision systems.

The balanced scorecard forces managers to put their goals and organizational strategy into operation by specifying the measurements they will use to evaluate the success of the strategy implementation. Incorporating environmental management into the balanced scorecard format obliges the managers to develop specific ways to measure success. Thus, a company needs to do far more than just establish a goal of being environmentally sensitive—it must specify the measurable goals. It needs to develop goals and performance measures for the corporation, for its business units and facilities, and for its teams, managers, and staff.

Kaplan and Norton include four perspectives in their balanced scorecard: financial, customer, internal, and learning and improvement. All relate to the core values of the company. A company that develops a corporate environmental strategy as part of the overall corporate strategy must develop measures of success. As increased environmental sensitivity becomes a core corporate value, this value should be an overlay on the balanced scorecard and should be an additional goal within each of the four scorecard perspectives. It must be seen as relating to:

- Increased financial profitability;
- Increased customer satisfaction;
- Increased operating effectiveness;
- Increased innovation and learning.

Alternatively, environmental responsibility and performance could be viewed as a fifth perspective rather than as a core corporate value. In either case, goals and performance measures must be developed and specified.

The balanced scorecard model fits in well with the Environmental Strategy Implementation framework used in this book. It examines the importance of the performance measures in the implementation of strategy. By integrating environment as a core corporate value, the balanced scorecard can become an important component of the overall implementation of a corporate environmental strategy.

SUMMARY

Some of the approaches above have been developed specifically to improve corporate environmental performance. Others are frameworks that can be adapted to the implementation of an environmental strategy. All require the development of a strategy, setting corporate environmental goals, and developing performance measures. Developing relevant performance measures often can be the necessary link between the development of a company's environmental strategy and the successful implementation of that strategy and excellent environmental performance.

These frameworks all can be used as part of the Environmental Strategy Implementation discussed in this book. Whether one is using a corporate social audit, LCA, ESI, or other approach, a broad identification of environmental impacts is necessary, as is a recognition of those impacts on the company's various stakeholders. The Total Stakeholder Analysis approach described in this chapter can be used. First, the strategy and a corporate structure to implement it must be developed. Then impacts and performance measures need to be identified. Finally, an information system should be developed to provide the information needed for various internal and external decisions. The discussion of various corporate designs of environmental information systems is the subject of Chapter 5.

Chapter Five

Internal Reporting
Information Systems

B uilding on the development of a corporate environmental strategy, in Chapter 4 we examined how companies can organize the environmental management function to better identify, organize, and manage corporate environmental impacts. In this chapter we survey some corporate attempts at developing environmental information systems and discuss issues related to the integration of that information into both financial reporting and management accounting systems and ultimately into management decisions. Exhibit 5–1 lists various decisions managers need to make that require improved information related to environmental impacts. It also lists the type of environmental information usually required. In most cases, more than one item of environmental information is required to properly make the environmental management decisions.

This study reports on both the state of the art and best practices in measuring corporate environmental performance. Unfortunately, corporate environmental information is not generally available for effective management. The most commonly available information relates to physical data on waste production, toxicity, and waste reduction, but many companies do not have accurate data even in this area and do not know their total waste generation or the causes of that waste.

Moving further down the list in Exhibit 5–1, information is even more scarce. Most companies do not track their environmental costs adequately and certainly do not have them broken down by activity, facility, and products. To manage these costs, better information is needed about past, present, and forecasted future environmental operating costs and capital expenditures. The success of an Environmental Strategy Implementation depends on accumulating, aggregating, measuring, and reporting infor-

EXHIBIT 5–1

The Integration of Environmental Information into Management Decisions

Environmental Information Required	Decisions
• Physical data related to the reduction of toxicity and waste	• Capital investments for environmental projects
• Accumulation of current environmental costs for past sins by activity, facility, and product	• Capital investments for nonenvironmental projects
• Accumulation of current environmental costs for current sins by activity, facility, and product	• Financial reporting • Process design
• Present and future capital expenditures for pollution prevention	• Purchasing • Cost control
• Present and future capital expenditures for pollution control	• Product design • Product packaging
• Present and future costs for product redesign	• Product costing • Product pricing
• Present and future costs for process redesign	• Evaluation of performance of corporation, facilities, and products
• Estimates of future environmental costs	• Evaluation of performance of managers
• Estimates of future environmental benefits	• Risk assessments and risk management

mation related to corporate environmental impacts to various managers within the corporation. Thus the development and improvement of these systems is critical.

WASTE MANAGEMENT INFORMATION SYSTEMS

In 1992 Ciba-Geigy established a set of waste management guidelines that formally specify a waste hierarchy for all international operations: (1)

avoid; (2) reduce; (3) recycle; (4) treat; (5) dispose. This system provides direction to various divisions so that Ciba recycles more than 80% of the waste generated by operations. Facilities worldwide run their own waste tracking systems "so that they can account for and monitor waste from generation to safe disposal." This method takes a life cycle approach to production and exceeds the regulatory requirements of many countries, which require tracking only from the time waste leaves the facility. Here, in what is likely to be the near-term trend, Ciba is focusing on the generation of the waste. This approach leads to paying attention to product design to reduce production of the waste so that disposal will not be necessary.

Because informational needs in multinational organizations often differ based on particular national regulatory requirements, many companies have difficulty standardizing environmental information across national boundaries to implement an environmental strategy. In 1990 Ciba introduced a standardized annual report on Safety, Energy, and Environmental Protection (SEEP) for use throughout its worldwide organization. The report includes:

- Some data that all sites must provide and some that are site-specific;
- Environmental cost data in a fixed format;
- A discussion of cases of improvement in environmental performance along with failures, providing the information for a transfer of knowledge throughout the organization;
- Any other matters of significance.

The SEEP report provides information for decision making at the local level and is an important input for developing, monitoring, and implementing the environmental strategy.

Since 1975, the 3M Company has been tracking its waste and waste reduction for the amount of waste eliminated and the amount of money saved, which has been in excess of $700 million. The Pollution Prevention Pays (3P) program encourages technical innovation to prevent pollution at the source through four methods: product reformulation, process modification, equipment redesign, and resource recovery. The program encourages all employees to submit proposals for completed projects for pollution prevention and recognizes them for doing so. Each 3P project submittal form includes a description of the project and the technology used and an estimate of the amount of pollutants prevented from being generated or released the first year. Also included is the first year of cost savings resulting from the project. The form in Exhibit 5–2 is used to track the company's pollution prevention efforts. 3M has information in various databases, such as in the 3P program. When the databases are integrated the information is used to calculate the waste that is generated. One of the advantages of this system is that it demonstrates the advantages of pollution prevention over remediation.

Duke Power has developed a corporate environmental strategic plan for internal use. It has identified seven areas of strategic focus and has specified goals, measures, targets, and programs for each area and a system to provide the information for decisions. The waste and emission focus has developed the principles of ALARAC (as low as reasonably achievable and cost effective) to reduce waste, liquid discharges, and emissions. The company has developed programs to define and integrate the ALARAC principles. Those programs include source reduction, recycling and resource recovery, and ash reuse. Specific measures have been established for each of these programs and target goals. For example, within ash reuse, the company measures the amount of ash reused as a percentage of the ash generated on a per ton basis, with a targeted goal of 40% reuse of ash. The company also provides environmental information to be used in employee performance appraisals and gives specific environmental goals and measures of environmental performance achieved.

THE DEVELOPMENT OF ONE ENVIRONMENTAL ACCOUNTING AND REPORTING SYSTEM

In response to growing public pressure for increased environmental responsibility and corporate concerns for environmental impacts Polaroid Corporation in 1987 set up what is now considered one of the best environmental information systems presently in use.[1] The Toxic Use and Waste Reduction (TUWR) program is "based on the premise that reducing the use of toxics and sources of waste, per unit of production, reduces the need to manage waste and thus prevents pollution." It sets clear priorities for change in manufacturing operations and in the design of new processes and facilities (see Exhibit 5–3).

---

1. This section draws on, and more detailed information on the Polaroid system can be obtained from, Mary E. Barth, Marc J. Epstein, and Richard D. Stark, "Polaroid: Managing Environmental Responsibilities and their Costs," Harvard Business School Case #9-194-052, Boston, 1994.

EXHIBIT 5–2
3M Pollution Prevention Pays

Pollution Prevention
Pays (3P) Submittal

Form 25956 - A - PWO

Environmental Engineering
and Pollution Control/3M

21-2W-05 3M Center
St. Paul, MN 55144

3M

Project Name (NAME)	Submittal Date (SDATE)

Division/Dept. (DIV)	Product Affected (PROD)	Plant Location (PLANT) (STATE)

Project Contact (PNAME)	EE & PC Contact (ENAME)

Project Origin (ORIG)
(Check one or more;) 1 ☐ Lab   2 ☐ Engineering   3 ☐ Manufacturing   4 ☐ Other (List) _____

Project Description (Be concise)

Project Measurement Criteria

Type of Pollution Prevented (Check one or more)	First Year Quantity Prevented	Characteristics
☐ Air Pollution (QAIR)	Tons	
☐ Water Pollution (QWAT)	Tons	
☐ Wastewater (QWW)	Million Gallons	
☐ Solid Waste (QSOL)	Tons	

☐ Check here if pollution prevented was a hazardous waste (QHAZ) _____ tons first year

Technical Accomplishment (Describe)

Method used to prevent pollution (TECH)
   1 ☐ Product Reformulation   3 ☐ Equipment Redesign
   2 ☐ Process Modification   4 ☐ Recovery and/or Reuse

Additional Considerations

Capital Cost of Implementation (TCOST)

Annual Estimated Operating Cost (OCOST)

Related P for P (if applicable) (PFP)

Additional Information

Monetary Benefit
Include All First Year Savings

Capital (CSAVE) _____

Operation & Maintenance (OSAVE) _____

Energy (ESAVE) _____

Sales (SSAVE) _____

Other (OTSAVE) _____

Total (Tsave) _____

Project Committment
(Signed AFE, etc.) _____

— For Office Use Only —

	Review Date (RDATE)	Notification Date	Project Number (NO)
Action Plan	Project Status (STAT) ▶ 1 ☐ Accepted 2 ☐ On Hold 3 ☐ Rejected		
	Comments:		

Pollution Prevention Pays (3P) Submittal Form

EXHIBIT 5–3
Polaroid Corporation (Toxic Use and Waste Reduction Flow Diagram)

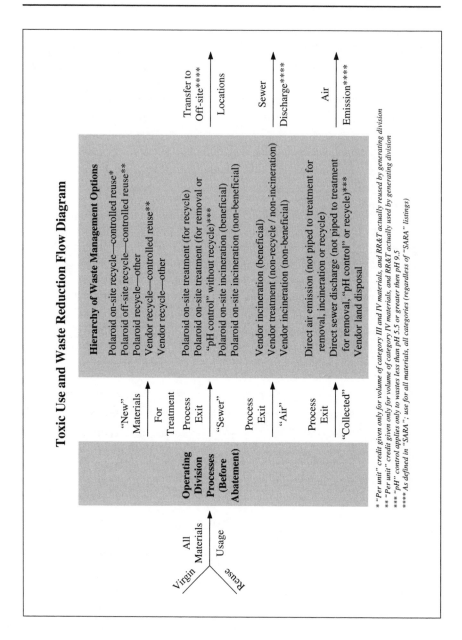

The program measures the use of all chemicals and generation of all waste, charts the success of waste reduction efforts, and targets areas for further improvement. A hierarchy of waste management options was established that ranks options as:

- Recycle at Polaroid;
- Recycle at vendor;
- Treatment;
- Incineration;
- Direct air emission or sewer discharge;
- Vendor land disposal.

The goal is to move waste management activities up the hierarchy to reduce the overall amount of waste that must be managed. One of the most important benefits of the TUWR program is the overall emphasis on reducing toxicity and waste. The program is integrated with the work of the product design staff so that changes can be made through capital improvements, process improvements, and product improvements to reduce environmental impacts. TUWR is a tool for Polaroid's Research and Development Division to set priorities for the design of new manufacturing processes and the redesign of existing ones.

The most cost-effective way to reduce environmental impacts and their related costs is through changes in the process and product designs. This method reduces the amount of waste produced and the costs of environmental cleanup.

The centralized measurement system that supports TUWR is the environmental accounting and reporting system (EARS). The system produces corporate and divisional reports that monitor existing production and predict the impact of new chemicals on TUWR performance. The system monitors the toxic use and waste generation for five categories of materials including 1,700 chemicals. (Category I materials are ones that pose the greatest threats to health and the environment.) It tracks all releases to air, water, and land by chemical and site, providing operational management with a comprehensive measure of environmental releases, some of which are then reported to the government. Among the benefits of the system are the accumulation of data for ease of reporting to government regulators. A more significant benefit is the decrease in cost for the production and ultimate cleanup of waste. Because less waste is produced, Polaroid has been able to reduce its landfill and incinerator needs and recently canceled plans to build an incinerator, saving extensive permitting, capital, and operating costs.

The EARS system uses credits as incentives for the consideration of alternative materials in product production and design so as to reduce waste and toxicity and eliminate the use of the most toxic chemicals. For example, EARS credits are given for recycling category III, IV, and V materials. All the TUWR data are used to establish divisional and corporate indices for measuring progress toward environmental goals.

As new products are introduced, Polaroid has shifted away from using the most toxic chemicals, to less toxic alternatives wherever possible. For instance, EARS classified mercury used in batteries for film packs as a Category I material, and TUWR provided strong incentives to redesign the battery to eliminate the use of mercury. Polaroid's management believes that the system has produced cost savings through reduced material wastage, improved yields, and reduced spending on compliance. Management estimates that return on investment, based solely on wastage and yields, increased markedly because of the changes caused by the TUWR program.

The EARS system is an advanced system for accumulating data for internal and external reporting of information on the use of materials and the discharge of waste. Though this system is important for environmental management, it is not integrated into the financial reporting system to be used in determining environmental liabilities to be shown on external financial statements. Nor is it integrated into the management accounting system to be used in accumulating environmental costs or for product costing and capital investment decisions.

The question is whether this detailed information about existing environmental problems and the expertise of a well-respected EH&S department should be used to determine environmental liabilities and to gain a better understanding of what the scope of future environmental impacts is likely to be, based on current production. Likewise, the EH&S department's understanding of present and future environmental impacts may be useful in integrating present and future environmental impacts into present product costing and capital investment decisions for both environmentally related projects and capital projects in general. Continued development and integration of systems such as Polaroid's EARS system are necessary to improve the quality of internal and external reporting of environmental impacts and the quality of environmental management decisions.

OTHER ENVIRONMENTAL INFORMATION SYSTEMS

To achieve the benefits available from transferring technologies within large, decentralized organizations, information systems must be developed that collect information in a standard format for ease of comparability. United Technologies, for example, has developed a data management system to monitor environmental performance at its business units and collect the data in a standardized format. The system helps identify potential environmental problems and establishes criteria for developing and monitoring corporate environmental standards. The company's Otis Elevator division has a clearly articulated system for measuring EH&S performance, and employees are held accountable for that performance.

The data management system of United Technologies is a critical component for collecting information from the business units and for giving them information for the continuous monitoring of EH&S performance. It provides the information for senior managers to make adjustments and includes incentives to improve performance. At Otis, incentives have included adjustments in the division's incentive pay bonus pool based on fatality records. An incentive system is an important component of the overall environmental management system if a change in corporate culture is desired and if a new mission statement has established improved EH&S performance as a core value in corporate strategy.

Corporations need to develop a way to internalize environmental issues so that when issues arise they can deal with them in the best long-term interests of the corporation. Corporations need to be crisis prepared rather than crisis prone. An effective environmental information system is critical to that internalization. Many companies have developed information systems that collect data and help guide responses to dealing with various environmental impacts and crises. Amoco Corporation, for example, has a detailed Crisis Management Plan and associated management structure to ensure that the company can respond promptly and effectively to any emergency. Drills are held regularly to improve its crisis management and emergency response capabilities. "The issue at stake is how to ensure that the firm, when confronted with any environmental issue, will by default pick the response that leads to the outcome of corporate environmental behavior that best fits its long-term goals and responds most appropriately to internal and external constraints. Outcomes of corporate environmental behavior result from the way the firm monitors and assesses environmental issues, the way it deals with different stakeholders, and the programs and policies it finally decides to implement" (Corbett and Van Wassenhove, 1993, 117).

IBM has developed and installed comprehensive chemical management systems at all facilities. The company established mini-teams that provide a multifunctional approach to chemical management and waste minimization, resulting in annual savings exceeding $500,000. A hazardous waste management system at IBM uses bar coding to track the waste from generation to disposal, making the trash system more efficient and reducing waste.

Continuous improvements and company-wide benefits cannot be achieved without adequate internal communications. Though many companies have developed innovative methods for reducing waste and redesigning products and processes to reduce environmental impacts, many of these companies have not shared the cost-saving discoveries throughout their industries or even their companies. Communication and the transfer of technology within multinational companies are critical to reducing the environmental impacts of company activities on both the community and the company.

AT&T is developing information systems that will make it easier to integrate environmental considerations into management decision making, including the product design decisions. The company also has been examining the implementation of various aspects of environmental accounting and the use of activity-based costing to help incorporate environmental concerns into management decisions.

Chevron's Save Money and Reduce Toxics (SMART) program "has brought together 26 waste specialists from all parts of the company to swap ideas, brainstorm, and discuss ways to minimize future waste-handling costs" (Surma, 1992, 14). With increased sharing of techniques for reducing environmental impacts and their related costs, companies can significantly improve the quality of their environmental management.

MANAGEMENT ACCOUNTING SYSTEMS AND FINANCIAL REPORTING SYSTEMS

The development of an environmental information system is necessary but not sufficient to improve environmental management. The physical data related to waste production, waste reduction, production yields, and toxicity are certainly important. They must fit into a system of waste accounting that provides management with the costing information necessary for improved analysis and for the decisions related to the design and evaluation of product and process improvements.

An environmental information system must feed information to various management accounting and financial reporting systems already in the corporation. For management accounting, information is needed to make proper costing, capital budgeting, and performance evaluation decisions as seen in Exhibit 5–1. Similarly, information is needed to make decisions related to the appropriate accrual of environmental liability and the appropriate external disclosures in both corporate annual reports and environmental reports. This disclosure surely will include both physical and monetized information. Overall, it is important that a complete environmental information system be developed and that the system collect data for measuring and reporting environmental information to both internal and external users.

According to the Business Charter for Sustainable Development (BCSD) of the International Chamber of Commerce, management accounting systems must include the environmental costs that are part of the production, distribution, marketing, use, and disposal of goods. This information is necessary for an Environmental Strategy Implementation or a life cycle assessment. Unfortunately, traditional management accounting systems have not tracked, accumulated, measured, or reported the information related to either the costs or benefits of these activities. The BCSD seeks a system of full-cost accounting that takes into account both internal and external costs, expecting that it will result in better commercial decisions and be a boon for business and the global environment alike (Business Council for Sustainable Development, 1993).

Companies are accumulating more information about their EH&S systems and are disclosing more of this information to both governmental agencies and stakeholders. The 16th principle of the BCSD requires companies "to measure environmental performance; to conduct regular environmental audits and assessments of compliance with company requirements, legal requirements and these principles; and periodically to provide appropriate information to the Board of Directors, shareholders, employees, the authorities, and the public." This increased disclosure of information can be in voluntary compliance with these principles or in regulatory compliance with FASB and SEC rules. In either case, more information is necessary related to current and future environmental costs.

It is needed to identify and assess impacts, to integrate them, and to report them to external users.

IS A LINK NECESSARY OR DESIRABLE?

Most manufacturing companies for many years have been using information systems designed to track wastes. Chevron, for example, has been tracking yields per pound of raw materials for more than 20 years. Costs associated with wastes are assigned to the process that generated the waste. Even the costs of waste incineration are assigned back to the relevant processes. Chevron is typical of many companies that began to develop information systems to improve operational efficiency by reducing wastes and improving production yields using standard control charts and efficiency measures.[2]

In many companies, these early systems served as the basis for the development of more sophisticated systems for managing environmental impacts. Though most companies have developed or are developing systems to track waste reduction or toxicity, very few have related these improvements in efficiency and environmental responsibility to a measurement of cost savings. The next step for most of these companies is the integration of these systems with the financial reporting and management accounting systems in their organizations.

With such integration, information can be provided that facilitates the consideration of environmental costs and benefits in decisions related to financial reporting, financial analysis, capital investments, product costing, product pricing, product and process design, and performance evaluation. Managers throughout the organization would benefit from a broad identification of the current and future environmental impacts of products and processes and a better understanding of how these impacts are likely to affect other company operations. In some cases, a broader understanding of the impacts of new environmental regulations causes companies to reevaluate their accruals in financial statements and disclosure in MD&A sections of annual reports. In most cases, it also improves product costing, product design, capital budgeting, and performance evaluation decisions.

---

2. The material in this section is drawn from Dorfman, Muir, and Miller, 1992.

Is a link necessary? No. Is it desirable? In most cases, yes! Integrating the physical data and cost data related to wastes and other environmental impacts into the management accounting and reporting systems gives decision makers more complete information with which to make improved decisions. In too many organizations, EH&S personnel have made substantial efforts to gather useful environmental data that have not been passed along to operations, legal, accounting, and senior management for critical decisions. A linking of these systems and better communication and coordination among affected personnel is easily attained, with little financial or personnel costs, and has significant organizational benefits.

SUMMARY

As corporations move toward increased environmental responsibility, information technology can be either a facilitator or a barrier to the management of environmentally sensitive corporations. The information system should make it easier for an organization to comply with environmental regulations and implement its environmental strategy. Unfortunately, most corporate environmental information systems generally are not well developed. Further, where useful systems are in place, they supply information only to EH&S personnel and do not affect the primary financial reporting, management accounting, and management control functions in organizations. Potentially useful information typically is not used in making major management decisions in operations and capital expenditures. For environmental management to improve, the development and integration of environmental information into management decisions is critical.

Chapter Six

Internal Environmental Auditing Systems

The 1989 International Chamber of Commerce Position Paper on Environmental Auditing defines environmental auditing as follows:

> A management tool comprising a systematic, documented, periodic and objective evaluation of how well environmental organization, management, and equipment are performing with the aim of helping to safeguard the environment by: (i) facilitating management control of environmental practices; and (ii) assessing compliance with company policies, which would include meeting regulatory requirements (International Chamber of Commerce, 1991, 3).

Internal auditing departments have been an integral part of corporations for many years. Their primary mission is to monitor, evaluate, and control company risks. As environmental liabilities became more prominent, auditing departments were faced with the task of developing systems and procedures to audit environmental risks and compliance.

The need for increased internal controls for pollution prevention and for compliance with environmental regulations has obliged internal audit departments to include the evaluation of environmental risks in their scope. Separate board-level committees that focus on environmental affairs are now common. Environmental auditing programs are becoming a more integral part of corporate internal control systems.

WHAT IS ENVIRONMENTAL AUDITING?

Auditing has been defined as "a systematic process of objectively obtaining and evaluating evidence regarding a verifiable assertion about activities and events to ascertain the degree of correspondence between the assertion and established criteria and then communicating the results [of the process] to interested users" (Canadian Institute of Chartered Accountants, 1992, 34).

In a study for The Institute of Internal Auditors, CH2M Hill (1993, xi) defined environmental auditing as follows:

An environmental management system is defined as an organization's structure of responsibilities and policies, practices, procedures, processes, and resources for protecting the environment and managing the environmental issues. Environmental auditing is an integral part of an environmental management system whereby management determines whether the organization's environmental control systems are adequate to ensure compliance with regulatory requirements and internal policies.

TYPES OF ENVIRONMENTAL AUDITS[1]

Environmental auditing practices vary widely among organizations depending on the objectives of the audit and the types of environmental risks faced. CH2M Hill categorizes environmental audits in seven primary types, based on their objectives:

- Compliance audits;
- Environmental management systems audits;
- Transactional audits (also known as due diligence audits);
- Treatment, storage, and disposal facility audits;
- Pollution prevention audits;
- Environmental liability accrual audits;
- Product audits (CH2M Hill, 1993, 6).

Compliance Audit

The most common environmental audit is the compliance audit. Environmental laws can impose joint and several liability, retroactive liability, and civil and criminal penalties for noncompliance. The compliance audit procedure includes a detailed, site-specific audit of current, past, and future operations. In general, locations or facilities are prioritized and

---

1. This section draws heavily on and relies on the description of audit types in CH2M Hill, 1993.

scheduled for audit on the basis of the potential risks involved. Compliance audits normally are programmatic and deal with many issues such as reviewing all environmental components the site may affect: air, water, land, and waste water.

Environmental Management Systems Audit

Due to the retroactive aspect of the Comprehensive Environmental Response, Compensation, and Liability Act (CERCLA), companies at present are faced with the expense of resolving environmental issues arising from practices that were legal at the time they were undertaken. Thus companies now are beginning to focus on anticipating future regulatory trends and reflecting them in their current environmental management systems. As companies become more certain that they are in compliance with regulations, the audit emphasis shifts to environmental management systems. These audits focus on whether systems are in place and operating properly to manage future environmental risks.

Due Diligence Audit

Due diligence audits or transactional audits are conducted for the purpose of assessing the environmental risks and liabilities of land or facilities prior to a real estate acquisition. They are important because under CERCLA the current landowner can be held responsible for environmental contamination without regard to who caused the contamination. Transactional audits are an environmental risk management tool for banks, land buyers, lending agencies, charitable organizations, investors, and any other organization purchasing land. These interested parties need to understand the environmental risk associated with the property they are purchasing, lending on, or accepting as a gift, because the environmental liability can easily exceed the market value of the asset. (This issue is further discussed in the section below on business acquisitions and divestments.)

Treatment, Storage, and Disposal Facility Audit

In many instances EPA regulations require that hazardous material be tracked from "cradle to grave." Companies that produce hazardous waste material may contract with other companies to store, treat, or dispose of that material. Yet companies are still liable for any environmental damage that might be caused by the "handling" company. Some companies conduct audits on the facilities they own and on facilities that handle hazardous waste material with which they contract. These audits must cover all the issues raised by the Resource Conservation and Recovery Act (RCRA) in the handling of these waste materials.

Pollution Prevention Audit

Pollution prevention audits are designed to minimize waste at the source rather than at the "end of pipe." The areas examined include source elimination, energy conservation, recovery, recyclability, treatment, disposal, and release. Companies examine whether pollution can be prevented through capital improvements, process improvements, or product improvements. Companies conduct these audits because they recognize that eliminating or reducing the production of waste is usually much less expensive in total environmental and company costs than cleaning it up at the end of the production process.

Environmental Liability Accrual Audit

Internal audits that address the issues of reasonable, probable, and estimable in determining the environmental liabilities to be accrued for financial reporting are important obligations of accounting professionals. Often the auditors seek assistance from independent technical professionals, such as consulting engineers, for verification and to demonstrate due diligence. Too often, however, it is the chief legal professional who determines the accrual rather than a combination of the accounting, operations, EH&S, and legal officers.

Product Audit

Some companies perform audits on specific products to determine whether more should be done to make them environmentally friendly and to confirm that product and chemical restrictions are being met. These audits have resulted in the development of products such as refrigerators and automobiles with higher recyclable contents. The product audit examines the environmental impacts of the product including packaging and distribution. Packaging materials are assessed for their ability to be recycled or recovered and for the use of recycled materials. This audit is often a significant part of a life cycle assessment.

INTERNAL ENVIRONMENTAL AUDIT DEPARTMENTS

Internal auditors are involved in risk management. With the enormous potential risk from environmental issues, internal auditors have begun to use their skills to identify environmental risks and bring them to the attention of management. Corporate internal audits are conducted for compliance with government regulations, corporate goals, corporate procedures, and practices. Internal audits for compliance with environmental regulations recently have become more important due to stricter environmental regulations.

The Environmental Auditing Department at BFI is responsible for conducting environmental audits of all facilities on a regular basis and validating the effectiveness of the company's other environmental management systems. The department is separate from the operations and compliance support groups of the company and reports directly to the general counsel. Though compliance is certainly a primary function of an internal audit group, planning also is considered in the internal audit recommendations.

It is critical that internal environmental auditors be familiar with federal, state, and local regulations and permits, and monitor compliance with those regulations and permits. It is also important that compliance with company policies and procedures be monitored. At BFI, "all data related to audit findings, actions taken or planned and follow-up activity are computerized...allowing ongoing monitoring of progress and long-term performance trend analysis."

At Bristol-Myers Squibb, the Corporate Technical Evaluation and Services Department audits each company facility every 18 to 24 months for compliance with EH&S regulations, good manufacturing practices, proper conservation and use of energy, and corporate policies. Reports are forwarded to appropriate senior management personnel for review.

THE IMPORTANCE OF THE SELF-AUDIT

The internal audit process is not intended to monitor or implement daily compliance. At BFI, "facilities have their own management systems designed to ensure compliance and achieve environmental excellence when auditors and government inspectors are not present. Because direct responsibility rests with the district managers, a system of self-audits or self-inspections is integral to the EHS program." Managers must conduct facility inspections personally on a regular basis to ensure that operations comply with regulations and company policies. Further, all employees must be trained to identify potential and existing environmental violations and hazards for corrective and preventive action. It is only in this way that an EH&S management system can be implemented effectively because an internal audit department cannot effectively monitor daily compliance.

ASSURANCE LETTERS

Many companies use assurance letters to help monitor and improve corporate environmental performance. Typically, the CEO requests a letter from business unit managers stating that there are no deficiencies or problems related to matters of EH&S that could have a significant impact on the company. If problems do exist, then the letters serve to provide notice of the problems and the corrective action being taken. The letters filter up to senior management and down to the plant manager, so that all managers in positions of authority recognize their responsibility for EH&S performance. Letters received by the CEO are a commitment from all levels of management on EH&S responsibility and often are used in business unit and manager performance reviews.

THE ROLE OF ENVIRONMENTAL AUDITING IN BUSINESS ACQUISITIONS AND DIVESTMENTS

The dramatic increase in environmental costs and broadened court rulings on the assignment of environmental liabilities have caused companies to be much more sensitive to potential environmental problems related to business acquisitions. In the Fleet Factors case (*United States* v. *Fleet Factors Corp.*) the Eleventh Circuit Court of Appeals held that the bank was liable as an "operator" for the cleanup of the property even though it did not cause or contribute to the hazardous waste. The Court found that a lender could be liable "by participating in the financial management of a facility to a degree indicating a capacity to influence the corporation's treatment of hazardous waste" (Shanker, 1994, 104).

Like more and more companies, Sun Company requires the EH&S department to review the company's environmental exposure on all acquisitions and divestments of company assets. As part of the requirement for EH&S to sign off, the department performs an environmental audit. It completes a due diligence report that identifies the current environmental status of the assets and potential future liabilities. This audit is important for the buyer and seller because both may acquire or retain some environmental liability. Careful audits of the facilities are necessary for both the buyer and seller to evaluate the acquisition or divestment fully.

Bristol-Myers Squibb has prepared a due diligence manual to assist management in assessing environmental, health, and safety issues associated with acquisition and divestment transactions. The company's approach to due diligence includes defining, identifying, and quantifying those issues that will have an impact on EH&S. It also emphasizes the importance of having multidisciplinary teams, including employees from accounting, operations, legal, finance, and EH&S, involved in the EH&S aspects of acquisitions and divestments. The manual includes detailed questionnaires for transactions involving real estate and manufacturing site acquisitions that can be sent to sellers and landlords to aid in determining EH&S impacts. These questionnaires assist in gathering information for the due diligence process.

The Bristol-Myers Squibb manual also provides guidelines, shown in Exhibit 6–1, to aid managers in the purchasing process.

Many companies have reported a common practice of setting aside enough funds on any acquisition to bring an acquired company into environmental compliance. This goal typically is accomplished through an immediate credit, a fund that can be drawn on, or an indemnification for some period of time. Companies have set up different incentives for managers' use of these funds to encourage both an accurate evaluation of environmental needs and a responsible correction of environmental deficiencies. In many cases, managers can use the funds set aside through the acquisition only for immediate compliance costs. After that, any environmental expenditures not previously identified and budgeted for in the acquisition affect the business unit's bottom line and the manager's performance evaluation. In some cases, this stipulation causes managers to overreport projected environmental expenditures.

These holdbacks and indemnifications also force companies to be even more careful about whom they do business with—buyers, sellers, and joint venturers as well as customers and suppliers. Because of the

EXHIBIT 6–1
Bristol-Myers Squibb (Techniques for Minimizing Environmental Liability When Buying)

Techniques for Minimizing Environmental Liability When Buying (Note: Not all techniques are applicable in all situations).

• Background Information	Seller provides information about the property or business.
• Letter of Intent	Environmental problems give buyer right to terminate purchase.
• Environmental Assessment	Conduct assessment to identify problems and to potentially gain the benefit of any defenses under CERCLA.
• Seller's Indemnification	Seller indemnifies buyer against liabilities and third party claims, including associated legal, investigatory and remedial fees and expenses associated with the environmental condition of the property. (Note: Ensure seller has the financial strength to back up the indemnification).
• Representations and Warranties	Seller warrants the property is free from contamination and the business is free from liability; all necessary permits are available and up-to-date; and operations comply with all applicable laws and regulations. Seller further warrants that no condition or circumstance exists which may interfere with or prevent continued compliance with such regulations in the future.
• Remedial Actions	Seller undertakes remedial actions for liabilities subject to seller's indemnification; seller conducts remediation as a pre-condition to the sale.
• Operational Deficiencies	Seller corrects before the sale or adjusts the purchase price, and indemnifies for any past noncompliance problems or contamination which may result from pre-closing conditions or activities. (Note: Ensure seller has the financial strength to back up the indemnification).
• Pollution Control Equipment	Seller agrees to reimburse buyer for necessary capital items, or buyer and seller agree upon a cost allocation.
• Purchase Price	Adjust the price to cover environmental costs (where adequate information for firm cost estimates is available).
• Liability Insurance	Purchase insurance or require seller to insure buyer against future liabilities (if available at a reasonable cost). (Note: To the extent possible, make sure the insurance actually covers the expected liabilities, not that it is assumed to provide coverage).
• Environmental Contingency Fund	In lieu of insurance, have seller set up a trust fund or account to provide a letter of credit. (Note: Make sure that such a fund is actually accessible and not just for window-dressing).
• Subdivide Property	Seller retains contaminated portion of the property (where the contamination is adequately identified and effectively contained).

increased penalties for environmental violations, swift action often is taken if concerns for environmental liability are not addressed adequately in a timely manner. Multinational companies increasingly are terminating relationships with those buyers, sellers, joint venturers, customers, and suppliers rather than be exposed to additional liability that may flow to them because of the long reach of many environmental laws. These companies also have been establishing commitments to environmental responsibility that would be violated by dealing with entities that do not meet a company's worldwide environmental standards.

ENVIRONMENTAL AUDITING PRACTICES AND PROGRAMS

Internal environmental auditing is probably the best-developed environmental system in place in organizations. Basic systems are in general use, although improvements could be implemented that would broaden the focus and provide more benefits to environmental planning and control. In most organizations, an environmental audit program is well developed and routine. It typically is conducted by some combination of central staff from the EH&S department and staff from the facilities or business units, with wide variation in reporting responsibilities. Many companies send the results of the environmental audits to the business unit managers who set the action plans and the schedules for reporting deficiencies. Others report to a central EH&S office, which coordinates environmental improvements.

More comprehensive reporting programs do produce improved results. Environmental audits should be independent of the business units. A report to the head of EH&S and to a member of the board of directors, along with the business unit manager, is important. In addition, the audit should be part of a more comprehensive program of evaluating the environmental performance of the business unit, the facility, the business unit manager, and other management and staff. It also should be part of a comprehensive performance evaluation system in the organization to provide the incentives necessary to motivate improved corporate environmental performance.

A recent survey of the S&P 500 by the Washington-based Investor Responsibility Research Center found that 80 percent of the respondents conducted some environmental auditing, but just 6 percent release summaries to shareholders and then only on special request (*The Wall Street Journal*, 12/13/93). The recent Price Waterhouse study reported that 73 percent of the respondents audit primarily for compliance with environmental regulations and that 64 percent of internal environmental auditing is completed by internal corporate environmental staff (Price Waterhouse, 1994, 31–32).

Typical of many corporations, Ciba-Geigy has been conducting environmental audits since 1980. Major production sites are audited every three to five years. Many other facilities conduct audits annually. The audit is intended as an internal management tool to improve environmental performance.

There is no generally accepted model of environmental auditing and no expectation that there should be one for all companies to use. Companies develop systems and procedures for auditing that fit their production processes, facilities, products, and environmental impacts.

In 1992, The Southern Company developed a system-wide environmental auditing task force and established a set of common environmental auditing criteria. Each environmental auditing program in The Southern Company must meet or exceed the criteria shown in Exhibit 6–2.

Pacific Gas & Electric instructs its own personnel to conduct self-audits of their facilities. In 1993 the company conducted 130 audits of facilities. It has developed an auditing database that allows "statistical tracking and analysis" of audit results. The company also began a re-inspection program to ensure that adequate corrective action has been taken and documented. A Compliance Guidance Working Group, created in 1992 to address administrative and procedural violations, has been improving the communications between corporate environmental staff and the company's business units.

The environmental staff at Procter & Gamble conducts annual audits assessing the complexity of each site's processes and environmental performance requirements. The company then establishes a target rating for the site's management system and expects that by 1995, 90 percent of company sites will achieve their target environmental management ratings.

Union Carbide has conducted more than 1,000 environmental audits of facilities since its program began in 1986. Frequency of the audit depends on the size and risk related to the facility. With a strong commitment to environmental auditing, senior management contacts business unit and facility managers to get explanations and drive action on all audits with low scores.

The frequency of a site audit is based on an audit-scheduling algorithm. The audit timeliness index (ATI) is based on five components: hazard,

EXHIBIT 6–2
The Southern Company

Elements of an Effective Environmental Auditing Program for The Southern Company

An effective environmental auditing program will provide management with information relating to the effectiveness of its environmental management systems in achieving compliance with company policies and governmental requirements. The elements of such a program are defined in the following principles. Each environmental auditing program in The Southern Company system must meet or exceed these criteria.

1. The audit program must have explicit support from senior management.

2. The environmental auditing function must have proper independence of the activities it audits.

3. Auditors must have the necessary qualifications and training to accomplish the audit program objectives.

4. The auditing program must define explicitly its objectives, scope, resources to be committed, and the auditing methodology.

5. The audit protocol should document information that is sufficient, reliable, and useful to support an assessment of overall management effectiveness and to provide a sound basis for audit findings and recommendations.

6. The audit process should include specific procedures for the prompt preparation of clear, candid reports that incorporate audit findings, corrective actions, and schedules for implementation. During the audit, the auditor(s) shall immediately notify management of any situation or event reportable to state or federal agencies, any practice with unacceptable environmental impact, or any perceived violation of state or federal regulations.

7. A sound quality assurance program shall be established to ensure the accuracy and thoroughness of environmental auditing.

prior audit, time since last audit, special site specific, and plant population. After determining that a site is to be audited, the company applies an audit classification system that determines measures for EH&S issues and evaluates the improvement in performance from one year to the next. The audits are rated in four categories: Meets (M), Substantially Meets (SM), Generally Meets (GM), and Requires Substantial Improvement (RSI). For an audit to get a rating of Meets, at least 75 percent of the functional areas must be Meets. Typical of the functional areas are operational safety, waste management, product risk assessment, product quality and distribution, emergency planning, and surface water protection. The development of an action plan to correct all deficiencies is expected.

Union Carbide has showed steady improvement in its corporate environmental performance. The improvement is due, in part, to a comprehensive set of companywide, international environmental standards and a strong audit program. The use of Arthur D. Little, Inc. (ADL) as its external environmental auditor also has benefited the company by providing an external evaluation and attestation of the internal audit system that aids both internal and external users of financial and environmental information. The audit lets the company benchmark its performance—ADL can compare Union Carbide's performance against the performance of others, which helps in the general improvement of its audit system.

Union Carbide's ATI includes a hazard component based on a location's score in the company's hazard ranking model. The audits include reviews of programs related to episodic risk management and community emergency response. Such audits have become more commonplace as companies, particularly in the chemical and oil industries, have attempted to be crisis prepared rather than crisis prone.

ECO-AUDITING

The European Community has been developing and implementing eco-auditing for many years. On a voluntary basis companies are encouraged to set up an environmental management system that covers all the key areas of their environmental impacts including site audits every three years subject to independent verification. This Eco-Management and Audit Scheme (EMAS) permits companies, upon completion, to use the EMAS logo, which signals that they are an environmentally concerned company (Naimon, 1994, 59).

A European Eco-Audit Regulation adopted in March 1993, although voluntary, will be an important tool in the disclosure of relevant environmental information to key stakeholders. It attempts to standardize good-quality environmental management. The regulation requires an assessment of the environmental impact of products, processes, and new activities on the local environment. Preventing and reducing pollution, toxic emissions, and waste generation are of prime importance, along with monitoring and measuring these activities. The eco-audit establishes audit procedures for specific sites rather than for entire companies and also specific guidelines on the disclosure of information to the public. Public disclosure of information related to a company's environmental activities is sought to obtain feedback from the public regarding the company's handling of environmental issues.

Companies are required to display a Statement of Participation that indicates the registration of a site in the eco-audit scheme. Following an audit the site must prepare an independently verified statement that describes the activities and environmental impacts at the site. The regulation also requires the employment of an outside "environmental verifier" to check independently whether the company is in compliance. The auditor gives company management a report. It includes instances of noncompliance, defects in the environmental management system, and recommendations to the company.

The U.N. Business Council for Sustainable Development has established a Strategic Advisory Group on the Environment (SAGE) to establish standards for eco-labeling. This group also will look into standards for auditing, environmental management systems, environmental performance evaluation, life cycle analysis, and products.

BROADER CORPORATE ENVIRONMENTAL INTERNAL AUDITS

An environmental audit of a corporate facility usually is completed to determine levels of pollution, compliance with governmental standards, and health and safety risks to employees from pollution and also to validate whether management control systems for pollution prevention are in place and operative. Probably the most comprehensive work on environmental auditing has been completed by ADL. The company likely has completed the most environmental audits of any independent outside company or auditor. Ladd Greeno and his associates at ADL have written an authoritative and widely quoted book on the fundamentals of environmental auditing (Greeno et al., 1987). The main components of the audit procedure they propose are cited below:

"Prior to the audit itself, there are several issues involved in the planning that need to be completed:

1. Site and facilities selection

2. Assemble audit team

3. Develop audit plan

"Once the audit team is on site there are five basic steps in the audit procedure:

1. Develop an understanding of internal management systems and procedures.

2. Assess strengths and weaknesses.

3. Gather audit evidence.

4. Evaluate audit findings.

5. Report audit findings" (Greeno et al., 1987, 23–25)

The field research results reported in this study indicate that the accounting and auditing community must be more involved in the development and practice of environmental auditing. These professions bring established measurement frameworks and auditing procedures that can improve environmental auditing practices substantially. In a study on *Environmental Auditing and the Role of the Accounting Profession* (Canadian Institute of Chartered Accountants, 1992), the CICA grouped environmentally related services into four categories:

• Environmental consulting services;

• Site assessments;

• Operational compliance assessments;

• Environmental management system assessments.

While Canadian firms are not required to carry out environmental audits, more audits are being conducted in response to the increasing scope of pollution control legislation and regulation, accompanied by increasingly burdensome fines, penalties, and orders that can be imposed under much of the legislation. The CICA study describes the state of the art of environmental auditing and how it differs from the types of audits typically conducted by accountants and auditors. It also provides recommendations on the role of accountants in the development and practice of the growing field of environmental auditing.

Two other useful books that provide guidance to the practice of environmental auditing are the ICC *Guide to Effective Environmental Auditing* (1991), cited earlier, and the Department of Energy's manual of the protocols involved in doing an environmental audit. The manual provides the structure to ensure that systems are in place "to correct existing environmental problems, to minimize risks to the environment or public health, and to anticipate and address potential environmental problems before they pose a threat to the quality of the environment or the public welfare. Finally, it is DOE's policy that efforts to meet environmental obligations be carried out consistently across all operations and among all field organizations and programs" (U.S. Department of Energy, 1).

LACK OF STANDARDS IN ENVIRONMENTAL AUDITING

The quality and quantity of environmental reporting, external environmental audits, and internal environmental audits all have increased significantly. Signatories of the CERES Principles agree that "[w]e will conduct an annual self-evaluation of our progress in implementing these Principles. We will support the timely creation of generally accepted environmental audit procedures. We will annually complete the CERES Report, which will be made available to the public."

But there are no generally accepted standards for the conduct of either internal or external environmental audits. To a large part it depends on who is doing the audit. The different organizations cited above may have different standards and guidelines and also a wide variety of methods and techniques. This fact has led to some struggles on the part of companies that are serious in their pursuit of compliance and environmental risk assessment.

The Arthur D. Little Center for Environmental Assurance also concurs that "there are no widely accepted standards which identify the necessary elements for conducting effective environmental, health, and safety audits. Yet, despite differences in audit approach and philosophy among audit practitioners, a number of fundamental principles for conducting audits are beginning to emerge" (Arthur D. Little, 1989, 22). ADL sees that "future audit programs will shift their focus towards auditing the environmental management systems rather than the facility's compliance status at the time of the audit. Top management needs to be assured that the facility has the programs and procedures in place to manage for compliance before, during, and after the audit—not just that the facility was in good shape during the audit" (Greeno et al., 1987, 243–244).

The Environmental Protection Agency issued its own auditing standards in 1986. In July 1994 the agency began hearings to modify and improve those standards. The EPA has conducted these hearings so that interested parties can present arguments and evidence as to whether additional incentives are needed to encourage the self-disclosure and prompt correction of environmental violations uncovered during facility audits (EPA, 1994, 4).

Frank Friedman, who spent many years with Occidental Petroleum and was involved in its environmental auditing program, makes certain further distinctions. He believes that the environmental audit does not require outside independence as a financial audit does and should be called an assessment rather than an audit. He argues that "as long as there is a commitment to assure that problems surfaced are addressed, this program review can and should be done by qualified in-house people who are 'independent' of production responsibilities. An in-house individual, familiar with the operations and credible to the facility being audited, can determine far more about what is right or wrong with a facility than an outsider" (Friedman, 1993, 146).

The Canadian Institute of Chartered Accountants also looked at the lack of standards in the field. Its recommendations were that environmental audits should be conducted by one group so as to achieve comparability and standardization of methods and results. It found that at present most environmental audits are being conducted by internal corporate staff. Some of the audit functions are being satisfied by engineering and scientific consulting firms, management consulting divisions of public accounting firms, small specialty environmental consulting firms, and law firms. The law firms are being retained for the "due diligence" review of a property or asset before it is purchased (CICA, 1992, 31).

Some nonaccounting groups also have been attempting to create certification standards for environmental auditors. For example, the

Association of Environmental Consulting Firms (AECF) is trying to establish a certification process for environmental auditors, and the Board of Certified Safety Professionals has developed a code of professional conduct. A similar code has been developed by the Institute of Internal Auditors. The American Society for Testing and Materials has given its approval to a set of standards that would aid those seeking protection under Superfund's innocent landowner defense (Friedman, 1993, 146–147).

SUMMARY

The growth of environmental costs and the recognition by corporate managers of the need to better manage corporate environmental impacts has dramatically increased the demands for both internal and external environmental audits. Improved self-audits and internal audits are necessary to monitor and reduce environmental impact, but external audits provide additional benefits.

The external audits increase stakeholder confidence in the quality of corporate environmental controls, planning, and performance. They also provide senior management with an independent verification and analysis of the strengths and deficiencies of the environmental management program and additional confidence that hazards and violations will be minimized.

Though no standards exist at present for either internal or external environmental auditing, it is likely that both will be developed soon. Stakeholders want more verification of corporate environmental responsibility to determine managers' sensitivity to this area of increased public concern. They want to understand corporate plans to reduce both environmental impacts and company costs. Shareholders and financial analysts desire more information that will permit them to assess a company's future environmental liabilities. Managers need more information about these same issues to develop a corporate environmental strategy and manage environmental impacts better.

It is expected that both internal and external accountants and auditors will need to expand the scope of their services to provide the assistance desired by both corporate managers and external users. They also will need to be involved in integrating environmental considerations throughout the organization through multifunctional teams such as the environmental accrual committees discussed earlier. Such teams include accounting, operations, legal, product design, and EH&S personnel. Only through such multifunctional integration can environmental impacts be understood throughout a company, appropriate environmental measurements and disclosures be developed, and environmental impacts be reduced through capital improvements, process improvements, and product improvements.

Companies must use internal environmental audits to monitor corporate environmental performance. But they also must use these systems to consider broader environmental impacts and ways to reduce those impacts. Environmental planning must be as much a part of the environmental audit process as environmental compliance. Companies need to consider existing and pending legislation and possible product and process redesigns. They must integrate a broadened internal environmental audit system, including self-audits and external audits, into the basic management systems in the organization. Only in this way can they achieve the maximum benefits of reduced environmental impacts and reduced company costs.

Chapter Seven

External Reporting Systems and Environmental Audits

C orporate responses to increased stakeholder demands for information on corporate environmental performance vary widely. Some companies have expanded their coverage of environmental issues in their corporate annual report to satisfy both increased financial disclosure requirements and demands by financial analysts, environmental activists, and other stakeholders. Many companies in addition or alternatively have produced separate corporate environmental reports. It is clear, however, that the number of corporate environmental progress reports is increasing dramatically, about doubling every year. It is also clear that the companies that have been producing them see very substantial benefits both to their companies and various stakeholders.

Noranda Forest's CEO, K. Linn Macdonald, has stated that environmental reporting "can only foster a better public understanding of the environmental challenges particular to the forest products industry, not to mention the considerable accomplishments of the entire industry in dealing with them." But this communication to outside stakeholders makes sense only when the external report is backed by substantive internal progress. As discussed later in this chapter, Noranda Forest has an aggressive internal environmental audit program that includes an external auditor who conducts an independent review of its practices. In addition, the company has been working on life cycle assessments to evaluate the environmental impacts of its products and processes.

THE VARIETY OF ENVIRONMENTAL DISCLOSURES IN CORPORATE ANNUAL REPORTS AND CORPORATE ENVIRONMENTAL REPORTS

Various pressures have caused companies to increase their environmental disclosures in corporate annual reports and the quantity and quality of disclosures in environmental reports. The diversity of environmental information in annual reports and EH&S reports can be classified according to the choice of various disclosure strategies. Those disclosure choices include:

- No accrual or disclosure of environmental liability;
- Disclosure of current environmental operating costs;
- Disclosure of current environmental capital expenditures;
- Accrual of an environmental liability that is included in "other liabilities" and not separately reported;
- Identification of the environmental liability as a separate line item on the balance sheet.

The choices listed above encompass numerous alternatives. Brief descriptions follow of the diversity of disclosure choices some companies select.

Environmental disclosures in annual reports are becoming more prevalent and are found in a variety of places. Most common are disclosures in the MD&A section, where companies often cite their pending environmental litigation, remediation costs, past costs, and any other unusual items. These disclosures also can be found in the Notes to the Financial Statements, where companies report their environmental operating and capital expenditures for the past year and current year and their expectations for the coming year. Rarely are environmental disclosures found as separate line items in the financial statements.

Some companies have issued environmental reports for various operating divisions or geographical areas. Dow Chemical has issued several environmental progress reports for Dow Europe and Dow Canada and now has issued its first global EH&S report. This 1993 report tracks the company's progress in pollution control and prevention, sustainability, environmental partnership programs, emissions reduction, energy efficiency, and health and safety issues. It reports the amounts of emissions for a variety of chemicals as well as progress toward the company's environmental goals. It states that Dow performs EH&S audits on a regular basis for use by management in measuring and reporting its progress against EH&S expectations and that Dow retains Arthur D. Little to review its auditing practices.

In the Dow Europe EH&S report for 1992, Dow discloses the amount of emissions from substances in its plants in the Dow Europe Priority List. The report includes an overview of the key hazard and environmental characteristics of each substance, the amounts emitted, and the percentage of throughput. Specific disclosures also are provided for each European plant, related to waste water, air, and waste emissions; the amounts of those emissions; and a comparison of those emission amounts with prior years and future expectations and goals. All this information is indexed to show reductions or increases in emissions on a percentage basis.

Dow Canada was the first of the Dow companies to produce an EH&S report, beginning in 1988. In its 1992 report the company discloses the amounts for capital expenditures for environmental projects for the years 1986–1992. The report also includes a detailed inventory of chemical emissions to air, water, and land, and chemicals in materials and waste sent off site for processing or treatment and disposal. The report further discloses the company's accomplishments and failures at each of its plants.

In both its 1993 corporate annual report and its environmental report, Sun Company disclosed the projected environmental capital spending for 1994 and 1995 in addition to its previous expenditures. These are the types of disclosures the SEC has contended should be included in the MD&A section of corporate annual reports under SEC Release 36, issued in 1989.

The SEC has been advocating the inclusion of forward-looking information in corporate annual reports. If companies have projections about corporate environmental impacts, liabilities, or performance that would be useful to external users of financial information, then that information should be disclosed in some form. Disclosing it will tell a more complete corporate story to the company's owners, analysts, and other stakeholders who are trying to understand the company's position and performance. Disclosure of this additional environmental information has been increasing dramatically, as any comparison of 1992 and 1993 annual reports demonstrates. This increased disclosure may be partially in response to the SEC's MD&A release and Staff Accounting Bulletin 92.

Union Carbide recognizes both the importance of and lack of precision in estimating environmental liabilities. In the MD&A section of its annual report, the company included an estimate that its expenses and capital expenditures related to environmental protection, in 1993 dollars, would average about $150 million and $65 million annually over the next five years. It further stated that any excesses over the averages would not be material over the five-year period but might have a material adverse effect in a given quarter or year. It is disclosures such as this that provide the additional information various stakeholders want.

British Petroleum has included an extensive section on environmental investments in its corporate annual report. The company discloses prior, current, and future capital investments in pollution abatement as well as operating expenses for current and past years. The reserve for remediation and dismantling of oil and gas related assets also is disclosed. The company acknowledges that much of its expenditures for EH&S are intended to comply with environmental and product quality regulations. By improving its EH&S performance, the company helps to protect its "license to operate." Though not to be measured for external reporting purposes, such improvements in corporate environmental performance may create an "environmental goodwill" or "environmental asset" as contrasted with the environmental liabilities most often discussed. Viewing environmental expenditures in this way provides companies with information related to the planning orientation advocated in this book.

Some companies have recognized that increased environmental measurement and reporting are necessary for both internal and external users to evaluate the company's performance. In this regard, Browning-Ferris Industries has been increasing the amount of accrued environmental liabilities disclosed in its corporate annual report and has looked at those liabilities more broadly than many companies that restrict their accruals only to Superfund liabilities. In the 1993 annual report, BFI's CEO William Ruckelshaus wrote:

> There is increasing focus by investors and regulators on company balance sheets, especially in the area of environmental liabilities and provisions for future environmental obligations like landfill closures and post-closure maintenance. We think on that score we have one of the strongest balance sheets in the industry. Further, our reserve policy on landfill issues considers the likely impact of Subtitle D [of RCRA, relating to standards for municipal solid waste landfills], the applicable provisions of the Clean Air Act and a template methodology confirmed by outside experts. This puts us in a strong position for the future.

BFI has included more detail in the corporate annual report than most companies.

EXHIBIT 7–1

Browning-Ferris Industries (Excerpts from Balance Sheet & Footnotes to Financial Statements)

EXCERPT FROM BALANCE SHEET		

Liabilities and common stockholders' equity	September 30	
(in thousands)	1993	1992
Accrued environmental and landfill costs	$631,690	$643,011

EXCERPT FROM FOOTNOTES TO FINANCIAL STATEMENT		

(7) Accrued environmental and landfill costs

Accrued environmental and landfill costs at September 30, 1993 and 1992 were as follows (in thousands):

	1993	1992
Accrued costs associated with open landfills (including landfills under expansion)	$ 414,021	$ 401,966
Accrued costs associated with closed landfills and corrective action costs (including Superfund sites)	125,162	110,948
Accrued costs of closure, post-closure and certain other liabilities associated with discontinued operations	189,947	223,315
Total	729,130	736,229
Less current portion (included in other accrued liabilities)	97,440	93,218
Accrued environmental and landfills costs	$ 631,690	$ 643,011

EXHIBIT 7–2
Cambrex Corporation (Notes to Consolidated Financial Statements)

CAMBREX CORPORATION AND SUBSIDIARIES

NOTES TO CONSOLIDATED FINANCIAL STATEMENTS — (Continued)
(dollars in thousands, except share data)

The following table exclusively addresses matters wherein the related liabilities are considered estimable. It summarizes the estimated range of the Company's share of costs associated with such matters, the related accruals, and activity associated with those accruals. Such ranges and accruals have not been reduced for recoveries, if any, under insurance policies or from third parties due to the numerous uncertainties associated with such claims. The changes in the estimated ranges from 1992 to 1993 represent revisions to estimates and the addition of matters that were quantified for the first time during 1993. The related accruals represent management's assessment of the aggregate liability associated with estimable matters.

	December 31,	
	1993	1992
Estimated range of the Company's share of costs associated with estimable matters:		
Minimum	$ 7,085	$ 6,107
Maximum	$14,835	$14,705
Accrual and related activity:		
Balance, beginning of year	$ 7,388	$ 3,868
Adjustment recorded in connection with acquisition activity *	1,320	—
Additions:		
Income statement charges....................................	1,029	1,747
Estimated liability recorded in connection with acquisition activity net of related deferred tax asset of $1,320........................	—	1,980
Deductions for expenditures	(679)	(207)
Balance, end of year	$ 9,058	$ 7,388
Classification of year end accrual:		
Current	$ 310	$ 800
Non-current	8,748	6,588
	$ 9,058	$ 7,388

---

* Effective January 1, 1993, the Company adopted Statement of Financial Accounting Standard #109, "Accounting for Income Taxes." At that date and in accordance with the provisions of that Statement, a deferred tax asset of $1,320 previously netted against this accrual was reclassified to non-current assets.

During 1991, income statement charges for additions to the accrual for environmental contingencies aggregated $3,190.

In addition, the company later disclosed estimates of future environmental compliance costs at its currently operating landfill operations. The company, which already had accrued $414 million for such costs (as shown in Exhibit 7–1), stated that it expects to spend another $765 million to $815 million between the present time and the time the dumps are closed. Most of those funds likely will not be needed for decades. BFI is an example of a company that is recognizing its environmental problems, disclosing them, and attempting to manage existing environmental problems better and avoid future ones.

Cambrex Corporation has taken a leadership role in external environmental disclosures through the disclosure of minimum and maximum ranges of its environmental liability (see Exhibit 7–2). As is often the case with companies that make voluntary disclosures, Cambrex believes that its disclosure strategy has improved its relationship with institutional investors. Financial analysts increasingly are concerned with the magnitude of environmental liabilities of the companies that they follow and sometimes overestimate the amount of those liabilities. It is increasingly important for companies to be forthcoming in their environmental disclosures for the sake of their own relationships with their investors, in addition to any growing concerns about the adequacy of their disclosures and compliance with FASB and SEC regulations.

In addition to the line item disclosures in the balance sheet and in footnotes, some companies have included environmental disclosures in the operating activities section of their statement of cash flows. For example, Sun Company included an "accrual for environmental remediation" and United Technologies included an "environmental remediation provision" and a change in "environmental liabilities" in their cash flow statements.

Weyerhaeuser Company has included estimates of future environmental capital expenditures in the MD&A section of its 1993 annual report. It states that "while it is difficult to isolate the environmental component of most manufacturing capital projects, the company estimates that capital expenditures for environmental compliance were approximately 8 percent of total capital expenditures in 1992 and 1993, and based on its understanding of current regulatory requirements, the company expects this percentage to increase to approximately 11 percent in 1994 and to range from 13 to 14 percent of total capital expenditures in 1995."

Monsanto has been widely recognized for its "Monsanto Pledge" to protect the environment. In 1987 the company announced a goal of reducing air emissions of toxic chemicals by 90 percent worldwide by 1992. That goal has been achieved, due to the closing of several plants in Europe and to large capital expenditures. The footnotes to the 1993 financial statements disclose expenditures of $233 million for management of environmental programs, including the operation and maintenance of facilities for environmental control, in addition to $53 million expended for capital projects. The company's balance sheet includes accrued liabilities of $266 million for the remediation of identified waste disposal sites.

EXHIBIT 7–3
Monsanto Emissions Reduction Program (E&H Report)

Table 3. 1993 Worldwide Releases and Transfers, by Plant Location

(millions)	Releases											
	Air		Water		Injection Wells		Land		Transfers		Total	
	lb.	kg.	lb.	kg.	lb.	kg.	lb.	kg.	lb.	kg.	lb.	kg.
Alvin, Texas	0.3	0.1	—	—	160.2	72.8	0.1	<0.1	0.1	<0.1	160.7	73.0
Sauget, Ill.	1.1	0.5	—	—	—	—	<0.1	<0.1	18.6	8.4	19.6	8.9
St. Louis, Mo.	<0.1	<0.1	—	—	—	—	—	—	7.7	3.5	7.8	3.5
Pensacola, Fla.	1.0	0.5	<0.1	<0.1	5.8	2.6	—	—	0.8	0.3	7.6	3.4
Decatur, Ala.	2.0	0.9	4.6	2.1	—	—	<0.1	<0.1	0.1	0.1	6.7	3.0
Luling, La.	2.0	0.9	<0.1	<0.1	2.6	1.2	—	—	0.4	0.2	5.0	2.3
Springfield, Mass.	0.3	0.2	<0.1	<0.1	—	—	—	—	3.8	1.7	4.2	1.9
Newport, Wales	1.2	0.6	1.1	0.5	—	—	—	—	<0.1	<0.1	2.3	1.0
University Park, Ill.	<0.1	<0.1	—	—	—	—	—	—	2.2	1.0	2.3	1.0
Augusta, Ga.	<0.1	<0.1	—	—	—	—	—	—	1.2	0.5	1.2	0.6
Muscatine, Iowa	0.6	0.3	<0.1	<0.1	—	—	—	—	0.2	0.1	0.8	0.4
Ruabon, Wales	0.8	0.4	<0.1	<0.1	—	—	—	—	<0.1	<0.1	0.8	0.4
All Others (24 plants)	2.2	1.0	0.1	0.1	<0.1	<0.1	<0.1	<0.1	2.4	1.1	4.8	2.1
Total, Worldwide	11.5	5.2	5.8	2.6	168.6	76.6	0.1	<0.1	37.6	17.1	223.6	101.6

Table 4. 1993 Worldwide Releases and Transfers, by Chemical

(millions)	Releases											
	Air		Water		Injection Wells		Land		Transfers		Total	
	lb.	kg.	lb.	kg.	lb.	kg.	lb.	kg.	lb.	kg.	lb.	kg.
Ammonium Sulfate	—	—	4.6	2.1	133.7	60.8	—	—	7.5	3.4	145.8	66.3
Ammonia	0.2	0.1	0.1	<0.1	22.4	10.2	<0.1	<0.1	1.1	0.5	23.9	10.8
Hydrochloric Acid	1.7	0.8	—	—	<0.1	<0.1	<0.1	<0.1	15.3	7.0	17.0	7.7
Methanol	0.2	0.1	0.2	0.1	1.7	0.8	—	—	4.5	2.0	6.5	3.0
Formaldehyde	<0.1	<0.1	0.6	0.3	2.7	1.2	—	—	1.6	0.7	5.0	2.3
Ammonium Nitrate (soln.)	—	—	—	—	4.7	2.1	—	—	—	—	4.7	2.1
Carbon Monoxide	4.0	1.8	—	—	—	—	—	—	—	—	4.0	1.8
Acrylonitrile	0.4	0.2	<0.1	<0.1	1.3	0.6	—	—	0.1	<0.1	1.8	0.8
n-Butyl Alcohol	<0.1	<0.1	<0.1	<0.1	0.6	0.3	—	—	0.8	0.3	1.3	0.6
Xylene (mixed isomers)	1.0	0.5	<0.1	<0.1	—	—	—	—	0.3	0.1	1.3	0.6
Chloromethane	0.9	0.4	—	—	<0.1	<0.1	—	—	—	—	0.9	0.4
4-Nitrophenol	<0.1	<0.1	—	—	—	—	—	—	0.9	0.4	0.9	0.4
Toluene	0.3	0.1	<0.1	<0.1	—	—	—	—	0.4	0.2	0.7	0.3
Maleic Anhydride	<0.1	<0.1	<0.1	<0.1	—	—	—	—	0.7	0.3	0.7	0.3
Copper	—	—	<0.1	<0.1	<0.1	<0.1	—	—	0.4	0.2	0.4	0.2
Styrene	0.2	0.1	<0.1	<0.1	—	—	—	—	0.2	0.1	0.4	0.2
Phenol	<0.1	<0.1	<0.1	<0.1	0.4	0.2	—	—	<0.1	<0.1	0.4	0.2
Vinyl Acetate	0.3	0.1	—	—	—	—	—	—	<0.1	<0.1	0.3	0.1
Dichloromethane	0.2	0.1	—	—	0.2	0.1	—	—	<0.1	<0.1	0.3	0.1
Benzyl Chloride	<0.1	<0.1	<0.1	<0.1	—	—	—	—	0.3	0.1	0.3	0.1
All Others (77 chemicals)	2.1	0.9	0.2	0.1	1.0	0.4	0.1	<0.1	3.6	1.6	6.9	3.2
Total, Worldwide	11.5	5.2	5.8	2.6	168.6	76.6	0.1	<0.1	37.6	17.1	223.6	101.6

Note: Data for individual chemicals not listed in this table are available from Monsanto's Corporate Communications Department at 800 North Lindbergh Boulevard, St. Louis, Missouri 63167. Data may not add up to totals shown due to independent rounding.

Monsanto also publishes a very informative EH&S report. It includes detail about the company's emissions, releases, and transfers of toxic chemicals by plant location and by chemical substance. It discusses the Monsanto goals and their attainment. Exhibit 7–3 is from the Air Emissions Reduction Program and is included in the EH&S report.

The type of emission information disclosed in Exhibit 7–3 is required by the EPA and is appearing more often in external corporate EH&S reports. Monsanto, as well as many other companies, has disclosed on a comparative basis its emissions of toxic chemicals based on a list of more than 300 chemicals designated as toxic under Title III of the Superfund Amendments and Reauthorization Act (SARA). The company also has included an extensive list of the 33/50 Program chemicals that have been tracked since 1987.[1] Exhibit 7–3 and the DuPont and Weyerhaeuser exhibits that follow (7–4 and 7–5) are good examples of the disclosures of physical environmental data that many stakeholders want to supplement the financial environmental data. One of the more extensive disclosures of environmental performance is found in the DuPont "Progress Report on Corporate Environmentalism." The report discloses both where progress is proceeding rapidly and those areas where by comparison it currently lags. DuPont's EH&S report includes exhibits related to air emissions similar to the Monsanto disclosures. It also includes easy-to-understand disclosures in 12 areas important to the environment. In addition to information regarding emissions and hazardous wastes, the company has included disclosures regarding packaging waste, energy use, double-hulled tankers, double-walled storage tanks, and wildlife habitat enhancement. These disclosures have been tracked for several years and are displayed with the goals set in each area.

Weyerhaeuser also participates in the EPA's 33/50 program, reports on emissions of SARA toxic chemicals, and discloses that information in its EH&S report. Using a slightly different form of disclosure, the company conveys the notion that reducing toxic chemicals is a top priority.

The Southern Company has made extensive disclosures that aim to satisfy the requirements of SEC Regulation S-K, Item 101. In the MD&A section of its annual report, the company discusses its proposed compliance with Phases I and II of the Clean Air Act. It estimates that approximately $275 million in additional construction expenditures will be

---

1. See Chapter 2 for a more extensive discussion of the 33/50 program.

EXHIBIT 7–4
DuPont (Progress Toward Goals)

PROGRESS TOWARD GOALS

**1. Toxic Air Emissions...
down 45%**

Toxic air emissions in the United States have been reduced by 45% from the base year of 1987. Outside the U.S., emissions have been reduced by 18% from the base year of 1990. The goal outside the U.S. is a 10% reduction per year from 1990 to 1993.

1987	1988	1989	1990	1991	1992	1993 Goal
100%	91%	87%	76%	73%	55%	40%

**2. Carcinogenic Air Emissions...
down 55%**

In the U.S., carcinogenic air emissions are down 55% from the base year of 1987. Outside the U.S., these emissions are down 25% from the base year of 1990. Our goal is the same: a 90% reduction by the year 2000.

1987	1988	1989	1990	1991	1992	2000 Goal
100%	83%	85%	55%	54%	45%	10%

**3. 33/50 Chemicals...
down 33%**

DuPont met the interim goal to reduce releases of 33/50 chemicals by 33% in the U.S. Sites outside the U.S. are not involved in this effort, which is a voluntary initiative of the U.S. Environmental Protection Agency.

1988	1989	1990	1991	1992	1995 Goal
100%	116%	92%	81%	67%	50%

**4. Hazardous Waste Generated...
down 35% and 6%**

Hazardous waste generated was reduced by 35%, indexed to production, at U.S. sites from 1982–90. The new goal is global and not indexed to production. On this basis, hazardous waste generated was reduced by 6% from the base year of 1990.

OLD GOAL				NEW GOAL			
1982	1985	1988	1990	1990	1991	1992	2000 Goal
100%	87%	73%	65%	100%	102%	94%	65%

**5. Land Disposal of Hazardous Waste...
up 56%**

Most programs are in place and the technical effort under way to make significant progress toward this goal after 1997. The goal is based on hazardous waste as defined by the U.S. Resource Conservation and Recovery Act; change is measured on a dry weight basis, though all material is injected with water (up to 98%) into EPA-permitted deepwells.

1987	1988	1989	1990	1991	1992	2000 Goal
100%	104%	114%	99%	148%	156%	0

**6. Packaging Waste...
a new goal**

The Environmentally Improved Packaging Program is a new initiative, and measurable progress is expected to begin in 1993.

1991	1992	1995 Interim Goal	1998 Interim Goal	2000 Goal
100%	100%	75%	65%	50%

(continued)

necessary to meet Phase I compliance through 1995. In addition, Phase II compliance could require total construction expenditures ranging from approximately $450 million to $800 million. The company further acknowledges that it cannot assure the recoverability of all Clean Air Act costs. As discussed earlier, the intent of the SEC disclosure rules related to MD&A are that trends and forward-looking events likely

EXHIBIT 7–4 *(concluded)*

---

7. Energy Use...
38% less per pound of product

Energy use in 1992 was 38% less than the base year of 1973, measured in BTUs per pound of product. In absolute terms, energy use was down by 13% and production up by 40% from 1973–92.

1973	1978	1983	1988	1992
100%	86%	78%	67%	62%

8. Chlorofluorocarbon Production...
down 55%

Production of chlorofluorocarbons (CFCs) for sale has been reduced by 55% from the base year of 1986.

1986	1987	1988	1989	1990	1991	1992	1995 Goal*
100%	117%	119%	112%	66%	51%	45%	0

*Based on a request from the U.S. government, DuPont could produce in 1995 as much as 25% of its 1986 CFC production levels in the U.S. DuPont will base production on customer commitments.

9. Nitrous Oxide...
down 9%

The technical programs are under way to essentially eliminate emissions of nitrous oxide, a greenhouse gas. Most of the reductions will occur in 1996.·

1990	1991	1992	1997 Goal
100%	94%	91%	10%

10. Double-hulled Tankers...
57% of fleet

DuPont's energy subsidiary, Conoco, now has four of seven tankers with double-hull construction as added protection against oil spills.

1991	1992	1993	1995 Interim Goal	2000 Goal
0	29%	57%	71%	100%

11. Double-walled Storage Tanks...
at 127 gasoline outlets

Since April 1990, double-walled underground storage tanks have been installed at all newly constructed or renovated Conoco-owned gasoline outlets in the U.S. and Western Europe. In the U.S., this represents more than 25% of all outlets.

1990	1991	1992	1993
39	92	119	127

12. Wildlife Habitat Enhancement...
21 plants certified

DuPont started a wildlife habitat enhancement program at its plants in 1983, and more than 160,000 acres are now under habitat management around the world. The number of plants with programs accredited by the U.S. Wildlife Habitat Enhancement Council has grown to 21.

1990	1991	1992	1993
5	12	17	21

Backup data and additional information on DuPont's environmental progress are provided in the charts and tables beginning on page 12.

---

to affect corporate shareholders should be disclosed. If a company knows of likely environmental impacts of its products and services, it has an obligation to disclose those impacts to external users of the financial statements. Fulfilling this obligation is the thrust of these environmental disclosures by The Southern Company.

The Southern Company also publishes an environmental audit. It is thorough in its assessments of accomplishments and the work still needed

EXHIBIT 7–5
Weyerhaeuser Company (EPA's 33/50 Program)

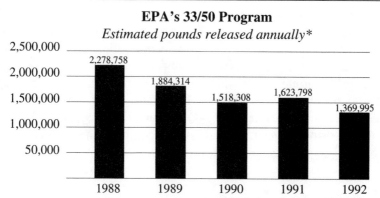

EPA's 33/50 Program
*Estimated pounds released annually**

Year	Value
1988	2,278,758
1989	1,884,314
1990	1,518,308
1991	1,623,798
1992	1,369,995

Includes chloroform, chromium compounds, lead, methylethylketone, perchloroethylene, toluene, 1-1-1-trichloroethane, and xylene. No reported releases for other chemicals.

SARA 313 Estimated Releases from Our Pulp and Paper Manufacturing Facilities
Estimated pounds released annually

	1988	1989	1990	1991	1992
Sulfuric Acid Used for Coliform Control	6,4000,000	8,170,000	8,370,000	474,000	0
Sulfuric Acid (Other)	144,000	316,374	342,500	583,987	630,450
Methanol	2,168,690	2,223,790	1,639,291	3,253,131	3,020,050
Chloroform	976,287	1,703,214	1,364,618	1,396,033	1,194,170
Hydrochloric Acid	319,700	386,400	404,500	1,160,809	1,033,090
Chlorine	680,133	500,800	408,800	394,333	189,920
Other Chemicals	804,512	784,289	905,907	824,382	999,469
Totals	11,493,322	14,084,867	13,435,616	8,086,675	7,067,149

The reporting of legal and permissible releases can be compared only roughly from year to year because of numerous changes, for example, in the methods of calculating releases, in the reporting format and content, and to the list of chemicals reported. These changes were required by regulatory agencies or were developed by the National Council on Air and Stream Improvement (NCASI) to improve accuracy. Other variables, such as variations in product mix, manufacturing processes and sampling methods, or different reporting methods from mill to mill, are a result of internal processes.

Compiled from data from pulp and paper manufacturing facilities only. 1992 data are preliminary and do not include two facilities that were acquired in December 1992. Data for 1993 will be compiled during April-June 1994. Results will be reported to the U.S. EPA on July 1,1994, in accordance with regulations.

to be done but is produced by internal company personnel and thus does not have the external attestation that some stakeholders want. It includes a 15-point strategic plan for implementing the company's environmental policy. Company President Edward L. Addison stated that "we view this environmental responsibility as an integral part of our business and a duty that each of us is obligated to uphold. And the chief executive of each of our companies is accountable for implementing the Southern Company's environmental strategic plan in that company."

E.B. Eddy Group, a Canadian pulp and paper manufacturer, is committed to sustainable development. Its EH&S annual report reflects this concern. The innovative report, "A Question of Balance: Status Report on Sustainable Development," focuses on the company's progress in relation to six indicators of sustainable development:

- Resources used;
- Efficiency of resource conversion;
- Wastes generated;
- Environmental effects;
- Research activities;
- Socio-economic impacts.

The company has reported on its paper making, pulp and bleaching process, sawmill operations, and forest management in terms of these six indicators. Its first report was published in 1993, and company executives hope to use the analysis and the report as a basis for improving future environmental performance with a goal of "fully sustainable operations."

In its EH&S report, Ontario Hydro extensively discusses its corporate activities in many areas of environmental concern including environmental audits, alternative energy technologies, air and water emissions, and recycling initiatives. Among Ontario Hydro's environmental objectives is its pledge "to develop Ontario specific estimates of the external costs and benefits associated with Hydro's activities, where possible, and to recommend the appropriate mechanism for incorporation into planning and decision making, in conjunction with the corporation's full-cost accounting research program."[2]

Rohm and Haas recently published its first EH&S report for Europe. For each of the seven plants the company operates in Europe, it has a

---

2. This subject is discussed more extensively in Chapter 8.

separate emissions report detailing the emissions of water, air, and waste pollutants on a three-year comparative basis.

The Toxic Release Inventory (TRI) came into existence as part of Section 313 of the Emergency Planning and Community Right to Know Act of 1986 (EPCRA), also known as SARA Title III. The regulations require U.S. plants to provide the TRI report to their states and the EPA annually. The TRI identifies specific chemical releases and off-site transfers listing all such releases to air, land, or water. Rules released in November 1994 expand the total number of chemicals to be reported to 654, effective January 1, 1995, for reports due January 1, 1996. The emissions reported include both those authorized by permit and those that do not require a permit. The TRI provides information on the quantities of hazardous substances released into the environment by various companies and facilities.

Many companies in the chemical industry have taken the initiative to publicly disclose information about their emissions of toxic substances included in the TRI. While the TRI report is required, there is no obligation to disclose this information publicly. ICI, which is a signatory to the ICC Business Charter for Sustainable Development and participates in Responsible Care, has included the TRI toxic emissions data in its EH&S report for 1993. The company also includes a section on total environmental expenditures in 1993 and compares 1993 and 1992 performance, openly discussing failures.

The EH&S report of Bristol-Myers Squibb includes a section on measuring performance. It discusses the company's emissions and reports that more than 90 percent of the emissions are recovered or treated on-site. The company has many programs to promote environmental management. The EH&S report is comprehensive and includes an estimate of future environmental capital expenditures.

Companies are increasing their disclosures in corporate annual reports and issuing environmental reports in significantly larger numbers. Though it appears that separate environmental reports and external environmental audits are becoming more prevalent, there is justification for including all disclosures in the corporate annual report, which is read more widely and is more central to the evaluation of corporate performance. Allied Signal, for example, has chosen to expand the discussion of corporate environmental performance in its corporate annual report rather than issue a separate environmental report. It is the company's way of signaling the importance of environmental impacts on the company's "overall business strategy and operations responsibility."

This description of the variety of environmental disclosures in corporate annual and environmental reports demonstrates the rapid rise in the quality and quantity of corporate environmental disclosures. The trend is for further improvement in both quality and quantity. Companies increasingly recognize their obligation to report on past and current activities related to environmental costs and project the liabilities for future programs aimed at pollution prevention, control, and remediation.

Companies are recognizing that disclosure requirements may encompass far more than only Superfund liabilities and are beginning to include liabilities related to other environmental obligations and regulations such as those associated with the Clean Air Act amendments. Companies also are starting to consider the impact of responsibility for post-consumer waste and the likely future obligation and possible ways to reduce that obligation. Effective planning related to environmental responsibilities for the future costs of current production encourages many companies to redesign products and processes to reduce both company and environmental costs.

We have seen examples of some companies that make modest disclosures and others that make extensive disclosures. The SEC and FASB are promoting fuller disclosures as are many other stakeholders including environmental activists and financial analysts. As this area continues to develop, more standardized disclosures in both corporate annual and environmental reports likely will develop. Until that time, voluntary disclosures provide an opportunity for forward-looking companies to explain the environmental problems they have created and the company's activities to remediate past problems and reduce future ones.

MOVING TOWARD A STANDARD ENVIRONMENTAL REPORT

Though standardized external environmental reporting has yet to be established, numerous organizations have been working diligently to develop a format that would be acceptable to the producers of the reports and useful to the various users. Others instead have been encouraging companies to increase disclosures without suggesting standardized formats.

ICC/BCSD

In 1991, the International Chamber of Commerce (ICC) formally presented the Business Charter for Sustainable Development containing

16 principles for environmental management. Well over 1,000 companies have endorsed the charter, and many companies have developed programs to measure progress toward achieving sustainable development. Bristol-Myers Squibb has retained an outside consultant, Environmental Resources Management (ERM), to assist it in implementing the ICC Charter. By benchmarking its performance against the Charter and the performance of other large companies, it has identified strengths and weaknesses in its existing programs and determined opportunities for improvement. Exhibit 7–6 depicts Bristol-Myers Squibb's progress toward achieving goals established by the 16 principles. Some of the particular programs and initiatives are discussed elsewhere in this book.

CERES

Among the most prominent approaches to standardized environmental reporting is that of the Coalition for Environmentally Responsible Economies (CERES). First released in 1989 as the Valdez Principles, the CERES Principles represent an "environmental ethic devised to encourage the development of positive programs to prevent environmental degradation, assist corporations in setting policy, and enable investors to make informed decisions regarding environmental issues." CERES is a nonprofit organization composed primarily of public interest groups, social investment professionals, and environmental groups promoting responsible economic activity for a "safe, just, and sustainable future." Companies that endorse these principles commit to monitor, publicly report in the CERES report, and improve performance in 10 areas:

- Protection of the biosphere;
- Sustainable use of natural resources;
- Reduction and disposal of wastes;
- Energy conservation;
- Risk reduction;
- Safe products and services;
- Environmental restoration;
- Informing the public;
- Management commitment;
- Audits and reports.

EXHIBIT 7–6

Bristol-Myers Squibb

Legend:
- ○ Developed and in the process of, or has completed, pilot implementation
- ◐ In the process of being implemented across the corporation
- ● Implemented worldwide

	Pledge & Policies		Manuals & Guidelines										
	Bristol-Myers Squibb Pledge	Environmental Protection Policy	Acquisition and Divestiture Manual	Capital Appropriations Request (CAR) Guideline	Contract Manufacturer / Suppliers Guidelines	Emergency Preparedness Guidelines	Environmental Manual	Hazardous Materials Transportation Guidelines	Packaging Guidelines	Purchasing Guidelines	Safety and Health Manual	Waste Minimization Guidelines
1. Corporate Priority	All are corporate priorities, but are at various stages of business level implementation.											
2. Integrated Management		◐					●	●	●	●		●
3. Process of Improvement		●										
4. Employee Education		●	○				●	●	●		●	
5. Prior Assessment		●	●	◐	○		●		●	●	●	●
6. Products and Services	●	●							●	●		
7. Customer Advice								●				
8. Facilities and Operations	●	●		●			●	●		●	●	●
9. Research									○	○		○
10. Precautionary Approach					○		●			●	●	●
11. Contractors and Suppliers					○				●	●		●
12. Emergency Preparedness						●	●	●			●	
13. Transfer of Technology									○	○		○
14. Contributing to the Common Effort	●											
15. Openness to Concerns	●											
16. Compliance and Reporting							●	●	●		●	

EXHIBIT 7–6 *(concluded)*

Legend:
- ○ Developed and in the process of, or has completed, pilot implementation
- ◐ In the process of being implemented across the corporation
- ● Implemented worldwide

Programs & Initiatives	Auditing Program	Common Effort Initiatives	Customer Communications	Employee Education Initiatives	Energy Management Program	Environmental Affairs Department	Environmental Self-Assessment Program (ESAP)	Management Systems Assessment	Office of Corporate Conduct	Product Life Cycle Reviews	Research Initiatives	Stakeholder Communications Initiatives	Technology Transfer Initiatives	Waste Contractor Evaluation Program
1. Corporate Priority	All are corporate priorities, but are at various stages of business level implementation.													
2. Integrated Management							○	○		○				
3. Process of Improvement	●			◐		◐	○	○		○	○	◐	○	
4. Employee Education				◐		◐		○		○			○	
5. Prior Assessment						●				○	○			●
6. Products and Services			○							○	○		○	
7. Customer Advice												◐		
8. Facilities and Operations	●			◐	◐			○		○	○		○	
9. Research										○	○		○	
10. Precautionary Approach										○	○		○	◐
11. Contractors and Suppliers														●
12. Emergency Preparedness				◐										
13. Transfer of Technology		◐					○		○	○	○		○	
14. Contributing to the Common Effort		◐	○			◐								
15. Openness to Concerns						●			●			◐		
16. Compliance and Reporting	◐					◐	○					◐		

The CERES report is completed annually by all CERES companies. It is an attempt to standardize information in a credible, simple, accessible, and widely disseminated format. CERES emphasizes the importance of both internal and external evaluations of corporate environmental performance as a means toward actual environmental improvements. It also emphasizes that a standardized report will aid in providing various stakeholders with the information they need to evaluate corporate environmental and financial performance.

In February 1993, the Sun Company became the first Fortune 500 company to endorse the CERES Principles. According to Sun's EH&S vice president, Bob Banks, signing on with CERES has given Sun an opportunity to build relationships and "have a seat at the table in a variety of meetings...with environmentalists, religious groups, social investors, regulators, academicians and the press." It also has helped to build relationships with customers and shareholders.

Numerous companies have indicated that becoming environmentally proactive has provided numerous benefits in addition to the obvious ones to both the company and the environment. They have reported that a commitment to improved corporate environmental performance had several effects. It has:

• Aided in preventing future legal and regulatory problems;

• Substantially improved relations with regulatory agencies;

• Reduced penalties in various court proceedings.

Underlying this commitment is the change in corporate culture reflected in changes in capital investment, product design, performance evaluation, and other management systems to integrate environmental sensitivity into management decision making. This commitment recognizes the need to balance economic growth and environmental improvements, as Sun is trying to do. According to Banks, the principles "demonstrate that environmental reporting and economic growth can co-exist."

Sun also believes that standards for environmental disclosure are likely to be established to provide common data for evaluating and comparing corporate environmental performance and that the CERES report may serve as the basic format for that standard. Banks has said that "public accountability and public disclosure is here—it's only a matter of time before voluntary reporting is standardized."

In February 1994, General Motors (GM) became the first major manufacturing company to endorse the CERES Principles. Its EH&S report was organized to provide information corresponding to the CERES report format and is fairly comprehensive. While the company has employed an environmental activities staff since 1971 and has been involved in environmental organizations for some time, the 1994 EH&S report was the first one it published.

Another signatory of the CERES Principles, Ben & Jerry's, has continued to put an independent, uncensored social assessment in its corporate annual report. An environmental audit is expected to be available in the near future. The goal of the external environmental assessment team is to "determine the actual and potential impacts Ben & Jerry's has on the environment, and to come up with methods we can use to minimize or eliminate those impacts."

PERI

The Public Environmental Reporting Initiative (PERI), like CERES, has developed a set of principles to guide companies in their reporting of company environmental policies and practices. The PERI guidelines provide a systematic framework for organizing environmental information and are designed to "improve, expand, and encourage environmental reporting to the public through the voluntary actions of individual organizations." The guidelines are intended to be voluntary and nonprescriptive, allowing each company to decide how, when, and to what extent it responds to each of 10 elements in the recommended content of the environmental reports. The guidelines also are based on the "merits of 'continuous improvement' and the principle of 'what gets measured get managed.'" Among the companies supporting the initiative are IBM, Polaroid, DuPont, Dow, Amoco, and British Petroleum. All have produced corporate environmental reports with widely different formats and content.

Amoco Corporation was one of the 10 companies that established PERI. Its first EH&S report following PERI guidelines was published in 1993. The company expects to continue publishing similar reports on an annual basis. Its report includes a discussion of the company's commitment to "continuous improvement by monitoring compliance with regulations and our internal standards and to strive for performance which compares favorably with industry leaders." Amoco has developed a

EXHIBIT 7–7
Amoco Corporation (International Standard of Care—Standards Issued)

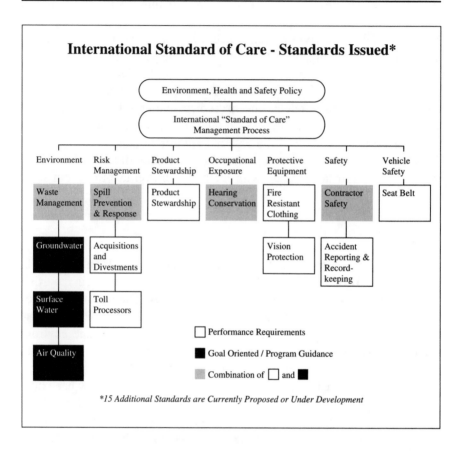

International Standard of Care - Standards Issued*

15 Additional Standards are Currently Proposed or Under Development

system to achieve its EH&S goals and a process for implementing its standards, called International Standard of Care (ISOC). The ISOC sets minimum standards for environment, health, and safety practices and procedures in the workplace. The ISOC management process, shown in Exhibit 7–7, provides a framework for EH&S policy and a system for achieving those policy goals, all within the PERI guidelines.

IRRC

The Investor Responsibility Research Center (IRRC), established in 1972, compiles and analyzes information on the activities of corporations and institutional investors in an effort to influence such activities and related public policies. Its Corporate Environmental Profiles Directory summarizes environmental information of companies in the Standard & Poor's 500. The information is compiled primarily from an IRRC environmental corporate survey, 10-K filings with the SEC, and EPA public data. The directory gives individual company profiles and contains an executive summary compiling the results of the individual profiles.

Each individual company profile is two pages long and includes information on environmental capital expenditures, amounts of toxic chemical releases, reported spills of oil and chemicals, data about compliance with EH&S regulations, consent decrees, and amounts of penalties. There are also short sections regarding the number of environmental staff, corporate policy, environmental auditing, and current achievements and projects related to the environment.

The IRRC in 1991 conducted research to determine the environmental information needs and attitudes of its institutional investor subscribers. It concluded that financially relevant environmental information was what institutional investors wanted most. More specifically, environmental liability was ranked at the top of the "Environmental Information Priorities." The study also concluded that investors want one- or two-page corporate environmental reports and that many environmental reports are too long. This finding supports arguments that other standardized report formats and guidelines provide more information than users want or can use easily to make evaluations and investment decisions.

Responsible Care Initiative

In 1988, the Chemical Manufacturers Association (CMA) launched the Responsible Care Initiative to improve the chemical industry's health, safety, and environmental performance record. The principles of responsible care are implemented through six codes of management practices:

- Pollution Prevention and Waste Reduction Code;
- Employee Health & Safety Code;
- Process Safety Code;
- Community Awareness and Emergency Response Code;
- Distribution and Transportation Code;
- Product Stewardship Code.

The CMA, whose members account for more than 90 percent of the U.S. productive capacity for basic industrial chemicals, requires adoption of Responsible Care as a requirement for membership in the association.

Union Carbide's report on EH&S, "Responsible Care Progress Report," is designed to report progress corresponding to the six codes listed above. The report provides extensive data on compliance with various environmental regulations, quantities of environmental releases, and progress toward company goals and industry codes. The company also has developed a very extensive manual that provides guidance on adherence to Responsible Care standards. It further has found that reporting compliance with Responsible Care and corporate environmental performance has provided other benefits. Though the intended audience was employees and the community, suppliers and customers were the most receptive audience. The Responsible Care report signaled the importance of this ethic in doing business with Union Carbide.

It is becoming commonplace for industry codes and standards to promote both expanded environmental responsibility and expanded disclosures on environmental progress. Such codes encourage corporate participation, provide guidance, and level the playing field.

ISO 9000/14000

Another approach to the standardization of environmental disclosures was taken by the International Organization for Standardization (ISO), established in Geneva in 1947. ISO 9000 is a series of quality assurance documents introduced in 1987 that attempts to create quality standards for products worldwide. "The standards that they propose while not regulated have become necessary prerequisites to two-party contractual negotiations at the national and international level" (Wolfe, 1994, 50). Conformance to international quality standards is fast becoming a condition for competing in the global marketplace. The ISO 9000 standards focus on the processes used in the design and production of goods and services and are intended to harmonize the large number of national and international standards in this field.

Currently 55 countries worldwide have adopted ISO 9000, and more than 40,000 certificates related to ISO 9000 have been issued worldwide (Batra et al., 1993, 54). But ISO is not well known and has not been well received in the United States. A recent survey of mid-sized U.S. manufacturers found that while they are familiar with ISO 9000, not many will seek certification (Midsized Manufacturers, 1993, 21). The survey determined that many of these companies feel they already meet or exceed those standards, although this attitude may change.

As a result of increased worldwide concern for the environment, ISO has undertaken the task of proposing international environmental management standards. The intent is to enable organizations to be more effective in meeting their environmental goals. The proposed ISO 14000 standards will cover six areas:

- Environmental management systems;
- Environmental auditing;
- Environmental performance evaluation;
- Environmental labeling;
- Life cycle assessment;
- Environmental aspects in product standards.

They will apply to all organization types in every country in the world (Harmon, 1994).

ISO 14001, the environmental management system standard, is now out in draft form and should be in use by the end of 1995. The ISO 14000 standards are expected to be compatible with requirements, standards, regulations, and systems currently in use. It is hoped any modifications to existing systems will be minor. While the ISO 9000 guidelines had several quality codes for registration, ISO 14001 will be the only registration code. The remaining ISO 14000 codes will be used as guidelines for implementation only.

PREPARATION OF THE EXTERNAL ENVIRONMENTAL REPORT AND THE ROLE OF EH&S PROFESSIONALS IN THE ACCRUAL PROCESS

The preparation of environmental reports for external use, whether it be the EH&S report or the inclusion of environmental liabilities and expenditures in the annual report, requires a specialized knowledge of environmental issues, law, and accounting. Generally, no one individual or department has that knowledge, and the process should be a joint effort of a variety of individuals and departments that collectively possess this

EXHIBIT 7–8

Union Carbide Corporation Environmental Protection (Capital Expenditures & Environmental Protection Expense US/PR)

$ THOUSANDS

	Air	Water	Residues	Remedial	Total Expenditures	Net Add'l Accruals	Deprec	Environ Admin Expense	Total Expense
A. CAPITAL									
Current Year									
Year 2									
Year 3									
Year 4									
Year 5									
Year 6									
Post Year 6									
B. EXPENSE									
Current Year									
Year 2									
Year 3									
Year 4									
Year 5									
Year 6									
Post Year 6									

COMPANY _____

LOCATION _____

knowledge. Some companies also have included feedback from stakeholders in making the decisions on what to disclose in the environmental report and the corporate annual report.

At Sun Company, the external environmental report is prepared by employees from corporate communications, finance, legal, and EH&S. The process for the accrual of environmental liabilities for the annual report also involves cross-functional integration. On a monthly basis, staff from EH&S, legal, and accounting meet to discuss present and future environmental liabilities and possible disclosures required to fulfill regulatory requirements.

At Union Carbide the various business groups and corporate departments collect and report data on actual environmental operating and capital expenditures for all sites for which they are responsible. This information is used for reporting to regulatory agencies, for internal planning and control, and for disclosure in the EH&S report. Exhibit 7–8 illustrates how the costs are calculated.

Costs are collected for each plant location and for the various categories such as air, water, solids, and remedial. For those locations involved in production rather than pollution control but that have pollution control equipment, managers must estimate the cost of the use of the equipment. Otherwise, actual costs are included. The research and development department also must submit this form separately for each project. This system allows EH&S to track and identify all environmental costs by location and type.

The various business units within Union Carbide also prepare a five-year forecast of environmental operating expenses and capital expenditures. These items include:

- Construction expenditures for pollution-control equipment;
- Operating costs of the equipment;
- Depreciation expenses of the equipment;
- General administrative expenses for environmental matters
  such as the centralized EH&S staff.

The data collected are used for the disclosures in the annual reports and for future estimates of environmental costs and environmental capital expenditures.

Exhibit 7–9 is a Union Carbide request form for accrual of an environmental project. The controller provides guidance on accounting requirements and informs the division's accounting environmental coordinator,

EXHIBIT 7–9

Union Carbide (Request for UCC Accrual of an Environmental Project)

PPB 401   EXHIBIT 1

REQUEST FOR UCC ACCRUAL OF AN ENVIRONMENTAL PROJECT

<u>Note:</u>
This form can not be used to request, nor does it grant, authority to expend funds on an environmental project.

Project Title: _____

Requesting Division/Location: _____

Estimated Project Expenditures: $ _____

Project Description (copy of EPR System Project Reports attached):

Requested By:

Accting. Envir. Coordinator _____ Date: _____

Endorsed By:

HS&EA Management _____ Date: _____

Plant/Location Management _____ Date: _____

Div/Function Management _____ Date: _____

Approved By:

UCC Controller _____ Date: _____

who issues a determination as to whether the project is likely to meet the established accrual criteria, namely "... if it is probable that a liability has been incurred and if the cost of the project can be reasonably estimated. If appropriate, the Coordinator submits the project to the Union Carbide Environmental Accrual Committee, which, comprised of all Division Accounting Environmental Coordinators, meets quarterly to review all projects with respect to meeting the criteria for accrual. The committee then presents its recommendations for accrual to the Union Carbide controller, who implements the recommendation and tracks the accrual."

At Dow Chemical, in-house specialists and outside environmental experts evaluate the probability and scope of environmental liabilities. Unfortunately, in far too many companies, it is the legal counsel's office or the CFO and controller who determine the environmental liability without the assistance of the EH&S professionals. The general counsel's office often argues that it monitors the status of corporate environmental litigation and is in the best position to estimate the company's likely environmental liability. But it is the EH&S department that should best understand company environmental programs and changing external pressures and best be able to assess the changes in environmental regulations, technology, and the cost of technology and the likely impacts of those changes on the future corporate environmental liabilities. That input is critical if a broad understanding of future environmental liabilities is desired for either internal decision making or external reporting.

An accrual committee provides an opportunity for a corporation to obtain a deeper and broader understanding of its present and future environmental liabilities. It brings together corporate staff from legal, accounting, operations, engineering, and EH&S to examine the possible alternatives for reducing future environmental liabilities. Often, when EH&S describes likely changes in environmental regulations, legal and accounting decide to consider broader environmental liability disclosures. More important, engineering and operations staff usually decide to examine possible redesign of products and processes to reduce potential exposure. Thus the development of a multidisciplinary environmental accrual committee often encourages more environmental planning and reduced corporate environmental costs.

In addition to the feedback companies obtain from meetings with stakeholder groups, many companies include a short questionnaire in their corporate environmental reports to determine user opinions on the quality and quantity of disclosures. In this way, they can help their own efforts to improve environmental disclosure.

EXTERNAL AUDITS OF ENVIRONMENTAL REPORTS

The earlier part of this chapter gave examples of the rapid rise in the quality and quantity of environmental disclosures and discussed attempts at standardizing environmental disclosures. Concurrently, companies have found it desirable to obtain independent verification and attestation of progress toward improved environmental management and performance. The growth of environmental auditing for both internal and external reporting has been significant.

The recognized leader in environmental auditing is Arthur D. Little, Inc. ADL has been instrumental in developing improved methods for internal environmental audits and has helped numerous companies develop and implement internal environmental audit systems. The company also has been the leader in external environmental audits and in providing a level of assurance to various stakeholders concerning the effectiveness of a company's environmental management program. Other consulting firms and accounting firms also have begun performing external environmental audits. Descriptions and examples of some of the audit reports follow. As can be seen readily by reviewing the wording of the five reports included here, no standard environmental audit principles, audit format, or audit report format have been developed.

Increasing numbers of corporations are expected to include environmental audit reports in various external documents in the coming years. The preceding section discussed alternative approaches to standardizing environmental reporting and internal environmental auditing. It is likely that stakeholder demands for increased external environmental reports and audits will influence the number of corporations providing them. It also likely will prompt the further development of the environmental auditing profession and the development of standards for improved comparability.

The 1993 Sun Environmental Report includes a Report of Independent Accountants as shown in Exhibit 7–10. The report was prepared by Coopers & Lybrand, which also audits Sun's financial reports.

In its report for British Petroleum's environmental report (see Exhibit 7–11), Ernst & Young acknowledges that "in due course this may lead to

EXHIBIT 7–10
Sun Company

Report of Independent Accountants

Sun Company, Inc.
Philadelphia, Pennsylvania

We have conducted a review of the accompanying Sun Company, Inc. "Assertion on Health, Environment and Safety Data Collection, Compilation & Validation Process" (the "Assertion") for the year ended December 31, 1993. Our review was conducted in accordance with standards established by the American Institute of Certified Public Accountants and, accordingly, included such procedures as we considered necessary in the circumstances.

The purpose of the review was a comparison of Sun Company, Inc.'s Health, Environment and Safety Data Collection, Compilation & Validation Process (the "HES Data Process") with the criteria set forth in the Assertion. A review consists principally of inquiries of company personnel, analytical procedures and consideration of the responses and results in the context of the Assertion. It is substantially less in scope than an examination, the objective of which is the expression of an opinion on the Assertion for the year ended December 31, 1993. Accordingly, we do not express such an opinion.

Based on our review, nothing came to our attention that caused us to believe that the HES Data Process for the year ended December 31, 1993, is not in conformity with the criteria set forth in the accompanying Assertion.

Coopers & Lybrand

Coopers & Lybrand
Philadelphia, Pennsylvania
February 18, 1994

---

an independent attestation" of future reports. Public accounting firms have begun a process of examining alternative approaches to external environmental audits. Though this process is in its infancy, there is some evidence that standard environmental reporting and a process for an independent attestation of some combination of environmental policies, procedures, programs, and performance will be forthcoming.

IBM's external environmental report includes a note that the international auditing firm of Price Waterhouse, which audits the company's financial statements, also performed certain procedures with respect to the

EXHIBIT 7–11
British Petroleum

---

report by
Ernst & Young

We have been asked by the British Petroleum Company plc (BP) to work with them to improve the efficiency and quality of their Health, Safety and Environmental (HSE) reporting. In due course this may lead to an independent attestation of future HSE reports. In the meantime, we have also been asked to review the accompanying statement of BP's HSE performance report entitled "New Horizons".

Our review this year has been less in scope than a full attestation on the HSE report, the objective of which would be the expression of an independent opinion on the statement of environmental policy objective, procedures and Focused Programmes. Accordingly, we do not express such an opinion this year.

We conducted our review by carrying out the following procedures:

→ Discussion with HSE executives on the framework and content of New Horizons, interviewing of HSE Executives and review of documents at the Corporate and Business level (documents include Board and HSE Audit Committee minutes, HSE Forum notes and HSE Audit Programmes).

→ Limited review of the underlying information that supports statements made in New Horizons.

→ Review of the performance measurement data collated by HSE Corporate personnel and the processes and procedures used to obtain such data which are set out on pages 14 to 25 in New Horizons, and agreement of the data with supporting information provided by the Business HSE groups. However, we have not made any site visits to test the system for reporting data from sites, nor sought to verify such data by means of test checking or re-performance.

→ Interviews with HSE personnel responsible for collating the data in the Corporate Centre and the Businesses regarding the consistency of measurement of reported data.

As a result of carrying out the above procedures, we are satisfied that the information reported on pages 14 to 25 has been properly collated from data produced by the individual Businesses and that statements made in New Horizons are supported by underlying information.

Based upon the procedures we have carried out, it is our perception that Senior Management within BP attach great importance to HSE performance and are committed to implementing quality HSE programmes throughout the group. They have developed programmes that address business HSE risks identified by BP, community concerns about HSE impacts of local facilities and employee concerns about HSE aspects of the working environment.

Ernst & Young
Chartered Accountants
London
8th April 1993

---

accumulation of data for inclusion in the environmental report. "Price Waterhouse's work was undertaken in accordance with the Standards for Attestation Engagements established by the American Institute of Certified Public Accountants. Price Waterhouse has reported to the Company's management on the results of those procedures, and IBM utilized the results to further improve its process."

Another approach is to obtain the benefit of an independent evaluation by an external environmental auditor but not to include the report in the corporate annual report. For example, Noranda Forest has developed a strong internal audit program and has retained Arthur D. Little to conduct an independent review of its environmental audit practices. Recommendations for improvement have been made, revisions completed, and improved auditing procedures put in place. Noranda Forest mentioned the external environmental audit and auditor but did not include an audit report. The company has gained a major benefit, however: an independent auditor has given internal managers quality assurance about the veracity of their practices, and appropriate changes have been made to improve environmental management.

Through similar processes, companies can implement their corporate environmental strategy and control environmental costs more effectively. As corporate environmental reports become more numerous, internal environmental auditing increases, and use of external environmental auditors continues, stakeholders are likely to become more sensitive to the value of an external environmental audit. The audit will become a commonplace part of corporate annual and environmental reports.

WMX Technologies, through its various subsidiaries including Waste Management and Chemical Waste Management, is the world's largest environmental services company. Its 73-page annual environmental report is among the most comprehensive reports produced. It includes a copy of an opinion letter by the external environmental auditor, ADL, assessing the environmental policies, procedures, programs, and systems at the company and placing WMX "among the leaders of industry as a whole with regard to corporate environmental management" (see Exhibit 7–12).

Body Shop has produced EH&S reports since 1992. The 1994 report includes a "verifier's statement" by the consulting firm Environmental Resource Management. The purpose of the audit was to verify that the EHS report is in compliance with the Eco Management and Audit Scheme of the European Union. The audit report details the scope and results of the audit.

McLaren Hart, an environmental engineering firm, also has been involved in environmental audits. The firm evaluated the environmental, health, and safety programs of Eastman Kodak on the basis of 10 program evaluation criteria, "which reflect generally accepted industry standards." The report's executive summary is contained in the 1993 EH&S report

EXHIBIT 7–12
WMX Technologies

Arthur D Little

Arthur D. Little, Inc.
Acorn Park
Cambridge, Massachusetts
02140-2390
USA

Main Number 617.498.5000
Fax 617 498 7200
Telex 921436

To the Management of WMX Technologies, Inc.

We have reviewed the appropriateness and quality of the environmental management systems in place during 1993 at WMX Technologies, Inc. and its principal operating subsidiaries.

Our review included an assessment of policies and procedures, organization, training programs, regulatory and management reporting systems, performance incentive and disciplinary action programs, regulatory surveillance systems, audit programs and corrective action systems, and other environmental management programs and systems in place throughout the Company. In conducting our review, we examined selected documents and interviewed key employees at the corporate and principal operating subsidiary levels, as well as at selected facilities within each of the principal operating subsidiaries. We conducted our review relying upon our judgment based on our extensive consulting experience in this area, as well as our familiarity with similar programs established by many other corporations.

In our opinion, WMX Technologies, Inc.'s corporate and subsidiary environmental management systems place it among the leaders of industry as a whole with regard to corporate environmental management.

Arthur D. Little, Inc.
April 1994

EXHIBIT 7–13
Eastman Kodak

THIRD-PARTY EVALUATION OF EASTMAN KODAK'S
CORPORATE HS&E ASSESSMENT PROGRAM
EXECUTIVE SUMMARY

August 1993

Kodak's Corporate HS&E Assessment Program meets and in some areas exceeds generally accepted standards and criteria for programs of this type found in other Fortune 200 companies. The Program provides an independent evaluation of facility compliance and thereby assures Company management that compliance issues are routinely identified and remedied. The company has continued to make improvements to the Program in all areas since it was started in 1988. The first assessments began in 1989 and as of the Fall of 1993 about 70 percent of Kodak's major facilities had been evaluated for HS&E compliance.

A detailed independent evaluation of all elements of the Program was conducted by McLaren/Hart Environmental Engineering Corporation in mid-1993 using ten criteria, which reflect generally accepted industry standards. A summary of the evaluation is provided in the table inset. Program strengths include explicit top management support and a demonstrated commitment to continuously improve the Program. The Assessment Program enjoys strong and effective leadership and a cadre of Kodak assessors who have competent HS&E technical skills. Assessments are conducted in an independent, objective manner with due professional care. There are third-party participants (i.e., outside consultants) on all audits.

The Kodak Program is well documented. Effective assessment tools, protocols, procedures and other support materials have been developed and continue to be produced. Assessment reports are well written and distributed in a timely manner. Kodak business units manage the corrective action process well and most findings are corrected within a year.

In 1993 the Kodak Program is in its fifth year of operation and, as could be expected, some mid-course adjustments are needed. Key areas that need more attention relate primarily to re-evaluating the Program objectives, analysis and measurement of its performance and disclosure of appropriate information to interested third parties. Kodak's HS&E Guiding Principles clearly call for measurement and disclosure of relevant information on performance. But how this specifically applies to the Kodak Corporate HS&E Assessment Program has not been evaluated. The Kodak Assessment Program also needs to better clarify its fundamental objectives, not an uncommon problem after a program has been up and running for five years. The distinction among "compliance assessments", "risk assessments" and "management systems assessments" have tended to become blurred.

KODAK CORPORATE HS&E ASSESSMENT PROGRAM
EVALUATION SUMMARY

No.	Program Evaluation Criteria	Below Standard	Meets Standard	Exceeds Standard
1	Explicit top management support and commitment for prompt corrective action of assessment findings			✔
2	Proper organizational structure of the Program to assure independence and objective assessments		✔	
3	Demonstrated assessor proficiency and exercise of due professional care		✔	
4	Clearly stated and consistently applied assessment program objectives		✔	
5	Existence of a written assessment plan including methodology, scope and committed resources			✔
6	Preparation of clearly written assessment reports and distribution to appropriate levels of management			✔
7	Implementation of an effective corrective action procedure for assessment findings			✔
8	Quality assurance mechanisms in place to assure accuracy and thoroughness		✔	
9	Measurement and analysis of performance and timely disclosure to customers, shareholders and the public		✔	
10	Frequency of assessments on a schedule to evaluate HS&E compliance across all major operations		✔	

In summary, the Kodak Corporate HS&E Assessment Program is one of the better programs in industry and after some work in the areas noted above should continue to be so in the future.

Lawrence B. Cahill
Vice President

McLaren Hart ®
ENVIRONMENTAL ENGINEERING CORPORATION

Raymond W. Kane, P.E.
Vice President

and indicates that McLaren Hart did an independent evaluation of all elements of the EH&S program. The Kodak Program Evaluation Summary and McLaren Hart Executive Summary are shown as Exhibit 7–13.

McLaren Hart in its evaluation of the Kodak Corporate EH&S Assessment Program, begun in 1988, acknowledges it is one of the better programs in the industry, although "some mid-course adjustments are needed." The engineering firm further suggests that the "key areas that need more attention relate primarily to re-evaluating the Program objectives, analysis and measurement of its performance and disclosure of appropriate information to interested third parties."

Addressing these corporate needs is among the objectives of this book. Corporate executives need better techniques for analyzing, measuring, and disclosing environmental information and for making business decisions regarding environmental investments. Executives need better ways to integrate the measurement of environmental risk and uncertainty and better ways to measure past, present, and future environmental costs and benefits. It is these needs, in part, that McLaren Hart addresses.

DuPont, the eighth-largest industrial corporation in the United States, also retained McLaren Hart to do a follow-up on a previous audit conducted in 1991. The 1991 report made recommendations to DuPont for improvements in its environmental audit program. The 1993 report indicates the progress that DuPont has made (see Exhibit 7–14).

THE COORDINATION OF EXTERNAL AUDIT, INTERNAL AUDIT, AND SELF-AUDIT PROCEDURES

As discussed in Chapter 6, the external environmental audit is most beneficial if it is supported by a comprehensive system of environmental auditing that includes strong internal audit and self-audit functions. Companies conduct internal compliance audits to ensure compliance with company goals, industry initiatives, and government regulations as well as to reduce current environmental costs and future environmental liabilities. Systems are established for both EH&S and operating personnel to conduct site visits on a regular basis. An efficient internal environmental audit system provides the basis for practical environmental planning and control and for an effective external audit that relies heavily on information submitted by the company and an evaluation of systems in

EXHIBIT 7–14
DuPont (Environmental Audit—McLaren Hart)

E N V I R O N M E N T A L   A U D I T
(Following is a precis of the environmental audit evaluation.)

ENVIRONMENTAL ENGINEERING CORPORATION

E. I. DU PONT DE NEMOURS AND COMPANY
Evaluation of the Corporate Environmental Audit Program
Evaluation Report October 11, 1993

1.0 INTRODUCTION

DuPont instituted a corporate Environmental Audit Program in 1985. As part of DuPont's quality assurance efforts, the Company commissioned a third-party, independent evaluation of the Program in 1991. The evaluation consisted of a review of records, including program documentation and audit reports; interviews with senior corporate managers, the Corporate environmental staff and numerous auditors; and observation of five audits. McLaren/Hart conducted the evaluation during the latter half of 1991 and issued a final report on March 16, 1992. The Executive Summary of the Evaluation Report was included in *Corporate Environmentalism—A 1992 Progress Report*, published by DuPont in early 1993.

In 1993, DuPont contracted with McLaren/Hart to conduct a follow-up evaluation of the Program. The objectives of this second evaluation were to assess whether, in the past two years, DuPont has responded appropriately to:
• The findings and recommendations of the first report;
• Any internal organizational and structural changes taking place over the two-year period that might impact the effectiveness of the Program; and
• Generally recognized and applicable improvements in the practice of environmental auditing.

2.0 PROGRAM OVERVIEW

"The objectives of [DuPont's] environmental audits are:

• To assess global compliance with corporate environmental policy and applicable environmental laws and regulations;
• To provide assurance that management systems are in place for continuing compliance; and
• To verify and document that appropriate action is being taken in order to safeguard our environment."[1]

DuPont's objective is to conduct environmental audits of all major facilities operating in the U.S. and overseas. The Program is relatively mature in the U.S., Canada and Europe but is evolving in the rest of the world. Audits generally involve a team leader and 1–8 auditors. The audits take from 2–5 days depending upon team size and the complexity of the facility. A fairly standard approach is used in preparing for, conducting and reporting the results of the audits.

DuPont reviews its facilities based on a risk-driven schedule, as stated in the Program Guidelines. Facilities are ranked and placed into one of four categories. Certain large, especially complex facilities may be defined as Category I, which requires annual audits of certain site areas or specific environmental media. Category II facilities are to be reviewed every two years; Category III, once every three years; and Category IV, once every four years.

3.0 EXECUTIVE SUMMARY

Overall, the DuPont Environmental Audit Program is an excellent one. Its structure, content and procedures continue to meet or exceed those of

Programs generally found in comparable *Fortune 200* Companies. In the past two years, since the initial third-party evaluation, substantial progress has been made in improving the Program.

Of particular note are the following:

• The policy for report and facility action plan schedules has been shortened considerably from 90 days to 45 days.
• The Corporate oversight function has been clearly defined in the Program's Guidance Manual. There is a much more systematic and thorough oversight of the Audit Programs, including monitoring of facility action plan status for individual audits.
• All Corporate audit protocols have been updated and improved in the past year.
• Audit reports are much improved and include a two-way classification of findings, which better defines the findings by type and provides priorities for developing corrective actions.
• All audited sites are now encouraged to complete site evaluations of the audit team's performance. An Audit Appraisal Questionnaire has been prepared by Corporate to assist in this process.

Notwithstanding these and other structural and procedural improvements in the Corporate Program, the execution of the Audit Programs has been somewhat adversely affected by the ongoing restructuring within DuPont. The recent decentralization of the Company into 19 Strategic Business Units (SBUs) has resulted in the creation of 16 separate business-level audit programs. Several of these programs have lost momentum during the organizational transition and

[1]DuPont U.S. Environmental Audit Guidelines Manual, Chapter 3, Organization and Staffing, p. 1, June 28, 1993.

(continued)

EXHIBIT 7–14 *(concluded)*

are not consistently meeting all Corporate Audit Program Guidelines. The restructuring has also resulted in the loss of some experienced auditors. Audit Program Managers are aware of these challenges and it is likely that in the next six to twelve months they will be addressed.

4.0 RESULTS OF THE EVALUATION

The principal focus of the evaluation was to determine the progress DuPont has made with respect to the 1991 findings. Therefore, this section is organized consistent with the listing of high- and medium-priority development needs presented in the Executive Summary of the 1991 report. Exhibit 1 provides a summary of the progress made for each of the development needs. In all cases, at least some progress has been made in rectifying the deficiencies.

4.1 THE AUDIT PROGRAM

The Program has experienced some major improvements in policies and procedures, specifically with respect to the development of better tools and tracking systems. Most notably the Corporate Guidance Manual and Audit Protocols have been upgraded and updated in 1993. The July 1993 upgrade of Program Manual is a significant improvement, specifically the guidance provided on: community participation, report writing, findings classification, the audit appraisal questionnaire, and how to handle repeat findings. However, not all of the improvements required or recommended in the Manual have been implemented fully among the SBUs.

EXHIBIT 1
Summary of Progress Against 1991 Evaluation

Finding	No Progress	Some Progress	Major Improvement	Fully Corrected
The Program...				
A1. Uneven follow-up for corrective actions among Businesses		✔		
A2. Limited Corporate oversight of corrective action status at Business level			✔	
B1. Too relaxed a policy for completion of reports & corrective action plans (90 days)				✔
B2. Inconsistency in meeting the report & corrective action plan schedules			✔	
C. Lack of true independence where Business SHEA staff audit sites where they have provided technical assistance		✔		
D. Lack of an independent review of state regulations prior to the audits			✔	
E. Outdated audit protocols				✔
F. No formal Audit Program Plans developed by the Businesses			✔	
G. No clearly articulated objectives for the Corporate oversight function				✔
H. Lack of consistency in providing legal review of audit reports			✔	
I. Audit team evaluations conducted only in one Business				✔
The Audits...				
A. Uncertainty among auditors over whether audits are compliance assessments or management systems reviews		✔		
B. Rambling, unstructured closing conferences			✔	
C. Varying, rambling report styles			✔	
D. Field verification techniques not always used appropriately		✔		
E. Ancillary activities (e.g., maintenance, warehouses, tollers, contractors) not always audited with same rigor as line operations		✔		
F. Multiple tenant site audits do not always get the full cooperation of all tenants		✔		
G. Sites conducting self-audits only sporadically		✔		

place. The entire system also depends on an audit program that empowers employees to look for, detect, and report potential and existing environmental hazards and violations. Even regular and effective internal and external audits cannot detect all violations that may occur. Typically, it is the facility employees who are in the best position to detect and report existing and potential hazards. Companies have begun to recognize that identifying potential environmental hazards before they occur is usually much less costly than later cleaning up environmental violations. An effective environmental audit system includes employee and facility self-audits along with extensive company internal audits and an external auditor. These systems are typically far less costly than the alternative costs related to hazards and violations.

Dow Chemical has used an EH&S auditing framework that recognizes the need to integrate a variety of types and frequencies of audits to monitor overall company compliance with government regulations, industry initiatives, and company standards. The audits range from daily self-assessments to a detailed external audit. The self-audits consist of equipment inspections, job procedure checklists, and other routine practices conducted on a daily basis. The external audits are conducted by the consulting firm ADL and also by government agencies and others for insurance or ISO certification purposes. In addition, comprehensive internal environmental audits are conducted on a periodic basis, and less comprehensive inspections and equipment checks as necessary.

SUMMARY

There is much discussion in industry about excessive disclosure requirements. Some companies are concerned that if they disclose all their environmental liabilities and think of the liabilities broadly as suggested in this book, they would signal information to external users that might be detrimental to the company. Some are concerned that environmentalists or other potentially responsible parties in Superfund cases might gain information that would be detrimental to the company in negotiation and litigation. Public accountants usually have gone along with this approach based on their interpretation of applicable FASB guidelines. Some accountants now are concerned that additional disclosures are indeed required, and disclosure has been increasing. Further, the legal exposure from inadequate disclosures of environmental liabilities may be greater from shareholder lawsuits than from other external users. Corporate general counsels I met with related no examples of situations where disclosure of environmental impacts in corporate annual reports or environmental reports increased legal liability or jeopardized a legal position.

Twenty years ago, numerous academics and companies attempted to develop a methodology alternatively called "social accounting" or "social audit" to report on corporate social performance. It failed to last because it was never institutionalized in organizations. Companies never integrated it into costing, capital budgeting, or performance evaluation systems in their organizations. External social reports were, in many cases, discussions of missions and desired programs and attitudes rather than accounts of actual company progress.

Today, companies and their stakeholders need to ensure that the flurry of activity of external environmental reporting and external environmental auditing is supported by actual company progress. The external report should not precede the integration of environmental considerations into product costing, capital budgeting, product design, or performance evaluation. External reporting is an opportunity for a company to tell the story about its performance. Good environmental performance should improve corporate financial performance, and that story is worthy of disclosure. Taking care of past sins and planning effectively to avoid future sins are also stories worth telling.

It is clear that with a thorough review of the environmental impacts of products and processes substantial improvements can be made that will benefit both the environment and the bottom line. It is those stories that are worth including in environmental reports along with other data that will allow external users to evaluate a corporation's environmental performance. But companies should not operate under the misconception that producing an external environmental report will make them more environmentally responsible. That goal can be accomplished only through a change in corporate culture and the identification, measurement, monitoring, reporting, and consideration of environmental impacts in all management decisions.

Chapter Eight

Costing Systems

C hapters 8 and 9 examine the development of cost systems related to environmental costs. To design a corporate Environmental Strategy Implementation (ESI) or initiate a complete life cycle assessment (LCA), companies need ways to measure the environmental costs and benefits of corporate activities. This chapter discusses the measurement of environmental costs for use in both product costing and capital investment decisions. Chapter 9 examines the measurement of benefits to facilitate choices among process improvements, product improvements, and capital improvements. Integrating a complete measurement of the costs and benefits as specified in the ESI permits more comprehensive analysis of capital investment alternatives and leads to improved decision making.

COSTING SYSTEMS

One of the most disturbing findings of this field research project was that most companies do not have an adequate system for identifying and measuring environmental costs. In most instances they do not track or accumulate these costs separately and thus do not know the total corporate environmental costs or their causes. Without accurate information about those costs, effective management is impossible.

The objective in this chapter is to examine some of the problems companies are experiencing in attempting to estimate and account effectively for the costs of dealing with environmental issues and how they are managing those problems. Among the difficulties companies face is that estimated costs that may be incurred in the future due to current processes and products typically are not included in current product costs and prices. The history of environmental law demonstrates that present-day processes and products may well be retroactively subject to regulations not yet written. It is difficult enough to estimate and book costs accurately when the business context is well understood, but constant shifting of focus between present and future makes these problems considerably different from those encountered in normal cost accounting practice.

Though companies have been slow to alter their costing practices to deal with this problem, accounting systems now are beginning to change. Many companies are investigating and beginning to implement systems that do a better job of accumulating and measuring the past, present, and future environmental costs related to production.

THE COSTS TO INCLUDE IN PRODUCT COSTS

One of the most controversial issues I encountered in the field research was the determination of which costs to include in product costs. Three categories of costs are generally discussed:

- Current costs for past sins;
- Current costs for current sins;
- Future costs for current sins.

Current Costs for Past Sins

A significant amount of some companies' total environmental costs relates to current expenditures to clean up pollution caused decades ago. Some of this pollution is related to Superfund and, though legal at the time, now must be cleaned up under the joint and several, strict, and retroactive provisions of the law. The amount of these corporate environmental liabilities is often substantial. Including them in product costs often has a dramatic effect on the profitability of products, facilities, and divisions.

Though many companies do include current operating costs that relate to past sins in current product costs, they recognize the related problems. Some companies justify the inclusion with the following logic: In prior years (maybe decades ago), other expenses that created benefits for the future were charged to product costs or corporate overhead including product development, research and development, and advertising expenses. Thus current products are benefitting from those prior expenditures. Now the product must bear the costs related to prior production just as it is reaping the benefits.

In many cases, however, the current products are improvements on those prior products. In many cases the prior products are no longer produced in any form, although a particular facility still is bearing the costs. Controversy develops when product costs are loaded with these costs. Many managers believe that including these costs in product costs does not accurately measure product, facility, or division profitability. More important to many managers, it negatively affects performance evaluations and compensation.

Many companies believe that a more appropriate treatment for these costs is to include them in corporate overhead or general and administrative expense accounts and not include them in any product costs. Other companies place them in overhead accounts and then spread them to products through some allocation system that has a less direct impact on a particular product. But even with an allocation of past costs, the performance evaluation of managers includes costs incurred possibly decades earlier. Traditional concepts of responsibility accounting would dictate that managers should not be held accountable for costs they have no ability to control. To measure the performance of products, facilities, divisions, and division managers effectively, many companies now believe that including current costs for past sins in current product costs is inappropriate.

From a management accounting viewpoint, another solution to this dilemma would be to charge these costs directly against shareholders' equity or to a corporate general and administrative account that is not allocated to divisions or products. Prior earnings still would be overstated, but current income would not be distorted. Thus, there would be no need to identify the costs as either product or period costs for internal purposes, and they would not affect current management decisions.

Many companies argue that because the past costs must be borne by the company, they should be assigned to facilities and products on some basis. Otherwise, the business units may show a profit and the corporate entity may show a loss. This controversy highlights the extensive costs incurred through a lack of effective planning for future impacts and failure to consider full life cycle costs.

Current Costs for Current Sins

Including current operating costs that relate to current production in product costs, by contrast, is not controversial. These costs are of many different types, but because they relate to current environmental impacts that result from the production of current corporate products and services, most people agree that they should be included in current product costs. Most companies, however, do not adequately separate or track their environmental costs so they are unable to determine product costs accurately. Most companies arbitrarily assign environmental costs, continuing the practice of undercosting some products and overcosting others. Analysis and cost reduction are difficult because the companies do not know which products cause the environmental costs.

Future Costs for Current Sins

One of the problems in the effective management of environmental impacts is the lack of accurate measurement and reporting. It generally is agreed that the lack of understanding decades ago of the eventual environmental impacts of products and services and the related legal liabilities caused companies to ignore the consideration of those impacts in calculating product costs. Remediation costs related to Superfund were caused decades ago but are being incurred today. Thus, the products that caused those costs were undercosted and probably underpriced. It is critical for companies to ensure that current costs include an estimate of total product costs so that future generations of managers and products are not encumbered by those costs when they occur.

Some companies have argued that current costs for past sins are included in product costs as a surrogate for the future costs of present production. But cost estimation models are available that provide better estimates of future environmental costs than past costs are likely to be. A few companies have contended that measuring future costs is so speculative that no number should be included in product costs. When pressed, those same companies are able to provide some estimate of likely impacts and possible categories and range of costs.

Identifying and measuring environmental impacts using various techniques described in this book certainly provides better information than no estimate at all. It also forces companies to design products and processes more carefully to reduce future environmental impacts. The process of broadly identifying impacts using approaches such as Total Stakeholder Analysis (TSA) described in Chapter 4 is certainly beneficial. Further, using the techniques described in Chapters 8 and 9 to measure future costs and benefits helps companies better understand the likely impacts of changing regulations, changing technology, and the changing cost of technology.

Some Comments on Cost Allocation

Most companies acknowledged that they do not have a system that adequately identifies and tracks environmental costs. Thus many environmental costs are hidden in other accounts, and no assignment is made to the activities or products that caused those costs.

Ignoring the problem is clearly improper, but compounding it through an inaccurate and arbitrary allocation often can be even more harmful. In many cases, managers reported that these arbitrary allocations were directly affecting compensation and that their excellent environmental performance was masked by this lack of proper costing. One company reported that $100 million of traced environmental costs were arbitrarily allocated equally to the company's five manufacturing facilities with no regard to when the pollution was caused, which facilities it related to, or which products caused the pollution. These current costs for past sins were being matched against revenue from totally unrelated products in zero waste modern facilities. Improved costing systems must be installed in organizations to properly identify, track, measure, and manage environmental costs.

IDENTIFYING AND TRACKING ENVIRONMENTAL COSTS

Many companies do not know how much their environmental costs are or what causes those costs. They need to define the activities, processes, and products that cause the environmental costs. When the costs are properly identified, traced, recalculated, and arrayed, these companies often find that some products have been undercosted and some overcosted. Companies then can manage their environmental costs better by examining available alternatives. Some of these alternatives may be:

- Change the process design to reduce costs;
- Change the product design to reduce costs:

- Increase the price;
- Accept a lower price temporarily with recognition that the full cost and full price ultimately must be obtained;
- Drop the product.

Arthur Andersen & Co. has developed a model and software program to help companies identify, track, accumulate, estimate, and manage total environmental costs and the significant cost components. This model, EcoAccounting[SM], does not replace current cost accounting systems but supplements them. "The model includes an activity dictionary with definitions for over 100 environmental activities, a cost matrix to capture and organize the data, and performance measures for all of the key environmental activities" (EcoAccounting, 1994, 1).

The EcoAccounting program uses a three-step approach that includes identifying environmental costs, establishing performance measures, and analyzing strategic alternatives. The identification step includes interviews with employees and a review of operating statements, general ledgers, and project logs. The intent is "to determine how employees spend their time and to quantify nonpayroll expenditures."

The second step requires the establishment of performance measures for outputs, i.e., fines, penalties or discharges. It also focuses on process measures, which might include the average time it takes to obtain a permit. The last step requires the use of cost and performance information to help the company analyze strategic alternatives for decision making and effectively manage its environmental costs. The EcoAccounting system might, for example, assign costs to product-level facilities that will help the company evaluate "the impact on product costs of switching from a chemical to a water-based solvent" (EcoAccounting, 1994, 2). The system focuses on five areas of environmental management: compliance, liability reduction, pollution prevention, remediation, and strategic positioning.

This cost management system includes a cost matrix model that categorizes environmental cost pools and activities (see Exhibit 8–1). One of the fundamental procedures involved in the process is to define an "activity list" (see Exhibit 8–2). Activity lists can be used to change the cost matrix and to help the company understand what drives those activities and costs. The assignment of environmental costs to various activities is the last function of EcoAccounting. It is important in integrating environmental strategy into organizations and in improving environmental management.

EXHIBIT 8–1

Arthur Andersen & Co. (EcoAccounting℠ Cost Matrix)

EcoAccounting℠ Cost Matrix

Strategic Positioning	Risk Prevention	Compliance	Remediation	Disposal & Claims
Publications & Community Relations	Product Design	Permitting Activities	Site Characterization	Hazardous Material Recycling
Public Policy	Process Changes	Capital Expenditures	Engineering & Project Mgmt.	Storage, Handling & Transportation
Environmental Business Strategy Development	Policies, Procedures & Systems	Records Reporting & Other	Construction	Pre-Disposal Treatment
Voluntary Programs	Performance Reviews	Training & Communications	Monitoring & Maintenance	Disposal Costs
Product Positioning	Product Stewardship	Regulatory Tracking	Valuation & Tax Issues	Non-Hazardous Handling & Disposal
	Maintenance	Internal Assessment	Transaction Costs	Packaging Costs
			Emergency Responses	Fines & Penalties
				Claims Mgmt. & Litigation

Total Environmental Costs

Strictly Confidential

ARTHUR ANDERSEN

EcoAccounting℠

Arthur Andersen & Co. SC

EXHIBIT 8–2
Arthur Andersen & Co. (Define Activity to Initialize Matrix)

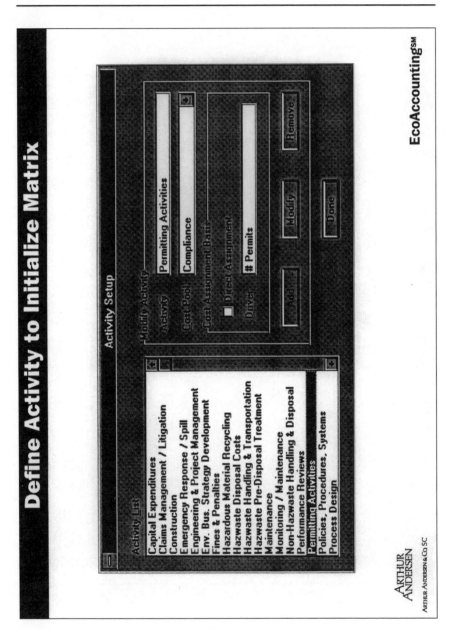

The Arthur Andersen EcoAccounting system is intended to benefit its corporate users in four ways:

- Provide an accurate picture of total environmental activities;
- Establish and improve internal accountability;
- Allow management to benchmark activities across facilities;
- Help management control future costs and assist with forecasting.

Though not the only approach to identifying and tracking environmental costs, the Arthur Andersen system is an effective tool to lead companies to better environmental cost management.

ADDITIONAL ISSUES RELATED TO COSTING

The question of when to capitalize environmental expenditures is not treated uniformly. Generally, an expenditure must be capitalized for tax purposes according to Internal Revenue Code Section 263, unless it meets the following four criteria:

- The expenditure is incidental.
- The expenditure does not materially add to the property's value.
- The expenditure does not appreciably prolong the property's useful life.
- The expenditure's purpose is to keep the property in ordinarily efficient operating condition (Gibby and Patella, 1993, 44–45).

In 1994, after taking various previous positions, the IRS issued a letter ruling (94–38). It held that cleanup efforts to restore and remediate the soil and groundwater treatment were costs that could be expensed. It did distinguish between cleanup costs and construction costs associated with groundwater treatment facilities that must be capitalized (Grant Thornton, 1994).

Union Carbide Corporation has specific guidelines regarding environmental costs that are distinguished from capital expenditures. Environmental expenses "cover all non-capitalized environmental costs charged to operations for the year." Union Carbide includes a measure of the benefits in determining the "net total cost" for the environmental expense as follows: "In all instances, the intention is to collect or estimate the net total costs involved in the environmental protection activity. To calculate net total costs, the value of any benefits derived through increased efficiency in manufacturing operations and/or by-products recovered as a result of installing pollution control equipment are to be deducted from the costs of operating these facilities."

Companies usually put current environmental operating costs directly into product costs. For example, one company's standard cost book acknowledges that the cost of materials includes the "cost of waste disposal which is accounted for as a by-product of the chemical process."

The 1994 Price Waterhouse Survey asked companies what environmental costs they included for accrual purposes. The costs most consistently included related directly to remediation. For example, more than 90% of respondents included contractor fees for remediation and study costs for accrual purposes. More than 65 percent of respondents included regulator's costs, outside legal costs, and perpetual care costs for accrual purposes. The internal costs of accumulating information and monitoring the remediation process such as Internal Administrative Costs and Write-Off to Site were accrued less often (Price Waterhouse, 1994, 14).

The Defense Contract Audit Agency has defined environmental costs. "Environmental costs are normal costs of doing business and are generally allowable costs if reasonable and allocable. Some environmental costs must be capitalized when the incurrence of such costs improves the property beyond its acquisition condition.... If environmental clean-up efforts resulted in contamination caused by contractor wrongdoing, the clean-up's costs are not allowable" (DCAA, 1994, 7157).

The categories included in this definition are costs to prevent environmental contamination, costs to clean up prior contamination, and costs directly associated with the first two categories including legal costs. The preferred method of accounting for pollution prevention is to assign the costs directly to specifically identifiable final cost objectives or to allocate the costs indirectly to final cost objectives in the period incurred. Costs for remediation are usually not allocable on a causal or beneficial basis and therefore often are charged to general and administrative expense, which is allocated to all contracts.

LIFE CYCLE COSTING

Life cycle costing is an attempt to identify all the environmental costs—internal and external—associated with a product, process, or activity throughout all stages of its life. The product stages in the life cycle

EXHIBIT 8–3
Example Life Cycle Cost Categories

Example Life Cycle Cost Categories

Conventional Costs	Liability Costs	Environmental Costs*
Capital	Legal Counsel	Global Warming
Equipment	Penalties / Fines	Ozone Depletion
Labor	Personal Injury	Photochemical Smog
Energy	Remediation Activities	Acid Deposition
Monitoring	Economic Loss	Resource Depletion
Regulatory Compliance	Property Damage	Water Pollution
Documents	Changes in Future Markets	Chronic Health Effects
Maintenance	Public Image Damage	Acute Health Effects
Insurance / Special Taxes		Habitat Alteration
Air Emission Control		Social Welfare Effects
Water Effluent Control		
Radioactive / Hazardous Waste Management		
Raw Materials / Supplies		
Waste Treatment / Disposal Costs		

* The boundary between environmental and liability costs can be vague. Environmental costs can lead to liability costs (e.g., water contamination may lead to personal injury).

process are raw materials acquisition; manufacturing; use, reuse, and maintenance; and recycling and waste management. The implementation of life cycle costing uses systems techniques.

Life cycle assessment (LCA) consists of four interrelated activities: goal setting, inventory analysis, impact assessment, and improvement assessment. In determining the costs to be included in the LCA at least three distinct categories can be identified: conventional costs, liability costs, and environmental costs. Exhibit 8–3 (Weitz et al., 1994, 2–10) provides examples of costs included in each category.

The life cycle cost of a product includes all costs incurred in the phases of research, development, testing, production, distribution, use, repair, and disposal of a product. These various costs need to be accounted for when using LCA to determine the total cost of a product. Conventional costs are those applied specifically to bringing the product to market. While each of the categories may have environmental components, it is the disposal phase of the product's life that bears much of the environmental cost.

In the past, manufacturers were not concerned with the ultimate disposal of their products or post-consumer waste. Corporate management delegated to the consumer the task of figuring out how to dispose of the product safely. The take-back principle has shifted this burden for disposal of products and the raw material components back to the manufacturer. Costs must be determined, allocated, and formally accounted for to ensure that products can be disposed of in an environmentally responsible manner after their useful life.

LCA also considers the liability costs to be future costs that can be measured through various methods such as option screening or scenario forecasting, described later in this book. The environmental cost category includes primarily externalities that must be assessed to include costs and benefits. Life cycle costing is an extension of the basic LCA. It requires measuring the present and future costs and benefits of a company's products, services, and activities. This book describes both frameworks and tools to implement an environmental strategy. Life cycle costing can be an important part of that implementation.

COST MANAGEMENT

An excellent example of a company that has produced significant benefits for both the environment and its bottom line is Hyde Tool. Located in Southbridge, Massachusetts, Hyde Tool is a small manufacturer of industrial and do-it-yourself tools with gross revenues of approximately $40 million. It demonstrates that the approach, frameworks, and techniques described in this book are applicable to large and small companies alike, whether in high-impact or low-impact industries. Hyde Tool has no full-time EH&S staff and approaches these environmental decisions as attempts to reduce total corporate costs.

Several years ago the company set an environmental goal of zero toxic emissions because it was concerned about the effect of waste water on the community. It also was concerned about potential environmental fines that, if imposed, could devastate the company financially.

Hyde believes all improvements should be based on solid, financially based business decisions rather than on environmental concerns alone. It attempts to integrate all financial impacts into its capital investment decisions, including the savings from avoidance of costs such as government fines. Hyde will not introduce any new toxic chemicals or other hazards into its facilities and tries aggressively to eliminate the use of the ones it has.

The company began working with environmental agencies in Massachusetts to devise a closed loop system to reduce waste water emissions. It also wanted to make sure that the system was cost effective and that it would result in a net reduction of costs to the company. Hyde sealed floor drains to avoid flushing waste water into the town's sewer system, installed filters to cleanse and recycle polluted water, and set up chillers to control coolant temperatures in the grinding operations and vacuum furnaces.

It has reduced annual waste water from 29 million to 1.25 million gallons. The total cost of the project changeover was $100,000. The company has saved twice that total amount and acknowledges that it would be bad business not to profit from such an effort. Hyde discovered that it was more cost effective to prevent the pollution before it occurred than to deal with an end-of-the-pipe problem later.

With this success behind it, Hyde Tool has pursued other avenues of waste reduction including recycling paper and cardboard and changing packing materials.

Activity-Based Costing

Traditional accounting systems have been criticized because they do not provide accurate environmental cost information. Two of the often-stated reasons for the inaccurate accounting data are the tendency to allocate environmental costs to overhead costs and to combine environmental costs in cost pools with nonenvironmental costs. This method hampers management's ability to assess environmental costs and make informed decisions.

Activity-based costing (ABC) is based on assumptions about the nature of costs. While traditional cost accounting assumes that producing products and services is what causes costs, ABC assumes that activities cause the costs. Those activities are performed for products, services, and customers. An ABC system attempts to track the costs of each. "ABC is a procedure that measures the costs of objects such as products, services, and customers. ABC first assigns resource costs to the activities performed by the organization. Then activity costs are assigned to the products, customers, and services that benefit from or are creating the demand for the activities" (Atkinson et al., 1995, 23).

Activity-based costing requires identifying activities, tracing the costs of resources to the activities, identifying the outputs by which costs vary, and tracing the costs to the products, processes, or customers that cause those costs. Better cost management requires environmental costs to be accumulated and traced to the activities that cause the costs. The causative products, processes, facilities, or other activities must be analyzed to determine whether a redesign would reduce the environmental costs. Arraying product costs usually demonstrates that many products have been undercosted while many others have been overcosted. Better information on how the growing past, present, and future environmental costs affect current product costs leads to significantly better product management decisions.

Identifying and measuring environmental impacts and fully investigating and analyzing the alternatives should result in improved cost management and reduced environmental effects. Activity-based costing and activity-based management fit well with the Environmental Strategy Implementation proposed in this book.

Strategic Cost Management

Strategic cost management (SCM) is another approach that could be used in applying environmental costs. SCM has been defined "as the managerial use of cost information explicitly directed at one or more of the four stages of the strategic management cycle" (Shank, 1989, 50). It relies on the interaction of value chain analysis, strategic positioning analysis, and cost driver analysis. The information obtained from these three kinds of analyses could be applied to various stages of the Environmental Strategy Implementation proposed in Chapter 4.

FULL-COST ACCOUNTING

Though no company has yet fully implemented a system that integrates all present and future environmental costs into the product costing system, many are expanding their systems to include a broader inventory of costs.

Full-cost accounting takes into consideration the future costs imposed on the environment by a product and allocates them back to the product itself. Dow Chemical Chairman Frank Popoff and EH&S Vice President David Buzzelli (1993) have written that full-cost accounting is really a new paradigm whose goal is to price goods and services in a way that reflects not only the production costs traditionally considered but also the true environmental costs of the use, recycling, and disposal of the goods and services. "If we accept pollution prevention as the ultimate in environmental reform," they note, "we must apply full-cost accounting to today's processes, including waste treatment, to justify the required new investment for pollution prevention. Prices in the interim may have to increase temporarily until the waste is eliminated."

Corporations are understandably uneasy about considering this approach to pricing products. Popoff and Buzzelli note that the issue of competition also arises in the full-cost pricing debate: "If a particular company, business, or industry moves forward too quickly, its ability to compete may immediately suffer. For example, if the plastics industry decided to build the entire environmental cost of its products into the price, while the paper industry decided not to do so, consumers would be more likely to select paper over plastic in competitive applications— a choice that might or might not be the best one for the environment" (Popoff and Buzzelli, 1993, 71).

If full-cost accounting may lead logically to going out of business, why should we (and several major corporations whose experiences will be documented here) be considering it? Popoff and Buzzelli argue further that air, water, and land are not the "free goods" that society once believed them to be. They are economic assets that must be paid for and allocated appropriately and efficiently. "Ultimately, the adoption of full-cost accounting may determine a company's long-term survival" (Popoff and Buzzelli, 1993, 71).

The life cycle assessments and Environmental Strategy Implementations discussed throughout this book rely on a broad identification and measurement of environmental impacts and the inclusion of those impacts in various management decisions including product costing and capital budgeting. The full-cost concept is incorporated in those decisions as it relates to costs that certainly will be internalized. It also should include an estimate of externalities that likely will be internalized through regulation. Other external costs should be considered but not necessarily included in product costs.

Product pricing is not required to change. Prices still can be primarily market based, but full product costs must be considered. A company's total profit from production should include present and future costs likely to be incurred related to those products. Corporations should adopt full costing so they will better understand both the present and future costs of current production.

Ontario Hydro is one company that has considered implementing full-cost accounting for decision making and reporting as part of its commitment to become an environmentally responsible business. Its system would allow for the consideration of internal and external costs (social costs) including present and future costs. It would require a new accounting system that not only includes product and overhead costs but also the internal and external environmental costs.

The company established a Task Force on Sustainable Energy Development to examine the implementation of full-cost accounting and to assess environmental externalities. (Monetizing of externalities is discussed in Chapter 9.)

Full costing at Ontario Hydro is still at the experimental stage. The Task Force's report and recommendations were accepted by the board of directors but have not yet been fully implemented. Until further internal development of external cost measurements, the company is using sustainable energy development decision criteria, more fully discussed in Chapter 9.

The concept of full-cost accounting is acknowledged in the British Petroleum corporate annual report, which states: "The cost of meeting society's environmental expectations is rising continuously and in the long run that cost must be reflected in the price the consumer pays. We do not believe our costs will differ significantly from those of other companies engaged in similar industries, or that our competitive position will be adversely affected as a result."

Because there are significant regional differences in environmental regulations, enforcement, and community concern, some companies must adjust both costing and pricing policies to compensate for those differences. For example, the waste management industry has faced decreasing margins in recent years. This situation is due in part to prior products and services being undercosted because environmental costs were ignored and not included in product costs. Companies thus were misled into believing that their margins were higher than they actually were. Further, the lower perceived margins today are a result of a matching problem when costs related to prior activities are included in current costs. Thus, margins have decreased because current operations are absorbing costs caused decades ago. A new costing system will assign costs properly and lead to better evaluation and management of operations.

One concern is whether full costing penalizes the more environmentally responsible companies. Many industries are concerned that the market will not bear the increased prices full costing might suggest and that regulations are driving up costs. Further, many companies don't comply with the regulations. In many cases, they may be small companies that believe they can avoid compliance and that regulators will focus on the major companies. The regional regulatory environment certainly will affect decisions concerning operations in a particular location and the likely expansion into new regions.

An interesting side note on the waste management industry is that the industry has seen the importance to its business of environmental responsibility because communities that establish waste collection and disposal policies must be convinced of the environmental sensitivities and activities of the disposal company. The increased concern for and development of policies promoting recycling, source reduction, waste minimization, and process and product improvements through redesign all contribute to the death spiral of the solid waste business. Companies in this industry must include these new approaches to waste and not limit their activities to disposal. They must look to provide services that focus on reducing, reusing, and recycling and that include organic recycling of waste and composting along with other alternatives to landfill and incineration.

Though I am aware of no company that has a complete full environmental costing system, many companies are using the Total Stakeholder Analysis (TSA) and Environmental Strategy Implementation (ESI) frameworks to improve environmental management. They also are using the broad identification and measurement of present and future environmental impacts that are integral to full costing. After completing an analysis of the full present and future product costs, some companies have determined that future environmental costs likely would be so significant that long-term product profitability was unlikely. In such cases, if product or process redesigns were not feasible, and cost decreases or price increases unlikely, the companies investigated product exit strategies. More complete identification and measurement of broadly defined environmental impacts and better accumulation, tracing, and assignment of environmental costs lead to better management decisions.

Legacy Costing

At the Allied Signal Aerospace Corporation facility in Kansas City, "legacy costing," an alternative approach to full costing, is being used to implement "environmentally conscious manufacturing techniques." Its definition is broad and includes an analysis of all corporate environmental impacts. "Legacy costs include costs incurred to minimize environmental impact (prevention costs), to assess environmental impact (assessment costs), and to remediate damage caused by the failure to avoid environmental insult (failure costs). Failure costs may be further classified as either voluntary failure costs or involuntary failure costs" (Lawrence and Butler, 1995, 2). Voluntary failure costs include costs that could be avoided through product (including the use of less toxic materials) or process redesigns and also legal and EH&S costs. Involuntary failure costs are associated with environmental damage from unintended spills and include fines and other costs.

Legacy costing is aimed in part at helping the company avoid any regulatory surprises. It attempts to get engineers and accountants working together to solve problems detected through the legacy costing process and process waste assessments. Legacy costing, like ESI and LCA, attempts to identify and measure all environmental costs and benefits of corporate activities. After identifying and measuring impacts, alternatives can be identified and evaluated and decisions can be made that provide the "greatest environmental improvement for the resources invested."

Both voluntary and involuntary failure costs are difficult to measure, and some companies have proposed using fuzzy logic, Monte Carlo simulations, contingent valuation, and other methods to measure environmental costs and benefits. These methods are described in Chapter 9.

ENVIRONMENTAL EXTERNALITIES

Some of the involuntary failure costs discussed above, such as fines, are paid for directly by the corporations and "internalized." Other costs, such as environmental damage, may not be identified completely and are costs to society and the environment. They are termed "external costs" because they are imposed on entities external to the corporation. Full-cost accounting and LCA models leave the question of how to include social costs in management decisions unresolved.

The Environmental Strategy Implementation approach dictates that all environmental impacts of company activities be identified. This approach includes all benefits and costs whether imposed on the company or on society. Using a Total Stakeholder Analysis, impacts should be examined and considered in management decisions. Whenever possible, those costs and benefits should be measured using techniques discussed in this book.

Companies will consider the external costs (alternatively called "externalities" or "social costs") differently in decision making. Companies increasingly recognize that many of these external costs become internal costs through increased regulation and penalties. Thus, in evaluating the long-run profitability of a product line, managers must consider that the total company costs likely will include some expenditures for what might, in the short run, be external costs. To satisfy the desire to be a good corporate citizen and environmentally responsible and to minimize long-run corporate costs, external costs must be identified, measured, and considered in all management decisions. To do otherwise leads to undercosted products, poor management decisions, and reduced corporate profitability.

The measurement of external costs and benefits, the monetizing of environmental externalities, and the variety of available methods are discussed in Chapter 9. Among the methods described are option screening, scenario forecasting, fuzzy logic, Monte Carlo simulations, decision trees, and contingent valuation. These methods are useful for estimating costs and benefits and for product costing and capital investment decisions.

SUMMARY

The integration of environmental costs into product costs is in its infancy. Companies only recently have realized that the current costs for past sins have produced incorrect product costs. They further have realized that they have not been accurately accumulating or tracking environmental costs. Thus, for many companies product profitability calculations are severely distorted.

Systems are available to identify and measure these environmental costs. This chapter has examined some of the frameworks for better costing and managing products and environmental impacts. In Chapter 9, the discussion of cost estimation models is expanded to focus on the estimation of benefits for both costing and capital investment decisions.

Chapter Nine

Capital Budgeting Systems

Our objective in this chapter is to present methods and procedures some companies are using to aid in the capital investment decision-making process for pollution prevention and pollution control equipment. We also discuss problems several companies are facing while attempting to come to grips with the actions they must take to comply with present and future environmental regulations. A primary problem in allocating funds for capital improvements is the difficulty in determining whether the amount of money being allocated for a particular purpose will be repaid in dollar-value measurements of improvements to the company and the environment. We will examine methods that can be used to measure the costs and benefits to both the company and the environment and how to integrate them into capital investment decisions.

For decades, business schools have been teaching and modern corporations have been using discounted cash flow techniques for capital investment decision making. But in too many corporations EH&S departments do not use these techniques regularly. In some cases it is due to the lack of financial background of some EH&S professionals. In other cases, it is due to a view that because many of these investments are required by regulations, evaluating the costs and benefits is unimportant—certainly not the case.

Numerous examples have been cited of cost savings, revenue increases, and competitive advantages that can be attained through proactive environmental management. Choices among process improvements, product improvements, and capital improvements can be evaluated properly only by completely identifying and measuring all environmental costs and benefits. That same analysis is necessary to make the choices between alternative capital investments. This analysis applies to plant locations, general capital projects, and environmental capital projects and to regulatory and voluntary projects. It requires projections of future revenues and costs and likely changes in environmental regulations, technology, and the cost of technology.

These projections are not easy to make and will not be precise, but they should produce some information for improved decisions. In all other segments of modern corporations, capital investment decisions are made that involve significant uncertainties and risks and long time horizons. Future revenues, competition, changing market forces, regulation, labor costs, material availability and costs, foreign currency stability, international political stability, and economic recessions all must be considered in making many major corporate investments. Evaluating the complete future environmental impacts for capital investments is no different and no less important. Numerous methods are available to aid companies in making these decisions. Some, such as scenario forecasting, option screening, Monte Carlo analysis, and decision trees, are used actively in many companies.

Continued use of the payback method rather than discounted cash flow is inadequate. Analyses that include only current costs and ignore the current benefits and all future costs and benefits are also inadequate. The complete examination of all impacts is required. Some managers continue to make decisions that minimize current capital costs related to project construction and ignore other long-term impacts and how changing regulations may require a rapid capital replacement. Other managers invest in capital projects that maximize short-term operating profits and have a quick payback but ignore longer-term impacts that may dramatically increase the company's long-term costs and ultimately produce a negative net present value. It is these types of improper decisions that the Environmental Strategy Implementation is designed to correct. Only through a complete analysis will proper costing and capital investment decisions be made.

THE CAPITAL EXPENDITURE APPROVAL PROCESS

Environmental issues have gained increased influence in many aspects of corporate life including the process of making capital investment decisions. In an increasing number of companies, decisions regarding new facilities, products, and equipment require the approval of or at least consideration by the EH&S department.

Many companies have completely decentralized the environmental capital investment decision-making process. For example, at BFI the central EH&S department does some evaluation of equipment for pollution prevention and control, conducts research, evaluates alternatives, and compares equipment specifications with regulatory requirements. The acquisition decisions are made at the district level.

In most companies that provide capital allocations to business units, EH&S gives support only if it is specifically requested by the business unit. In many cases, business unit and operations managers do not request such assistance. They make arbitrary decisions on choices among process improvements, product improvements, and capital improvements and do not adequately evaluate the choices between alternative capital investments. They do not broadly identify and measure all the relevant environmental and company costs and benefits and do not consider both present and future costs. They thus make inefficient and ineffective allocations of corporate funds.

Many companies, though, have recognized the significant value that can be added by fully integrating the identification and measurement of environmental impacts into capital investment decisions or, at a minimum, requiring an EH&S review of capital expenditures. Bristol-Myers Squibb includes EH&S in all its capital investment decisions. Capital appropriations requests (CARs) are required for all new processes, products, and facilities, and each facility has its own environmental coordinator, who must review all facility CARs. Capital expenditures of more than $4 million, as well as purchases and sales of land, must be approved by the corporate general finance committee, of which the corporate vice president of EH&S is a member.

Each CAR addresses the following environmental issues:

- Permitted environmental releases;
- Likelihood of sudden environmental releases, such as spills and explosions;
- Hazardous and nonhazardous waste generation, storage, and disposal;
- Disposal of raw materials, intermediates, and final products;
- Health and safety risks to employees;
- Energy consumption.

EXHIBIT 9–1
Union Carbide Corporation (Project Funding Proposal)

PPB 401 EXHIBIT 2 (PAGE 1 OF 2)

PROJECT FUNDING PROPOSAL

UNION CARBIDE CORPORATION

DATE:_____

PFP NUMBER _____
INITIAL OPR. DATE_____
(QTR./ YR.)

DIVISION_____

STRATEGIC PLANNING UNIT_____

PROJECT TITLE AND LOCATION_____

FINANCIAL SUMMARY

	PROJECT ACCRUAL ($M)	EXPENDITURES ($M)	PROJECT STAGE	($M)
CAPITAL	_____	_____	REMEDIAL INVESTIGATION	_____
EXPENSE	_____	_____	FEASIBILITY STUDY	_____
TOTAL	_____	_____	REMEDIAL ACTION	_____
			CLOSURE	_____
			POST CLOSURE	_____

PROJECT DESCRIPTION

SITE/PROJECT HISTORY

(continued)

EXHIBIT 9–1 *(concluded)*

PPB 401 EXHIBIT 2 (PAGE 2 OF 2)

PROJECT JUSTIFICATION

TECHNOLOGY (TREATMENT METHODOLOGY; ALTERNATIVES; RISK ANALYSIS)

ADDITIONAL FACTORS ASSOCIATED WITH PROJECT (PROJECT PLAN AND SCHEDULE; FUNDING)

SUBMITTED BY:_____

APPROVAL

DIVISION/FUNCTION_____

PLANT/DIVISION ENDORSEMENTS:
_____
_____
_____

AREA VP
(INT'L
PROJECTS)_____

UCC_____

Staff Endorsements:

LAW_____

FINANCE_____

HS&EA _____

_____

_____

CARs for new products or packaging must include an assessment of product life cycle impacts on the environment. Furthermore, CARs involving questions of acquisition and divestiture must include an evaluation of potential EH&S liabilities. The technical issues section of a CAR summarizes technical risks as well as issues such as environmental liabilities, costs and compliance problems, health and safety risks, and manpower requirements.

At Union Carbide all capital investment projects above the $2 million level require the approval of EH&S. This stipulation forces employees to consider EH&S concerns early in the conception and planning stages of any new capital investment project. Exhibit 9–1 is the project funding proposal form that must be submitted for environmental capital investments.

Union Carbide's approach has been to get all relevant departments together to assess and investigate the potential risks before a decision is made. This multifunctional approach is seen elsewhere at Union Carbide in the environmental accrual process. It generally improves environmental decisions dramatically.

Union Carbide also has developed a comprehensive capital project proposal screening checklist, which requires business unit and facility managers to consider environmental, safety and health, and product safety issues that may affect their location. This checklist (Exhibit 9–9) is given in its entirety at the end of this chapter.

ONE COMPANY'S CORPORATE ENVIRONMENTAL PLANNING PROCESS

In the late 1980s Ed Woolard, CEO of DuPont, decided that a change in corporate culture was necessary. He proposed a series of goals for improving the company's environmental performance that would be achievable within 10 years. The identification and implementation of those goals occurred after meetings with managers, environmental seminars to ascertain the public's expectations, and various meetings between advocacy groups and DuPont employees and between environmentalists and senior management. The identification of these goals was the result of consultation with the company's environmental professionals who indicated the areas where significant progress could be made and on which the company's technical and management strength could be brought to bear. The definition and quantification of the goals, however, were purely leadership decisions made by Woolard who was determined to establish goals that would "stretch" the capabilities of the company, require genuine "step change" in operations, and elevate environmental performance to a level of awareness comparable to that of safety and health in the company's culture. Those goals and progress toward reaching them are disclosed in the DuPont Progress Toward Goals report (see Exhibit 7–4). Woolard wanted employees to recognize that environmental stewardship and business success are interrelated.

DuPont has developed an information and resource allocation process called the Corporate Environmental Plan (CEP), begun in 1991. It is designed to integrate environmental thinking with business thinking. The CEP is an important part of those changes and is probably one of the most complete and extensive environmental planning processes ever developed. It produces extensive analyses of proposed capital investment projects and ranks them so that those with the greatest benefits will be funded. The CEP allows for integrating environmental planning and business planning as well as for identifying the initiatives required to achieve DuPont's goals. "The CEP is designed to translate environmental vision into action at the site level and to use the results to help shape both the corporation's annual business plan and establish its environmental strategies. Carried out annually, the CEP is a continuous improvement process" (Martin, 1994, 58).

DuPont believes that environmental responsibility begins at the site level. The environmental plan development guidelines are distributed annually to approximately 115 sites seeking proposals for environmental projects. Environmental goals, policies, and regulations are updated every year and are sent to the site levels along with examples of plans and guidance on database use. At each site, technical, regulatory, manufacturing, and business experts develop proposals for capital projects and operational changes in line with environmental compliance policies and goals. The proposals are sent to the strategic business unit leaders, who continue discussions and interactions with the site to revise and upgrade the proposals. Exhibit 9–2 is an example of the data submitted at the site level for each project to be considered. Specific information regarding costs and benefits is requested and later used to analyze the proposal at the corporate level.

DuPont managers believe that the integration of environmental and business issues occurs at the site level. The proposal then is evaluated at the corporate level in accordance with goals and affordability prerequisites. "Individual business environmental plans are modified and the resulting annual corporate business plan thus incorporates site, business,

EXHIBIT 9–2
DuPont (Table II Input: Initiative Information)

Table II Input: Initiative Information

Product Line: _____   Page _____

Site: _____

Initiative Name _____

CIMS #_____   Project #_____   Business Commitment? (Y/N) _____

Authorization Date: Month _____   Proof Year _____
                       Year _____

	Driver Code	Expected Reduction Quantity	Specify Units:
Primary Driver:	_____	_____	___ English
Other Drivers:	_____	_____	___ SI
	_____	_____	
	_____	_____	
	_____	_____	
	_____		

Capital Authorization ($M):* _____

Capital Spendout ($M) *(Optional)* :*

1994 _____   1997 _____   2000 _____
1995 _____   1998 _____   2001 _____
1996 _____   1999 _____   2002 _____

Noncapital Cost ($M):*

1994 _____   1997 _____   2000 _____
1995 _____   1998 _____   2001 _____
1996 _____   1999 _____   2002 _____

Estimated Operating Cost ($M/Year)* _____   Initiative Life (Years) _____

Estimated Benefit ($M/Year)*   _____   Initiative Status   _____

If costs are allocated between product lines:

Product Line	Cost Allocation %	Reduction Allocation %
_____	_____	_____
_____	_____	_____
_____	_____	_____
_____	_____	_____

Initiative Type _____   Initiative Subtype _____

Comments_____
_____
_____

*Estimate for 1994, 1995, and 1996 costs. For 1997–2002 only, engineering judgment is subject to a number of uncertainties, such as the developing nature of regulations, applications of environmental regulations, limited knowledge of uncertain conditions, and the nature of technology development and applications.

and corporate views" (Martin, 1994, 60). It appears that the 1994 CEP cycle has provided corporate decision makers with an exceptional amount of measurable environmental costs and benefits.

An 80/20 analysis is conducted to determine the projects most beneficial and most cost effective to the company. "Only environmental initiatives that benefit a corporate goal are included in this analysis. For each corporate goal, all of the initiatives that benefit the goal are ranked, based on the ratio of the initiative cost to the pounds of waste or emissions reduced. These selected projects can be compared and ranked in terms of cost and benefit" (Martin, 1994, 63). A ranking system nets the present implementation cost with the lifetime emission reductions in pounds for all projects. Only those projects with the highest ranking after the 80/20 analysis are approved. Other proposals are referred to the strategic business units themselves for consideration.

The company draws at least four conclusions from the 80/20 analysis:

- 80 percent of the environmental benefit comes from 20 percent of the cost.

- By weighting toward risk, the effectiveness of environmental projects can be further enhanced. It approaches 90 percent of the benefit at 10 percent of the cost.

- Regulation-driven waste reduction projects cost three times more than voluntarily driven ones for the same benefit.

- The freed-up resources then can be deployed to new U.S.-based facilities, creating both sustainable economic growth and environmental health.

Exhibit 9–3 reflects this thinking. This chart indicates that the incremental reduction in waste above the 80 percent level is not cost effective.

DuPont now is attempting to evolve into a "third phase" of corporate environmentalism, in which environmental performance is truly integrated with business performance. Unless a company dares to state such a vision and make demands on the organization accordingly, it will have difficulty transcending its past performance (Martin, 1994, 59).

THE NEED TO EXPAND THE ANALYSIS FOR ENVIRONMENTAL CAPITAL INVESTMENTS

DuPont's CEP process is an example of an attempt to integrate environmental strategy into all aspects of corporate decision making,

EXHIBIT 9–3

DuPont (Waste Reduction Cost/Benefit Performance)

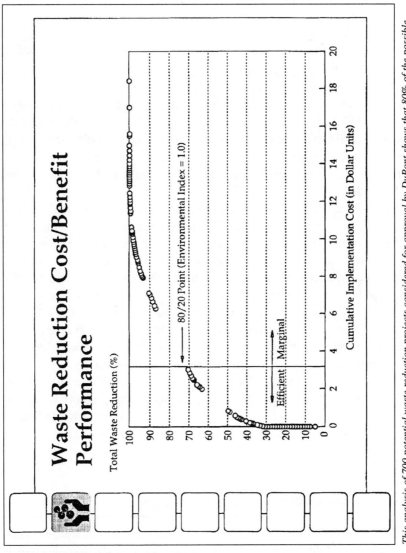

This analysis of 700 potential waste reduction projects considered for approval by DuPont shows that 80% of the possible environmental benefits can be achieved with the first 20% of the project cost.

including the capital budgeting process. The company thought out its options carefully. It developed an environmental strategy based on the principle that pollution prevention is more cost effective than remediation and has implemented it throughout the company.

Generally, though, a capital investment decision for environmental equipment is not analyzed thoroughly. Often it is approved automatically because it is seen to be regulatory rather than voluntary, so rigorous analysis is not completed. Further costs often are not fully identified, and benefits are ignored. The use of traditional cost-benefit analysis would improve most environmental capital decisions. Cost-benefit analysis attempts to quantify all impacts, even those that are subjective, value ridden, and difficult to monetize. Externalities and the willingness-to-pay concept have been used to duplicate the market value of a "good" to aid in the analysis. A further discussion of cost-benefit analysis can be found in Appendix B.

In this book I have introduced Total Stakeholder Analysis and Environmental Strategy Implementation. TSA provides a different and more comprehensive perspective on the impact of a company's activities, products, and services on various constituents at present and in the future. It provides a broader identification and measurement of costs and benefits. TSA can be applied to capital budgeting decisions by extending to future events the identification, measurement, and reporting of the costs and benefits of environmental impacts. The company can analyze the effects capital budgeting decisions will have on its various stakeholders and select those capital projects with the greatest net benefits.

ESI relies on a forward-looking strategy that is continually seeking process improvements. Analyzing capital budgeting projects using TSA and ESI gives a more complete understanding and weighting of all stakeholder interests and clearly defines benefits to the environment and the company.

COST ASSESSMENT METHODS

Total cost assessment aims to improve the capital budgeting decision-making process by assuring that the data gathered include all environmental costs, both direct and indirect, and all environmental risks. It is an investment tool that can help analyze the long-term costs and savings of pollution prevention projects. TCA considers a broader range of costs than

EXHIBIT 9–4
Environmental Protection Agency

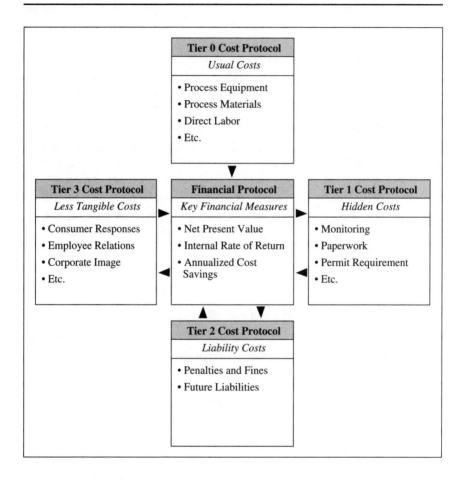

traditional capital investment analysis, including certain probable costs and savings.

The Environmental Protection Agency (EPA) has supported several studies to demonstrate how economic assessments and accounting systems can be modified to improve the competitiveness of investments for pollution prevention. This approach is based on EPA concerns that the traditional costing systems and capital budgeting systems are inadequate for the often complex analysis of pollution prevention projects. Such projects may have multiproduct or multiplant benefits, may require a longer time for the benefits to be measured adequately, and may provide benefits of a probable nature, many of which are difficult to estimate with any amount of certainty. Therefore, the EPA suggests that capital budgeting practices be modified to adequately evaluate environmental alternatives (EPA, 1992a, 58–59).

The EPA has developed cost management techniques to identify, track, and monitor environmental costs. This method for pollution prevention contains a four-tier hierarchy of costs and methods for the analysis of the costs (see Exhibit 9–4). "The hierarchy progresses from the most conventional and certain costs in Tier 0 to the most difficult to estimate and least certain costs in Tier 3. At each tier, the user first analyzes all costs associated with the current and alternative PP project, and then calculates key financial indicators of the economic viability of the PP project" (EPA, 1992b, 28). Many companies concerned with compliance have adopted the EPA method because they believe this method will be more acceptable for pollution prevention investment decisions than their own methods.

The analysis involved at the various tiers is as follows:

Tier 0–Usual Costs

> Step 1: Identify pollution-prevention alternatives.

> Step 2: Estimate usual costs of current and alternative practices.

> Step 3: Complete Tier 0 worksheet.

Tier 1–Hidden Costs

> Step 1: Establish facility's regulatory status.

> Step 2: Estimate hidden capital expenditures.

> Step 3: Estimate hidden expenses.

> Step 4: Complete Tier 1 cost worksheet.

Tier 2–Liability Costs

> Step 1: Identify regulatory programs under which penalties and/or fines could be incurred.

> Step 2: Estimate expected annual penalties and fines associated with each program and requirement.

> Step 3: Identify waste-management issues with which liabilities can be associated.

> Step 4: Estimate total expected liabilities.

EXHIBIT 9–5
Tellus Institute Total Cost Assessment

Table 5-1. Cost Inclusion Comparison: Company Versus TCA Analyses

X = Cost(s) Included P = Cost(s) Partially Included	Project 1[1] Company	TCA	Project 2[2] Company	TCA	Project 3[3] Company	TCA
Capital Costs						
Purchased Equipment	X	X	X	X	X	X
Materials (e.g. Piping, Elec.)					X	X
Utility Systems		X				
Site Preparation						
Installation				X		
Engineering/Contractor	X	X			X	X
Start-up/Training	X	X		X		
Contingency					X	X
Permitting						
Initial Chemicals						
Working Capital			X	X		
Salvage Value						
Other:						
Project Audit					X	X
Operating Costs						
Direct Costs:[4]						
Raw Materials/Supplies	P	X	X	X	X	X
Waste Disposal	P	X	P	X	X	X
Labor	X	X	X	X	X	X
Revenues - General					X	X
Revenues - By-products						
Other						
Transportation					X	X
Indirect Costs:[5]						
Waste Management						
Hauling		X		X	X	X
Storage		X				
Handling		X				
Waste-end Fees/Taxes		X				
Hauling Insurance				X		
Utilities						
Energy		X	X	X	X	X
Water		X		X		
Sewerage (POTW)		X		X		
Pollution Control/Solvent Recovery		X				
Regulatory Compliance		X				
Insurance						
Future Liability		X				X

Notes:

1. Solvent/heavy-metal to aqueous/heavy metal-free coating conversion at Paper Coating Company
2. Paint/water separator at Metal Fabrication Company
3. Byproduct recovery project at Diversified Chemical Company
4. We use the term "direct costs" to mean costs which are typically allocated to a product or process line (i.e. not charged to an overhead account) and are typically included in project financial analyses.
5. We use the term "indirect costs" to mean costs which are typically charged to an overhead account and typically not included in project financial analyses.

Step 5: Estimate expected years of liability incurrence.

Step 6: Estimate your share of total future liabilities.

Tier 3–Less Tangible Costs

Step 1: Identify qualitatively less tangible benefits of pollution prevention.

Step 2: Quantify less tangible benefits of pollution prevention (U.S. EPA, 1989).

After all steps for all tiers are completed, the EPA method calls for financial analysis of all current and proposed alternative practices. Calculated costs are compiled and analyzed to yield estimates of three financial indicators that form the basis for ranking practices. The three EPA-recommended financial indicators are:

- Total annualized savings (TAS);
- Net present value (NPV);
- Internal rate of return (IRR).

In research studies for the EPA's Office of Pollution Prevention, the Tellus Institute proposed four key elements in total cost assessment: cost inventory, cost allocation, time horizon, and financial indicators. "The effect of a TCA approach should be to 'level the playing field' such that prevention investments receive a balanced appraisal by managers responsible for allocating capital resources" (White, Savage, and Becker, 1993, 2).

The cost inventory element includes all the benefits and costs of a proposed capital investment—direct and indirect costs, future liability costs, less tangible benefits, and nonenvironmental costs. Exhibit 9–5 is an example of the categories in a cost inventory developed as part of a Tellus Institute study for the New Jersey Department of Environmental Protection.

Cost allocation in TCA requires understanding the manufacturing process so that all costs can be applied to a specific product or process. These allocations can become very difficult when the wastes from various products and processes are combined for disposal.

The choice of time horizon is also important in examining how long a project will take to become profitable. For pollution prevention projects, the avoidance of future liability from personal injury, property damage, or environmental regulation fines also should be considered in the time horizon element. Future benefits to be considered but harder to quantify might include increased revenues from better product quality, improved corporate and/or product image, and reduced health maintenance costs.

The financial indicator chosen for TCA should consider the other three elements. Typically, discounted cash flow methods such as net present value, profitability index, and internal rate of return are used for this analysis, with a payback period of five years. To implement TCA, the Tellus Institute has developed computer software, P2/Finance, that can perform the TCA analysis of pollution prevention projects.

These methods are useful for both costing and capital investment decisions. They can aid companies in more broadly identifying and measuring environmental costs for more effective management decisions. Though they generally are applied to evaluating alternatives for pollution prevention and pollution control equipment, they can be used to examine a broader cost inventory and drive those costs into the product costing system. In an activity-based costing context, determining what causes those costs is useful for both the costing and capital investment decisions and can be helpful in making choices among product improvements, process improvements, and capital improvements. It also can be useful in ensuring that companies do not continue to undercost their products because they ignore environmental costs in product costing.

The broad identification and measurement of environmental costs and benefits should be part of all capital investment decisions for plant locations and for purchases of general capital equipment, pollution prevention equipment, and pollution control equipment. The same NPV and IRR methods used elsewhere in the company ought to be used in environmental planning.

It is not that capital budgeting models are inadequate but rather that they often are not used in environmental capital investment decisions. Long time horizons, uncertainty, and risk are dealt with in other capital investments and need to be integrated here. The cost inventory described above as the first step in total cost assessment is also useful for the broader identification of costs specified by Environmental Strategy Implementation. The TCA and EPA methods are good first steps in more complete environmental capital decisions. The Total Stakeholder Analysis (TSA) and ESI provide the frameworks and procedures for making capital investment decisions that properly include present and future impacts. Their use also helps companies evaluate the uncertainties and risks related to those decisions.

OPTION ASSESSMENTS, OPTION SCREENING, AND SCENARIO FORECASTING

Option assessments and option screenings are designed to provide decision makers with all the available options regarding alternatives. "There is a three-phase methodology developed that helps decision makers assess, and act on, the relative attractiveness of options to reduce the environmental impact of substance chains" (Winsemius and Hahn, 1992, 252). The first phase is to generate options. This phase includes four steps:

- Drawing a flow diagram;
- Identifying the major environmental issues;
- Defining the options;
- Selecting the most likely options for further evaluation.

This selection step is based on cost effectiveness, relevance for decision makers, and environmental impact.

The next phase prioritizes the options by determining an economic and environmental profile of the effects. These effects are quantified in monetary terms and typically include the net changes in operating and capital costs. The options then are positioned on an "option map" based on the relative weight and importance of the costs and benefits of each option. The last phase requires the establishment of targets, resources, and responsibilities (Winsemius and Hahn, 1992).

The Niagara Mohawk Power Company (NMPC) of Syracuse, New York, is among the leaders in reporting on environmental externalities and using them in the capital investment decision process. The company defines environmental externalities in the context of electricity generation as "costs (or benefits) to society associated with electric supply or consumption that are not reflected in market prices (hence, they are 'external' to the market)."

The New York State Public Service Commission (NYPSC) sponsored a study to estimate the value of environmental externalities associated with electric supply-and-demand resource options. In addition to qualitative requirements, the quantitative requirements monetized the externalities as a specified dollar per ton of pollutant, cents per KWh, or percentage of avoided costs. The NYPSC has adopted dollar per ton externality values for sulfur dioxide, nitrogen oxides, and carbon dioxide. The values adopted are within a range of values established from low to midrange to high. Niagara Mohawk also has used dollar per ton values for these pollutants in its energy supply and demand side planning activities.

While New York State has required that externality factors be considered by utility companies in competitive bidding, Niagara Mohawk also decided to apply these externality costs in its 1991 Integrated Resource Plan. This plan evaluates future supply and demand scenarios for future energy requirements and is used in capital investment decisions. Niagara Mohawk typically uses a pollution control approach to valuation rather than a damage estimate approach. (These approaches are discussed more thoroughly later in this chapter.) This attempt to integrate the identification and measurement of options on both the demand and supply side is among the best of corporate practices. Tom Centore, manager of marketing and development for investment recovery at Niagara Mohawk has said, "We've stopped treating waste as a liability. We consider it an asset. When we sell, reuse, or recycle waste, we add value directly to the company's bottom line" (McCommons, 1992, 68).

In addition to the Integrated Resource Plan required by New York State, Niagara Mohawk also has completed a fossil optimization and capital utilization study (FOCUS), which attempts to look at similar issues from the company's perspective. FOCUS was undertaken to "develop a long-range plan for the future of the Company's fossil plants." FOCUS led to an on-going process of enhancing the framework for decision making regarding economic costs and benefits of Niagara Mohawk's fossil generation facilities. The company believes that in the long term, environmental constraints and societal impacts also will affect them.

The first step of the FOCUS process was a probable study of the difficulty of compliance with air emissions requirements for specific fossil generating units. The second step was a cost and benefit analysis of various emission-reduction technologies, involving the cost model PROMOD III(R).The third component of FOCUS was derivation of a total cost for each of the scenarios studied, based on unit shutdowns, production costs, capital savings, and allowance credits. The study gave Niagara Mohawk sufficient information to make budget decisions regarding the viability of several of its plants. The study methodology, option screening, continuously surveys the various managers and decision makers in the company to determine the available options.

Niagara Mohawk uses option screening to compare various potential environmental scenarios and associated costs resulting from environmental considerations. It implemented a system to identify and measure

EXHIBIT 9–6

Niagara Mohawk Power Company (Summary of Screening Results for the 800 MW Phased IGCC at Albany for the Base Need Scenario)

Summary of Screening Results for the 800 MW Phased IGCC at Albany for the Base Need Scenario			
	1991 dollars (millions)		
Category	**Case A**	**Case B**	**Case C**
Benefits			
Production Cost Savings	1,040	1,709	1,573
Generation Capacity Savings	304	471	566
Emissions Savings	155	232	235
Total Benefits	1,499	2,413	2,374
Costs			
Capital Costs	750	711	711
Operating Costs	881	1,402	1,347
Life Extension Costs	116	77	133
Waste Disposal Costs	21	24	24
Gas Supply Costs	0	0	0
Transmission Upgrade Costs	50	49	49
Total Costs	1,818	2,262	2,262
Net Present Value (Benefits – Costs)	(320)	160	110
Benefit / Cost Ratio	0.82	1.05	1.07

Note: Dollar amounts represent the present value of all impacts over the 1992-2014 study period for Case A and over the 1992-2030 study period for Cases B and C. Production cost savings are net of fuel and operating and maintenance costs for the option. Totals in the table may not add up due to rounding. Source: Integrated Electric Resource Plan 1991.

the options related to both the demand and supply side of electric power usage. The company uses option screening to determine the optimum mix of demand and supply strategies that provide electrical energy services at the lowest cost, within a set of various constraints. It used focus groups to determine the appropriate options and assign probabilities to the most likely scenarios.

Niagara Mohawk developed five separate measures of cost effectiveness to use in the screening analysis:

- The Rate Impact Measure Test;
- The Utility Revenue Requirements Test;
- The Total Resource Cost Test;
- The Societal Test;
- The DSM Participant Test.

The results of these tests are used in the screening process to determine all relevant costs and benefits and to choose the best option. The objective is to optimize and balance economic, financial, environmental, energy and engineering, and customer service objectives to determine the best resource plan considering trade-offs relative to numerous uncertainties, constraints, and policy objectives. The results of this analysis are seen in Exhibit 9–6, which is a summary of the screening results using three different options. The best option is the one with the highest benefit/cost ratio.

Niagara Mohawk also does a detailed cost benefit analysis for each proposed capital project. Exhibit 9–7 proceeds from assumptions regarding costs of emissions, externality costs, and benefits of reduced emissions to a detailed calculation of the net dollar benefits of the project. The company has adopted the specific monetary values per ton of pollutants determined by the NYPSC.

The EPA proposes an option rating weighted sum method for screening and ranking pollution prevention options. The method involves three steps. First, important criteria in terms of program goals and constraints are determined and each is given a relative weight. Then each option is rated on each criterion on a scale of 0–10. Lastly, the rating of each option for a particular criterion is multiplied by the weight of the criterion. The option with the best overall rating is chosen and may be subject to further technical and economic analysis (U.S. EPA, 1992a, 127).

Some companies also are using scenario forecasting techniques to help them examine the likely impacts on their total environmental costs of changing regulations, changing technologies, and the changing cost of technologies. In companies with high levels of uncertainty, where change is imminent and diversity of opinion exists, scenario forecasting can be useful to clearly identify the various choices for decision makers. Some have suggested that scenario forecasting aids in assessing and managing

EXHIBIT 9–7
Niagara Mohawk Power Company (R&D Summary Benefit Assessment Worksheet)

NIAGARA MOHAWK	R&D SUMMARY BENEFIT ASSESSMENT WORKSHEET

Project Name: Bioenergy From Willow

Project Number: 05-9020

Plans to Use:	__ Certain	_ Probable	__X__ Uncertain

Who Would Use: NMPC Dept(s):   Corporate Planning

Other: Other Utilities

Benefit Categories (P=Primary Benefit, S=Secondary Benefit)

S greater flexibility/capabilities   _ more efficient systems/components   _ better, timely information
_ avoided capital cost   _ greater system reliability/availability   _ greater safety
_ reduced O&M (non-fuel cost)   _ increased revenues   P regulatory or enviro. benefits
_ reduced fuel cost   _ external commercial potential   _ direct customer savings

Description of Application: The results of this project will be a report describing biomass production at the test site in Tully, New York. The report shall also address the viability of a commercial scale willow bioenergy production demonstration farm and report on its success at the test site.

Key Assumptions:

- Environmental externalities will have a significant impact on fossil-fired generating plants. The 1990 Clean Air Act (CAA) and the proposed New York State Department of Environmental Conservation (NYSDEC) and the State Energy Office (SEO) emission reduction regulations will impact fossil generation.

- CAA requires a reduction in SO_2 to meet Acid Rain (Title IV) requirements in years 1995 (Phase I) and 2000 (Phase II).

- Fossil units with marginal heat rates will be severely impacted when and if CO_2 emission reduction regulations are finalized.

- The Fossil Optimization & Capital Utilization Study (FOCUS) has determined that the Dunkirk Unit #2 could have some difficulty surviving because of proposed heat rate efficiency regulations and projected expenditures necessary to meet NO_x and SO_2 requirements.

- Co-firing biomass with coal reduces greenhouse gases. The net effect of CO_2 production from biomass is essentially neutral when grown and used as a fuel on a sustained basis.

- Burning biomass, such as wood, produces very little SO_2 (0.02 - 0.04 lb/MBTU). (EPRI 2612-13,9/91-pg4.11)

- Co-firing retrofit is usually less than $ 200 per Kw. (EPRI study 2612-13, 9/91-pg4-7)

- SO_2 allowances are approx. $ 175/ton. (Summer 93 EPA auction)

- 10 % co-firing wood with coal yield approx. 5 % reduction in NO_x emissions. (EPRI study 2612-13, 9/91, pg4-11)

- 1.5 cent per kilowatt-hour tax incentive for electric power generated in a closed-cycle-fuels production/utilization system provided by the National Energy Policy Act of 1992.

EXHIBIT 9–7 *(continued)*

NIAGARA MOHAWK	R&D SUMMARY BENEFIT ASSESSMENT WORKSHEET

Project Name: Bioenergy From Willow

Project Number: 05-9020

Benefit Calculation Summary:	
• Benefit resulting from reduction of SO_2 = \$607,832 (1994\$)	Net Research Benefit (PV in 1994) <u>\$2,642,650</u> Probability Benefit Will Be Achieved: <u>30%</u> Expected Research Benefit (PV in 1994) <u>\$792,795</u>
• Benefit resulting from 1.5¢/KWh tax credit = \$3,264,818 (1994\$)	__ One Time in year _____ and/or _X_ Continuing from year 1994 to year (end) 2007
• Cost of co-firing retrofit (-) = \$1,230,000 (1994\$)	Not Quantified: __ Conceptual Stage __ Not Quantifiable
• Net Research Benefit: \$607,832 + \$3,264,818 - \$1,230,000 = \$2,642,650 (1994\$)	__ Project Discontinued

Doc.A7.14.rhh

risk, broadens corporate thinking, and makes managers focus on the long-term impacts of their decisions.

Through methods such as those described in this chapter, available data are gathered, assembled, and processed to provide the best available information, the likely outcomes, and the likely impacts of those outcomes. These methods also push business unit managers to be proactive rather than to wait for regulatory or technology changes to affect their businesses. Option assessments, option screening, and scenario forecasting usually provide information useful to improve business and environmental planning, even though it may not be precise.

Fuzzy Logic

In the preceding chapter the legacy costing system at AlliedSignal was described. Fuzzy logic has been used to evaluate the failure costs related to environmentally conscious manufacturing at AlliedSignal (Lawrence, Fortune, and Butler, 1995, and Lawrence and Butler, 1995).

Decision trees and Bayesian probability analyses often have been used to improve decision making under uncertainty. Probabilities can be assigned to the various risks, assessments made, and options evaluated. The application of fuzzy logic is an attempt to apply additional tools

EXHIBIT 9–7 *(continued)*

NIAGARA MOHAWK	CALCULATION WORKSHEET

Project Name:	Bioenergy From Willow
Project Number:	05-9020

Benefit Calculation: Calculation Used: _X_ Incremental Benefit or ___ (Cost without R&D · Cost with R&D)

Operational data from the Environmental Emissions Minimization Study, Task 1: Benchmarking Current Environmental Emissions, 04-9443, 6/24/93, was used as a baseline for determining SO_2 reductions
During 1992, 619,120 MWh of energy was produced with 242,914 tons of coal. A total of 9,884 tons of SO_2 was produced as a result of those operations.

Since little or no SO_2 is produced when burning biomass, if 10% of the coal used in that plant was replaced by biomass, such as wood, a proportional reduction in SO_2 emissions would result.

• Benefits resulting from reduction in SO_2 were determined by:

A 10% reduction in the use of coal each year would result in a 10% reduction in the generation of SO_2.

10% of 9,884 tons of SO_2 = 988 tons of SO_2/year.

Dollar savings per year are = tons of SO_2 times EPA SO_2 allowance per ton.

988 tons SO_2 X $ 175/ton SO_2 = $ 172,900/yr (1994$)

• Benefit resulting from 1.5 cent/kWh tax credit:

If system is in place by 1999, the National Energy Policy Act of 1992 provides tax credit of 1.5 cent/kWh for production through 2007.

Tax Credit per year = Production for 1 year (ie.-1992, Dunkirk 2) X 10% X 1.5¢ per kWh

Tax Credit per year = 619,120,000 kWh X 0.10 X 1.5¢/kWh = $ 928,688/ year

TOTAL SAVINGS PER YEAR: $ 172,900 + $ 928,688 = $ 1,101,588

P/A (1999$) (10.2%, 9) = 5.7135   P/F (1994$) (10.2%, 5) = 0.6153
(factor of an annuity in 1999)   (present worth of a future single annuity)

Total P/F (1994$) = Total Savings/yr X [P/A (1999$)] X [P/F (1994$)]

••Total P/F (1994$) = $ 1,101,588 X 5.7135 X 0.6153 = $ 3,872,650 (1994$)

---

because of the significant uncertainty of the risks associated with environmental impacts.

Fuzzy set theory is a branch of mathematics dealing with sets of information that do not have precise boundaries. "Fuzzy set theory is built on the premise that 99.9 percent of human reasoning is not precise.

EXHIBIT 9–7 *(concluded)*

NIAGARA MOHAWK	CALCULATION WORKSHEET

- Cost of co-firing retrofit construction

Size of plant times 10% times $ 200 per KW.

Cost of co-firing retrofit = 100 MW X 0.10 X $ 200/KW = $ 2,000,000

Investment $ 2,000,000 (Buying 1999):

      P/F (1994$) (10.2, 5) = 0.6153

          Investment (1994$) = $ 2,000,000 X 0.6153
                         = $ 1,230,000 (1994$)

- •NET BENEFIT (1994$) = $ 3,872,650 (-) $ 1,230,000 = $ 2,642,650

- •Probability of benefit being achieved is 30%

- •Expected Research Benefit: 30% X $ 2,642,650 = $ 792,795

Because strategic decisions are full of uncertainty and therefore are inherently imprecise, it seems natural to use technologies based on fuzzy set theory for decision making" (Brewer, Gatian, and Reeve, 1993, 41).

To use fuzzy logic, identified possible magnitudes of future environmental liability independently are assigned a degree of belief (DOB), between 0 and 1. These future environmental liabilities might include various externalities such as water and air pollution of a residential area near a plant or internal disposal costs for chemicals used directly in the manufacturing process. DOBs also are assigned to possible interest-rate levels for each period. All possible combinations of circumstances that define the range of possible realizations of future financial liability are considered. NPV is calculated for each such realization, and a DOB is derived by combining the DOBs attached to each circumstance and associated with that NPV level. The fuzzy logic analysis results in a set of possible NPV levels, along with a DOB for each. One way to use the results of a fuzzy logic analysis is to rank the possible NPV levels according to DOB magnitudes. Though fuzzy logic has many limitations, it does provide an alternative approach to identifying and measuring future environmental impacts.

Monte Carlo Simulation and Decision Trees

"Monte Carlo analysis is a simulation technique that permits the probability distributions of outcomes to be calculated for complex decision trees. A computer is used to simulate the outcome of a series of probable events, over and over again, very rapidly" (Deloitte & Touche, 1991, 4). A decision tree is a visual portrayal of the structure of a decision problem, displaying the alternative courses of action, all possible outcomes, and the probability values of each decision.

Many companies have applied Monte Carlo analysis to the problem of comparing the possible costs of alternative environmental remediation options. Using Monte Carlo random sampling from an option's cost probability distribution, the probability that one option will cost more than another can be estimated and the most likely costs of each operation can be compared. Probabilities (i.e., confidence levels) can be assigned to a range of possible costs, leading to more credible and defendable comparisons.

Monte Carlo simulation assigns a probability distribution (rather than a fuzzy logic DOB) to environmental risk. That risk can increase or decrease depending on changes to environmental legislation. Once probability distributions are established for all inputs required for an NPV analysis, the Monte Carlo simulation is initiated. A computer program implementing the algebraic formula for NPV is written, except that when dollar value of future liabilities or interest rates is called for, it is replaced by random numbers drawn from the appropriate probability distributions.

The computer goes through the decision tree, drawing a sample from the relevant probability distributions at each point where an event occurs, and then applies simple logic to determine how to proceed through the tree. Where alternative technologies are available, the computer model will determine the probability distributions of the possible costs of the technologies and then choose the least costly option. If the decision tree has different possible events, the computer will model each event and the possible outcomes. This process is repeated until meaningful probability distributions can be established.

Deloitte & Touche has developed a case study of compliance with the Clean Air Act using a decision tree to analyze the cost alternatives regarding the installation of a scrubber (see Exhibit 9–8). A sensitivity analysis to determine how much of a change in probability values would result in a different alternative being selected also can be performed.

EXHIBIT 9–8
Deloitte & Touche (Clear Air Act Decision Tree)

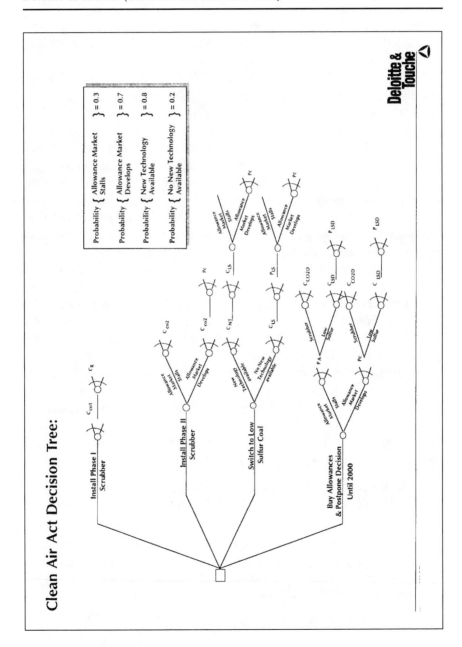

Clean Air Act Decision Tree:

MONETIZING ENVIRONMENTAL EXTERNALITIES

In Chapter 8 we discussed the use of environmental externalities in various costing approaches including full costing. We reviewed Niagara Mohawk's approach to option screening, including externalities in capital investment decisions. Ontario Hydro also has considered two major approaches to monetizing environmental externalities: the cost of control approach and the damage costing approach.

The cost of control approach is defined as the cost of reducing or avoiding pollution before it occurs. It avoids difficult-to-determine actual costs of environmental damage by replacing them with more easily estimated costs of installing, operating, and maintaining environmental control technologies. Advocates of this approach argue that compliance costs are a reasonable substitute for damage costs. Niagara Mohawk uses a pollution control approach that prevents pollution and avoids the difficulty in determining damage to the environment from pollution.

Ontario Hydro uses the damage costing approach, which focuses on attempting to assess actual cost incurred from environmental damage. This method is useful, for example, in assessing impacts on human health problems, animal-herd losses, and crop damage from toxic air and water emissions. The task force preferred this approach because they felt it provided a more realistic estimate of external damages, although it was more difficult to calculate. While there is some concern about the degree of uncertainty associated with monetary estimates of externalities, the task force found that uncertainty is pervasive in many areas of business and needs to be placed in that context.

Ontario Hydro suggests four specific methods to monetize these impacts:

- Market-price method: using information on market prices of, for example, crops that have been damaged or lost due to toxic emissions;

- Hedonic-pricing method, also known as the property-value approach: using geographical differences in real-estate values or wage rates, assuming that such differences are attributable to relative environmental quality;

- Travel-cost method: using information on cost of travel from polluted areas to recreational sites not affected by environmental damage;

- Contingent-valuation method: making use of survey responses on willingness-to-pay or willingness-to-accept from "perpetrators" and "victims" of environmental impact to express physical descriptions of environmental damage in dollar terms.

In March 1994 Ontario Hydro prepared a set of interim sustainable development decision criteria to assist in capital investment project evaluations. The analysis of capital projects in accordance with these criteria should include environmental impacts and alternatives that consider:

- Full life cycle, when possible, but at a minimum design, construction/production, operation/use, decommissioning, and disposal;
- Expected damage to ecosystems, communities, and human health and not the ability to meet existing or proposed environmental regulations;
- Identification and evaluation of the potential positive and negative environmental impacts of each of the alternatives, including impacts that may be common among the alternatives;
- Quantification and monetization of the potential impacts, when possible, but at a minimum a qualitative description of the impacts;
- The trade-offs in selecting the preferred alternatives.

Companies have begun to examine various alternative approaches to measuring current and future environmental costs and benefits. They have been considering alternatives for integrating those measurements into both product costing and capital investment decisions.

We can consider measuring environmental costs based on the cost to control pollution before it occurs, the cost to clean up pollution after it has occurred, or the cost of repairing damage to the environment caused by the pollution. Methods discussed in Chapters 8 and 9 provide guidance on approaches to those measurements. We continue with additional approaches, recognizing that those methods are imprecise but do produce results that improve decisions. Identifying and measuring external environmental costs is important for the environment and likely will be internalized through regulation.

We now turn to some additional approaches and considerations to improving the capital budgeting process.

CONTINGENT VALUATION

Contingent valuation (CV) is one way to measure environmental costs and benefits. It is a survey-based method that attempts to determine how individuals value nonmarketed goods in dollar terms. It is similar to market research, which attempts to predict how people will make decisions. "The CV method uses survey questions to elicit people's preferences for public goods by finding out what they would be willing to pay for specified improvements in them" (Mitchell and Carson, 1989, 2).

The contingent valuation concept has been in use for more than 30 years but became increasingly important with the passage of the Comprehensive Environmental Response Compensation and Liability Act (CERCLA) in 1980 and the Oil Pollution Act of 1990. "These laws created legal causes of action for the recovery of monetary damages for injuries to natural resources resulting from releases of hazardous substances and oil" (Carson, Meade, and Smith, 1993, 8). Thus, contingent valuation now is used widely in both government and industry. Most federal, state, and regulatory agencies responsible for natural resources or environmental assessments use CV. One of the recent uses of this concept was in the valuation of the environmental impact of the Exxon Valdez disaster. But the method also has been used to value environmental benefits created by, for example, the development of recreational facilities by a corporation as a byproduct of its commercial activities.

In addition, "in 1986, the U.S. Department of the Interior promulgated natural resource damage assessment (NRDA) regulations, allowing trustees (governmental agencies) to be compensated for damages resulting from a chemical or hazardous substance release. Under these regulations, trustees could recover foregone passive-use values only if no foregone use values could be estimated" (Desvousges, Gable, Dunford, and Hudson, 1993, 9).

One criticism of CV is that the survey methodology it uses, which asks hypothetical questions, gets only hypothetical responses. Survey respondents may not be able to provide useful estimates of how they value various natural resources, and their actual behavior may differ substantially from their opinions. Critics of CV also focus on the lack of reliability of survey respondents who have never experienced the commodity and on the fact that the survey results are quite sensitive to the design and statistical analysis used.

Experience has shown that in some cases a variation of the forced-to-pay approach (often called the "compelling payment approach") moves toward a solution to that problem and produces more reliable results. In these cases, the respondents still are asked what they would be willing to pay, but the questions are stated in relation to payments made through taxation, thus making the payment more comprehensible and real (Epstein, Epstein, and Weiss, 1977, 142).

Proponents of CV argue that the methodology does not require visiting or experiencing the commodity or resource. "Like all economic measures of welfare change, passive use value reflects changes in the satisfaction of people's preferences. The preferences relevant for passive use value are preferences about the state of the environment" (Randall, 1993, 12). Perhaps CV is not perfect, but it does provide useful information about the value of nonmarketed goods that we would not otherwise have.

RISK ASSESSMENT

The terms "uncertainty" and "risk" often are used interchangeably but are distinctly different. Uncertainty relates to a situation in which the probability distribution is not known. Risk relates to a situation in which the probability distribution of an event is known. To assess risk in environmental situations, it often is suggested that adjustments be made to the cost and benefit profiles rather than to the discount rate. A better approach to this problem is to test the sensitivity of the outcome of project evaluations to variation in the key parameters (Kula, 1992, 253–254).

Environmental decisions are considered complex and risky and have the potential for enormous financial impact. Remediation costs for environmental spills and other accidents, fines, penalties, legal costs, damages, and bad decisions have increased dramatically in the last several decades. Traditional financial analysis of uncertain future events as best and worst case scenarios is inadequate because it ignores risk components in the analysis. New techniques for risk analysis recently have been developed, and existing techniques increasingly have been applied to environmental issues.

Risk assessment is a technique that helps identify and measure the nature and magnitude of risk. The New York State Electric and Gas Corporation has used a site-screening and priority-setting system (SSPS) developed by the Electric Power Research Institute (EPRI) to assess risk at its various plants. The system ranked 17 manufactured gas plant sites over a five-year period using relative risk scores. Scores were calculated for actual risk, perceived risk, and the level of effort required for cleanup.

The SSPS plotted the actual risk versus the perceived risk at all of the sites, allowing the utility to group sites into risk categories of low, moderate, and high. The SSPS uses net present value analysis to demonstrate the estimated company savings from this approach.

In another EPRI project, utility companies were concerned about the risk of fires involving several groups of polychlorinated biphenyl (PCB) transformers. While fires were considered unlikely, they are expensive to clean up when they do occur. EPRI developed a model for evaluating the economic risk of PCB transformers and for analyzing the alternatives. The ASK model offers the best management options for reducing risk and is used to help the utility companies choose between alternative capital investments. The options available were to retain the transformers, replace them with new equipment, or retrofill them. A system such as this also can be used effectively to analyze options and impacts related to low-probability, high-cost events such as explosions and oil and chemical releases.

Another problem that EPRI research efforts dealt with was the formulation of a cost-effective policy for underground storage tank replacement decisions. The issues of when to replace or upgrade tanks, what form of leak detection to use, and which replacement tank options to choose were dealt with. EPRI analysts evaluated the costs of risk mitigation against the reductions in financial risk from potential tank leaks for two tank designs and five leak detection configurations.

This model also showed that early removal or replacement of four additional unprotected steel tanks at power-generating stations where leak detection is not possible is more cost effective than waiting until regulation requires action. The utility company, Union Electric, expected to save at least $1.26 million by adopting this early tank replacement program instead of keeping its bare steel tanks until required to replace them or upgrade them under the regulations. The utility now can explicitly consider the financial risk of potential tank leakage. Thus, methods do exist to improve the evaluation of alternatives and make better decisions based on a clearer understanding and assessment of environmental risk.

This contribution is certainly important. Broader and more complete identification and measurement of costs and benefits produce different results as different risk assessments are made. Using net present value calculations and the models developed for risk assessment as part of the ESI proposed in this book should lead managers to better capital investment decisions based on a clearer understanding of available alternatives.

OPTION PRICING THEORY

Koechlin and Muller (1993) argue that discounted cash flows are insufficient for evaluating environmental risks and alternatives, in part because of the long time horizon. They propose the use of option pricing, which is a way of calculating the expected market value of an option. It models the time series interaction between investments and has been used most often in the financial markets (stock options).

The value of a stock option is determined primarily by the volatility of the underlying stock. They propose the same kind of methodology be applied to environmental investment decisions. As environmental regulations and information about the environment change, so do options, processes, and products. The value of the strategic environmental option increases with the riskiness of the underlying cash flows. Koechlin and Muller acknowledge that while the theory of option pricing is relatively easy to apply to environmental issues, "it remains very difficult to actually place a monetary value on the options embedded in environmental management" (Koechlin and Muller, 1993, 126).

OTHER ISSUES IN CAPITAL BUDGETING UNDER UNCERTAINTY

Traditional capital budgeting techniques make use of an internal discount rate to compare alternatives in investment decisions. The choice of the discount rate obviously affects the outcome of the decision. "Most companies discount all future cash flows at the same rate, usually the firm's cost of capital. In most cases this is appropriate, however there may be compelling arguments why the costs and benefits of some pollution prevention projects should be discounted at a lower rate" (Environmental Law Institute, 1993, 29). Many of the more traditional analyses use short-term payback methods, while environmental decisions may require a longer time horizon.

Gray (1990) and Gray et al., (1993) propose that "all new investments should meet environmental criteria" as well as other corporate criteria in the investment decision process. They suggest the use of an "environmental hurdle rate" through which all investment decisions should be filtered. They acknowledge that this interest rate is more difficult to ascertain because of the long-term nature of environmental decisions.

Environmental capital budgeting must use the same techniques for decision making that other areas use throughout modern corporations. Payback is inadequate, so discounted cash flow methods should be used. Risk analysis should be incorporated into the decision and appropriate discount rates used. Whereas certain hurdle rates generally are established for all other capital investments, they usually are ignored for environmental capital investments because companies believe incorrectly that a positive return on investment is not achievable. The biggest improvement in environmental capital investment decisions, however, probably will be made through a broader identification and measurement of costs and benefits. By including all environmental impacts, companies can apply the same discount rates as they do for other projects. They can complete proper analyses that consider all stakeholders and all impacts in an attempt to minimize environmental impacts and maximize corporate profits.

There is ample reason to be concerned about the extent of uncertainty associated with monetary estimates of externalities. Not only is the nature of most externalities uncertain, but the dollar value of their environmental impacts and the estimated cost required to remediate them are also uncertain. The key to producing a set of worthwhile results is to apply well-established, appropriate tools of risk analysis that express the impact of uncertainty in terms of the decisions that have to be made. Decision makers need information on both probable frequency of occurrence of an adverse event and the dollar value of its impact. They have to determine whether or not the risks identified are acceptable and, if not acceptable, what the dollar costs of avoidance or mitigation are.

HOW TO ESTIMATE FUTURE LIABILITY FUZZILY OR STATISTICALLY

Uncertainty about the future exists for various reasons, including the following:

- Technology: a method for disposing of certain toxic materials may be unavailable, insufficiently tested, or not certified;
- Programmatic requirements: it may take longer than anticipated to complete staffing or to obtain government approval for cleanup processes;

• Unforeseen events: changes in law, redetermination of toxicity categories of particular substances.

An organized methodology for quantifying uncertainty in risk assessment and their NPVs must comprise technical evaluations, programmatic interpretations, and mathematical computations, with the joint goal of measuring the degree of confidence with which the estimate is held. Every estimate of risk is in actuality the sum of estimates of risk levels of a large number of contributing factors, each of which is itself uncertain to some extent. In fact, the simple act of conducting such an analysis often calls attention to possible risks that previously had been unnoticed.

After making qualitative assessments of likely sources of environmental liability attributable to various aspects of company operations, the next step is to determine quantitative impacts on the company. To account for uncertainty, a "best" estimate is provided to establish the "most likely" dollar value that will be required to cover the foreseeable consequences and the most probable to occur of the uncertain consequences. Next, the most optimistic (best case) and pessimistic (worst case) dollar value limits are estimated. Detailed investigations must be conducted to assess technical and financial risks associated with toxicity of materials being handled in connection with normal operations of the company. Specific areas of investigation include uncertainty about the impact of toxicity on long-term health, short-term safety of employees, and the public. Buried somewhere within these two kinds of uncertainty may be fundamental uncertainties about toxicity of materials themselves. A formal research program, perhaps conducted by an independent organization, may be required to establish the true level of the toxicity involved.

SUMMARY

Companies need to incorporate environmental considerations into their capital budgeting and investment decisions. Total Stakeholder Analysis and Environmental Strategy Implementation will provide the company with additional perspectives with which to make those decisions. All environmental costs and benefits need to be identified and measured before investment decisions are made and strategy implemented. A trend is emerging whereby companies have gone beyond regulatory requirements in meeting their environmental obligations. They are beginning to understand that being proactive and planning for pollution prevention rather than reactive and settling for mere compliance is the most cost effective and most responsible strategy. The Environmental Strategy Implementation can be most effective if it is included in all corporate systems. ESI is a forward-looking system that aids in developing environmental goals and policies. Those environmental goals can be enhanced further by the capital projects the company decides to pursue. Many of those decisions must be made under conditions of ambiguity and uncertainty. Information and measurement techniques continually are sought that will reduce the amount of uncertainty in the decision-making process.

Frameworks and measurement techniques are available to incorporate environmental risks and uncertainties effectively into the capital decision process. This chapter has reviewed many of them. Though not without their limitations, these approaches represent significant improvement for environmental management over the approaches used at present in most corporations. These approaches should reduce environmental impacts and increase corporate profits. They definitely will improve management decisions.

Exhibit 9–9 Union Carbide Corporation

199

EXHIBIT 9–9
Union Carbide Corporation (Capital Project Proposal HS&E Checklist)

PG 2.3.2
CAPITAL PROJECT PROPOSAL   PROJECT:_____
HS&E CHECKLIST

LOCATION:_____

HS&E SCREENING CHECKLIST

If all the questions for any of the three sections can be answered "No." then that section of the HS&E checklist can be excluded from further consideration by indicating on the first page of that section under "Comments" that all responses to that section of the Screening Checklist were negative. The questions should be answered in the context "as a result of this project."

Environmental

1. Will there be any increase in air emissions, any new source of air emissions, or any increase in _____
   episodic emission potential?

2. Will there be any increase in materials discharged to the process or clean sewer systems? _____

3. Are there any plans to dispose of wastewater by underground injection? _____

4. Are there any or will there be any wastes generated, stored, treated or disposed of at the project site _____
   that would be classified special?

5. Is there presently any soil or groundwater contamination at the project site or does the project _____
   increase the potential to contaminate soil or groundwater?

6. Will underground storage tanks be used for this project? _____

Safety and Health

1. Will flammable, toxic, corrosive, reactive or otherwise hazardous substances be transported, stored, _____
   processed or produced at the project site?

2. Are extremes of pressure (500 psig) or temperature (400°C) present anywhere in the new facility? _____

3. Will this project use any new process technology or adversely affect reliability of existing facilities? _____

4. Are any process intermediates isolated that are not included on the governing chemical control law _____
   (TSCA in U.S.) inventory listing for the location?

Product Safety

1. Are any new products manufactured or will any existing products be directed toward a new market? _____

2. Will distribution schemes cause new or additional public exposures to this product? _____

3. Will this project introduce new contaminants, increase existing hazardous contaminant level, or _____
   otherwise increase the hazardous nature of the products?

Reviewer _____   Date _____

Union Carbide Corporation/**Responsible Care Programs and Guidelines Manual**   (5/95)

EXHIBIT 9–9 *(continued)*

PG 2.3.2
CAPITAL PROJECT PROPOSAL   PROJECT:_____
HS&E CHECKLIST
                                                 LOCATION:_____
ENVIRONMENTAL

1.   GENERAL   YES   NO   OTHER   COMMENTS:

1.1   Does the geographic location of the project   (__) ___ (__) _____
      present any potential interstate or international   _____
      air pollution liabilities or unusual water   _____
      (surface or groundwater) pollution liabilities?   _____

1.2   Is process technology design derived from   ___ (__) (__) _____
      either proven commercial-scale facilities or six   _____
      months or more of successful pilot-scale   _____
      operations?   _____

1.3   Is there a high degree of confidence that the ___ (__) (__) _____
      predicted composition and quantities of air   _____
      and water pollutants and residues generated   _____
      from operation of the project have not omitted   _____
      any chemical more toxic than those   _____
      documented and have not understated any   _____
      quantities by more than 50%?   _____

1.4   Are any of the residuals from either   (__) ___ (__) _____
      environmental discharges or disposed wastes   _____
      resulting from operation of the completed   _____
      project believed to be a potential subject of   _____
      future governmental rule-making that could   _____
      cause future unfavorable economics or   _____
      publicity for the project, location or   _____
      Corporation?

1.5   Has the design inventory of hazardous and   ___ (__) (__) _____
      toxic chemicals been minimized to the extent   _____
      practicable?   _____

1.6   Will the design and operation of the project be ___ (__) (__) _____
      consistent with the location's waste and   _____
      release reduction program?   _____

1.7   Will the facility be staffed, or have readily   ___ (__) (__) _____
      available, personnel fully aware of the   _____
      environmental consequences of operational   _____
      problems and trained to implement timely and   _____
      proper response actions?   _____

2.   AIR EMISSIONS

2.1   Have all significant air emissions (point,   ___ (__) (__) _____
      fugitive & secondary) been identified and   _____
      described with respect to quantity,   _____
      composition and their ultimate treatment?   _____
      (Consider start-up/shutdown and abnormal   _____
      operating conditions.)

                              HSE pg. 1

Union Carbide Corporation/**Responsible Care Programs and Guidelines Manual**   (5/95)

Exhibit 9–9 Union Carbide Corporation   201

EXHIBIT 9–9 *(continued)*

PG 2.3.2
CAPITAL PROJECT PROPOSAL
HS&E CHECKLIST (CONTINUED)

		YES	NO	OTHER	COMMENTS:
2.2	Do proposed air emissions contain any material classified as hazardous under Federal, State or local regulations? (Pay special attention to Hazardous Air Pollutants (HAP's) identified in the Clean Air Act.)	(__)	__	(__)	_____
2.3	Does the project design satisfy the design objectives in TMS Criteria ET-1100 (Environmental Guidelines for Project Endorsement Review) for both routine (continuous & intermittent) emissions and episodic air emissions? (Pay special attention to known and suspected carcinogens.)	__	(__)	(__)	_____
2.4	Will proposed air emissions require Prevention of Significant Deterioration (PSD) Review and/or New Source Review?	(__)	__	(__)	_____
2.5	Do any proposed air emission sources require new control systems or upgrading of existing systems?	(__)	__	(__)	_____
2.6	Are the air pollution control systems designed to meet applicable governmental technological levels and UCC requirements?	__	(__)	(__)	_____
2.7	Are there any air pollution control systems that have not been reviewed to assure conformance with Federal, State or local regulations?	(__)	__	(__)	_____

3.   SURFACE/GROUNDWATER
      PROTECTION

3.1	Have all significant water discharges been identified and described with respect to quantity, composition and their ultimate treatment and/or disposal? (Consider start-up/shutdown conditions and abnormal operating conditions.)	__	(__)	(__)	_____
3.2	Do proposed wastewater discharges contain any substances on EPA's priority pollutant list?	(__)	__	(__)	_____
3.3	Will wastewater discharges be restricted by water quality limits of the receiving stream or by the capacity of a Publicly-Owned Treatment Works (POTW)?	(__)	__	(__)	_____

HSE pg. 2

EXHIBIT 9–9 *(continued)*

PG 2.3.2
CAPITAL PROJECT PROPOSAL
HS&E CHECKLIST (CONTINUED)

		YES	NO	OTHER	COMMENTS:
3.4	Does the operation handle any compounds having EPA Reportable Quantities (RQ's)?	(_)	___	(_)	_____
3.5	Are adequate leak/spill prevention and detection measures provided?	___	(_)	(_)	_____
3.6	Will secondary containment be provided for all new and modified oil and chemical handling or storage areas?	___	(_)	(_)	_____
3.7	Are modifications to an existing or an entirely new Spill Prevention. Control and Countermeasures (SPCC) Plan required?	(_)	___	(_)	_____
3.8	Will underground tanks be used for this project?	(_)	___	(_)	_____
3.9	Are there any plans to dispose of wastewater by underground injection?	(_)	___	(_)	_____
3.10	Do any proposed wastewater discharges require new control systems or upgrading of existing systems?	(_)	___	(_)	_____
3.11	Are the water pollution control systems. underground tanks and injection wells designed to meet applicable governmental technological levels and UCC requirements?	___	(_)	(_)	_____
3.12	Are there any containment, storage, treatment or disposal design plans that have not been reviewed to assure conformance with Federal. State or local regulations?	(_)	___	(_)	_____

4.   **WASTE MANAGEMENT**

		YES	NO	OTHER	COMMENTS:
4.1	Have all significant special wastes been identified and described with respect to quantity, composition and their ultimate treatment and/or disposal? (Consider start-up/shutdown conditions and abnormal operating conditions.)	___	(_)	(_)	_____
4.2	Have all special waste conservation/ minimization alternatives been reviewed and used where feasible?	___	(_)	(_)	_____
4.3	Are the off-site locations that are managing special wastes approved in accordance with UCC Responsible Care Standard 5.1?	___	(_)	(_)	_____

HSE pg. 3

Exhibit 9–9 Union Carbide Corporation   **203**

EXHIBIT 9–9 *(continued)*

PG 2.3.2
CAPITAL PROJECT PROPOSAL
HS&E CHECKLIST (CONTINUED)

		YES	NO	OTHER	COMMENTS:

4.4 Has land application of special wastes been minimized to the extent feasible?   (__) (__) _____

4.5 Are any proposed wastes classified as hazardous under Federal, State or local regulations?   (__) __ (__) _____

4.6 Will the project necessitate the storage, treatment or disposal of hazardous waste, either on-site or off-site?   (__) __ (__) _____

4.7 Are the hazardous waste storage, treatment and disposal systems designed to meet applicable governmental technological levels and UCC requirements?   ___ (__) (__) _____

4.8 Are there any storage, treatment or disposal design plans that have not been reviewed to assure conformance with Federal, State or local regulations?   (__) __ (__) _____

5.   COMPLIANCE/PERMITS

5.1 If the project is associated with an existing facility, has the facility experienced any incidents of non-compliance with air, wastewater, storm water, solid/hazardous waste permits or regulations, or received any pollution-related citizen complaints in the past 12 months that may affect the project? Describe impact.   (__) __ (__) _____

5.2 Are there any Compliance Orders or other legal actions that may affect the project? Describe impact.   (__) __ (__) _____

5.3 Will the predicted air and water discharges from operation of the completed project comply with all applicable governmental rules? List significant applicable regulations.   (__) (__) (__) _____

5.4 Will the planned storage, treatment and disposal of hazardous wastes comply with all applicable governmental rules? List significant applicable regulations.   (__) (__) (__) _____

5.5 Have all required air, wastewater, storm water and solid/hazardous waste permits and permit modifications been identified? List new permits/modifications needed.   (__) (__) (__) _____

HSE pg. 4

EXHIBIT 9–9 *(continued)*

PG 2.3.2
CAPITAL PROJECT PROPOSAL
HS&E CHECKLIST (CONTINUED)

		YES	NO	OTHER	COMMENTS:

5.6   Are there any other environmental permits needed or which require modification (ex.. underground storage tanks. Corps of Engineers, wetlands...)? List new permits/modifications needed.   (__) __ (__) _____

5.7   Are any delays in construction or operation start-up likely due to permitting or other regulatory requirements?   (__) __ (__) _____

6.   SITE CONDITION

6.1   Is background air quality monitoring data available for the past 12 months at the project site?   __ (__) (__) _____

6.2   If there are proposed wastewater or storm water discharges to surface water, is background water quality data available?   __ (__) (__) _____

6.3   Is the proposed project site to be located within ½ mile of any existing or potential surface or underground source of drinking water?   (__) __ (__) _____

6.4   Is there presently any known or suspected soil and/or groundwater contamination at the project site?   (__) __ (__) _____

6.5   Are there any inactive or active waste storage. treatment or disposal facilities located on the project site?   (__) __ (__) _____

6.6   Are there ongoing or past site investigations and/or remedial actions for present and/or past solid waste units that pose(d) a significant threat of release of hazardous constituents to the environment at the project site?   (__) __ (__) _____

6.7   Is there any material containing PCB's located on the project site?   (__) __ (__) _____

6.8   Are underground tanks located on the project site?   (__) __ (__) _____

6.9   Does the project site contain U.S. Coast Guard designated wetlands?   (__) __ (__) _____

_____   _____
Reviewer   Date

HSE pg. 5

Union Carbide Corporation/**Responsible Care Programs and Guidelines Manual**   (5/95)

Exhibit 9–9 Union Carbide Corporation   205

EXHIBIT 9–9 *(continued)*

PG 2.3.2
CAPITAL PROJECT PROPOSAL   PROJECT: _____
HS&E CHECKLIST
                                     LOCATION:_____

SAFETY AND HEALTH

| | | YES | NO | OTHER | COMMENTS: |

1.   GENERAL

1.1   Will toxic, flammable, corrosive or otherwise hazardous substances be transported, stored, processed or produced in facilities affected by this project?   (__) __ (__) _____

1.2   Will high noise levels (85 dBA and higher), radiation sources, heat stress, repetitive motion, or other new or unusual physical hazards be introduced by this project?   (__) __ (__) _____

1.3   Could any of the substances handled in facilities affected by this project cause an explosion if heated, contaminated, concentrated or otherwise mishandled?   (__) __ (__) _____

1.4   Is all necessary safety and health data known for each substance handled? (Include isolated intermediates.)   __ (__) (__) _____

1.5   Do up-to-date Material Safety Data Sheets exist for each substance handled? (Include any stream or mixture handled or stored.)   __ (__) (__) _____

1.6   Will this project introduce new chemicals that are highly reactive with other chemicals already handled at the location?   (__) __ (__) _____

1.7   Is there potential for mixing of incompatible chemicals in process, storage or waste disposal areas (in/outside boundaries) of this facility?   (__) __ (__) _____

1.8   Has an HS&EA Definition of Technology (DOT) Report, or an HS&EA Section of a Process DOT Report (forms A through G) been prepared for this project?   __ (__) (__) _____

1.9   Are Operational Safety Standards required, and will they be prepared before startup?   __ (__) (__) _____

1.10   Are inventories of hazardous or toxic materials minimized?   __ (__) (__) _____

2.   COMPLIANCE

2.1   Will any new safety or health programs be required to meet regulations?   (__) __ (__) _____

HSE pg. 6

EXHIBIT 9–9 *(continued)*

PG 2.3.2
CAPITAL PROJECT PROPOSAL
HS&E CHECKLIST (CONTINUED)

		YES	NO	OTHER	COMMENTS:
2.2	Have all Department of Transportation (or equivalent) requirements been identified for substances that will be shipped either to or from the plant location?	___	(__)	(__)	
2.3	Are there any proposed changes to safety and health regulations that could affect design or operation of project facilities?	(__)	___	(__)	
2.4	Will the following be required to comply with safety and health regulations:				
	a) Monitoring of employee exposure?	(__)	___	(__)	
	b) Ventilation, noise suppression or other engineering controls?	(__)	___	(__)	
	c) Special personal protective equipment?	(__)	___	(__)	
	d) Special medical examinations or a medical surveillance program?	(__)	___	(__)	
	e) Special operating or maintenance procedures?	(__)	___	(__)	
	f) Regulated areas?	(__)	___	(__)	
2.5	Will employees need supplemental training beyond normal corporate or business programs to assure safe operation?	(__)	___	(__)	
2.6	Will any variances to UCC Safety/Health TMS Mandatory Standards be required?	(__)	___	(__)	
2.7	Do any State or local regulations supersede Federal safety and health regulations?	(__)	___	(__)	
2.8	Are all chemicals that will be handled included in the governing chemical control law (TSCA in U.S.)inventory or equivalent (including isolated intermediates)?	___	(__)	(__)	
2.9	Will this project involve installation or removal of asbestos or PCB materials?	(__)	___	(__)	
2.10	Are new occupied buildings or expansions of existing occupied buildings planned?	(__)	___	(__)	
2.11	Will occupied buildings be affected by process changes that:				
	a) Decrease the separation distance?	(__)	___	(__)	
	b) Increase the hazard classification?	(__)	___	(__)	
	c) Significantly increase the risk above current level (i.e., process complexity)?	(__)	___	(__)	

HSE pg. 7

Union Carbide Corporation/**Responsible Care Programs and Guidelines Manual**   (5/95)

Exhibit 9–9 Union Carbide Corporation 207

EXHIBIT 9–9 *(continued)*

PG 2.3.2
CAPITAL PROJECT PROPOSAL
HS&E CHECKLIST (CONTINUED)

	YES	NO	OTHER	COMMENTS:
2.12 Will contractors be used for on-site work? (If so, the UCC On-Site Contractor HS&E Program applies.)	(__)	___	(__)	

3. **PUBLIC IMPACT**

3.1 Will emergency relief devices that protect facilities affected by this project discharge directly to the atmosphere? (__) ___ (__)

3.2 Could releases from the emergency relief devices that discharge directly to the atmosphere have an adverse impact on the health or safety of the public? (__) ___ (__)

3.3 Could a process upset or other emergency situation (fire, explosion, spill, etc.) occur in the project facilities that could have an adverse impact on the public? (__) ___ (__)

3.4 In the event of the release of toxic chemicals from facilities affected by this project, would existing or planned monitoring, detection, and/or alarm systems be adequate? ___ (__) (__)

4. **FACILITY DESIGN**

4.1 Will extremes of temperature or pressure (i.e., temperatures above 400°C or pressure over 500 psig) exist in facilities affected by this project? (__) ___ (__)

4.2 Will there be any new ignition sources associated with this project? (__) ___ (__)

4.3 Will recognized industry practices be followed in the layout of the facility? ___ (__) (__)

4.4 Will the pressure vessels, storage tanks, safety valves, piping, valves and fittings that are part of the project facilities conform to applicable industry codes and standards and Federal, State, and local laws and regulations? ___ (__) (__)

4.5 Will all normal project safety and health reviews be performed? ___ (__) (__)

4.6 Is there a need for a Process Hazard Analysis (PHA) of the facilities? (__) (__) (__)

HSE pg. 8

EXHIBIT 9–9 *(continued)*

PG 2.3.2
CAPITAL PROJECT PROPOSAL
HS&E CHECKLIST (CONTINUED)

		YES	NO	OTHER	COMMENTS:
4.7	Could the loss of any utility that supplies project facilities create a possible hazardous situation?	(__)	__	(__)	_____
4.8	Will flammable gas detectors be installed as part of this project?	(__)	(__)	(__)	_____
4.9	For facilities affected by this project, is any reaction sufficiently exothermic to result in a runaway reaction under any operating conditions that could occur?	(__)	__	(__)	_____
4.10	Does this project introduce a new process or incorporate process technology new to this location?	(__)	__	(__)	_____
4.11	Are process monitoring and control devices adequate to prevent upsets leading to hazardous operation or toxic releases?	__	(__)	(__)	_____
4.12	Would increased use of automation or advanced process control effectively reduce the risks of employee exposures?	(__)	__	(__)	_____
4.13	Will water spray protection be provided for processing, storage and distribution areas in accordance with UCC criteria?	__	(__)	(__)	_____
4.14	Are fire water supplies and distribution systems adequate to provide sufficient fire water to this facility?	__	(__)	(__)	_____
4.15	Could this project adversely impact on or be impacted by other facilities?	(__)	__	(__)	_____
4.16	Were there any areas considered for inherent safety that were rejected?	(__)	__	(__)	_____
4.17	Were there areas where inherent safety was incorporated? (If yes, where?)	__	(__)	(__)	_____
4.18	Have seismic zones been considered, and appropriate design requirements used?	__	(__)	(__)	_____
4.19	Are considerations of ergonomic principles included in the facility and process design?	__	(__)	(__)	_____

HSE pg. 9

Exhibit 9–9 Union Carbide Corporation 209

EXHIBIT 9–9 *(continued)*

PG 2.3.2
CAPITAL PROJECT PROPOSAL
HS&E CHECKLIST (CONTINUED)

	YES	NO	OTHER	COMMENTS:

5. EMERGENCY RESPONSE

5.1 Will additional fire and emergency response equipment, personnel or procedures be required as a result of this project? (__) ___ (__) _____

5.2 Will any changes to the location's Community Emergency Response Plan (evacuation, etc.) be required as a result of this project? (__) ___ (__) _____

6. ERMS COMPLIANCE

6.1 Will this project change the ERMS Hazard Ranking Model (HRM) data? (__) ___ (__) _____

6.2 Has a consequence or other type analysis been conducted to evaluate potential for off-site fatality events? ___ (__) (__) _____

6.3 Have there been prior Risk Reviews done for this facility? ___ (__) (__) _____

6.4 Is a Risk Review required for this project (e.g., does off-site fatality potential exist)? (__) ___ (__) _____

6.5 Have all scenarios identified by a Risk Review or Third Tier Study been mitigated as required by ERMS? ___ (__) (__) _____

_____   _____
Reviewer   Date

HSE pg. 10

EXHIBIT 9–9 *(continued)*

PG 2.3.2
CAPITAL PROJECT PROPOSAL   PROJECT:_____
HS&E CHECKLIST

                                      LOCATION:_____
PRODUCT SAFETY

                                      YES   NO   OTHER   COMMENTS:

1.   GENERAL

1.1 Will any of the products from this facility be   (__) ___ (__) _____
     marketed as a consumer product?

1.2 Will any of the products be used as an   (__) ___ (__) _____
     intermediate by UCC or others to formulate a   _____
     product that will be marketed as a consumer   _____
     product?

1.3 Are any of the products intended for use in the   (__) ___ (__) _____
     manufacture of food, drugs or their packaging   _____
     materials?

1.4 Are any of the products classified by the Food   (__) ___ (__) _____
     and Drug Administration as medical devices?

1.5 Are any of the products subject to regulation   (__) ___ (__) _____
     under Federal Insecticide, Fungicide,   _____
     Rodenticide Act; Toxic Substances Control   _____
     Act; Consumer Product Safety Commission;   _____
     or Federal Food, Drug and Cosmetic Act?

1.6 Are any of the products classified as toxic,   (__) ___ (__) _____
     explosive, corrosive, flammable or otherwise   _____
     hazardous?

1.7 Can any product harm persons or property in   (__) ___ (__) _____
     normal use or any potential misuse?

1.8 Does the product, or any component in the   (__) ___ (__) _____
     product, appear on any listing of chemicals   _____
     requiring customer, employee or public   _____
     notification?

2.   PRODUCT DESIGN

2.1 Has the product undergone a product safety   ___ (__) (__) _____
     risk analysis to evaluate downstream   _____
     exposure/health risk potential?

2.2 Are any Premanufacture Notifications   (__) ___ (__) _____
     necessary for any of the products or   _____
     intermediates?

2.3 Does any product require certification or   (__) ___ (__) _____
     testing by Federal, State or local   _____
     governmental agencies?

2.4 Does any product require testing or approval   (__) ___ (__) _____
     by a nationally recognized testing agency?

HSE pg. 11

Union Carbide Corporation/**Responsible Care Programs and Guidelines Manual**   (5/95)

Exhibit 9–9 Union Carbide Corporation   211

EXHIBIT 9–9 *(concluded)*

PG 2.3.2
CAPITAL PROJECT PROPOSAL
HS&E CHECKLIST (CONTINUED)

		YES	NO	OTHER	COMMENTS:

2.5   Will this project introduce new contaminants,   (__) ___ (__) _____
increase existing hazardous contaminant level,   _____
or otherwise increase the hazardous nature of   _____
the product?   _____

2.6   Is this a new or modified product, or a   (__) ___ (__) _____
product directed toward a new market?

3.   DISTRIBUTION

3.1   Will distribution cause new or additional   (__) ___ (__) _____
public exposure to this product?

3.2   Have all regulatory requirements for shipping   ___ (__) (__) _____
the products been identified?

3.3   Has all labeling and Material Safety Data   ___ (__) (__) _____
Sheet data been obtained for all products?

3.4   Will any special handling, storage or shipping   (__) ___ (__) _____
equipment or procedures be required for any   _____
of the products?

4.   PRODUCT IMAGE

4.1   Is there any history of product liability with   (__) ___ (__) _____
any of these products or similar products?   _____

4.2   Could any of the products be viewed by the   (__) ___ (__) _____
public or regulatory agencies as presenting an   _____
unacceptable risk to health, safety or the   _____
environment?   _____

4.3   Will communication with any regulatory   (__) ___ (__) _____
agency be required regarding the safety of any   _____
of the products?

_____   _____
Reviewer   Date

HSE pg. 12

Chapter Ten

Performance Evaluation Systems

The company can talk about compliance, but if the infrastructure doesn't exist to support it, it is just lip service.

Bruce E. Ranck, president and COO
Browning-Ferris Industries

In the early chapters of this book, I chronicled the failures of social accounting in the 1970s and blamed them in part on the lack of institutionalization in industry. With the increasing importance of environmental costs and the development of environmental strategies, the integration of improved approaches to decision making is imperative. It can be accomplished only if employees throughout the organization believe that their performance on environmental issues affects the evaluation of their individual performance. Earlier I discussed the need for better methods of measuring and reporting corporate environmental performance for external reporting purposes. Financial analysts, shareholders, and various other stakeholders need this information. They need it not only for environmental reasons but also to make informed decisions about the current financial performance and current financial position of the company. Some stakeholders believe that increased external disclosure of environmental performance will motivate improved corporate performance.

The issue we discuss in this chapter is how to motivate individual employee behavior to align it with the environmental goals of the organization. Those goals are related to improved environmental sensitivity and performance and a recognition that improved environmental performance often will lead to improved long-term corporate financial performance. So we move from evaluating the corporation's performance to investigating the environmental performance of business units, facilities, senior managers, lower level managers, and staff.

Many questions need to be answered. How explicit should the goals be? How explicit should the measurements be? How should the goals and measurements be included in performance evaluation, salary, and bonuses? Companies have been trying to improve their management of environmental impacts and to develop and implement environmental strategies. Many are beginning to recognize the importance of integrating environmental measurements into performance evaluation systems. Such integration will ensure that statements of environmental responsibility articulated by the CEO and in corporate mission statements are implemented properly.

EVALUATING CORPORATIONS, STRATEGIC BUSINESS UNITS, AND FACILITIES

Numerous organizations develop environmental performance indexes to help them gauge the performance of strategic business units and company facilities. The development is sometimes prompted by external evaluators. Sometimes it is part of a comprehensive performance evaluation system used to motivate improved environmental performance. The Kansas City Division of AlliedSignal Aerospace Corporation has developed a system that responds to a rating of its performance by its sole customer, which determines a large portion of its fee based on EH&S performance.

The Kansas City plant is operated for the U.S. Department of Energy (DOE) by AlliedSignal under a long-term contract. DOE formally evaluates the performance of the division twice a year, and the evaluation provides the basis for the contract award fee determination. A description of the performance ratings and the 1993–94 scores of the Kansas City Division are shown in Exhibit 10–1. Based on these ratings, the Division earned an award fee of approximately $4.5 million for the first half of 1994.

The EH&S score accounts for 55 percent of the performance criteria that make up AlliedSignal's performance rating (with the other four areas

EXHIBIT 10–1
U.S. Department of Energy Performance Evaluation Report of AlliedSignal Aerospace Corporation's Kansas City Division

Performance Ratings

Grade	Grade	Criteria
Outstanding	96-100	Substantially exceeds expected levels of performance
Good	86-95	Exceeds expected levels of performance
Satisfactory	76-85	Meets expected levels of performance
Marginal	66-75	Less than expected
Unsatisfactory	65 or below	Below minimum acceptable levels

Scores by Principal Assessment Area

Performance Area	Weighting	1st Half 1994	2nd Half 1993
General Management	10%	95	95
EH&S	55%	88.86	90.18
Operations & Weapons	15%	95	94
Safeguards & Securities	10%	92	92
Resources & Business Management	10%	93	93
Numeric Grade		91.0	91.7

making up the 45 percent balance). With such a large part of the Division's fee based on environmental performance, a change in corporate culture was necessary. Management motivated a change in focus through performance evaluations. Though product quality and on-time delivery remain important, sensitivity to environmental issues is also important to managers and staff alike. Responding to good but not outstanding ratings on environmental performance, the company stated that "our challenge...will be to raise our EH&S ratings without compromising our scores in other areas." In part, this goal is accomplished through innovative programs such as the legacy costing work described in Chapter 8. Through innovative evaluation programs, the Department of Energy and

AlliedSignal have motivated improved environmental performance. The company constantly measures and monitors environmental performance and reports it to both internal and external stakeholders.

Niagara Mohawk Power began to develop a comprehensive self-assessment program as part of a 1989 settlement with the New York State Public Service Commission. The assessment concluded, in part, that to sustain long-term improvement, corporate culture had to change. To implement that change, Niagara Mohawk Power developed the measured equity return incentive term (MERIT). The company identified three performance areas that affect the creation of value for various stakeholders and developed measures for them. The areas are:

- Responsiveness to customer needs;
- Efficiency through cost management, improved operations, employee empowerment, and safety;
- Aggressive, responsible leadership in addressing environmental issues.

The degree of success in reaching these three goals determines the level of the financial award available for distribution to company employees. The company developed an environmental performance index (EPI) and chose targets to focus on consistent and measurable improvements from a baseline of environmental performance. Establishing solid benchmarks against which environmental performance can be measured encourages management and staff to improve compliance with environmental regulations. It also leads to a decrease in costly noncompliance issues and corrective actions. Three categories of performance were measured: emissions/waste, compliance, and environmental enhancements. For two of the categories weights were assigned and benchmarks established for continuous improvement. For example, weights were assigned in the compliance category based on relative importance, such as the number of notices of violation and the number of environmental audits performed.

In the emissions/waste category the weights were "subjectively assigned to reflect the relative environmental externalities costs based on currently available information." So, for example, weights and benchmarks for sulfur dioxide and nitric oxides have been established and are used in the scoring system (Miakisz, 1992, 190–191).

The enhancement category is scored based on the amount of money invested in the enhancement. Every $200,000 invested scores an additional point. The scores for these three categories are added up to determine a composite index score, which is used for yearly comparisons. If at least 50 percent of the category point total is not achieved, no MERIT award will be earned for that category.

Explicitly identifying corporate goals and setting specific targets likely does improve corporate environmental performance and focuses attention on areas of concern and priority. Niagara Mohawk managers believe that the company's environmental performance has improved through the application of MERIT and the EPI. Driving this system to individual performance indicators and to individual compensation might be desirable, however. An explicit system directly affecting individual pay often will provide stronger individual incentives that will have a more powerful impact on corporate culture.

Environmental strategy is linked most powerfully to environmental performance through the development of performance measures. The environmental performance of corporations, business units, facilities, teams, managers, and all other employees must be measured and must be part of the way they are evaluated for success. In addition, incentives should be established to encourage environmental excellence.

Chapter 11 of this book suggests a corporate environmental performance scorecard and measures of environmental leadership to provide benchmarks and guidance for corporate environmental improvement. The next section examines how providing individual incentives improves environmental performance through individual employee participation.

INCENTIVES FOR INDIVIDUAL ENVIRONMENTAL RESPONSIBILITY

The traditional accounting system in most organizations I observed has provided a negative incentive (disincentive) to report potential hazards or violations of environmental laws, corporate goals, and corporate practices. Employees sometimes believe they will be penalized if they notify a manager of a potential hazard because eliminating the hazard might cause the business unit to suffer a short-term financial loss. This expenditure typically is viewed as an expense rather than an asset and often has a negative impact on a manager's overall rewards.

To confront this concern, Chevron enacted worldwide Policy 530, "Protecting People and the Environment." The policy requires each operating company to:

develop and maintain a process whereby employees at all levels are encouraged to freely report existing or potential compliance problems with management. The process must be designed to ensure that each alleged problem is documented and responded to, that the employee has the ability to reach a responsive level of management, and that the employee will have no fear of retribution. The process must include alternate channels of reporting for situations where employees perceive that their supervisors are not being responsive to their compliance concerns. There must also be a process by which employees can elevate their concerns beyond local management in the event that the local reporting system is perceived to be nonresponsive.

The Chevron policy was designed as a proactive guide to foster integration of environmental issues into everyday business decisions. The policy has encouraged a system where "employees and managers are rewarded for identifying and dealing with potential environmental hazards. For example, at the time when the old underground gasoline tanks at service stations were replaced with double-walled fiberglass tanks, such tanks were not required. But an expenditure of $25,000–50,000 to replace a tank costs the company far less than the $250,000 or more needed to remediate the contamination from a leaking tank" (Surma, 1992, 15).

Chevron has been integrating environmental performance into the performance management process and has been developing performance accountability metrics for senior management. This is a top-down process. Though each employee has a performance plan, environmental performance may not be a major factor. The system is based on the view that by integrating environmental performance into the evaluation of senior management, it will be pushed down through the organization. Though the system is not fully integrated nor explicit, it is an excellent first step toward getting employees throughout the organization to become more sensitive to environmental concerns. It will encourage managers to discuss both corporate environmental performance and individual environmental performance in performance reviews.

In addition to boldly discouraging negative incentives, some performance systems are neutral in that they relate no positive or negative incentives to reporting potential or existing hazards. A few companies have tied individual performance reviews and compensation explicitly to environmental performance. They have established environmental performance as a critical variable for compensation in positive incentive systems.

Many companies do encourage excellence in environmental performance by establishing individual environmental goals and tracking progress toward those goals. Often, specific environmental attributes are listed on a performance evaluation form. This comparison of performance with goals ensures that both the employee and the evaluator consider environmental impacts in the performance evaluation process.

Poor environmental performance should affect pay, but most companies show no evidence that it does. Only a fully integrated, explicit system can do that. As noted below, some companies intentionally have opted for an implicit system to allow managers discretion to make the tradeoffs between environmental performance and financial performance. If a company views environmental performance as a core value and wants to change the corporate culture, an explicit performance evaluation system is likely to produce more powerful results.

One way to improve environmental performance is to involve employees throughout the organization. They can be encouraged to seek out violations and report them quickly or, in some cases, can be empowered to repair the problem. Some companies have developed extensive training programs that sensitize employees to the environmental and financial impacts of various projects and products and demonstrate what employees can do to aid themselves, the corporation, and the environment. Some companies have progressed one step further and moved much of the internal environmental audit work (discussed in detail in Chapter 6) from the central internal environmental audit staff to local employees at the manufacturing facilities. These employees conduct self-audits and report or repair the problems. This method drives home to the employees the importance of environmental compliance to the corporation, to their individual welfare, and to their jobs.

If developed properly, the system can affect the pay of the factory workers, their supervisors, and senior managers. Divisional performance evaluations will have an environmental component in addition to the standard profit component. The system also can:

- Substantially reduce fines related to violations of environmental laws;
- Increase efficiency through improved monitoring of process performance;
- Reduce the amount of work the central environmental audit staff must perform.

As the system is pushed to the local staff, suggested process improvements are more noticeable, waste frequently is reduced, and profits often increase. Employees can even be given small monetary rewards for discovering and reporting potential or existing hazards.

Some companies have programs that are neutral and do not affect employee performance evaluations but even so are effective. Many companies have established employee hotlines for possible compliance violations of government regulations, corporate goals, or corporate practices. Employees can call the compliance hotline anonymously 24 hours a day, seven days a week, to report possible violations. In this way, the company obtains the necessary information from the employee who observes the violation without the employee's being penalized for the report. Making this method work requires employees who are motivated to report such violations because of concern for the welfare of the corporation or the environment.

First a corporation needs an established mission statement that includes a desire to take a leadership role in corporate environmental performance. It needs a CEO who has made statements that set the tone at the top as wanting to reduce and minimize negative corporate environmental impacts. Then the performance evaluation system must be revised to make salary, bonus, and promotion policies consistent with the stated corporate goals. If goal congruency does not exist, employees quickly recognize the variables in their performance that are critical to their success. A company should not claim to want to be "the leading environmentally responsible company" and reward employees strictly on financial performance. If environmental performance is truly important, evaluations and rewards should highlight that component. A company that sincerely wants to change its corporate culture and establish and maintain a position of environmental leadership must make the environmental performance of individuals, facilities, and divisions an integral part of the performance evaluation.

Using an Environmental Multiplier to Drive Performance

Among the most advanced and explicit integrations of environmental performance into performance evaluation systems is that used by Browning-Ferris Industries (BFI). With 37,000 employees, BFI is one of the largest companies involved in the collection and disposal of solid wastes. In the late 1980s, the company decided a change in corporate direction was necessary, and former EPA administrator, William Ruckelshaus, was brought in as CEO. He recognized that the company

EXHIBIT 10–2
Browning-Ferris Industries (Mission Statement)

Mission Statement

Our mission is to provide the highest quality waste collection, transportation, processing, disposal and related services to both public and private customers worldwide. We will carry out our mission efficiently, safely and in an environmentally responsible manner with respect for the role of government in protecting the public interest.

---

needed to view society's changing requirements for corporate environmental responsibility as new opportunities for BFI rather than as regulations to battle. In attempting to reposition itself for future growth, the company decided in 1990 that a fundamental change in the corporate culture was necessary. The decision to become "truly compliant" at almost any cost became an obsession. Whether the initial impetus for that decision was improved public relations, regulatory pressure, concern for the long-term profitability of the enterprise, a new understanding of the concerns of the various corporate stakeholders, or a new mandate from senior corporate executives is not at present critical. What is important is that a successful change in corporate culture requires a bold implementation strategy. Though the company did develop a new mission statement (see Exhibit 10–2) that includes environmental compliance as a critical element, it recognized that a new strategy was necessary to effect this change in corporate culture.

Among the first steps was the development of Awareness & Compliance Tools (ACT) for Environmental Responsibility. They provide specific guidance for the training necessary to meet newly established corporate environmental objectives (see Exhibit 10–3). The objectives used for measuring environmental performance are very specific. They include both core corporate objectives and regional objectives that apply both to specific business needs and community needs. A different set of ACT tools was developed for each of the three major lines of business: landfill operations, solid waste, and medical waste. In addition, a detailed training manual of more than 200 pages describes the objectives and explains the problems and the role of all employees in achieving corpo-

EXHIBIT 10–3
Browning-Ferris Industries (ACT Performance Objectives)

A.C.T.
— for —
Environmental
Responsibility

BFI Landfill
Awareness & Compliance Tools

PERFORMANCE OBJECTIVES

Participants in this program need these fundamental job performance skills to be able to act for environmental compliance in their day-to-day work.

1 — Perspective on Compliance
- Understand BFI's compliance program and management's support for compliance.
- Be aware of the impact noncompliance can have on our landfill.
- Begin working as a cross-functional team to achieve compliance at your site.

2 — The Law
- Be aware of basic federal laws that apply to landfill business.
- Be aware of BFI's commitment to complying with those laws.
- Learn how to look up basic state and local laws that govern landfill operations.

3 — Surface Water Management Overview
- Understand your site surface water management plan.
- Identify surface water management problems.

4 — Ground Water
- Become aware of ground water's importance.
- Understand the concept of ground water quality.
- Obtain a basic knowledge of ground water monitoring.

5 — Leachate
- Be aware of what leachate is and the importance of controlling it.
- Understand how BFI manages leachate.
- Know your role in detecting leaks and preventing spills.

6 — UST/AST
- Be aware of the hazards of aboveground and underground storage tanks.
- Understand the basics about your site's UST Management Plan and SPCC Plan.
- Be aware of record keeping requirements.
- Know your role in detecting leaks and preventing spills.

7 — Air Quality
- Be aware of air quality issues that relate to landfills.
- Identify possible air emission sources at your site.

---

rate environmental compliance and responsibility. ACT tools include training videos and extensive, detailed tools to aid all employees in meeting the performance objectives. Exhibit 10–4 shows one of the tools, a Leak Detection Guide. It is a self-adhesive sticker listing changes that might indicate troublesome leaks.

EXHIBIT 10–4
Browning-Ferris Industries (Leak Detection Guide)

Leak Detection Guide

**Watch for and report any
of these changes. They could
be signs of leaks.**

✓ Dead grass and plants

✓ More odor or vapor than normal

✓ Oil or fuel stains on concrete or in soil

✓ Problems in dispensing fuel

✓ Unexplained level change inside a tank

✓ Water in a tank

✓ Caved-in pavement

✓ Oil sheen on surface water or in
  storm drain

✓ Smell of petroleum (oil) in basements

✓ Oil or fuel buildup in pavement joints

✓ Leak detection alarm going off

✓ Presence of oil or fuel in containment
  structure

A.C.T.
Environmental
Responsibility

Senior corporate officers recognized that to implement this change in strategy effectively, they needed to change incentives. The company needed to tie environmental performance directly to employee pay. A new system was implemented beginning in fiscal year 1991. It provided that one-third of total compensation was at-risk pay and integrated an environmental compliance component into the total bonus calculation. Exhibits 10–5 and 10–6 are the multiplier scale and the computation worksheet used in the performance evaluation system. The scale is used to convert the total points earned on the environmental compliance goals to the environmental multiplier. Thus, a score of 70 will permit an employee to receive only 25 percent of the incentive pay related to financial and revenue objectives as described below. A score of less than 70

EXHIBIT 10–5
Browning-Ferris Industries (Multiplier Scale)

Points Earned	District Environmental Multiplier
95-100	1.00
90-94	0.90
85-89	0.80
80-84	0.75
75-79	0.50
70-74	0.25
below 70	0.00

produces a multiplier of 0. This scoring method is obviously a powerful motivator of performance for a company that desires to change corporate culture to produce a more environmentally sensitive company.

The district manager work plan for collection/solid waste again shows the importance of meeting the performance objectives discussed above. The maximum incentive award is shown to be 50 percent of the base salary. Then the scoring of the environmental performance is recorded to determine the environmental multiplier. The scoring is a very explicit determination comparing actual performance with preset corporate, regional, and district goals. In collection/solid waste, financial objectives make up 45 percent of the incentive plan after a minimum threshold return on asset is achieved. Another 15 percent of the incentive award depends on a quality-of-revenue calculation with both revenue and cost per unit components. The total of these two elements is multiplied by the environmental multiplier. Nonfinancial objectives such as customer retention, which do not relate to environmental performance, are calculated separately and added to the previous total to determine the total employee bonus award. The first two categories are multiplied by the environmental multiplier to encourage employees to make the proper trade-offs when authorizing expenditures on environmental projects. Attempting to reduce spending on environmental projects can have a seriously detrimental

EXHIBIT 10–6
Browning-Ferris Industries (Computation Worksheet)

**1994 DISTRICT MANAGER COLLECTION/SOLID WASTE INCENTIVE PLAN
WORKPLAN**   Recycled paper

Name:_____   District:_____ Region:_____

Base Salary Effective 9/30/94 $_____   Maximum Total Award 50% x Base Sal $_____

DIVISIONAL FINANCIAL THRESHOLD: FY'94 RODAAC must exceed FY'93 RODAAC for plan eligibility.
                          FY'93 RODAAC:_____   FY'94 RODAAC:_____

Environmental Multiplier			
Performance on Environmental Goals:	Maximum Points Available 100	Actual Points Earned	Environmental Multiplier

FINANCIAL OBJECTIVES (45%)

1. Div Revenue Growth	Maximum Component Weight of 15% and Max $ Award of $_____ Revenue Threshold = $_____ (Actual FY'93 Revenue) Maximum Payout at $_____ Revenue Actual FY'94 Revenue = $_____ Actual Performance = ___% Actual $ Award = Actual Performance % x Max $ Award = $_____	
2. Divisional EBNOT	Max Component Weight of 30% and Max $ Award of $_____ EBNOT Threshold = $_____ (Actual FY'93 EBNOT) Maximum Payout at $_____ EBNOT Actual FY'94 EBNOT = $_____ Actual Performance = ___% Actual $ Award = Actual Performance % x Max $ Award = $_____	
	Total Award: Financial Performance	$

DISTRICT SPECIFIC QUALITY OF REVENUE OBJECTIVES (15%)

District Specific Quality of Revenue	Max Component Weight of 15% and Max $ Award of $_____					
	Net Rev/Unit Target	Maximum Weight	Maximum $ Award	Actual Peformance %	Total $ Award	
	Net Cost/Unit Target	Maximum Weight	Maximum $ Award	Actual Peformance %	Total $ Award	
	Total Award: Quality of Revenue Performance					$
	Subtotal of Financial & Quality of Rev Awards:					$
	x Environmental Multiplier:					
						$

NON-FINANCIAL OBJECTIVES (40%)

Objectives	Maximum Weight	Maximum $ Award	Target	Actual Performance	Total $ Award	
1. Customer Retention	10%					
2. District Specific Objectives:						
a)_____	10%					
b)_____	10%					
c)_____	10%					
	30%					
Total Award: Non-Financial Performance						$

TOTAL 1994 BONUS AWARD (Financial + Quality of Revenue + Non-Financial Awards)	$

_____   _____   _____   _____
(District Manager)   (Date)   (Division Vice President)   (Date)

effect on an employee bonus if environmental performance does not meet objectives.

The advantage of a compound incentive plan like the one in use at BFI is clear. When multiple performance measures are used, an additive system would permit employees to focus on one or two goals at the expense of the others, without severe penalty. Under a compound plan, the multiplicative effect encourages employees to consider all company objectives and goals rather than to ignore some performance measures and still receive a bonus. But the weights on each performance measure might indeed focus more attention on one or two goals.

The performance evaluation system is applied to district and division managers because it is these managers who can control the outcome of their decisions. The system is intended to encourage these managers to be proactive rather than reactive. It encourages them to plan and budget for environmental responsibility rather than react to crises and be concerned only with minimum compliance. The scores are evaluated by regional environmental compliance managers, regional vice presidents, and the vice president of operations. If an employee receives a score of less than 70, this very explicit system allows for no bonus to be earned under the Financial and Quality of Revenue Objectives. It is also quite likely that the employee will be terminated. According to the established corporate culture, employees with low environmental performance scores are not exhibiting the type of behavior the company desires.

The company believes that this emphasis on environmental compliance helps its public image, will affect what the community is saying about BFI (in turn affecting the success of BFI salespeople), and ultimately will have an important impact on corporate financial performance. The system works, in part, because employees throughout the organization understand that environmental compliance is not negotiable and is a critical success variable for both the company's performance and their own performance. Though this system of incentive pay does not apply to anyone below the district manager level, those district managers have incentives to encourage their subordinates to be environmentally responsible so as to make their bonus achievable.

All company employees are trained under the ACT program described above and are reminded constantly of the importance of environmental performance to BFI. On new corporate acquisitions or new appointments, specific budget allocations can be made in addition to any holdbacks inserted in the acquisition documents. Providing a specific budget allocation ensures that a prior lack of compliance by a previous company that causes substantial expenditures on the part of BFI does not affect the reduced division profit and the performance evaluation of the manager.

At BFI, as at other progressive companies, some unintended benefits do arise.[1] This environmental performance evaluation system has been entered into evidence in various court or regulatory proceedings regarding environmental compliance to document the company's commitment to the environment. Courts and regulators have been more responsive to requests and more sympathetic to concerns because the company has demonstrated through past actions and company programs that it indeed is trying to improve its corporate environmental performance.

OTHER EXAMPLES OF THE INTEGRATION OF ENVIRONMENTAL RESPONSIBILITY INTO PERFORMANCE EVALUATIONS

DuPont has determined that environmental performance should be used in determining total compensation and has identified three broad categories for consideration:

- Compliance with corporate policy;
- Proactive initiation of programs;
- Incidents with adverse potential.

Though an explicit percentage of total compensation is not predetermined, business unit managers are expected to develop written and measurable objectives consistent with corporate goals. Through this approach, DuPont uses performance evaluation to move closer to its goal of becoming more environmentally responsible.

Polaroid has established a strong policy statement and goals for improved environmental performance. Environmental management is one of seven specific performance criteria used for assessing managers' effectiveness. (The other six are cost, quality, scheduling, inventory, safety, and diversity.) Though environmental management is included in the performance evaluation system, no specific weightings are determined. Management has significant discretion as to its importance in a

---

1. See the related discussion in Chapter 7 of Sun Company's signing the CERES Principles.

particular manager's evaluation. The combination of the Toxic Use and Waste Reduction framework, the corporate infrastructure, and corporate efforts to involve every employee in the process of reducing waste and toxicity are helping Polaroid achieve its current goals and move toward continuous improvement in environmental performance.

At Sun Company, environmental performance does affect bonuses, but as at Polaroid the amount or extent is not explicit. Employees understand that achieving environmental goals is important to the company and affects corporate financial performance and individual compensation.

STRIVING FOR ENVIRONMENTAL RESPONSIBILITY IN A GLOBAL ENTERPRISE

ABB, with more than 200,000 employees worldwide in the business of producing and distributing electricity, comprises 1,300 companies and 5,000 profit centers with clearly defined accountability. This large number poses a challenge for change in any corporate culture and for the establishment of a uniform performance evaluation system. Using a matrix structure for its organization, ABB has developed a general format for management incentive plans, but particular geographic and business-specific changes can be made as needed.

In its mission statement, ABB commits itself to "meeting societal goals for sustainable development and clean energy." The challenge is how to develop and implement an environmental strategy that achieves those goals. For ABB, developing cost-effective technology to maintain "the delicate balance between meeting the world's needs and protecting the environment" is central to the company's business. ABB Service in the United States, which provides various environmental services, provides incentives to employees to meet environmental goals by generally allocating 20 percent of incentive pay to environmental performance. In other companies within ABB, the percentage allocated to environmental performance goals ranges from 0–20 percent. Though such a system is explicit and establishes specific goals, at least 80 percent of total incentive pay and a far greater percentage of total pay depends on profit and revenue growth in the company and the region. Thus, individuals may choose to trade off environmental performance for profit or revenue growth. They still achieve a high level of incentive pay and are evaluated favorably by superiors because of strong growth.

We have argued here that it is difficult to achieve maximum environmental performance and goals of sustainability or environmental excellence unless management sends a clear message that environmental performance is critical to the company. If performance is evaluated based on profit or revenue contributions, employees quickly recognize that trade-offs on the environment are acceptable: any desired change in corporate culture becomes impossible.

Ciba-Geigy makes environmental protection an integral part of performance evaluation and of the incentive system. It defines targets in various ways and measures performance against those targets. The system is not necessarily applied uniformly throughout the organization. It differs based on an employee's level of responsibility in the organization and on the business unit's goals themselves. Each business unit has environmental objectives, and the rewards will be based on the performance of both the business unit and the individual. The system is explicit, it measures environmental performance in physical units rather than dollars, and the environmental goals do not necessarily have equal weights. Overall business unit performance used in performance evaluation decisions is affected by environmental performance, but managers are given discretion to override a poor environmental performance in the overall performance evaluation and bonus system.

This system is in contrast to the BFI system described above, in which bonuses are eliminated if environmental performance is not at least at a minimal level. In addition, the possibility of a manager's overriding a performance appraisal provides the benefit of discretion in the system but may communicate less of a commitment to employees if excellent financial performance can compensate for poor environmental performance. The decision of how explicit to make environmental performance in performance evaluation systems thus has several components. It must be tailored to each company's specific orientation, organization, and needs.

Some companies make the environmental goals explicit for each business unit so that monitoring for continuous improvement is encouraged. Alcan Aluminum, for example, requires that compliance reviews be conducted every three years on every operating entity and location. It then requires the management of each business unit to provide an annual representation letter based on the compliance review and other business unit information. The letter reports on "its current environmental status, identifies changing requirements, risks, and hazards, and outlines environmental plans and financial requirements for that business unit."

This representation letter is submitted to the environmental committee of the board of directors and the CEO. It helps the company understand the corporate capital needs for environmental protection along with needed research and development and required process improvements. With approaches such as this, a company can encourage managers to focus on environmental status, risks, and plans. They are held accountable for the results of that analysis and planning.

ICI uses another approach. It views environmental improvement as one of six key performance objectives that affect its top 100 people. While the overall approach is to use quantitative measures applicable to all employees, each affected employee's performance criteria are individualized. The individual criteria are specified in an agreement between the operating unit's chief executive and the employee.

For most senior managers, ICI multiplies a base bonus contingent on the company's overall performance by a factor of between 0 and 1.5. This factor depends on the employee's success in fulfilling six corporate performance objectives and their relative importance to the employee's particular job.

Since it instituted a formal waste management program in 1983, Amoco Corporation has reduced the amount of hazardous wastes produced within its chemical company by 95 percent. This feat has been accomplished, in part, through a program that established specific performance goals for facility managers and holds senior managers accountable for environmental performance. The program is administered by a Waste Management Committee that balances the costs and liabilities associated with the "generation, recycling, reclamation, and disposal of wastes." The program is critical for Amoco, which has annual environmental expenditures of $1 billion.

THE USE OF COMPANY ENVIRONMENTAL AWARDS FOR EMPLOYEES

Many companies have programs that provide awards to employees for exemplary environmental performance. In some cases awards are given to teams rather than individuals. They vary from cash gifts and various methods of acknowledging the achievement to banquets, plaques, and so on. Chevron, for example, has a recognition and awards program that provides rewards for doing things right. It is a positive incentive for employees to go beyond their job responsibility and to become eligible for a cash award of $500 to $5,000. Awards can be useful but only in connection with a more comprehensive program of performance evaluation that includes other motivations for improved environmental performance among divisions, their managers, and their support staff.

THE USE OF INTERNAL WASTE AND ENVIRONMENTAL TAXES

One way to motivate behavior is through the use of a waste tax. Dow Chemical built a waste landfill at its Michigan division that was expected to last until 2007. Over the last several years, the company began charging each plant a fee according to the actual waste it brings to the landfill. Plants discovered that it was more economical to introduce process improvements to reduce the quantity of waste. This Dow internal waste tax has reduced solid waste by 50 percent. The Michigan landfill now is expected to last until 2034. The combination of integrating environmental impacts into product costs and then driving those costs into the performance evaluation system can be a powerful motivator of individual behavior.

An Ontario Hydro study recommended the establishment of a "liability fund." This fund would comprise monies collected from customers for asset removal, decommissioning, irradiated fuel disposal, and radioactive waste disposal. In addition, a provision for the amounts in prior years, including interest, would be fully funded.

Some companies have argued that a waste tax might work better in highly centralized organizations than in less centralized ones. In decentralized organizations there is the concern that a central tax imposed on business units would not fit in with the corporate culture and would meet with resistance. The orientation is often to allow the managers to make their own trade-offs of business and environmental improvements if such must be made rather than obtaining penalties or extra funds through internal taxes and redistributing those funds. But such waste taxes have provided information to business units on the costs of environmental pollution and often motivate managers to reduce waste.

SUMMARY

Union Carbide has set an explicit 1996 goal for environmental compliance. Top management has signed on, and the goal has been made public.

If it is not achieved, the corporation and its officers and employees expect to be held accountable. Corporations, their officers, and employees should be rewarded for significant environmental improvements.

For companies that indeed want to improve corporate environmental performance, the development of incentives is important. The performance of all employees, teams, facilities, and business units must include an environmental performance component. Environmental successes must be included along with financial successes. In the long run, environmental performance and financial performance are interrelated. One cannot continue to strive for environmental excellence while evaluating and rewarding performance strictly on short-term financial indicators.

Chapter Eleven

Implementing a Corporate Environmental Strategy

This research project began as an attempt to survey and document integration of environmental impacts into various corporate management decisions. It evolved into a comprehensive examination of not only corporate environmental management practices but also corporate management accounting practices. By looking closely at what may be the most pressing problem in our society—and certainly one of the most costly problems in American business—we can view the way management decisions are made for rapidly evolving management issues.

Environmental costs have grown very large very fast, and most managers and their corporations found themselves unprepared to deal with them. Many of the corporations were crisis prone rather than crisis prepared. Most were using significantly out-of-date techniques in environmental management and costing. They were not making decisions based on the same rational evaluation of options that would be required for other capital investment decisions. They were taking a compliance approach, reacting to environmental crises and government regulations, rather than a planning approach. Few companies were attempting to manage the corporation and its environmental impacts by considering uncertainties and risks and factoring them into forecasts. They were not evaluating alternatives that considered the costs and benefits of environmental improvements.

Environmental management was in a sorry state, and management accountants had not been of much assistance. Environmental staffs often were headed by someone in middle management and reported to a member of the legal counsel's staff. Management accountants typically were not involved in environmental management decisions because those decisions were considered regulatory rather than voluntary, and extensive analysis seemed unnecessary.

In the two and a half years that I devoted to this project, corporate attitudes and practices about corporate environmental performance and corporate environmental impacts have changed dramatically. The concepts of take-back, sustainable development, and the corporation's ultimate responsibility for post-consumer waste are becoming well accepted. Senior corporate executives recognize that a sound corporate environmental strategy is critical to the long-term financial success of most corporations. They view the minimization of negative environmental impacts as a core corporate value.

Now environmental staffs typically are headed by a professional with either significant environmental experience or significant operations experience, or both. Environmental management increasingly is seen as a planning function rather than a compliance function. The senior environmental executive typically has direct access to the corporate CEO and board of directors, and the accounting and finance functions are becoming more involved in EH&S analyses and decisions.

Corporations have begun to recognize that accounting and financial analysis and evaluation techniques are very useful in developing alternatives. Proper decisions can be made only if environmental costs are tracked and assigned properly. The large increase in environmental costs had produced incorrect product costs, causing the corporation to make improper costing and pricing decisions. As companies have begun to integrate environmental impacts into product costing, capital investment, and performance evaluation decisions, they typically have seen environmental performance and financial performance improve.

Increasingly, analysis demonstrated how some products were undercosted and some overcosted because significant environmental costs caused by a few products were being spread to all. Corporations noticed that identifying environmental impacts and carrying out rigorous financial analyses increased profitability. Costs were better controlled, and companies could evaluate whether process improvements, product improvements, or capital improvements would best reduce long-term product costs. This process was aided by the involvement of the operations, legal, accounting, and engineering departments. They assisted the environmental department in evaluating alternatives that would reduce environmental impacts.

These evaluations also aided companies in making decisions about alternative capital improvements of both pollution prevention and control equipment and general capital investment, project investment, and facility design and location. The more advanced analyses now often include formal analyses of the uncertainties related to the future changes in environmental regulations, changing technologies, and changing costs of technologies.

All these decisions require the involvement of accounting and finance staff. Corporate accountants have had to change their focus from determining the minimum amount of environmental liability to be accrued to examining the likely future impacts of existing production on both the environment and the company. Management accountants now also must consider the likely impact of regulations, technology, and competition on a corporate environmental strategy and the effect of those factors on future product costs and future profitability.

In this rapidly changing business environment, minimizing environmental impacts and redesigning products and processes often can create a competitive advantage. The way companies have adapted to this evolving issue indicates the quality and foresight of their management and their willingness and ability to change the corporate culture when necessary and appropriate. This study served as an excellent opportunity to observe how corporate accounting and accountants and corporations and their managers can adapt to changing internal and external needs, demands, and pressures.

SCORING CORPORATE ENVIRONMENTAL PERFORMANCE

Over and over again, corporate officers asked me how their environmental performance compared to that of others in their industry. This book describes various approaches companies have taken to improve environmental performance and integrate corporate environmental impacts into management decisions. It will permit companies to benchmark their performance. But this area is changing as rapidly as any evolving area in corporate decision making and planning I have ever seen. Corporate environmental leaders will not remain leaders if they do not continue to develop and progress continuously.

This extensive field research has allowed me to identify the 10 components of corporate environmental integration described in this book, corresponding to Chapters 2 through 11. They are indicators of corporate environmental performance. The Measures of Corporate Environmental

EXHIBIT 11–1
Corporate Environmental Performance Scorecard

TEN COMPONENTS OF CORPORATE ENVIRONMENTAL INTEGRATION		MEASURES OF ENVIRONMENTAL LEADERSHIP
1. Development of a corporate environmental strategy	CORPORATE ENVIRONMENTAL LEADER	1.0 Implementation of corporate environmental strategy Significant integration of corporate environmental impacts into management decisions Moving toward sustainable development
2. Integrating environmental concerns into product design systems		
3. Systems for identifying, organizing, and managing environmental impacts		2.0 Significant progress in at least five components and at least modest progress in two others
4. Information systems for internal reporting		3.0 Significant progress in at least three or four components and modest progress in at least two others
5. Internal environmental auditing systems		4.0 Modest progress in at least three or four components and some progress in at least two others
6. External environmental reporting and external environmental audits		5.0 Development of environmental goals Beginnings of an action plan Some progress in at least one or two components
7. Costing systems		
8. Capital budgeting systems		6.0 Development of approach to environmental problems but with compliance orientation Minimal sensitivity to corporate environmental impacts
9. Integrating environmental impacts into performance evaluation systems		
10. Implementing a corporate environmental strategy	CORPORATE ENVIRONMENTAL LAGGARD	7.0 No recognition of environmental impacts and minimal compliance with regulations Continuous violations of regulations

Leadership are summarized, with the 10 components of corporate environmental integration, on a Corporate Environmental Performance Scorecard in Exhibit 11–1 and are described in detail in Exhibit 11–2. These measures should prove useful to corporations as they evaluate their performance.

EXHIBIT 11–2

Measures of Corporate Environmental Leadership

1.0 **Corporate Environmental Leadership**
    Significant performance in at least six or seven components of corporate environmental integration
    Some progress in at least three additional components
    Life cycle assessments of present and future products and services
    Sensitivity and integration of environmental impacts into management decisions throughout organization—at all levels, in all facilities, in all business units, and in all geographic regions.
    Evaluation of all environmental impacts of corporate investments, processes, and products
    Moving toward sustainable development

2.0 *Significant* performance in at least five components of corporate environmental integration
    Some or modest progress in at least two additional components
    Plans for improved progress in all components
    Some progress on integration of functional disciplines for long-term corporate environmental improvement
    Significant transfer of technologies and analysis techniques across divisions and facilities

3.0 *Significant* progress in at least three or four components of corporate environmental integration
    Modest progress in at least two additional components
    Significant focus on corporate environmental planning in addition to compliance

4.0 *Modest* progress in at least three or four components of corporate environmental integration
    Some progress in at least one or two additional components
    Some two-way communication with various corporate stakeholders including employees, suppliers, customers, and the community
    Broad identification of corporate environmental impacts—some measurement and reporting of those impacts

5.0 Development of corporate environmental goals
    Beginning of a system for implementation of action plan
    Beginning of development of an action plan to compare corporate environmental performance
    Inclusion of environmental sensitivity in corporate mission
    Some progress in at least one or two components of corporate environmental integration
    Beginning to develop and standardize internal documents and manuals for improved environmental education and management.

EXHIBIT 11–2 *(concluded)*

6.0   Minimal general sensitivity to environmental impacts
      Initial development of general approach and organization for confronting
           environmental problems
      Some focus on compliance with existing regulations
      No formulation of solutions to long-term corporate environmental problems

7.0   **Corporate Environmental Laggard**
      No corporate recognition of environmental impacts
      Minimal compliance with environmental regulations
      Continuous violations of some environmental regulations.

Scoring corporate environmental performance is going to surprise many people. Many of the companies we often think of as environmental laggards are progressing rapidly. They are confronting their environmental problems and dealing with them aggressively. Some of these companies are in industries that have been heavy polluters for decades. They are making significant strides in developing strong corporate environmental strategies, changing their corporate cultures, and improving their environmental performance. They often are becoming environmental leaders.

So this scorecard is more a predictor of future environmental performance than it is a measure of past performance. It also may measure a company's management and control of potential future liabilities. To the extent that environmental impacts and corporate profitability are linked, it may be useful in forecasting future financial performance. Many of the companies I visited only now are beginning to integrate environmental impacts into management decisions. Thus, this scorecard measures environmental leadership by evaluating a company's integration of environmental concerns into corporate culture and management decisions. Numerous measures already exist that evaluate how well companies have performed using different environmental variables. What should interest both financial analysts and environmentalists more is how well a company is positioned for future environmental performance.

Readers also should be cautious in comparing performance across industries. Some companies have more difficult environmental problems because of their industries and products, while others have problems due to the age of their facilities. Neither financial analysts nor environmentalists can reasonably expect companies to abandon old production facilities or change production processes radically overnight, but it is reasonable to expect that companies are planning effectively to minimize both present and future environmental impacts.

Not only will many corporate executives, government regulators, and environmentalists be surprised by some of the leaders, but so will many financial analysts and shareholders. Those companies that are environmental laggards also may be laggards in other areas of corporate planning and in confronting and dealing with changing societal needs and pressures. They may be failing to meet customer needs as they fail to meet government and societal needs. These scores may indicate the foresight of corporate management in dealing with emerging corporate issues. They may be a sign that the managers of environmental laggards are generally less nimble as managers than are managers of the corporate environmental leaders.

Financial analysts, shareholders, and corporate managers should be concerned for other reasons. Regulators (EPA, FASB, and SEC) are encouraging companies to evaluate their present and future environmental liabilities better for both internal and external decision making. Many companies have hundreds of millions or billions of dollars' worth of environmental liabilities that are not at present on their corporate financial statements. As financial analysts' understanding of and interest in these contingent environmental liabilities increase, the share prices of companies not adequately confronting their environmental impacts likely will be affected.

These liabilities are greater than the current environmental liabilities associated with Superfund. A company may need to recognize the liabilities on its balance sheet. More important, the size of these liabilities demands the integration of environmental impacts into the core management decisions being made daily. A company must consider the likely future responsibility for reuse, recycling, or ultimate disposal of its products. It must take into account the impact of present and likely future regulations, including the Clean Air Act Amendments and the Clean Water Act. The potential future liabilities and likely management actions to minimize those impacts are apt to affect corporate share prices and cost of capital.

SOME SURPRISES FROM THE FIELD RESEARCH

The book includes throughout descriptions of both the state of the art and best practices in corporate environmental management and the

EXHIBIT 11–3
Some Surprises from the Field Research

Some Disappointments

1. Available financial tools are seldom used in corporate environmental decisions though often used elsewhere in the company.

2. There is little functional cooperation between EH&S and other departments.

3. Proven environmental technologies are seldom transferred across divisions and facilities within corporations.

4. There is little broad thinking about the future impacts of corporate products on various stakeholders and on both the environment and long-term corporate profitability.

5. Most companies narrowly define environmental liabilities for both external reporting and internal decision making; limited to Superfund and ignoring Clean Water Act, Clean Air Act, and other regulations.

6. Most companies have compliance orientation rather than planning orientation for environmental impacts.

7. Most companies do not know the amount of their environmental costs because they are hidden in various overhead accounts.

8. Most companies have made little or no attempt to motivate employees for improved environmental performance.

Some Pleasant Surprises

1. Some of the most environmentally sensitive and most progressive companies are the ones often thought to be the worst polluters. They often have the best environmental management systems and are likely to make the most progress in reducing future environmental impacts.

2. An increasing number of companies are making significant efforts to improve environmental decision making using available analytical approaches.

3. An increasing number of companies have adopted the concept of sustainable development as a core value.

4. An increasing number of companies are using life cycle analysis to examine the impacts of their products from cradle to grave.

5. The quantity and quality of external environmental reporting in both corporate annual reports and in separate environmental reports has increased dramatically.

6. An increasing number of companies are trying to get accounting, operations, legal, and EH&S managers together to aid in analyzing and planning for reduced environmental impacts through process and product redesign.

7. CEOs generally recognize the concept of product take-back and acknowledge the need to integrate the ultimate responsibility for product disposition into costing and capital investment decisions.

8. Internal environmental audit practices generally are well developed and are constantly being improved.

measurement of corporate environmental performance. The field research brought many surprises. They are summarized in Exhibit 11–3 and discussed below.

Disappointments

I was disappointed that most companies that do use sophisticated financial tools for capital investment decisions throughout their organizations do not transfer these tools to the EH&S departments for use in environmentally related decisions.

I was disappointed to find very little functional cooperation between EH&S and other departments and divisions. In most organizations accounting and finance personnel participate very little in environmentally related decisions. When improved scientific and financial methods for planning for and reducing environmental impacts are determined, many decentralized organizations do not implement those methods effectively or widely. In some cases, the divisions do not see the benefit, and in others the environment is not seen as a core corporate value.

Most companies were not as far along as I had expected in improving their environmental management practices. The tremendous increase in environmental costs should have moved companies to tackle these costs much earlier. Few companies have been estimating the future costs and benefits of environmental impacts for use in costing or capital budgeting decisions. Thus many project evaluations are incomplete and investment decisions incorrect. Products continually are being undercosted if foreseeable environmental costs are ignored, leading to a decrease in future corporate profitability.

For improved internal decision making, companies need better methods for identifying, measuring, monitoring, and reporting environmental impacts. For proper reporting of environmental liabilities to external decision makers, companies need better ways to evaluate the liabilities. Public accounting, auditing, and consulting firms are capable of performing these services but often have not been servicing their clients adequately. The liability of both corporate management and public accounting firms to corporate shareholders is going to increase steadily because of the lack of adequate disclosure of environmental liabilities. Those environmental liabilities must include a broad concept of likely environmental impacts rather than a narrow consideration of impacts under Superfund. Companies need to consider environmental performance as a variable in evaluating total corporate performance.

In many companies the EH&S function has a compliance orientation rather than a planning orientation. It focuses too much on past and present regulations, technology, and performance and not enough on future regulations, technology, and performance. This orientation sometimes is shown by direct control of the environmental function by the chief legal counsel.

Companies generally are not thinking broadly enough about their likely environmental impacts. They need to look at the impacts on their various stakeholders and then measure those impacts. Most companies have no inventory of their environmental costs and thus do not even know how much they are spending. Those costs too often are lumped in various overhead accounts and not assigned to the products or facilities that caused them.

We know that if companies do indeed want to drive superior environmental performance throughout the organization, they need to integrate it into the performance evaluation system to motivate employees adequately. Companies cannot expect employees to integrate environmental impacts into management decisions if the rewards are based entirely on division profits. They must ensure that all employees view corporate environmental performance as critical to the long-run financial success of the corporation. The only way to do so is by integrating measures of corporate environmental performance throughout the organization.

Pleasant Surprises

I was surprised to find that many of the companies that are often thought to be among the worst polluters are currently also among the most environmentally sensitive and have developed the best systems for minimizing future environmental impacts.

I was surprised to see how many companies are making substantial efforts to develop better systems for the costing and capital budgeting of environmentally related projects. Companies recognize increasingly that better measures are required to improve reporting and decision making in this area so as to reduce environmental impacts and improve long-term corporate performance.

I was pleased to see that a remarkable number of companies have recognized the importance of the concept of sustainable development and are applying that concept to corporate planning. Many of these companies are trying sincerely to change a corporate culture that has existed for 100 years or more and to make the company more environmentally sensitive.

I was surprised to see the substantial number of companies that are using life cycle analysis to help them understand the likely impacts of their products from "cradle to cradle" (a term that implies "from creation to re-creation," through recycling). By broadly identifying impacts, trying to measure those impacts, considering both present and future effects, and integrating these considerations into decisions, companies do reduce long-term effects on the environment and improve corporate profits.

I was pleased to see the rapid increase in environmental reporting in both corporate annual reports and environmental reports. The quality of disclosures has improved, and the number of corporations that make substantive disclosures has increased dramatically, with the numbers almost doubling every year.

I was pleased to see that some companies have developed environmental accrual committees composed of managers from EH&S, accounting, operations, and legal to determine the accrual of the environmental contingent liability. These enlightened companies have seen the benefit of:

- Coordinating across functions;
- Analyzing possible impacts on the company of pending regulations;
- Considering the company's possible responses through redesign of products and processes.

These benefits can be achieved if solutions are discussed by staff members who understand the impacts, who design the products and processes, who are aware of the legal liabilities, and who understand the financial impacts. The advantages of these group meetings cannot be overstated.

I was surprised to see that a number of companies do recognize that decision making is improved by attempting scientific evaluations using various forecasting methods. Predictions of future impacts are speculative and risk assessments and analyses of uncertainties are difficult, but the information obtained from scenario forecasting, option screening, Monte Carlo simulations, and decision tree analysis is a better basis for decision making than no information at all. Techniques are available that improve decisions when companies are concerned with changing regulations, changing technology, and the changing cost of technology. They also can help companies choose among various capital investments or choose among capital improvements, process improvements, or product improvements.

I was pleased to hear from corporate CEOs that they generally recognize and accept that their companies likely will be held responsible for post-consumer waste through some concept such as the "take-back principle." They also acknowledged that they need to be thinking about the design of their products to minimize the costs of product disassembly and the ultimate responsibility for the reuse, recycling, or ultimate disposition of their products. These executives now need to consider estimating those future costs and bringing them into the costing and capital budgeting decisions through full costing, life cycle analysis, or Environmental Strategic Implementation.

I was pleased to see that the general area of environmental auditing is well developed in industry. But substantially more work needs to be done on coordinating the internal environmental audit function and the burgeoning area of external audits, which are becoming more popular. Further, companies need to empower their employees in a self-audit function because many environmental planning and compliance issues can be discovered most easily by workers dealing with the production and distribution process on a daily basis. Compliance has moved environmental auditing forward. Now, long-term profitability and the reduction of environmental impacts should advance the coordination of external audit, internal audit, and self-audit and the full integration of environmental impacts into management decision making.

The number of examples of reduction, reuse, and recycling of waste is much larger than I imagined. There are hundreds of examples of changes in the design of both products and processes to reduce waste, though not by any means in every company.

Overall, I am convinced that companies are making significant strides in integrating corporate environmental impacts into management decisions. I also am convinced that the combination of regulatory and societal pressures, attempts at gaining competitive advantage, and the need to manage growing costs better will all encourage companies to continue to make progress in improving corporate environmental management systems and corporate environmental performance.

FIFTEEN STEPS TO ENVIRONMENTAL STRATEGY IMPLEMENTATION

This book has centered around how companies can integrate environmental impacts into management decisions and implement a corporate

EXHIBIT 11–4
Fifteen Steps to Environmental Strategy Implementation (ESI)

1. Develop environmental strategy. The corporate CEO should set the tone at the top.

2. Develop organizational structure to effectively implement and measure the success of the environmental strategy. The EH&S department should have direct access to senior corporate officers and a member of the board of directors. EH&S should be charged with the development and implementation of corporate environmental strategy and improved management of resources rather than only legal compliance. It should not be a part of the legal department.

3. Communicate to all stakeholders the importance of good corporate environmental performance on both corporate citizenship and corporate profits. Establish it as a core corporate value.

4. Integrate environmental information into the financial and managerial information systems so that managers can integrate environmental impacts into all management decisions.

5. Identify environmental impacts including benefits and costs. Think broadly and consider both current and future impacts. Consider impacts on both the company and society. Complete Total Stakeholder Analysis (TSA) as part of a life cycle assessment.

6. Measure impacts.

7. Prepare an inventory of current environmental activities related to pollution prevention and control. Track and accumulate current environmental costs related to current production.

8. Integrate current and future environmental impacts (costs and benefits) into all corporate decisions including product costing, product pricing, product design, and capital investments.

9. Integrate accounting and financial analysis techniques including risk assessment into environmental decisions. This integration will permit improved analysis of choices among product improvements, process improvements, and capital improvements and greater understanding of uncertainties related to changing regulations, technology, and the cost of technology. Existing cost estimation models are available to assist in this analysis.

10. Estimate future environmental costs related to current production including ultimate responsibility for product disposal.

11. Develop and implement a reporting strategy for both internal and external stakeholders and decision makers. EH&S, legal, accounting, and operations executives should be involved in an accrual committee to determine liabilities and consider environmental improvements.

EXHIBIT 11–4 *(concluded)*

12. Develop a monitoring system for environmental impacts so that the size of environmental contingent liabilities will not be a surprise to internal or external decision makers and can be better managed and controlled. This monitoring often leads to substantial cost savings as processes are improved.

13. Integrate corporate environmental performance into performance evaluation systems already in the organization. Incentives based totally on division profits provide a signal that environmental performance is unimportant. Consider environmental performance as a variable in the evaluation of total corporate performance. All employees must view corporate environmental performance as critical to the long-run financial success of the corporation.

14. Provide incentives for employees to suggest environmental improvements. These suggestions ultimately will lead to corporate profit improvements.

15. Provide feedback throughout the organization related to the impacts of various decisions so that environmental strategy can be updated continuously as corporate impacts, regulations, and technology change.

---

environmental strategy. Chapters 2 through 11 discussed the 10 components of corporate environmental integration summarized on the scorecard. They provided guidance on the state of the art, best corporate practices, and ways to implement an environmental strategy. Exhibit 11–4 is more explicit, providing 15 steps to the Environmental Strategy Implementation discussed throughout the book. Moving through a format such as this provides the guidance many companies find helpful in getting started or progressing in this critical area.

ADDITIONAL GUIDELINES FOR MANAGERS AND MANAGEMENT ACCOUNTANTS

In this book, we have presented many new opportunities for accounting personnel to contribute to improved management decisions by providing better information on the environmental impacts of corporate activities. Bristol-Myers Squibb included several checklists in its pollution prevention initiative. One checklist provides suggested items for managers to consider that will increase environmental sensitivity (see Exhibit 11–5).

EXHIBIT 11–5
Bristol-Myers Squibb (General Management Checklist)

General Management Checklist

❑ Establish pollution prevention through product life cycle analysis and environmental protection as a priority in the highest levels of management.

❑ Appoint a senior manager to be directly responsible for environmental issues and pollution prevention.

❑ Ensure that environmental goals are in sync with financial and production strategies and organizational structure.

❑ Establish environmental goals which are measurable and which are monitored on a regular basis.

❑ Establish a system for rewarding effective pollution prevention ideas.

❑ Design company-wide training courses to teach basic environmental awareness and pollution prevention techniques.

❑ Foster an "esprit de corps" and pride in setting an example in environmental matters at all organizational levels.

❑ Hold public meetings with the surrounding community to discuss mutually acceptable environmental initiatives.

❑ Consider long-term financial benefits of pollution prevention efforts arising from short-term capital expenditures.

❑ Consider sponsoring community-based environmental initiatives to conserve land, species, and the quality of air and water.

❑ Link environmental performance to existing quality programs.

A second checklist (Exhibit 11–6) provides useful items for internal and external accountants to consider in viewing their potential roles and responsibilities in this area. Going through this checklist would help management accountants provide useful information for management decision making. With the checklist external accountants, auditors, and consultants could bring better quality and expanded services to their clients.

Information is required to make improved decisions related to product costing, product pricing, product and process design, capital investments, and performance evaluations for corporations, their business units, and

EXHIBIT 11–6
Bristol-Myers Squibb (Purchasing, Finance, and Accounting Checklist)

Purchasing, Finance, and Accounting Checklist

❑ Estimate the costs of pollution prevention projects.

❑ Determine the benefits of a pollution prevention project by utilizing return on investment, payback period, and net present value techniques, together with other non-routine corporate benefits.

❑ Utilize financial and accounting personnel to determine whether incurred costs are capital or operating in nature.

❑ Utilize financial and accounting personnel to determine the appropriate timing of the recording of incurred costs.

❑ Involve financial and accounting personnel in development of project tracking systems.

❑ Subject all investments to ecological evaluation:
  • Will it increase pollution?
  • Will it increase ecological risks?
  • Will it protect the environment?

❑ Consider the financial dimensions of costs and risks involved if a particular investment is likely to cause or increase pollution. Factors that can be costly to ignore include:
  • Probable future costs for disposal of wastes, and
  • Possible changes in regulatory thresholds.

their employees. Managers need better information to handle environmental and other rapidly changing, critical issues. Company personnel from accounting, finance, legal, engineering, operations, and EH&S should be coordinated to gather information and provide inputs. They then can improve the decisions related to products and processes that can minimize environmental impacts and their related costs.

Management accountants have a critical role to play in this process. In many cases it will require additional training in new methods of analysis. But it is essential that management accountants improve the quality and quantity of information they are providing to managers. Financial accountants and auditors need to improve the quality and quantity of external disclosures related to environmental liabilities.

Managers need the information to make better internal decisions, and external users need the information to better evaluate the current and future financial condition of the company. Corporations and their accountants and managers should recognize that the approaches suggested in this book provide opportunities to get started in improving environmental management and to progress incrementally.

CONCLUDING REMARKS

Some have argued that most of the environmental win-win opportunities have been seized and that it will now be much more difficult to achieve benefits through careful environmental management. That idea is contrary to my findings. Most companies are just beginning their analyses of pollution-prevention opportunities. They have not yet fully investigated the areas where redesign of products and processes can lead to significant reductions in environmental costs. Even companies that have been more proactive than reactive generally have not been measuring the costs and benefits adequately.

When corporations more broadly identify the costs and benefits to their various stakeholders through a Total Stakeholder Analysis and measure those costs and benefits, they often find that the positive payoffs are far greater than they ever imagined. Using modern capital budgeting and forecasting techniques further accentuates the benefits of the analysis. Putting these techniques all together in the framework of an Environmental Strategy Implementation has let companies array their products and services and better understand the total environmental impact and product costs. The total costs of current production are likely to include both the total current costs of current production, through better tracking and assignment of environmental costs and activities, and the likely future costs of current production. This knowledge has led to a better understanding of which products do indeed produce long-run profitability.

Many savings and decisions remain easy to make. But a process must be in place to focus attention on company products and processes and to reduce environmental impacts and the related financial costs. The life cycle assessment approach has been suggested, and some discussion of this approach has been included here. The result of constant corporate monitoring and feedback mechanisms aimed at continuous improvement can be improved product quality, improved production yields through reduced waste, and increased profitability.

The approaches suggested in this book can be adapted and implemented by companies in high-impact and low-impact industries, in one location or globally, small or large, with large EH&S staffs or no full-time EH&S personnel. The approaches are meant to improve corporate environmental management practices to minimize corporate environmental negative impacts and also to improve corporate financial performance. The development and implementation of a corporate environmental strategy that integrates environmental impacts into all relevant management decisions is essential for all progressive companies.

The Regulations That Govern Environmental Reporting

I n many instances, the internal measurement, reporting, and management of environmental impacts is dictated by externally imposed regulations. This appendix reviews some of the environmental regulations that govern corporate environmental conduct, and reporting and accounting regulations that guide corporate environmental disclosures.[1] It also provides an update on the latest surveys of environmental practice and discusses some of the latest academic research related to environmental measurement and reporting. Though the regulations, surveys, and research focus primarily on external environmental disclosures, they do provide a foundation for this study's focus on the integration of corporate environmental impacts into management decisions.

Environmental regulations have at least two primary goals—to determine and assess the liability among the parties and to assist in repairing environmental damage. The environmental laws at the federal, state, and local levels can be classified in two categories. One category includes those laws that establish responsibility and the responsible parties for cleanup and remediation of hazardous waste sites. The other category includes those laws that monitor how hazardous wastes are handled, establish compliance standards and liability for personal or property damage, and assess punitive damages for violations of those laws and regulations.

---

1. This appendix draws heavily on and relies on the description of environmental regulations and financial reporting regulations in AICPA, 1993; Johnson, 1993; Barth et al, 1994; Rabinowitz and Murphy, 1992; Selling, 1993; and CH2M Hill, 1993.

ENVIRONMENTAL REGULATIONS

The rapid increase in environmental regulations began in the 1970s. Among the primary laws are the Clean Air Act (CAA), the Clean Water Act (CWA), the Resources Conservation and Recovery Act (RCRA), the Comprehensive Environmental Response, Compensation, and Liability Act (CERCLA), and the Superfund Amendments and Reauthorization Act (SARA). Responsibility for supervision and enforcement of these laws generally belongs to the EPA and environmental state agencies. Since the 1970s environmental legislation has become increasingly more stringent, with absolute liability being imposed on an ever-widening circle of participants.

Clean Air Act

The Clean Air Act, originally enacted in 1955, is preventative in nature. Its objective is to reduce air pollution by establishing air quality standards and requiring limitations on emissions by utility companies. The CAA was amended in 1970, 1977, and 1990. The 1990 amendments established specific requirements for the electric utility industry. They restrict the use of chemicals that cause acid rain and ozone depletion. They also require that costs be incurred primarily for abatement and prevention. Operating permits are required for major sources of pollution, and the penalty provisions of the CAA were greatly enhanced. Further, most violations previously classified as misdemeanors were upgraded to felonies, and fines and imprisonment times were increased. These programs are enforced through federally approved state implementation plans.

The emissions limits for electric utilities provide an annual allowance (authorization to emit one ton of sulfur dioxide) for emissions of pollutants. The utilities may not emit pollutants in excess of the allowances held, but they may buy and sell allowances. Thus one way a utility not in compliance with the regulations may meet its emissions limits is by acquiring additional allowances. These "pollution rights" were designed as an incentive for business to earn revenue by cutting pollution levels.

The market for the sale of pollution rights has been small due to some concern that those who buy these rights will not be allowed to include the cost in their rate base, which is set by state public utility commissions. Though utility companies are reluctant to buy or sell these allowances, there is some internal trading among various facilities and numerous transactions between utilities have been reported. In Southern California, securities firms, with the backing of the South Coast Air Quality Management District, proposed private auctions of rights to emit air pollutants.

Clean Water Act

The Clean Water Act was established in 1972 to restore and maintain the biological, chemical, and physical integrity of U.S. waters. The CWA Amendments of 1987 regulate both conventional and toxic pollutants. They established a comprehensive program for controlling discharges of pollutants into waterways. In addition, ambient water quality standards were used to set individual permit limitations and technology based limitations that impose the most cost effective pollution control technology on dischargers. The law also authorizes, cleanup and cost recovery actions where an imminent pollution hazard exists. It also prohibits the discharge of oil and other hazardous substances into United States navigable waters and imposes a criminal penalty for failure to notify the authorities of such discharges.

RCRA

The emphasis of both the CAA and CWA is on regulating air and water emissions. The Resource Conservation and Recovery Act of 1976 attempts to prevent pollution before it occurs. It provides comprehensive federal regulation of hazardous wastes from point of generation to final disposal. This "cradle to grave" approach involves the disposal, recycling, and management of hazardous waste. The law applies to all generators of hazardous waste, transporters of hazardous waste, and owners and operators of hazardous waste treatment, storage, and disposal facilities. The statute also includes specific guidelines for identifying hazardous waste. Once waste is identified as hazardous, anyone who handles the material must comply with a variety of notification, permission, and record-keeping requirements. In this way the EPA can better track and control the disposition of this material.

RCRA also contains rules related to solid waste landfills and underground storage tanks. Compliance is monitored by both the EPA and state agencies, with civil and criminal penalties authorized for noncompliance. RCRA was enacted to prevent events that lead to contamination and result in the need for future remediation and cleanup.

CERCLA and SARA

The assessment of liability and the remediation of hazardous waste sites is found in the Comprehensive Environmental Response, Compensation and Liability Act of 1980 (CERCLA, commonly known as the Superfund Act) and its amendment, the Superfund Amendment and Reauthorization Act (SARA) of 1986. CERCLA imposes severe and strict liability as a means to inhibit pollution and to encourage companies to find new and better "best available technologies." It has been seen as the centerpiece of environmental legislation in the 1980s and 1990s. It does not have its own cleanup standards but relies on the standards of other regulations. Cleanup funds come from the Superfund, which was created and is increased continuously by taxes on chemicals and other hazardous waste. The EPA recovers its costs of cleanup by assessing charges on the responsible parties involved.

An optional rule under CERCLA provides for the use of externalities in determining liability and damages. The Natural Resource Damage Assessment (NRDA) provision calls for determining monetary damages to natural resources as a result of the release of hazardous substances. The specified determination procedures include an assessment of the past, present, and future damages and a statement of those damages in monetary terms. An economic valuation and analysis of all costs and benefits to the environment and the monetization of that analysis is required.

Part of the SARA legislation is Section 313, which requires the EPA to establish an inventory of routine toxic chemical emissions for certain facilities. Companies subject to this reporting requirement must complete and publish an annual toxic release inventory (TRI) of 654 chemicals used at their facilities. The purpose of this inventory is to inform the EPA and the public of chemicals being emitted into the environment. (Additional information about TRI reporting can be found in Chapter 7.)

CERCLA is very broad in its coverage of who can be held liable for remediation, the types of contamination covered, and the unlimited monetary liability that can be imposed. CERCLA imposes liability on a broadly defined group of potentially responsible parties (PRPs), which could include a site's current or past owners and operators, those who generated substances disposed of at the site, those who transported the substances to the site, and even those who arranged these transactions. Past owners who can show they are "innocent landowners," having made careful and appropriate investigation of the property, its prior owners, and their practices, typically would not be held liable for the remediation.

The liability imposed by CERCLA is strict, retroactive, and joint and several. Strict liability means that any involvement is sufficient to establish liability. It is not necessary to prove negligence. Retroactive liability means that liability can be imposed after the fact for actions that may not have violated the law at the time they were committed. Joint and several liability means that any PRP who is partially responsible can be held liable for the full cost of cleanup.

A responsible PRP can sue other PRPs, if any, for their share of cleanup costs. The costs to a PRP may include cleanup costs, legal costs, claims to third parties (referred to as toxic torts), and natural resource costs. No fault needs to be established, nor will all parties that contributed to the site's contamination necessarily be held proportionately responsible for the costs.

In some cases, banks that have foreclosed on properties have been held liable. In a 1986 court case a Maryland district court found that when Maryland Bank and Trust foreclosed on its security it became the "owner or operator" of a contaminated facility. In a subsequent case in 1990, a federal Court of Appeals found that Fleet Factors Corporation, the nation's 14th largest bank, by acting as an "operator" could become liable for the environmental wrongs of a borrower merely by having the capacity to influence the treatment of hazardous waste. The bank's potential liability under CERCLA was not limited to the amount of the loan that it made on the property but actually could extend to the full cost of remediation. The EPA issued a ruling in 1992 that provided a range of activities in which secured creditors could engage to manage and protect their security interest while maintaining their "lender liability" exemption.

THE PROCESS OF ASSESSING LIABILITY UNDER CERCLA

The regulatory process of enforcing CERCLA is initiated when the Environmental Protection Agency (EPA) identifies a site containing pollutants that constitutes a potential threat to public health and safety. Since 1980, when CERCLA became law, approximately 1,500 Superfund sites have been identified and placed on the National Priority List (NPL). They constitute the most hazardous sites, so designated after a preliminary EPA investigation of the sites's characteristics.

The EPA notifies those parties that may be potentially responsible for contamination at the site. A Remedial Investigation and Feasibility Study (RI/FS) then is conducted, which results in a complete analysis of the environmental problems at the site and proposed alternatives for remediation. A record of decision (ROD) summarizing the findings and recommendations of the RI/FS, including estimated costs to implement the recommended remediation technology, then is filed with the EPA. During and following the RI/FS, the potentially responsible parties negotiate or litigate their share of the remediation costs, and a consent decree is filed. Often PRPs negotiate in groups with the EPA. Engineers then prepare detailed plans for the cleanup, after which the cleanup is begun. The cleanup phase could last a few years or many years depending on the nature of the problems and the solutions applied for the remediation.

While CERCLA, RCRA, SARA, CWA, and CAA do not constitute the totality of environmental regulations, they do illustrate the nature of those regulations. In addition to the federal laws, many states have enacted parallel legislation that, although differing in detail, generally adopts similar principles of strict, joint and several, and retroactive liability. The costs are often material and have an impact on accounting and financial reporting practices.

ACCOUNTING REGULATIONS

Though the focus of this study is primarily on the integration of environmental measurements in the management decision-making process, some discussion of the regulations driving external environmental disclosures is necessary. New accounting issues have emerged such as the expensing or capitalizing of treatment costs, the timing of disclosures of contingent environmental liabilities, and the content of those disclosures in the Management Discussion and Analysis section of annual reports. The questions raised relate to the quantity and quality of environmental information that should be made available to various corporate stakeholders. The Financial Accounting Standards Board (FASB), the Securities and Exchange Commission (SEC), and the American Institute of Certified Public Accountants (AICPA) have attempted to address some of these issues with a variety of rules and recommendations.

SFAS 5

The FASB issued its Statement on Financial Accounting Standards 5 (SFAS 5), "Accounting for Contingent Liabilities," in 1975. The

Statement was not intended to address environmental contingent liabilities in particular but rather to address contingencies in general. SFAS 5 defines a loss contingency as "an existing condition, situation, or set of circumstances involving uncertainty...that will be resolved when one or more future events occur or fail to occur." It requires accrual of a liability if: (1) it is probable that a liability has been incurred or an asset impaired and (2) the amount of the loss can be reasonably estimated. While SFAS 5 provides guidance for recognizing losses, it does not provide guidance for measuring them (Johnson, 1993, 118–119).

Some believe that SFAS 5 has some problems when applied to environmental liabilities. "An enterprise's environmental remediation obligation that results in a liability generally does not become determinable as a distinct event, nor is the amount of the liability generally fixed and determinable at a specific point in time. Rather, the existence of a liability for environmental remediation costs becomes determinable and the amount of the liability becomes estimable over a continuum of events and activities that help to frame, define, and verify the liability" (AICPA 1994, 45).

Other criticisms of the applicability of SFAS 5 to environmental issues often refer to the subjectivity involved in the disclosure. "SFAS 5 was not written with environmental issues in mind, and these guidelines are inadequate in practice because they are vague and open to subjective interpretation. Because environmental liabilities present a different order of risk altogether, wording such as 'probable,' 'reasonably estimated' leaves latitude for subjectivity and judgment. This latitude allows management to report bad effects when earnings are high, thereby misleading investors" (Williams and Phillips, 1994, 30).

FIN 14

The Financial Accounting Standards Board Interpretation 14 (FIN 14), "Reasonable Estimation of the Amount of a Loss—An Interpretation of FASB No 5," was introduced in 1976. The Interpretation provides the following guidance concerning the accrual of loss contingencies. "When some amount within the range appears at the time to be a better estimate than any other amount within the range, the best estimate shall be accrued" (AICPA, 1994, 88). If all estimates in a range are equally likely, then the minimum loss should be accrued. If a liability is not accrued because it is not probable or because there is no reasonable estimate, the nature of the liability still should be disclosed in the footnotes to the financial statements, if there is a reasonable possibility that a financial loss may have been incurred. Thus FIN 14 requires recording a liability even if it is possible only to estimate a range of probable costs.

SFAS 5 and FIN 14 remained the two primary accounting pronouncements related to environmental liabilities until 1989. As environmental accounting issues became more frequent and more prominent, the Emerging Issues Task Force further addressed these issues.

Emerging Issues Task Force

The FASB's Emerging Issues Task Force (EITF) dealt with the question of how to disclose environmental costs when it reached consensus on two issues focusing on whether to capitalize or expense certain environmental contamination treatment costs. The first consensus, reached in Issue 89–13, "Accounting for the Cost of Asbestos Removal," allowed for the capitalization of costs incurred to treat asbestos when they are incurred within a reasonable time period after the acquisition of the property. "The consensus reached in Issue No. 90–8, 'Capitalization of Costs to Treat Environmental Contamination,' generally calls for expensing costs of containment. However, it permits their capitalization (subject to recoverability) if the costs (a) extend the asset's life, increase its capacity, or improve its efficiency relative to the property's condition when originally constructed or acquired, (b) mitigate or prevent future contamination or (c) are incurred in preparing the property for sale" (Johnson, 1993, 119).

In these two issues, 89–13 and 90–8, the EITF reached a consensus that environmental contamination treatment costs generally should be charged to expense unless the three criteria above are met.

> Rather than penalizing a company for taking preventive measures, financial rules should encourage investment in prevention. Allowing capitalization of certain contamination prevention costs would be a good start. Extending this guideline to all environmental prevention procedures, even those not identified with a particular asset would allow companies to spread environmental expenses and not take a large hit at one time. Thus companies could manage better because the expense incurred today would lower costs tomorrow by minimizing the potential for disaster. A company either will pay now in prevention or pay later in clean up costs (Williams and Phillips, 1994, 32).

Most recently, in Issue 93–5, "Accounting for Environmental Liabilities," the consensus requires that an environmental liability be evaluated independently from any potential claim for recovery and that the loss arising from the recognition of an environmental liability be reduced only when a claim for recovery has a probability of realization. In addition, the EITF allows for the discounting of environmental liabilities at a specific cleanup site only if the entire amount of the obligation and the amount and timing of the payments for that site are fixed or reliably determinable.

SEC SAB 92

The Securities and Exchange Commission also has made pronouncements that affect the accounting for environmental liabilities. In June 1993 the SEC issued Staff Accounting Bulletin 92 (SAB 92), "Accounting and Disclosures Relating to Loss Contingencies," making it inappropriate to present environmental liabilities net of claims for insurance recovery. SAB 92, issued after the EITF consensus 93–5, indicated that "the rate used to discount the cash payments should be the rate that will produce an amount at which the environmental or product liability could be settled in an arm's-length transaction with a third party. If that rate is not readily determinable, the discount rate used to discount the cash payments should not exceed the interest rate on monetary assets that are essentially risk free and have maturities comparable to that of the environmental or product liability" (SEC, SAB 92, 10).

Commissioner Richard Y. Roberts of the SEC recently expressed his views regarding recent accounting developments in the area of environmental liability. He believes that SAB 92 and EITF 93–5 should be interpreted collectively and that issuers should follow the agreed-upon position or be able to justify any departures from it. "The SAB presents the view of Commission staff regarding: (1) the manner in which a contingent and any related asset representing claims for recovery should be displayed in the financial statements; (2) the appropriate discount rate to be used for recognition of a contingent liability presented at its present value to reflect the time value of money; and (3) the disclosures that are likely to be of particular significance to investors in their assessment of these contingencies" (Roberts, 1993, 6). "The SEC staff regards it as unacceptable to accrue nothing whatever when involvement in remediating a site is probable" (Price Waterhouse, 1994, 12).

Regulation S-K

SEC requirements for disclosure of environmental obligations by public companies arise from several laws and regulations. The Securities Act of 1933 establishes disclosure requirements to be met when securities are issued, and the Securities Exchange Act of 1934 establishes periodic disclosure requirements. These laws provide for liability for material misstatements of fact or omission of material information. Several provisions of Regulation S-K are particularly significant for registrants subject to potential environmental liabilities and risks.

Regulation S-K, Item 303, requires that the Management Discussion and Analysis section of Form 10K include discussion of any known demands, commitments, events, or uncertainties reasonably likely to have a material effect on the registrant's liquidity or capital resources. Regulation S-K, Item 101, requires a general description of the business and specific disclosures of those material items affected by compliance with environmental laws and the effect of the compliance on the capital expenditures, earnings, and competitive position of the registrant. Those disclosures include estimates of capital expenditures for the current and succeeding fiscal years and for any further periods in which those expenditures may be material, including the costs of bringing an entity into compliance with environmental regulations.

Regulation S-K, Item 103, requires disclosure of pending legal actions, including those arising under environmental laws that are material; or when the claim exceeds 10 percent of the registrant's current assets; or when a governmental authority is a party and for which sanctions may be more than $100,000.

MD&A

The Securities and Exchange Commission in 1980 required that the annual reports of registrants include a Management Discussion and Analysis (MD&A) section that assesses the company's liquidity, capital resources, and operations in a way investors can understand. One of the goals was to make information available to the public about predictable future events and trends that may affect future operations of the business.

Many companies do a good job of describing historical events, but very few provide useful and accurate forecasts and projections. When forward-looking data are disclosed, the bias is strong in favor of correctly projecting positive trends, while negative trends tend to be either ignored or not fully reported (Pava and Epstein, 1993). It is likely that continued monitoring and pressure by various regulators, including the SEC, will increase the disclosure of material forward-looking events in the MD&A

sections of external reports. If not, the SEC could file an enforcement action for increased disclosure of environmental liabilities in the MD&A section as it did in the Caterpillar case related to other MD&A disclosures in 1992.

"Financial Reporting Release No. 36 is an interpretive release to Regulation S-K, Item 303, and addresses environmental disclosures in Management Discussion and Analysis. It requires a discussion of all effects on results of operations, liquidity, and capital resources unless management can determine that a material effect is not likely to occur. Companies that have been correctly designated by the Environmental Protection Agency as potentially responsible parties (PRP) in most cases must disclose the effects of that PRP status, quantified to the extent reasonably practicable" (Johnson, 1993, 120). Disclosure should include the total potential cleanup costs required. It also should include an analysis of forward-looking events and significant effects of all environmental laws, including CAA, CWA, CERCLA, SARA, and RCRA, on future operations.

Another SEC statement, Release 6835 (May 1989), requires management to disclose any environmental problems likely to have a material effect on its operations. Management also should quantify any liabilities as far as is "reasonably practical." Relevant future trends, demands, commitments, events, or uncertainties also must be disclosed.

SEC and EPA Coordination and Enforcement

SEC Commissioner Richard Roberts has stated that cooperation between the SEC and the EPA will continue to grow and become more intense. The increasing amounts of future and current environmental liability costs have resulted in closer monitoring of environmental disclosures in SEC filings.

In order to enhance the disclosure in the environmental liability area, a dialogue has been developed between the staffs of the Commission and the Environmental Protection Agency ("EPA"). The Commission now utilizes EPA staff to help train Commission staff in the environmental liability disclosure review area. Further, through an informal understanding, Commission staff receives from the EPA lists of all companies that have been named as PRPs on hazardous waste sites. Information also is received concerning companies subject to the cleanup requirements under RCRA. Commission staff currently utilize this information in its review process (Roberts, 1993, 4).

SURVEYS AND STUDIES OF EXTERNAL FINANCIAL REPORTING OF ENVIRONMENTAL LIABILITIES

Though no previous study has surveyed the state of the art and best practices in environmental measurement and reporting through field research as extensively as this one, numerous recent studies have used mail surveys to gain an understanding of the general practices in external environmental reporting. Survey research does provide a general understanding of the state of the art, and a general review of those surveys is warranted. But it is also important to recognize the limitations of the surveys.

First, the field studies reported here indicate that no one person in most organizations knows the full range of the company's activities in environmental measurement and reporting. When the research concerns are narrowly limited to external environmental reporting, success is more likely, but some difficulty in obtaining useful information remains. Second, survey respondents are somewhat reluctant to provide honest and complete responses, given the concerns over potential litigation that always arise in discussions about the quality and quantity of environmental disclosures. Third, and probably most important, is the rapidly changing landscape of environmental disclosures and management. Since the late 1980s, activity in both internal and external corporate environmental measurement and reporting has increased significantly. By some measures, disclosures have been doubling on a yearly basis. Thus, though the survey data are somewhat useful as an independent look at the state of the art, they are probably more useful in tracking the trends over time.

Price Waterhouse has conducted three surveys of accounting for environmental compliance, in 1990, 1992, and 1994. The 1994 survey indicates a trend toward increased corporate accrual and disclosure of liabilities. The survey respondents, consisting primarily of SEC registrants, are becoming more concerned and aware of environmental liabilities. An increasing percentage of corporations have board level committees to oversee environmental compliance, and 83 percent of the respondents have an environmental affairs department. Approximately 63 percent of companies surveyed have written environmental accounting policies, a dramatic increase over 1992 (33 %) and 1990 (11%). Seventy-two percent of respondents disclose their environmental accounting policy in the accounting policies footnote to their financial statements—a significant increase over 1992 (26%) and 1990 (4%). Measurement remains difficult and practice remains mixed with regard to the timing of recording environmental cleanup liabilities, but it appears that companies are recognizing their liabilities sooner (Price Waterhouse, 1994).

The study also confirmed that when environmental liability already exists, companies are less likely to hide the fact from the public. In the past companies tried to hide under SFAS 5, claiming that the "event" had not occurred until initial notification of a pending infraction by regulatory authorities. The 1994 Price Waterhouse survey indicated a clear trend toward more disclosure, with 70 percent of respondents with significant environmental exposure disclosing those accruals in the financial statements. For companies with less significant exposure, only 46 percent disclosed their accrued liability. Some users have argued that a standard is needed that requires companies to do an annual assessment and accrual of estimated cleanup and restoration costs at the balance sheet date.

Academic research on environmental disclosure has focused on what is being disclosed, why it is being disclosed, and what should be disclosed. In terms of what firms are disclosing some studies have focused on the fact that firms in the same industry or with the same problem (e.g., Superfund) make different disclosures. A study by Freedman and Stagliano (1994) discovered that although firms are affected similarly by Superfund they make a whole range of disclosures, from monetary disclosures of the risk at each site to no mention of Superfund at all. All these firms face the same SEC and FASB accounting reporting rules.

KPMG Peat Marwick completed a major international survey of environmental reporting in 1993. Six hundred and ninety companies in 10 countries responded to the survey, which was designed to explore current practices in environmental reporting. More than 400 of these companies referred to environmental issues somewhere in their annual report, while 105 companies produced a separate environmental report. The survey found that a large number of companies report on environmental issues in the Management Discussion and Analysis section of the annual report. The study also reports a trend toward increased environmental reporting internationally.

In 1993, the AICPA published a survey of public companies and their compliance with environmental disclosure regulations. Drawn from more than 20,000 annual reports, the survey provides examples of environmental accounting policy statements and examples of how companies have dealt with issues related to compliance, litigation, and the acknowledgement of liability for environmental issues. The survey serves as a useful guide to corporations about environmental disclosures. But as mentioned earlier, because the quantity and quality of environmental disclosures are increasing so rapidly, the usefulness of this survey is limited.

Another major survey of corporate environmental reporting practices was completed by Deloitte & Touche, International Institute for Sustainable Development (IISD), and SustainAbility. The study report, *Coming Clean*, was published in 1993 and focuses on the reporting practices, motives, and views of 70 companies. It concludes that the demand for environmental disclosures will continue, broaden, and intensify and that environmental reports will be subject to increasingly rigorous analysis.

The survey also found that legislation forcing business to disclose environmental information is multiplying and that environmental reports are becoming the norm for corporate reporting rather than the exception. The study describes the evolution of environmental and sustainable development reporting in the following five stages:

Stage 1: Green glossies, newsletters, videos.
Short statement in annual report.

Stage 2: One-off environmental report, often linked to first formal policy statement.

Stage 3: Annual reporting, linked to environmental management system, but more text than figures.

Stage 4: Provision of full TRI-style performance data on annual basis. Available on diskette or on-line. Environment report referred to in annual report.

Stage 5: Sustainable development reporting linking environmental, economic, and social aspects of corporate performance, supported by indicators of sustainability.

(Deloitte & Touche et al., 1993, 10)

Chapter 7 of this book provides examples of disclosures in corporate annual reports and corporate environmental reports and describes the trends in corporate environmental reporting.

SUMMARY

The review of the previous research in this area described in Appendix B along with this review of both the environmental regulations and the applicable accounting guidelines provides necessary background for understanding the regulatory pressures that are part of the impetus for improved corporate environmental performance. As discussed throughout the book, additional benefits including increased competitive advantages, reduced environmental impacts, and increased corporate profitability through improved product quality and production yields provide additional impetus.

Appendix B

A Brief Review of the Social Audit, Environmental Accounting, and Cost-Benefit Analysis

The core of this book is the extensive field research on how corporations are integrating environmental impacts into management decision making. To understand the results of that research, readers may want some background and introduction to the social audit, environmental accounting, and cost-benefit analysis. This appendix is designed to provide that review.

SOCIAL RESPONSIBILITY AND THE SOCIAL AUDIT[1]—THE DEVELOPMENT OF FRAMEWORKS AND MODELS

As mentioned in Chapter 1, the concern for measuring and reporting corporate environmental performance follows on some important earlier developments. In the 1960s, corporate social responsibility became a concern among both corporate executives and academic researchers. Many argued that corporations had obligations to other interested parties in society in addition to obligations to shareholders to produce a profit. To put this concept into operation, many determined they needed guidance

---

1. This section of the book specifically and the balance of the literature review generally draws heavily on an early book on social accounting by Epstein, Epstein, and Weiss. That book provides extensive discussions of the early developments and history of social accounting and the social audit for those who are interested.

on measuring, monitoring, and reporting corporate social impacts. They needed a framework both to aid in making management decisions that would include consideration of societal interests and to communicate corporate social performance to interested external users. The social audit was developed in the early 1970s as a response to corporate needs for better information for both internal decision making and external reporting.

Ray Bauer and Dan Fenn (1972, 1973) of Harvard University were among the founders of the social audit. They proposed that companies conduct inventories and internal audits of corporate social activities including programs related to minority hiring and pollution control. They recommended that the true costs for each activity be determined including opportunity costs along with those costs assigned to overhead accounts. These costs then would be compared with performance data on the projects including the benefits to both the community and the company and would be assembled in an assessment and evaluation format called a process audit.

Other important early contributors to the development of social accounting were David Linowes and Ralph Estes. Linowes, a partner in a national accounting firm, saw a need to broaden the scope of public accounting to include social measurements and the evaluation of social programs. He proposed socio-economic accounting principles as guidelines for developing social auditing techniques that would yield a "socio-economic operating statement." The statement included voluntary company expenditures for social programs that benefited employees, customers, the environment, and the community. Detriments or negative charges were included, but involuntary actions such as compliance with pollution laws were ignored because they were required by law and were necessary costs of business. All measurements were in dollars so total socio-economic deficits or improvements could be calculated.

During the 1970s, Professor Ralph Estes developed a comprehensive corporate reporting model that included the disclosure of all social costs and benefits. The bottom line produced was a net social surplus or deficit that reflected benefits and detriments to society rather than to the organization. The model was intended to "serve as a useful framework for internal reporting in organizations concerned with social responsibility issues and interested in determining their full impact on society" (Estes, 1974, 19).

Estes has been continuing his work on the expansion of corporate reporting to include items of interest to other stakeholders in addition to the corporate shareholder. He has proposed that Congress pass a Corporate Accountability Act. It would redesignate the SEC as the Corporate Accountability Commission, which would determine stakeholder information needs and specify disclosure requirements that would better serve stakeholder needs. It also would consolidate corporate reporting to most of the federal agencies into a corporate report to be filed with the Commission, which would simplify much of the present corporate filings (Estes, 1994).

Another innovative approach was an attempt to develop a model expanding the traditional income statement into a "multi-dimensional income statement" (Charnes et al., 1974). It expanded the usual financial dimensions of an income statement to include variables related to the physical and social environment.

Epstein developed models for both the internal and external reporting of corporate social performance and implemented those models in numerous organizations during the 1970s.[2] The models included formats for internal reports including a "social activities inventory report" and a "social and economic impact report" and external reports including a "social report" (Epstein et al., 1977a, 127, 131, 165). They also included steps for developing and implementing a system for measuring and reporting corporate social performance. It included the following steps:

1. Set goals for social responsibility programs and for the social accounting process.

2. Conduct inventory of social responsibility programs.

3. Perform evaluation of the effectiveness of social programs and the benefits.

4. Present suggestions for change in corporate social program goals and priorities.

5. Identify impacts of organization on society.

6. Measure impacts of the organization on society.

7. Identify and measure future impacts of the organization on society. Develop a monitoring system for continuous reassessment of future impacts.

8. Compile all information into a useful report to management on the impact of the organization on society.

---

2. Though much of this development work was completed while Epstein was doing primarily academic work, some was a part of his work as a consultant and then director of social measurement services at Abt Accociates, Inc.

9. Analyze alternative management approaches for redirecting social costs and suggest feasible courses of action.

10. Redefine goals for social responsibility programs.
(Epstein et al., 1977a, 124, 125)

With James Post, Epstein also investigated the development of a social accounting information system to aid management in continuous identifying and monitoring of actual social demands and public expectations. The system included an environmental scanning activity that permitted management to assess the social environment in which it operated. Using an "activity" approach and an "overview" approach, the system created an "integrated" approach. It in turn provided the framework for determining the information needs for management decisions. An agenda of relevant public issues, an assessment of social trends, and an evaluation of an organization's current social performance were among the needs included (Post and Epstein, 1977).

SOCIAL ACCOUNTING AND THE SOCIAL AUDIT—COMPANY IMPLEMENTATIONS

Beginning in 1970, Abt Associates, Inc., began to explore the development of the corporate social audit. Headed by Dr. Clark Abt, Abt Associates became one of the largest social science research firms in the world. The company had expertise in evaluating social programs for government and saw an opportunity to transfer these methods to the private sector.

Abt Associates began to produce a corporate social audit in its annual report. The system for data collection and the social audit were the most comprehensive ever designed. Using a constituent impact approach, the audit attempted to determine the impact of the total company on its employees, customers, community, and the general public. All items were measured in monetary terms and were reported in a balance sheet and income statement format. Abt's approach was to make an explicit analogy to financial accounting because such "integration of social and financial reports allows for a more direct comparison of social benefits with associated financial costs, or financial benefits with related social costs" (Abt, 1973). The goal was to assess the total impact of a company on its environment. An estimation of the financial return on social investment, patterned after traditional return on investment calculations, also was included.

Another company active in corporate social reporting was First National Bank of Minneapolis. To carry out the company's social programs, it was necessary to assess community needs and establish priorities. The social auditing process and the ultimate social-environmental audit, which were incorporated in the company's annual report, included social indicators of the quality of life and included both monetary and nonmonetary measures.

Scovill Manufacturing Company included a social action report in its 1972 corporate annual report (see Exhibit B–1). The report described the company's activities in areas of employment opportunities, environmental controls, community involvement, and consumerism. A balance sheet format was used for brevity and to emphasize the strengths and weaknesses in each area.

Phillips Screw Company chose to do a partial social audit related to environmental concerns. Phillips, like many other companies, tried to respond to community pressure by evaluating the impact of corporate activities on the environment and measuring compliance with government regulations. Included in this manufacturing firm's 1973 annual report was a pollution audit. The audit, conducted by an independent consulting firm, Resource Planning Associates, Inc., examined the Phillips Metallurgical, Inc., and Shell Cast Corporation, subsidiaries of Phillips Screw. It attempted to measure the environmental impacts of the foundries' operations and to compare the amount of measured effluents to federal and state environmental quality standards for air and water quality, noise emissions, and solid wastes.

This voluntary audit was unusual because it stated for the public record that the company had exceeded certain environmental quality standards and detailed the required capital investment costs (see Exhibit B–2).

ENVIRONMENTAL ECONOMICS AND COST-BENEFIT ANALYSIS

In the 1970s, as accountants, business executives, and business school professors were attempting to develop a framework for measuring and reporting corporate social and environmental performance, economists also were trying to improve the methods for measuring environmental impacts. Drawing on some basic welfare economics concepts, they were developing the field of environmental economics and models that would be useful for measuring those impacts. It was expected that this work

EXHIBIT B–1

Scovill Manufacturing Company (Corporate Annual Report)

A Social Action Report: This is an admittedly imperfect attempt to report on our corporate social action. We have used the balance sheet method of reporting — not because it is possible to attach monetary values to all of the things we are doing or should be doing, but aren't — but because it allows for brevity in highlighting strengths and weaknesses in this area. We will welcome comments on the contents and on whether to continue this report.

Employment Opportunities

Assets	Liabilities
Company expansion has provided approximately 10,000 new jobs since 1963.	Fluctuating employment levels still a problem at some plant locations.
One of first members of Plans for Progress (3/17/64), a voluntary program to provide more job opportunities for minorities.	Need more upgrading of minority employees into higher labor grade jobs.
Minority employment has grown from 6% in 1963 to 19% in 1972.	Need more upgrading of women employees into higher labor grade jobs.
Women now constitute about 40% of total employment.	Closing of Waterbury work training center after Scovill investment of $33,000. State & Federal grants to support it were terminated.
Established National Alliance of Businessmen training program which resulted in hiring of 280 disadvantaged and 170 veterans in last 18 months in Waterbury area.	
Began first major pre-retirement counseling program for employees with U.A.W. in 1964.	
Established one of first effective alcoholism control programs for employees in 1954. (now includes drug control program)	

Environmental Controls

Assets	Liabilities
$3,500,000 Waterbury water treatment plant completed Nov. 1972.	Problem of disposing of semi-solid sludge from new Waterbury water treatment plant still being researched for a solution.
$3,000,000 air filtering systems for Waterbury mills 80% completed.	New brass chip dryer ($700,000) installed one year ago to reduce air pollution in Waterbury must be modified to comply with new state standards.
$55,000 water treatment facility for Canadian plant completed March, 1972.	
$1,100,000 water treatment facility 70% completed at Clarkesville, Ga. plant.	New OSHA (Occupational Safety and Health Act) standards may require additional expenditures.
All 10 new plants added since 1959 were built with all necessary pollution control equipment.	Intermittent nitrogen dioxide emissions from Waterbury plant a problem requiring further research.

EXHIBIT B–1 *(concluded)*

Community Involvement

Assets	Liabilities
Scovill charitable contributions averaged 1.2% of company pre-tax net income over past 5 years (1972 contributions were 8% of common stock dividends)	Programs to provide more low income housing have not been productive enough for time and money expended.
Local non-profit group to which Scovill contributed $163,000 has sponsored 174 units of subsidized housing.	Not enough rehabilitation of inner city neighborhoods.
Scovill partnership with minority businessman is rebuilding 12 vacant apartments and 4 storefronts to demonstrate benefits of rehabilitating deteriorating neighborhoods.	Still much to be accomplished in revitalizing core cities, controlling drug addiction, extending educational opportunities to the disadvantaged, etc. . . .
Support other such community projects as alcohol & drug control centers, inner city parks, recreational programs, public safety committees. . . .	Failure of programs to help youth groups establish minority owned businesses after Scovill investment of $20,000.
Employee participation in such community activities as selectmen, state representatives, school board members . . .	
Scovill loaned executives to federal, state and local governments in 1972.	

Consumerism

Assets	Liabilities
Corporate programs utilizing more effective quality control procedures throughout the company have upgraded product performance.	New and improved procedures to upgrade quality and service to insure customer satisfaction not foolproof — problems still occur and are corrected as soon as possible.
"Dial NuTone" established — a nationwide telephone network to speed up service and customer communications.	Improper use of products despite more informative product tags and installation instructions.
NuTone added over 100 authorized service stations to its national network in the past year — and expanded its Parts & Service Dept.	Pending or future legislation which may impose more stringent standards for quality and performance.
NuTone simplified its product installation books and added a new Consumer Assurance Laboratory.	
Hamilton Beach made its product tags more informative and simplified and clarified its warranties.	
Hamilton Beach established new nationwide service organization — trained factory personnel contact independent service stations weekly to insure warranties are enforced.	

EXHIBIT B–2
Phillips Screw Company (Pollution Audit)

Pollution Audit

The information herein has been extracted from a comprehensive pollution audit conducted by the undersigned on the Phillips Screw Company subsidiary Phillips Metallurgical, Inc. (PMI) and its subsidiary, Shell Cast Corp. (SCC).

The audit included consideration of air, water, noise and solid waste effluents and consisted of engineering and economic segments. Preliminary technical equipment needs and costs were projected to provide management with parameters for determining the economic impact on the Company and its operations. Experience suggests that these preliminary cost estimates will prove to be within normally accepted deviation ranges.

Where required, effluent testing was conducted in accordance with standardized techniques applicable to the circumstances encountered at each site. For the business/economic analysis, not presented in this summary, Company financial data on PMI and SCC were provided and integrated with proposed abatement equipment capital and operating costs as estimated by the undersigned.

Based upon our technical and economic analysis, the following significant conclusions have been drawn:

PMI has two effluent liabilities.

1. The plant exceeds Vermont air pollution standards — particulate emissions calculated at 7.0 lbs/hr compared to a maximum allowable level of 2.8 lbs/hr.

2. The plant exceeds Federal OSHA air contaminant standards — particulate concentration of at 25.2 mg/m3 compared to a maximum allowable level of 10.0 mg/m3.

SCC has two effluent liabilities.

1. The plant exceeds Connecticut air pollution standards — particulate emissions calculated at 3.0 lbs/hr compared to a maximum allowable level of 1.53 lbs/hr.

2. The plant emits at the Federal OSHA air contaminant standard — particulate concentration of at 10.0 mg/m3 compared to a maximum allowable level of 10 mg/m3.

No effluent liabilities in the areas of water, solid waste or noise pollution were observed.

Financial liabilities are as follows:

1. PMI to meet State and Federal air pollution standards requires a capital investment of $32,500 and annual operating expenses of $3,700.

2. SCC to meet State and Federal air pollution standards requires a capital investment of $25,500 and annual operating expenses of $3,200.

(These estimated costs are before tax and do not include amortization of capital equipment.)

In our opinion, expenditures of the levels cited for a remedial program of air pollution control will bring the current foundry operations into compliance with the respective State and Federal standards as they now exist. Furthermore, these expenditures are expected to provide sufficient margin to permit continued compliance in the event of any change in air pollution standards which we consider reasonably forseeable. Additionally, the nature and volume of solid waste effluents from current operations provide a sufficient margin for continued compliance in the event of reasonable changes to those standards.

Resource Planning Associates, Inc.

Resource Planning Associates, Inc.

Cambridge, Mass.
June 1, 1973

---

would serve as an input to the development of government policy and would help organizations to understand the social choices that individuals, businesses, and governments make in using various resources.

Much of environmental economics analysis is performed through cost-benefit analysis. Cost-benefit analysis is an attempt to analyze reasonable alternatives in dollar terms. It is used, for example, to examine the effect of a pollutant on both society and on individual members in society and then is used for decision making related to the allocation of resources. It has been applied extensively in the areas of pollution, urban renewal, conservation, and health care. "Externalities" (costs external to the firm) such as the social cost of pollution are included in the analysis as the cost of production borne by society rather than as part of a corporation's internal product cost. Then in the analysis of corporate impacts, the attempt is to internalize the externalities so that the company producing the impacts brings the costs into the costing system. The analysis also would include social benefits to measure the positive impacts of company activities. Such impacts would include recreational benefits a company may create for a community by allowing public use of company-owned forest land or waterways. All social costs and benefits are measured and included in the analysis.

One of the founders of modern-day cost-benefit analysis, E. J. Mishan, argued that cost-benefit analysis was an application of welfare economics and that the rationale of cost-benefit analysis was based on a potential Pareto improvement (Mishan, 1971). He defined a potential Pareto improvement as "a change which produces gains that exceed in value the accompanying losses; a change, therefore, such that gainers can (through costless transfers) fully compensate all the losers and remain themselves better off than before" (Mishan, 1972). Thus, a change not only should have the potential of making society better off but also should have the potential of doing so without making anyone worse off (Epstein et al, 1977a, 133–134).

One of the difficulties of using cost-benefit analysis is deciding which measurement tools are appropriate. Techniques for measuring the impacts of an organization on society include travel time estimates, actual value of loss, being forced to pay, property value appraisal, willingness to pay, aesthetic value loss, decrease in market value, and avoidance of loss. Some rely on economic concepts of consumer surplus, while others use various market valuation and contingent valuation methods. Some observers argue that it is difficult to determine the most appropriate measure, and others contend that all these methods have serious deficiencies. Still others feel that any methods that rely on community surveys to determine individual or societal views on social costs or benefits lack a scientific basis. Proponents of cost-benefit analysis recognize the deficiencies but argue that the estimates are good approximations of these impacts. The results they produce are better than no information at all and are very useful for decision making at the government policy and the corporate levels. In Chapter 9 we discussed the use of contingent valuation methods and cost-benefit analysis to estimate social costs and benefits and to estimate future corporate costs and benefits.

PREVIOUS STUDIES BY THE INSTITUTE OF MANAGEMENT ACCOUNTANTS

The National Association of Accountants (NAA), the precursor to the Institute of Management Accountants (the sponsoring organization for this study), was involved with social accounting beginning in the early 1970s. The NAA's Committee on Accounting for Corporate Social Performance issued a report in 1974 that stated objectives and procedures for developing corporate social accounting. The NAA sponsored two additional studies at that time. It previously had supported a study on human resource accounting (Caplan and Landekich, 1973) that fit into the Committee's general framework on social accounting.

The first study, *The Measurement of Corporate Environmental Activity*, examined the measurement of corporate environmental activity and its impact on decision making. The second, *Corporate Social Performance: The Measurement of Product and Service Contributions*, focused on measuring corporate product and service contributions. Of the many benefits derived from this research, the results of surveys conducted for each study contributed significantly to a better understanding of corporate social accounting.

The environmental measurement research project was conducted by Nikolai, Bazley, and Brummet (1976). Though the responding companies indicated that measuring environmental benefits in monetary terms generally was not prevalent, the four benefits most often measured were reduced production costs, conservation of physical resources, reduced pollution by the company, and avoidance of legal costs. Besides the benefit of avoiding legal costs, the most important reason for measuring these four benefits was improving the decision-making process concerning self-imposed social responsibilities.

The project also included case studies of nine companies demonstrating expertise in environmental measurement. These studies resulted in the following findings:

- Strong direction from top management is the major reason for active measurement of environmental impacts.

- While environmental research and development, engineering, and legal costs are treated as expenses, environmental capital expenditures are limited to equipment costs.
- The overriding benefit of avoiding being shut down for failure to comply with pollution control laws tends to eliminate the need to measure any other benefits.
- A narrative basis is used by some companies to evaluate benefits.
- Some companies use pollution control bonds for financing environmental expenditures because of lower interest rates, while others do not because of the additional costs of paperwork and complexities.
- Most companies do not separately categorize and measure pollution control operating costs, but believe they could if necessary.
- Systems are built with enough flexibility to make modifications if necessary as a result of changes in pollution control laws (Nikolai et al., 1976).

The second NAA study, by Epstein et al (1977b), consisted of an in-depth examination of the accounting for product and service contributions. The survey responses revealed that 57 percent of the companies had an employee responsible for social performance and that approximately 68 percent of these persons were at the level of vice president or above.

The survey also covered each company's degree of interest in and level of involvement with the four major social performance areas: product and service contributions, community involvement, human resources, and physical resources and environmental contributions.

Customers ranked product and service contributions first among the four areas of social performance in terms of organizational involvement but ranked this area fourth in terms of accounting for social performance. Though the corporations were involved in activities associated with product and service contributions, there was a significant lack of accounting for such involvement.

The book also included field studies to examine actual systems of measuring product and service contributions. These studies demonstrated that product and service impact was a central part of corporate social responsibility and accounting. But the study concludes with prescience:

Realistically we must conclude that the prospect for widespread development of operational corporate social accounting systems is problematic. This conclusion is based on two observations:

1. The momentum with which social accounting entered the 1970s has been effectively blunted.

2. At the present, neither of the management people (the corporate accountant or the corporate public affairs officer) within the organization on whose shoulders the principal burden of initiation and impetus rests is actively committed to its development.

Perhaps the most significant result of the survey is the limited extent to which the pioneering efforts described in the literature indicated a wider and more pervasive movement within industry toward the development of corporate social accounting systems. The survey revealed neither the existence of additional pioneering efforts nor any significant level of adoption of existing approaches (Epstein et al., 1977b, 67).

FURTHER THOUGHTS ON THE FAILURE OF SOCIAL ACCOUNTING

Some of the reasons for the failure of social accounting were discussed in Chapter 1. Social accounting focused on external reporting that in many cases did not have internal corporate activities to back up those reports. It was neither institutionalized nor part of the central core of most organizations. It was driven primarily by public relations personnel and used only secondarily as a management tool. Incentives typically were not in place to drive corporate social responsibility throughout the organization. Neither corporate management nor the accounting staff were committed to implementing corporate social accounting. Thus social accounting was dropped as the social tides changed with no resulting permanent change in corporate culture.

This book provides evidence of a growing level of institutional support for the integration of corporate environmental impacts into management decisions. Organizations support such a movement because they need to do a better job of managing a very large and growing corporate expense. They want to minimize corporate environmental impacts and increase corporate profitability. We hope this book will advance that integration and improve the quality of corporate environmental management.

Appendix C

Companies Cited

ABB Asea Brown Boveri Ltd. is a holding company for more than 1,300 companies. It has 200,000 employees worldwide in the business of producing, distributing, and applying electricity.

Alcan Aluminum, with 44,000 employees, is headquartered in Montreal and is involved in all stages of the aluminum industry with operations throughout the world.

Alcoa is the world's leading producer of aluminum with worldwide operations at 164 locations in 24 countries and 60,000 employees supplying fabricated and finished products.

AlliedSignal operates 400 facilities worldwide with more than 85,000 employees in the aerospace, automotive, and engineered materials businesses.

Amoco, with more than 46,000 employees, is a worldwide integrated petroleum and chemical company and the largest producer of natural gas in North America.

AT&T, with more than 300,000 employees, provides communications services and products as well as network equipment and computer systems to businesses, consumers, telecommunications service providers, and government agencies in about 200 countries.

Ben & Jerry's Homemade Inc. is a $140 million corporation operating throughout the United States and several other countries. It produces super premium ice cream, frozen yogurt, and ice cream novelties.

The Body Shop is a manufacturer and retailer of skin and hair care products made of natural ingredients. It operates worldwide in more than 45 countries and 1,000 stores.

Bristol-Myers Squibb is the third largest pharmaceutical company in the world and one of the world's largest diversified makers of healthcare products. It has 50,000 employees and operations in 35 countries.

British Petroleum, headquartered in London, is one of the world's largest petroleum and petrochemical companies and the largest producer of crude oil in the United States and United Kingdom, operating in 70 countries with 100,000 employees.

British Telecommunications, with more than 150,000 employees, supplies telecommunications services and equipment throughout the United Kingdom.

Browning-Ferris Industries (BFI) processes commercial, industrial, medical, and residential solid wastes for recycling, transport, and disposal. It has more than 30,000 employees throughout the world.

Cambrex is a $200 million, publicly held company that manufactures a broad line of specialty chemicals, fine chemicals, and commodity chemical intermediates. It has approximately 800 employees.

Chevron is one of the leading integrated oil companies engaging in all phases of the petroleum industry as well as chemicals, minerals, and land development. It operates in about 100 countries through more than 500 entities and 45,000 employees.

Ciba-Geigy, headquartered in Switzerland, has 87,000 employees in the health-care, pharmaceuticals, agriculture, and chemicals businesses.

Cracker Barrel owns and operates more than 180 full-service "country store" family restaurants throughout the United States featuring moderately priced home-style country cooking and separate gift shops.

Dexter Corporation is a specialty materials company in global markets in aerospace, automotive, electronics, food packaging, and medical. Founded in 1767, it is the oldest company on the New York Stock Exchange.

Dow Chemical is a diversified, worldwide manufacturer and supplier of chemicals, plastics, and consumer specialties. It operates in 33 countries and employs 55,000 people.

Duke Power, with 17,000 employees, is engaged in the generation, transmission, distribution, and sale of electric energy to 1.6 million customers in parts of North and South Carolina.

DuPont, with principal businesses in chemicals, fibers, polymers, and petroleum, has more than 200 manufacturing and processing facilities and 110,000 employees worldwide.

Eastman Kodak employs more than 110,000 people worldwide, primarily in the imaging (films, cameras, etc.) and health (X-ray films and pharmaceuticals) businesses.

E. B. Eddy is a Canadian-based forest management company with
sawmills and pulp and paper mills. It is a leading manufacturer of
fine, specialty and packaging grade papers, with 2,500 employees.

Ford Motor Company is the world's third-largest industrial corporation
and the second-largest producer of cars and trucks, with 322,000
employees worldwide.

General Motors, the largest U.S. corporation, has more than 700,000
employees worldwide and is involved in vehicle manufacturing,
automotive, space, and defense electronics, information technologies,
and financing and insurance.

Hyde Tools, a 120-year-old, privately held manufacturer of small
surface-preparation tools and knives, is located in Southbridge,
Massachusetts, with 300 employees.

IBM, with more than 200,000 employees, provides advanced information services, products, and technologies to customers throughout the
world.

ICI, with 65,000 employees, is a world leader in the manufacture of
paints, industrial chemicals, materials, and explosives.

McDonald's is the largest food service organization in the world. It
operates 14,000 restaurants in 70 countries through franchisees, joint-
venture partners, and company-operated restaurants.

Migros Cooperatives, founded in 1925, is Switzerland's largest retail
trading company, with more than 50,000 employees selling both food
and non-food items through more than 500 stores.

Herman Miller is involved primarily in manufacturing and selling office
furniture and related products throughout the world.

Minnesota Mining & Manufacturing, 3M, is a worldwide manufacturer
serving industrial, commercial, healthcare, and consumer markets
with more than 60,000 products and more than 80,000 employees.

Mobil Corporation, with more than 60,000 employees, is a major oil and
gas, petrochemicals, and plastics company with operations in more
than 100 countries.

Monsanto has 30,000 employees worldwide who are involved in the
discovery, manufacturing, and marketing of agricultural products,
performance chemicals used in consumer products, prescription pharmaceuticals, and food ingredients.

Motorola, with 110,000 employees, is one of the world's leading
providers of wireless communications (including cellular telephones),
semiconductors, and advanced electrical systems and services.

Niagara Mohawk Power, headquartered in Syracuse, New York, is an electric and gas utility serving more than 1.5 million customers in upstate New York. It supplies power from hydroelectric, coal, oil, natural gas, and nuclear-generated sources.

Noranda Forest, with 8,000 employees at operations in Canada, the United States, and the United Kingdom, is one of Canada's largest producers of forest products including building materials, papers, and pulp.

Northern Telecom Ltd. is a leading global designer, manufacturer, and supplier of telecommunications equipment to telephone, cable television, and other companies through 48 manufacturing facilities and 60,000 employees.

Ontario Hydro is the largest electric utility in Canada and one of the largest in North America. Its more than 20,000 employees serve more than 2.6 million customers.

Pacific Gas and Electric is the nation's largest investor-owned gas and electric utility. It serves more than 12 million customers in Northern and Central California through more than 20,000 employees.

Polaroid, with 12,000 employees, designs, manufactures, and markets worldwide a variety of products in the area of instant imaging photographic cameras and films and electronic imaging recording devices used for amateur and professional photography, industry, science, and medicine.

Procter & Gamble is one of the world's leading consumer products marketing companies. It manufactures and sells more than 250 brands and operates in more than 50 countries with about 100,000 employees.

Rohm and Haas is a multinational producer of specialty polymers and biologically active compounds. It has more than 13,000 employees upgrading petrochemical commodities to differentiated specialty products.

Rockwell International is a diversified, high-technology company with 77,000 employees working primarily in the electronics, aerospace, and automotive industries.

Southern Company is one of the largest investor-owned electric utilities in the nation, serving more than 3 million customers in Georgia, Florida, Mississippi, and Alabama.

Sun Company is one of the largest U.S. oil companies and the largest independent U.S. refiner/marketer. It operates under the SUNOCO brand name, with 14,000 employees.

Union Carbide is one of the major marketers of petrochemicals throughout the world with 13,000 employees in approximately 50 plants, factories, and laboratories manufacturing and distributing chemicals and plastics.

Unocal is a fully integrated energy resources company with operations throughout the world. It operates primarily under the Union Oil Company name, with more than 10,000 employees.

United Technologies produces a broad range of high-technology products and services worldwide including Pratt & Whitney aircraft engines, Otis elevators, Carrier air conditioning, and Sikorsky helicopters.

Weyerhaeuser, with more than 35,000 employees, is one of North America's largest producers of forest products and grower and harvester of timber with additional major operations in real estate development, financial services, and recycling of paper products.

WMX Technologies, with more than 70,000 employees, is the worldwide leader in providing comprehensive environmental, waste management, and related services to industry, government, and consumers.

Xerox is one of the world's largest producers of office equipment, servicing the document processing market in 130 countries with 100,000 employees.

Glossary of Acronyms

ABB Asea Brown Boveri Ltd.

ACT awareness and compliance tools

ALARAC as low as reasonably achievable and cost effective

ART Alcoa Remediation Team

ATI audit timeliness index

BCSD Business Council for Sustainable Development

BFI Browning-Ferris Industries

BT British Telecommunications

CAA Clean Air Act

CAR capital appropriations request

CEE customer energy efficiency

CEP Corporate Environmental Plan

CERES Coalition for Environmentally Responsible Economies

CFC chlorofluorocarbons

CGLI Council of Great Lakes Industries

CMA Chemical Manufacturers' Association

CV contingent valuation

CWA Clean Water Act

DOB degree of belief

DOD Department of Defense

DOE Department of Energy

EARS environmental accounting and reporting system

EC European Community

EH&S environment, health, and safety

EITF Emerging Issues Task Force

EMAS eco-management and audit scheme

EPA Environmental Protection Agency

EPCRA Emergency Planning and Community Right to Know Act of 1986

EPI environmental performance index

EPRI Electric Power Research Institute

ERM Environmental Resources Management

ERPM environmental remediation process model

ESAP environmental self-assessment program

ESI Environmental Strategy Implementation

FASB Financial Accounting Standards Board

FOCUS fossil optimization and capital utilization study

GATT General Agreement on Tariffs and Trade

GEMI Global Environmental Management Initiative

IRR internal rate of return

IRRC Investor Responsibility Research Center

ISO International Organization for Standardization

ISOC International Standard of Care

LCA life cycle assessment

MERIT measured equity return incentive term

NAFTA North American Free Trade Agreement

NMPC Niagara Mohawk Power Co.

NPL National Priorities List

NPV net present value

NRDA Natural Resource Damage Assessment

PCB polychlorinated biphenyl

PCEQ President's Commission on Environmental Quality

PERI Public Environmental Reporting Initiative

PLCM product life cycle management

PRP potentially responsible party

RCRA Resource Conservation and Recovery Act

RI/FS Remedial Investigation and Feasibility Study

ROD record of decision

SAGE Strategic Advisory Group on the Environment

SARA Superfund Amendment and Reauthorization Act

SEC Securities and Exchange Commission

SEEP safety, energy, and environmental protection

SEP supplemental environmental project

SETAC Society of Environmental Toxicology and Chemistry

SMART save money and reduce toxics

SSPS site-screening and priority-setting system

TAS total annualized savings

TSA Total Stakeholder Analysis

TQEM total quality environmental management

TQM total quality management

TRI toxic release inventory

TUWR toxic use and waste reduction

UST underground storage tank

Bibliography

Acton, J.P., and L.S. Dixon. 1992. *Superfund and Transaction Costs: The Experience of Insurers and Very Large Industrial Firms.* Santa Monica, CA: RAND, The Institute for Civil Justice.

Adams, J. 1992. "Liability and the Financial Statement." *Directors and Boards.* Summer: 33–36.

American Accounting Association. 1975. Committee on Social Costs. *Accounting Review Supplement.*

_____. 1976. Report of the Committee on Accounting for Social Performance. *Accounting Review Supplement.*

American Institute of Certified Public Accountants. 1977. *The Measurement of Corporate Social Performance: Determining the Impact of Business Actions on Areas of Social Concern.* New York: AICPA.

American Institute of Certified Public Accountants, Financial Report Survey. 1993. *Illustrations of Accounting for Environmental Costs.* New York: AICPA.

American Institute of Certified Public Accountants, Environmental Accounting Task Force, Accounting Standards Division. 1994. Environmental Remediation Liabilities.

Anderberg, M.R. 1994. "Environmental Costs: A New Element in Life-Cycle Cost Estimates for DOD Acquisition Programs." Presented to Environmental Life-Cycle Assessment (LCA) Model User Requirements Workshop, Arlington, Virginia, October 6–7.

Aoi, J. 1994. "To Whom Does the Company Belong?: A New Management Mission for the Information Age." *Journal of Applied Corporate Finance*, Winter: 25–31.

Arnold, F. 1993. "Life Cycle Doesn't Work." *The Environmental Forum*, September/October: 19–23.

Arrow, K., R. Solow, P.R. Portney, E.E. Leamer, R. Radner, and H. Schuman. 1993. Report of the NOAA Panel on Contingent Valuation. *Federal Register*, 58: 4601–14.

Arthur Andersen & Co. 1994. *EcoAccounting.* Chicago: Arthur Andersen & Co.

Arthur D. Little. 1989. *Environmental Auditing: An Overview*. Cambridge, MA: Arthur D. Little, Inc.

Atkinson, A.A., R.D. Banker, R.S. Kaplan, and S.M.Young. 1995. *Management Accounting*. Englewood Cliffs, NJ: Prentice-Hall, Inc.

Avila, J.A., and B.W. Whitehead. 1993. "What is Environmental Strategy?" *The McKinsey Quarterly*, No. 4: 53–68.

Barrett, S. 1992. "Strategy and the Environment." *The Columbia Journal of World Business*, Summer and Winter: 203–208.

Barth, M.E., M. Epstein, and R.D. Stark. 1994. *Polaroid: Managing Environmental Responsibilities and Costs*. Boston, MA: Harvard Business School Case 9-194-052.

Barth, M., and M. McNichols. 1994. "Estimation and Market Valuation of Environmental Liabilities Relating to Superfund Sites." *Journal of Accounting Research*, forthcoming.

Batra, S.P., D.K. Singh, and B.M. Willborg. 1993. "Roadmap to Successful ISO 9000 Registration." *Industrial Engineering*, October: 54–55.

Bauer, R.A., and D. Fenn, Jr. 1972. *The Corporate Social Audit*. New York: Russell Sage Foundation.

_____. 1973. "What Is a Corporate Social Audit?" *Harvard Business Review*, January–February.

Bechtel, F.K., and M.S. Koellner. 1992. "Due Diligence: What Every CPA Should Know About Environmental Liability." *Pennsylvania CPA Journal*, Winter: 8–11.

Bell, S. 1992. "Environmentally Sensitive: Practical Audit and Accounting Concerns Associated with Environmental Liability." *Pennsylvania CPA Journal*, Winter: 19–22.

Bennett, S.J., R. Freierman, and S. George. 1993. *Corporate Realities and Environmental Truths: Strategies for Leading Your Business in the Environmental Era*. New York: John Wiley & Sons, Inc.

Bhushan, A., and J.C. Mackenzie. 1994. *Environmental Leadership Plus Total Quality Management Equals Continuous Improvement*. New York: Executive Enterprises Publications.

Birchard, B. 1993. "The Right to Know." *CFO*, November.

Bloom, G.F., and M.S. Scott Morton. 1991. "Hazardous Waste Is Every Manager's Problem." *Sloan Management Review*, Summer: 75–84.

Brewer, P.C., A.W. Gatian, and J.M. Reeve. 1993. "Managing Uncertainty." *Management Accounting*, October: 39–45.

Breyer, S. 1993. *Breaking the Vicious Circle: Toward Effective Risk Regulation*. Cambridge, MA: Harvard University Press.

Brooks, P.L., L.J. Davidson, and J.H. Palmides. 1993. "Environmental Compliance: You Better Know Your ABCs." *Occupational Hazards*, February.

Business Council for Sustainable Development (BCSD). 1993. Internalizing Environmental Costs to Promote Eco Efficiency. Draft document, September 14, 1993.

Callenbach, E., F. Capra, L. Goldman, R. Lutz, and S. Marburg. 1993. *Eco Management: The Elmwood Guide to Ecological Auditing and Sustainable Business*. San Francisco, CA: Berrett-Koehler Publishers.

Cairncross, F. 1992a. *Costing the Earth*. Boston, MA: Harvard Business School Press.

_____. 1992b. "UNCED, Environmentalism and Beyond." *Columbia Journal of World Business*, Fall and Winter: 13–17.

Canadian Institute of Chartered Accountants. 1992. *Environmental Auditing and the Role of the Accounting Profession*. Toronto: The Canadian Institute of Chartered Accountants.

_____. 1993a. *Environmental Costs and Liabilities: Accounting and Financial Reporting Issues*. Toronto: The Canadian Institute of Chartered Accountants.

_____. 1993b. *Reporting on Environmental Performance: A Discussion Paper*. Toronto: The Canadian Institute of Chartered Accountants.

Caplan, E.H., and S. Landekich. 1974. *Human Resource Accounting: Past, Present and Future*. New York: National Association of Accountants.

Carnegie Commission on Science, Technology, and Government. 1993. *Risk and the Environment: Improving Regulatory Decision Making*. New York: Carnegie Commission on Science, Technology, and Government.

Carson, P., and J. Moulden. 1991. *Green Is Gold: Business Talking to Business About Environmental Revolution*. New York: Harper Business.

Carson, R.T., N.F. Meade, and V.K. Smith. 1993. "Introducing the Issues." *Choices*, 2nd Quarter: 5–8.

Chadick, B., R.W. Rouse, and J. Surma. 1993. "Perspectives on Environmental Accounting." *The CPA Journal*, January.

Charnes, A., W.W. Cooper, and G. Kozmetsky. 1974. "TIMS in Perspective 1954, 1964, 1974, 1984?" *Interfaces*, February.

CH2M HILL. 1993. *The Role of Internal Auditors in Environmental Issues*. Altamonte Springs, FL: The Institute of Internal Auditors Research Foundation.

Cooper, R., R.S. Kaplan, L.S. Maisel, E. Morrissey, and R.M. Oehm. 1992. *Implementing Activity-Based Cost Management: Moving from Analysis to Action*. Montvale, NJ: Institute of Management Accountants.

Corbett, C.J., and L.N. Van Wassenhove. 1993. "The Green Fee: Internalizing and Operationalizing Environmental Issues." *California Management Review*, Fall: 116–135.

Council of Great Lakes Industries (CGLI). 1993. *TQEM Primer and Self-Assessment Matrix.*

Davis, J. 1991. *Greening Business: Managing for Sustainable Development.* Cambridge, MA: Basil Blackwell.

Defense Contract Audit Agency. 1994. *Environmental Costs in DCAA Audit Manual*, Chapter 7. Washington, DC: DCAA.

Deloitte & Touche. 1991. Public Utility Executive Briefs, April 26: 1–7.

Deloitte Touche Tohmatsu International, International Institute for Sustainable Development, and SustainAbility. 1993. *Coming Clean: Corporate Environmental Reporting.* London: Deloitte Touche Tohmatsu International.

Desvousges, W.H., A.R. Gable, R.W. Dunford, and S.P. Hudson. 1993. "Contingent Valuation: The Wrong Tool to Measure Passive Use Loss." *Choices*, 2nd Quarter: 9–11.

Desvousges, W.H., F.R. Johnson, R.W. Dunford, K.J. Boyle, S.P. Hudson, and K.N. Wilson. 1992. *Measuring Nonuse Damages Using Contingent Valuation: An Experimental Evaluation of Accuracy.* Research Triangle Park, NC: Research Triangle Institute.

Dewhurst, P. 1993. "Product Design for Manufacture: Design for Disassembly." *Industrial Engineering*, September: 26–28.

Di Lorenzo, T. 1993. "The Mirage of Sustainable Development." *The Futurist*, September/October: 14–19.

Dorfman, M.H., W.R. Muir, and C.G. Miller. 1992. *Environmental Dividends: Cutting More Chemical Wastes.* New York: INFORM.

Dutta, S. 1993. "Fuzzy Logic Applications: Technological and Strategic Issues." *IEEE Transactions on Engineering Management*, Vol. 40, No. 3, August: 237–254.

Eccles, R. 1991. "The Performance Measurement Manifesto." *Harvard Business Review*, January–February: 131–137.

Eccles, R., and P.J. Pyburn. 1992. "Creating a Comprehensive System to Measure Performance." *Management Accounting*, October: 41–44.

Elkington, J., and N. Robins. 1993. *The Corporate Environment Report: Measuring Industry's Progress Towards Sustainable Development.* London: SustainAbility Ltd.

Environmental Law Institute. 1993. A Framework for Understanding the Relationship between Environmental Liability and Managerial Decisions Affecting Pollution Prevention: 1–46.

Epstein, M. 1975. Testimony before the Securities and Exchange Commission. Public Proceeding on Disclosure of Certain Environmental, Equal Employment and Other Matters of Primarily Social Rather than Financial Significance. Washington, DC. May 8: 1711–1888.

_____. 1991. "What Shareholders Really Want." *New York Times*, April 28, 1991, Sec. F: 11.

_____. 1993. "The Expanding Role of Accountants in Society." *Management Accounting*, April.

_____. 1994. "The Integration of Environmental Measurements into Management Decision Making." Unpublished paper presented at European Accounting Association, April, Venice, Italy.

_____. 1994. "A Formal Plan for Environmental Costs." *New York Times*, April 3, 1994, Sec. F: 11.

Epstein, M., J. Epstein, and E. Weiss. 1977. *Introduction to Social Accounting*. Los Angeles, CA: California State University, Los Angeles.

Epstein, M., E. Flamholtz, and J.J. McDonough. 1976. "Corporate Social Accounting in the United States of America: State of the Art and Future Prospects." *Accounting, Organizations and Society*, Vol. 1, No. 1: 23–42.

_____. 1977. *Corporate Social Performance: The Measurement of Product and Service Contributions*. New York: National Association of Accountants.

Epstein, M.J., and M.L. Pava. 1992. "Corporations and the Environment: Shareholders Demand Accountability." *USA Today*, November: 32–33.

Estes, R.W. 1974. "A Comprehensive Corporate Social Reporting Model." *The Federal Accountant*, December.

_____. 1976. *Corporate Social Accounting*. New York: John Wiley & Sons, Inc.

_____. 1995. *Tyranny of the Bottom Line: Calling the Corporation to Account*. San Francisco: Berrett-Koehler Publishers, Inc. Forthcoming.

European Community Committee of the American Chamber of Commerce. 1994. *EC Environment Guide*. Belgium: EC Committee of the ACC.

Executive Enterprises Publications. 1992. *Understanding Environmental Accounting and Disclosure Today*. New York: Executive Enterprises Publications Co.

_____. 1994. *Understanding Total Quality Environmental Management*. 2d ed. New York: Executive Enterprises Publications Co.

Fenn, S.A. 1993. "Environmental Information Needs An Institutional Investment Perspective." Unpublished paper. Environmental Law Institute, Washington, DC, June 15.

Fiksel, J., and K. Wapman. 1994. "How to Design for Environment and Minimize Life Cycle Cost." Presented at IEEE Symposium on Electronics and the Environment. San Francisco, CA.

Fischer, K., and J. Schot, eds. 1993. *Environmental Strategies for Industry: International Perspectives on Research Needs and Policy Implications.* Washington, DC: Island Press.

Frank, P.B., M.J. Wagner, and R.L Weil. 1994. *Litigation Services Handbook: The Role of the Accountant as Expert Witness. 1994 Cumulative Supplement.* New York: John Wiley & Sons, Inc.

Freedman, M., and A.J. Stagliano. 1994. "Disclosure of Environmental Cleanup Costs: The Impact of the Superfund Act." *Advances in Public Interest Accounting.*

Freeman, M.A. 1993. *The Measurement of Environmental and Resource Values: Theory and Methods.* Washington, DC: Resources for the Future.

Friedman, F.B. 1993. *Practical Guide to Environmental Management.* Washington, DC: Environmental Law Institute.

Gavin, J. G. 1992. "Environmental Protection and the GATT: A Business View." *Columbia Journal of World Business,* Fall and Winter: 75–83.

Gibby, D.J., and R. Patella. 1993. "Deductibility of Environmental Remediation Costs." *Journal of Accountancy,* December: 44–49.

Global Environmental Management Initiative. 1993. Business Environmental Cost Accounting Practices Survey, Summary of Responses, March 16.

Global Environmental Management Initiative. 1992. *Environmental Self Assessment Program.* Washington, DC: GEMI.

———. 1994. *Finding Cost Effective Pollution Prevention Initiatives: Incorporating Environmental Costs into Business Decision Making. A Primer.* Washington, DC: GEMI.

———. 1993. *Total Quality Environmental Management: The Primer.* Washington, DC: GEMI.

Graedel, T.E., and B.R. Allenby. 1995. *Industrial Ecology.* Englewood Cliffs, NJ: Prentice-Hall.

Graham, J., and K.D. Walker. 1992. "Role of Exposure Databases in Risk Assessment." *Archives of Environmental Health,* November/December 47: 408–420.

Grant Thornton. 1994. "Manufacturing Becomes 'Greener' as Companies Adopt Environmentally Sound Practices." *Grant Thornton Manufacturing Issues,* Winter, Vol. 5, No. 1.

Gray, G.M., and J.D. Graham. 1991. "Risk Assessment and Clean Air Policy." *Journal of Policy Analysis and Management,* Vol. 10, No. 2: 286–295.

Gray, R.H. 1990. *The Greening of Accountancy: The Profession after Pearce.* London: Certified Accountants Publications Ltd.

Gray, R.H., J. Bebbington, and D. Walters. 1993. *Accounting for the Environment.* London: Paul Chapman Publishing Ltd.

Gray, R.H., and D. Collison. 1991. "The Environmental Audit: Green-Gauge or Whitewash?" *Managerial Auditing Journal*, Vol. 6, No. 5: 17–25.

Gray, R.H., D. Owen, and K. Maunders. 1987. *Corporate Social Reporting: Accounting and Accountability.* London: Prentice-Hall, Inc.

Greenberg, R.S., and C.A. Unger. 1993/1994. "Environmental Management, Internal Control, and TQEM." *Total Quality Environmental Management*, Winter: 223–229.

Greeno, J.L., G.S. Hedstrom, and M. Diberto. 1987. *Environmental Auditing: Fundamentals and Techniques.* Cambridge, MA: Arthur D. Little, Inc.

Greeno, J.L., and S.N. Robinson. 1992. "Rethinking Corporate Environmental Management." *The Columbia Journal of World Business.* Fall & Winter: 222–232.

Hahn, R. 1992. "An Economic Analysis of Scrappage." Paper, Kennedy School of Government, Harvard University, July, unpublished.

Harmon, M. 1994. "First There Was ISO 9000, Now There's ISO 14000." *Quality Digest*, July.

Harrison, L.L, ed. 1984. *The McGraw-Hill Environmental Auditing Handbook: A Guide to Corporate and Environmental Risk Management.* New York: McGraw-Hill Book Company.

Hawken, P. 1993. *The Ecology of Commerce: A Declaration of Sustainability.* New York: Harper Business.

Hayes, D.J. 1993. "Beyond Cradle to Grave." *The Environmental Forum*, September/October: 14–17.

Hector, Gary. 1992. "A New Reason You Can't Get a Loan." *Fortune*, September 21: 107–112.

Hedstrom, G.S. 1992. "Environmental Audit Information Management and Communication: Satisfying Your Stakeholders," presented at Corporate Quality/Environmental Management II Conference, Arlington, Virginia. March 16–18: 217–221.

Henn, C.L. 1993. "The New Economics of Life Cycle Thinking," published by Institute for Electrical and Electronics Engineers: 184–188.

Henn, C.L., and J.A. Fava. 1993. "Life Cycle Analysis and Resource Management" in R.V. Kolluru, ed., *Environmental Strategies Handbook.* New York: McGraw-Hill, Inc: 542–641.

Hetland, J.L. 1974. "The Social Audit, First National Bank's Experience," presented at the Public Affairs Conference, Bank Marketing Association/ American Bankers Association, February 11.

Himelstein, L., and M.B. Regan. 1993. "Fresh Ammo for the Eco-Cops." *Business Week*, November 29: 136–138.

Hochman, S., R.P. Wells, P.A. O'Connell, and M.N. Hochman. 1993. "Total Quality Management: A Tool to Move from Compliance to Strategy." *Greener Management International* 1, January: 59–71.

International Chamber of Commerce. 1991. *ICC Guide to Effective Environmental Auditing*. Paris: ICC Publishing, S.A.

International Institute for Sustainable Development (IISD). 1992. *Business Strategy for Sustainable Development: Leadership and Accountability for the '90's*. Winnipeg, Manitoba: IISD.

Jaffe, A.B, S.R. Peterson, P.R. Portney, and R.N. Stavins. 1994. "Environmental Regulation and the Competitiveness of U.S. Manufacturing: What the Evidence Tells Us." *Journal of Economic Literature*, forthcoming.

Jain, R.K., L.V. Urban, G.S. Stacey, and H.E. Balbach. 1993. *Environmental Assessment*. New York: McGraw-Hill, Inc.

Johnson, L.T. 1993. "Research on Environmental Reporting." *Accounting Horizons*, Vol. 7, No. 3, September: 118–123.

Kaplan, J.M., L.S. Dakin, and M.R. Smolin. 1993. "Living with the Organizational Sentencing Guidelines." *California Management Review*, Fall: 136–146.

Kaplan, R.S., and D.P. Norton. 1992. "The Balanced Scorecard—Measures That Drive Performance." *Harvard Business Review*, January–February: 71–79.

_____. 1993. "Putting the Balanced Scorecard to Work." *Harvard Business Review*, September-October: 134–147.

Karch, K. 1994. "Getting Organizational Buy-In for Benchmarking: Environmental Management at Weyerhaeuser." *Total Quality Environmental Management*, Vol. 3, No. 3, Spring: 297–307.

Kinder, P., S.D. Lydenberg, and A.L. Domini. 1993. *Investing for Good: Making Money While Being Socially Responsible*. New York: HarperCollins Publishers, Inc.

Kinzer, S. 1994. "Germany Upholds Tax on Fast-Food Containers." *New York Times*, August 22.

Kleiner, A. 1991. "What Does It Mean to be Green?" *Harvard Business Review*, July–August: 38–47.

Kleiner, B.M. 1994. "Benchmarking for Continuous Performance Improvement: Tactics for Success." *Total Quality Environmental Management*, Vol. 3, No. 3, Spring: 283–295.

KPMG. 1993. *International Survey of Environmental Reporting*. New York: KPMG.

Koechlin, D., and K. Muller, eds. 1993. *Green Business Opportunities: The Profit Potential*. London: Pitman Publishing.

Kolluru, R.V. ed. 1993. *Environmental Strategies Handbook*. New York: McGraw-Hill, Inc.

Kreuze, J., and G.E. Newell. 1994. "ABC and Life-Cycle Costing for Environmental Expenditures." *Management Accounting*, February: 38–42.

Krutilla, J.V. 1967. "Conservation Reconsidered." *American Economic Review* 57, September: 777–786.

Kula, E. 1992. *Economics of Natural Resources, The Environment and Policies*. London: Chapman & Hall.

Lawrence, C.A., and A.C. Butler. 1995. "Legacy Costing, Fuzzy Systems Theory, and Environmentally Conscious Manufacturing." *Advances in Management Accounting*, Vol. 4. Forthcoming.

Lawrence, C.M., M. Fortune, and A.C. Butler. 1995. "A Fuzzy Decision Model for Environmental Risk Assessment," in P.H. Siegel, A. de Korvin, and K. Omer, eds. *Applications of Fuzzy Sets and the Theory of Evidence to Accounting*. Greenwich, CT: JAI Press. Forthcoming.

Ledgerwood, G., E. Street, and R. Therivel. 1992. *The Environmental Audit and Business Strategy*. London: Pitman Publishing.

Lent, T., and R.P. Wells. 1992. "Corporate Environmental Management Study Shows Shift from Compliance to Strategy." *Total Quality Environmental Management*, Summer: 379–394.

Lind, R.C. 1977. *Discounting for Time and Risk in Energy Policy*. Washington, DC: Resources for the Future.

Linowes, D.F. 1968. "Socio-Economic Accounting." *Journal of Accountancy*, November.

_____. 1972. "Measuring Social Programs in Business—A Social Audit Proposal for Immediate Implementation," address before the American Accounting Association, Louisiana State University, Baton Rouge, LA, April 28.

_____. 1974. *The Corporate Conscience*. New York: Hawthorn Books.

Lorensen, L. 1993. "Illustrations of Accounting for Environmental Costs." *AICPA Financial Report Survey*, July.

Lucas, A., and M. Roberts. 1994. "Environmental Management Standards Set of 1995 Debut." *Chemical Week*, November: 9–33.

Macve, R., and A. Carey, eds. 1992. *Business, Accountancy and The Environment: A Policy and Research Agenda*. London: The Institute of Chartered Accountants in England and Wales.

Makower, J. 1993. *The E Factor*. New York: The Tilden Press.

Marchant, G.E. 1994. "Environmental Legal Liabilities: Prevention and Control," in R.V. Kolluru, ed. *Environmental Strategies Handbook: A Guide to Effective Policies and Practices*. New York: McGraw Hill, Inc.

Marcil, A. 1992. "Environmentally Friendly Development: Can the Private Sector Succeed Where Others Have Failed?" *Columbia Journal of World Business* 27, Nos. 3&4, Fall/Winter: 195–200.

Martin, Dale. 1994. "Environmental Planning: Balancing Environmental Commitments with Economic Realities." *GEMI 1994 Conference Proceedings*. March 16–17: 57–64.

McCommons, J. 1992. "Niagara Mohawk Turns Its Waste Streams Into Cash Flow." *Trilogy*, July/August.

Merchant, K.A. 1989. *Rewarding Results: Motivating Profit Center Managers*. Boston, MA: Harvard Business School Press.

Meyer, S.M. 1992. "Environmentalism and Economic Prosperity: Testing the Environmental Impact Hypothesis." Unpublished, MIT.

Mezzo, L. 1994. "The Continuing Saga of Environmental Cleanup Costs." *Grant Thornton Manufacturing Issues*, Summer, Vol. 5, No. 3: 13.

Miakisz, J. 1992. "Developing a Composite Index for Measuring and Communicating Environmental Performance." *GEMI Conference Proceedings on Corporate Quality/Environmental Management II*: 189–193.

"Midsized Manufacturers are Familiar with ISO 9000, but Few will Register Soon." 1993. *Journal of Accountancy*, October: 21–22.

Mishan, E.J. 1971. *Cost-Benefit Analysis*. London: George Allen & Unwin, Ltd.

_____. 1972. *Economics for Social Decision: Elements of Cost-Benefit Analysis*. New York: Praeger Publishers.

Mitchell, R.C., and R.T. Carson. 1989. *Using Surveys to Value Public Goods: The Contingent Valuation Method*. Washington, DC: Resources for the Future.

Mullins, M.L. 1994. "Industry Perspective: Environmental Health and Safety Challenges and Social Responsibilities," in R.V. Kolluru, Ed., *Environmental Strategies Handbook: A Guide to Effective Policies and Practices*. New York: McGraw Hill, Inc, pp.s 201–238.

Naimon, J.S. 1994. "Lifting the Veil." *Tomorrow*, January-March, Vol. 1: 58–66.

Nikolai, A., J.D. Bazley, and R.L. Brummet. 1976. *The Measurement of Corporate Environmental Activity*. New York: National Association of Accountants.

Northeast Waste Management Officials' Association (NEWMOA). 1992. Costing and Financial Analysis of Pollution Prevention Projects: A Training Packet. Boston, MA: NEWMOA.

Owen, D., ed. 1992. *Green Reporting: Accountancy and the Challenge of the Nineties*. London: Chapman & Hall.

Pariser, D.B., and A. Neidermeyer. 1991. "Environmental Due Diligence: The Internal Auditor's Role." *Journal of Bank Accounting and Auditing*, Winter.

Pava, M. and M. Epstein. 1993. "How Good is MD&A as an Investment Tool?" *Journal of Accountancy*, March.

Popoff, F. and D.T. Buzzelli. 1993. "Viewpoint: Full-Cost Accounting." *Prism*, Third Quarter: 69–76.

Porter, M.E. 1980. *Competitive Strategy*. New York: Free Press.

_____. 1985. *Competitive Advantage*. New York: Free Press.

_____. 1990. *The Competitive Advantage of Nations*. New York: Free Press.

_____. 1991. "America's Green Strategy." *Scientific American*, April: 168.

_____. 1992. "Capital Disadvantage: America's Failing Capital Investment System." *Harvard Business Review*, September/October.

Porter, M.E., and C. van der Linde. 1994. "Towards a New Conception of the Environment-Competitiveness Relationship." Unpublished.

Post, J.F., and M. Epstein. 1977. "The Development of a Social Accounting Information System." *Academy of Management Review*, January.

President's Commission on Environmental Quality (PCEQ). 1993. *Total Quality Management: A Framework for Pollution Prevention*. Washington, DC: PCEQ.

Price Waterhouse. 1992a. *Environmental Costs: Accounting and Disclosure*. New York: Price Waterhouse.

_____. 1992b. *Accounting for Environmental Compliance: Crossroad of GAAP, Engineering, and Government*. New York: Price Waterhouse.

_____. 1994. *Progress on the Environmental Challenge: A Survey of Corporate America's Environmental Accounting and Management*. New York: Price Waterhouse.

Protzman, F. 1993. "Germany's Push to Expand the Scope of Recycling." *New York Times*, July 4.

Rabinowitz, D.L., and M. Murphy. 1992. "Environmental Disclosure: What the SEC Requires," in *Understanding Environmental Accounting and Disclosure Today*. New York: Executive Enterprises Publications Co.

Randall, A. 1993. "Passive-Use Values and Contingent Valuation—Valid for Damage Assessment." *Choices*, 2nd Quarter: 12–14.

Rappaport, A. 1993. "Industry and Regulatory Agency: A Non-Traditional Partnership," presented at the Seventh Talloires Seminar on International Environmental Issues, Strengthening Partnerships for Technological Cooperation. Talloires, France, June 10-12.

Rice, F. 1993. "Who Scores Best on the Environment." *Fortune*, July 26: 114–122.

Rice, V.R. 1994. "Regulating Reasonably." *The Environmental Forum*, May/June: 16–23.

Riordan, D.E., and S.N. Cairns. 1994. "Deduction of Toxic Waste Cleanup Costs May be a Hazardous Position." *Management Accounting*, February: 34–37.

Roberts, R.Y. 1993. "Environmental Liability Accounting Developments," speech to the American Bar Association Fourth Annual Joint Conference on Environmental Aspects of Corporate and Real Estate Transactions, New Orleans, Louisiana, June 10.

Robinson, S.N., R. Earle III, and R.A.N. McLean. 1994. "Transnational Corporations and Global Environmental Policy." *Prism*, First Quarter: 51–63.

Roussey, R.S. 1992. "Auditing Environmental Liabilities." *Auditing*, Vol. 11, No. 1, Spring: 47–57.

Rubenstein, D.B. 1994. *Environmental Accounting for the Sustainable Corporation: Strategies and Techniques*. Westport, CT: Quorum Books.

Russell, M., E.W. Colglazier, and M.R. English. 1991. *Hazardous Waste Remediation: The Task Ahead*. Knoxville, TN: Waste Management Research and Education Institute.

Russell, W.G., S.L. Skalak, and G. Miller. 1994. "Environmental Cost Accounting: The Bottom Line for Environmental Quality Management." *Total Quality Environmental Management*, Spring: 255–268.

Sarokin, D.J., W.R. Muir, C.G. Miller, S.R. Sperber. 1985. *Cutting Chemical Wastes*. New York: INFORM.

Saunders, T., and L. McGovern. 1993. *The Bottom Line of Green Is Black*. New York: Harper Collins.

Schmidheiny, S. 1992. "The Business Logic of Sustainable Development." *Columbia Journal of World Business*, Fall and Winter: 19–24.

_____.1992. *Changing Course: A Global Business Perspective on Development and the Environment*. Cambridge, MA: MIT Press.

SETAC News. 1993. "Life-Cycle Assessment." November, Vol. 3, No. 6.

Selling, T.I. 1993. *The SEC and Financial Statement Reporting of Environmental Contingencies.* Presentation at the 86th Annual Meeting and Exhibition of the Air and Waste Management Association, Denver, CO, June 13–18.

Shank, J.K. 1989. "Strategic Cost Management: New Wine, or Just New Bottles?" *Journal of Management Accounting Research*, Fall, Vol. 1: 47–65.

Shanker, H.M. 1994. "Lenders Beware...Are You Environmentally Liable?" *National Real Estate Investor*, August: 99–104.

Silverstein, M. 1990. *The Environmental Factor: Its Impact on the Future of the World Economy and Your Investments.* Chicago: Longman Financial Services Publishing.

Smart, B., ed. 1992. *Beyond Compliance: A New Industry View of the Environment.* New York: World Resources Institute.

Society of Management Accountants of Canada. 1995a. Management Accounting Guideline #37, "Implementing Corporate Environmental Strategies." Hamilton, Ontario: The Society of Management Accountants of Canada.

_____. 1995b. Management Accounting Guidelline #40, "Tools and Techniques of Environmental Accounting." Hamilton, Ontario: The Society of Management Accountants of Canada.

Spitzer, M.A. 1992. "Pollution Prevention." *Pollution Engineering*, September 1: 33–38.

Spitzer, M.A., R. Pojasek, F.L. Robertaccio, and J. Nelson. 1993. "Accounting and Capital Budgeting for Pollution Prevention." Presented at Engineering Foundation Conference, San Diego, CA, January 24–29.

"Superfund Site Spawns a Spate of Litigation Though Not a Cleanup." *The Wall Street Journal*, February 9, 1994.

Surma, J.P. 1992. "A Survey of How Corporate America Is Accounting for Environmental Costs," in *Understanding Environmental Accounting and Disclosure Today.* New York: Executive Enterprises Publications Co., Inc.

Surma, J.P., and A.A. Vondra. 1992. "Accounting for Environmental Costs: A Hazardous Subject." *Journal of Accountancy*, March: 51–55.

Thomas, L. 1992. "The Business Community and the Environment: An Important Partnership." *Business Horizons*, March/April, Vol. 35, No. 2: 21–24.

Tuppen, C. 1993. "An Environmental Policy for British Telecommunications." *Long Range Planning*, Vol. 26, No. 5, October: 24–30.

U.S. Department of Energy, Office of Environmental Audit. *Protocols for Conducting Environmental Management Assessments of DOE Organizations.* Washington: U.S. Department of Energy.

U.S. Environmental Protection Agency. 1989. *Pollution Prevention Benefits Manual*. Washington, DC: EPA.

_____. 1992a. *Facility Pollution Prevention Guide*. Washington, DC: EPA.

_____. 1992b. *Total Cost Assessment: Accelerating Industrial Pollution Prevention Through Innovative Project Financial Analysis*. Washington, DC: EPA.

_____. 1993. *Green Lights: An Enlightened Approach to Energy Efficiency and Pollution Prevention*. Washington, DC: EPA.

_____. 1994. Notice of Public Meeting on Auditing. *Federal Register*, June 14.

U.S. Securities and Exchange Commission. 1993. Staff Accounting Bulletin 92, "Accounting and Disclosures Relating to Loss Contingencies." Washington, DC: SEC.

U.S. Sentencing Commission. 1993. Memorandum from Phyllis J. Newton, staff director to Advisory Group on Environmental Sanctions, December 6.

Wald, M.L. 1992. "Utility is Selling Right to Pollute." *New York Times*, May 13.

Walley, N., and B. Whitehead. 1994. "It's Not Easy Being Green." *Harvard Business Review*, May/June, No. 3.

Weitz, K.A., J.K. Smith, B.F. Fagg, J.L. Warren, D. Adolphson, K. Tschritter, and B. Odegard. 1994. *DOE/SNL/EPA Joint Effort to Develop Waste Minimization Techniques for DOE R&D Laboratories*. Research Triangle Park, NC: Research Triangle Institute.

Wells, R.P., M.N. Hochman, S.D. Hochman, and P.A. O'Connell. 1992. "Measuring Environmental Success." *Total Quality Environmental Management*, Summer: 315–327.

White, A.L. 1993. "Accounting for Pollution Prevention." *EPA Journal*, July–September: 23–25.

White, A.L., M. Becker, and J. Goldstein. 1991. *Alternative Approaches to the Financial Evaluation of Industrial Pollution Prevention Investments*. Boston, MA: Tellus Institute.

White, A.L., D. Savage, and M. Becker. 1993a. Revised Executive Summary, June 1993. *Alternative Approaches to the Financial Evaluation of Industrial Pollution Prevention Investments*. Prepared for New Jersey Department of Environmental Protection.

_____. 1993b. Revised Executive Summary, June 1993. *Total Cost Assessment: Accelerating Industrial Pollution Prevention Through Innovative Project Financial Analysis with Applications to the Paper Industry*. Prepared for U.S. Environmental Protection Agency.

White, T.M. 1994. "Measure for Measure." *Environmental Forum*, July/August: 16–20.

Williams, G., and T.J. Phillips. 1994. "Cleaning up Our Act: Accounting for Environmental Liabilities." *Management Accounting*, February.

Willig, J.T., ed. 1994. *Understanding Total Quality Environmental Management.* New York: Executive Enterprises Publications Co.

Willits, S.D., and R. Giuntini. 1994. "Helping Your Company 'Go Green'." *Management Accounting*, February: 43–47.

Winsemius, P., and W. Hahn. 1992. "Environmental Option Assessment." *The Columbia Journal of World Business*, Fall and Winter: 249–266.

Wise, M., and L. Kenworth. 1993. *Preventing Industrial Toxic Hazards: A Guide for Communities.* New York: INFORM.

Wolfe, J. 1994. "Standard Bearers." *CA Magazine*, June/July.

World Commission on Environment and Development. 1987. *Our Common Future.* Oxford: Oxford University Press.

Index

A

ABB (Asea Brown Boveri Ltd.), 8, 279
  EH&S organizational structure, 60–62
  performance evaluation systems,
    227–228
Abt Associates, Inc., 3
  social audit, development of, 270–271
  TQEM (total quality environmental
    management) and, 66, 68
Accounting
  environmental, 78–82
  ESI (environmental strategy implemen-
    tation), checklist, 246
  regulations; see Regulations
Acquisition and divestments, internal
    auditing systems and, 93–96
Acronyms, glossary of, 285–288
Activity-based costing (ABC), 157–158
Acton, J.P., 289
Adams, J., 289
Addison, Edward L., 118
Adolphson, D., 303
AICPA (American Institute of Certified
    Public Accountants), regulations,
    256–260
Alcan Aluminum, 279
  performance evaluation systems, 228
Alcoa, 279
  Alcoa Remediation Team (ART), 70–71
Allenby, B.R., 294
AlliedSignal, 279
  legacy costing and, 162
  performance evaluation, 213–215
Allocation, of costs, 149
American Society for Testing and
    Materials, 104

Amoco, 21, 279
  information systems, 83–84
  IRRC (Investor Responsibility Research
    Center), 126–128
  partnership programs and, 22
  performance evaluation systems, 229
  PERI (Public Environmental Reporting
    Initiative) and, 125–126
Anderberg, M.R., 35–36, 289
Aoi, Joichi, 63, 289
Arnold, F., 289
Arrow, K., 289
Arthur Andersen & Co., EcoAccounting
    program, 150–153
Arthur D. Little, Inc. (ADL), 99, 101, 108
  Center for Environmental Assurance,
    102
  external audits of external environmen-
    tal reports, 134, 137, 138
Association of Environmental Consulting
    Firms (AECF), 104
Assurance letters, internal environmental
    auditing and, 93
Atkinson, A.A., 158, 290
AT&T, 279
  information systems, environmental, 84
  waste management, 44–45
Auditing; see Internal environmental
    auditing systems
Audit timeliness index (ATI), 99
Avila, J.A., 289
Awards
  Malcolm Baldrige National Quality, 70
  MERIT (measured equity return incen-
    tive term), 215–216
  performance evaluation and, 229

Awareness Compliance Tools (ACT) for Environmental Responsibility, 220

B

Balanced scorecard, corporate environmental impacts and, 72–74
Balbach, H.E., 296
Banker, R.D., 290
Banks, Bob, 124
Barrett, Scott, 25, 290
Barth, Mary E., 78n, 251n, 290
Batra, S.P., 290
Bauer, R.A., 268, 290
Bazley, J.D., 276, 299
Bebbington, J., 295
Bechtel, F.K., 290
Becker, M., 178, 302
Bell, S., 290
Ben & Jerry's Homemade, Inc., 299
  standards for environmental reports, 125
Bennett, S.J., 290
Bhushan, A., 46, 290
Birchard, B., 290
Bloom, G.F., 290
Blueprint for Sustainable Development in Virginia, 8
BMW, take-back programs, 32
Board of directors, EH&S organizational structure and, 54–56
The Body Shop, 279
  external audits of external environmental reports, 137
  life cycle assessment (LCA), 40
  waste reduction, 47
Boston Park Plaza Hotel, 47
Boyle, K.J., 292
Brewer, P.C., 187, 290
Breyer, Stephen, 18, 290
Bristol-Myers Squibb, 20, 58, 279
  acquisition and divestments, 94, 95
  capital expenditure approval process, 166–169
  corporate environmental strategy implementation, 245–248

Bristol-Myers Squibb *(continued)*
  disclosures, financial, 119
  Environment 2000, life cycle assessment (LCA), 37–40
  internal environmental auditing departments, 92
  self-audits, importance of, 93
  standard environmental reports and, 121, 122–123
  waste reduction, 47
British Petroleum, 125, 280
  disclosures, financial, 109
  full-cost accounting and, 160
British Telecommunications (BT), 280
  environmental purchasing and, 48
Brooks, P.L., 291
Browning-Ferris Industries (BFI), 58, 212, 280
  capital expenditure approval process, 166
  community interests and, 65
  disclosures, financial, 109–111
  EH&S organization, 56
  environmental multipliers in performance appraisals, 219–226, 228
  environmental self-assessment program (ESAP), 69
  internal environmental auditing departments, 92
  take-back programs, 33
  TQEM (total quality environmental management) and, 67
Brummet, R.L., 276, 299
Brundtland, Gro Harlem, 1–2, 7
Bush, George, 67
Business acquisition and divestments, internal environmental auditing systems and, 93–96
Business Council for Sustainable Development (BCSD), 15, 23
  life cycle assessments (LCAs) and, 35
  management accounting and financial reporting systems, 85
  standard environmental reports and, 120–121
Butler, A.C., 185, 297
Buzzelli, David T., 159, 299

C

Cairncross, F., 24, 291
Cairns, S.N., 300
Callenbach, E., 291
Cambrex Corp., 280
  disclosures, financial, 111, 112
Canadian Institute of Chartered
    Accountants (CICA), 101
Capital budgeting
  alternatives, selecting, 180–189
  contingent valuation (CV) and, 199,
    200–201
  cost assessment methods, 174–179
  cost of control approach, 190
  damage costing approach, 190–191
  decision trees and Monte Carlo simula-
    tion, 188–189
  DuPont environmental planning process,
    169–174
  80/20 analysis, 172
  EH&S checklist, 199–211
  expanded, for environmental capital
    investments, 172, 174
  expenditure approval process, 165–169
  fuzzy logic and, 185–187, 196–197
  liability, future, estimated, 196–197
  monetizing environmental externalities,
    190–191
  Monte Carlo simulation, 188–189
  Niagara Mohawk Power (NMPC),
    185–187, 193–194, 195–196
  option assessment, and screening,
    180–189
  option pricing theory, 195
  risk assessment, 193–194
  systems, 164–198
  uncertainty, other issues with, 195–196
Capitalization, of costs, 153–154
Caplan, E.H., 291
Capra, F., 291
Carey, A., 298
CARs (capital appropriations requests),
    166–169
Carson, P., 192, 291
Carson, R.T., 291, 298
CEOs, EH&S organization and, 56

CERCLA (Comprehensive Environmental
    Response, Compensation, and
    Liability Act), 90, 192, 254–255
CERES (Coalition for Environmentally
    Responsible Economies), 7,
    102–103
  standard environmental reports and,
    121, 124–125
Chadick, B., 291
Changing Course, 15
Charnes, A., 291
Chemical Manufacturers Association, 66
Chevron, 280
  information systems, 84
  performance evaluation and, 217,
    229–230
CH2M Hill, 89
Chrysler, waste management at, 43–44
Ciba-Geigy, 8–9, 17, 280
  environmental audits and, 97
  life cycle assessments (LCAs) and, 36
  performance evaluation systems, 228
  waste management information systems,
    76–77
Clean Air Act (CAA), 252–253
Clean-up incentives, 7
Clean Water Act (CWA), 253
Colglazier, E.W., 300
Collison, D., 294
Common Sense Initiative, 21
Community interests, total stakeholder
    analysis (TSA) and, 63–64, 66
Competitiveness, international
    competitors, 64
  environmental strategy and, 13–15,
    25–26
Compliance audits, 89–90
Contingent-valuation method, 191,
    200–201
Cooper, R., 291
Cooper, W.W., 291
Coopers & Lybrand, external audits of
    external environmental reports,
    134–135
Corbett, C.J., 84, 292
Corporate Accountability Commission,
    269

Corporate environmental impacts, 18,
50–74
balanced scorecard and, 72–74
EH&S organizational structure; *see*
EH&S departments
ESI (environmental strategy implementation) and, 50–53
minimizing, 31–49
Bristol-Myers Squibb, 37–40
life cycle assessments (LCAs) and,
34–43
life cycle costing, 35–36
recycling and the take-back
principle, 32–34
3Rs for, 31
waste reduction
through operations and purchasing,
46–48
product and process redesign
for, 43–45
tools and framework for analysis, 67–73
environmental remediation process
model (ERPM), 70–73
self-assessment
matrix, 68–70
program (ESAP), 69–70
TQEM (total quality environmental
management), 66–69
total stakeholder analysis (TSA), 62–66
Corporate environmental leadership,
236–237
Corporate environmental performance,
research report, 9–13
Corporate environmental strategy, 13–30
and competitiveness, international,
13–15, 25–26
development of, 25–27
ESI; *see* ESI (environmental strategy
implementation)
government partnerships and, 17–20
Green Lights Program (EPA), 19, 21
implementation; *see* ESI (environmental
strategy implementation)
mission statements and, 27–28
regulations, international, and multinational corporations, 15–17

Corporate environmental strategy *(cont'd)*
specific partnerships programs, 20–22
sustainable development and, 22–25
33/50 program (EPA), 20–21
Corporations, performance evaluation
systems for, 213–215
Cost-benefit analyses, social accounting
and, 271–276
Cost of control approach, 190
Costs/Costing systems, 24, 145–163
activity-based (ABC), 157–158
allocation of costs, 149
capitalization of costs, 153–154
cost assessment methods, capital budgeting systems, 174–179
current costs for current sins, 147–148
current costs for past sins, 146–147
EcoAccounting program, 150–153
externalities and, 162
full-cost accounting, 158–162
future costs for current sins, 148–149
identifying and tracking, 149–153
legacy costing, 162–163
life cycle costing, 154–156
management of costs, 156–158
product costs and, 146–147
strategic cost management (SCM), 158
Cracker Barrel, 47, 280
Criminal liability, environmental performance and, 5–6
Current costs
for current sins, 147–148
for past sins, 146–147
Customers, 64
satisfaction of, balanced scorecard
and, 73

D

Dakin, L.S., 296
Damage costing approach, 190–191
Davidson, L.J., 291
Davis, J., 292
Decision trees and Monte Carlo simula-
tion, 188–189

Defense, U.S. Department of, (DOD), life
cycle costing and, 35–36
Defense Contract Audit Agency, 154
de Korvin, A., 305
Deloitte & Touche, 69, 188, 189
external environmental reports, surveys
of, 264
Deming, W. Edwards, 66
Department of Defense (DOD), life cycle
costing and, 35–36
Desvousges, W.H., 192, 292
Dewhurst, P., 292
The Dexter Corp., 7–8, 280
Diberto, M., 295
Di Lorenzo, T., 292
Disclosures, financial, 107–120
Bristol-Myers Squibb, 119
British Petroleum, 109
Browning-Ferris Industries (BFI),
109–111
Cambrex Corp., 111, 112
Dow Chemical, 107–108
DuPont, 114–115
E.B. Eddy, 118
EPA, 114
ICI, 119
Monsanto, 112–114, 116
Ontario Hydro, 118
Rohm and Haas, 118–119
SEC and, 108–109
Southern Co., 114–118
Sun Co., 112
Union Carbide, 108
United Technologies, 112
Weyerhaeuser, 112–114
Dixon, L.S., 289
DOB (degree of belief), 187
Domini, A.L., 296
Dorfman, M.H., 86n, 292
Dow Chemical, 17–18, 36, 125, 280
community interests and, 65
disclosures, financial, 107–108
external environmental reports, 133
full-cost accounting and, 158–162
waste management program, 31
waste taxes, internal, 230
Due diligence audits, 90

Duke Power, 280
waste management information systems,
78
Dunford, R.W., 192, 292
DuPont, 28, 29, 58, 125, 172, 174, 280
disclosures, financial, 114,115
80/20 analysis, 20
environmental planning process,
169–174
performance evaluation systems,
226–227
Dutta, S., 292

E

Earle, R., III, 300
EARS (environmental accounting and
reporting system), 81–82
Earth Day, 2
Earth Summit (1992), 7
Eastman Kodak, 72, 280
environmental principles at, 28, 30
external audits of external environmental reports, 137–138
take-back programs, 33
TQEM (total quality environmental
management) and, 66
E.B. Eddy, 23–24, 281
disclosures, financial, 118
Eccles, R., 292
EC (European Community), 16
take-back programs, 33
EcoAccounting program, 150–153
Eco-auditing, 99–100
Eco-Management and Audit Scheme
(EMAS), 99
EH&S departments, 9–11, 51
at Bristol-Myers Squibb, 20
capital budgeting and; *see* Capital
budgeting
centralized vs. decentralized management, 59–60
at Eastman Kodak, 28
at E.B. Eddy, 23–24
and external environmental report
preparation, 129–134

EH&S departments *(continued)*
  information systems for; *see*
      Information systems, environ-
      mental
  organizational structure, 27, 53–63
    board of directors and, 54–56
    centralized vs. decentralized manage-
        ment, 59–60
    and CEOs, 56
    EH&S vice president, 58–59
    general counsel and, 56–58
    and international companies, 60–62
    management and, 59–60
    staff support of, 59
  reports from, Dow Chemical, 107–108
  vice presidents and, 58–59
80/20 analysis, DuPont environmental
    planning process, 172
Electric Power Research Institute (EPRI),
    193–194
Elkington, J., 292
Employees, 64
  awards for, 229–230
  involvement of, performance evaluation
      systems, 218
Energy, U.S. Department of, performance
    evaluation and, 213–215
Energy Policy Act (1992), 27
Energy prices, 26
English, M.R., 300
Environment 2000, Bristol-Myers Squibb,
    life cycle assessment (LCA),
    37–40
*Environmental Auditing and the Role of
    the Accounting Profession*, 101
Environmental economics, social
    accounting and, 271–276
Environmental impacts; *see* Corporate
    environmental impacts
Environmental Law Institute, 195
Environmental multipliers, performance
    evaluation, 219–226
Environmental Protection Agency;
    see EPA
Environmental remediation process model
    (ERPM), 70–73

Environmental reporting, 2–5
  external; *see* External environmental
      reports
Environmental Resources Management,
    Inc. (ERM), 37, 121
Environmental self-assessment
  matrix, 69–70
  program (ESAP), 69
Environmental strategy; *see* Corporate
    environmental strategy
EPA
  cost assessment methods, capital
      budgeting systems, 174–179
  Design for the Environment Program,
      43
  disclosures, financial, 114
  environmental auditing standards, 103
  Green Lights Program, 19, 21
  initiatives and programs, other, 21–22
  regulations; *see* Regulations
  SEC, coordination with, 261–262
  33/50 program, 20–21
  treatment, storage, and disposal facility
      audit, 90–91
EPI (environmental performance index),
    215–216
Epstein, J., 193, 267n, 293
Epstein, M.J., 76n, 193, 260, 267n, 269,
    270, 275, 277, 290, 293, 299
Ernst & Young, 134, 136
ESI (environmental strategy implementa-
    tion), 36, 232–249; *see also*
    Corporate environmental strategy
  Bristol-Myers Squibb, 245–248
  capital budgeting and, 172, 174
  corporate leadership in, 236–237
  corporate performance, scoring,
      234–238
  environmental impacts and, 50–53
  fifteen steps for, 243–244
  full-cost accounting and, 161–163
  life cycle assessments (LCAs) and,
      42–43
  managers and management accountants,
      guidelines, 245–248
  research surprises, 238–243

ESI *(continued)*
total stakeholder analysis (TSA); *see*
Total stakeholder analysis (TSA)
Estes, R.W., 268–269, 283
External environmental reports, 106–149
coordination of, 140–143
disclosures, financial; *see* Disclosures,
financial
EH&S department role, 129–134
external audits of, 139–140
preparation of, 129–134
standards for, 120–129
CERES and, 121, 124–125
ICC/BCSD, 120–121
IRRC (Investor Responsibility
Research Center), 126–128
ISO 9000/14000, 128–129
PERI (Public Environmental
Reporting Initiative), 125–126
responsible care initiative, 127
surveys and studies of, 262–264
Externalities
costing systems and, 162–163
monetizing, 190–191
Exxon Valdez, 192

F

Facilities, performance evaluation systems
for, 213–216
Fagg, B.P., 302
FASB, 3
regulations, 256–260
Fava, J.A., 295
Fenn, D., Jr., 268, 290
Fenn, S.A., 293
Fiksel, J., 294
FIN 14, 257–258
Finance checklist, corporate strategy
implementation, 246
Financial Accounting Standards Board
(FASB); *see* FASB
Financial reporting systems, 84–86
First National Bank of Minneapolis, cor-
porate social reporting and, 271
Fischer, K., 294
Fisher, George, 72

Flamholtz, E., 293
Ford Motor Co., 281
waste management, 43–44
Forecasting, capital budgeting and;
see Capital budgeting
Fortune, M., 185, 297
Frank, P.B., 294
Freedman, M., 294
Freeman, M.A., 294
Freierman, R., 290
Friedman, Frank B., 103, 104, 294
Full-cost accounting, 158–162
Full-cost pricing, 158–160
Future costs for current sins, 148–149
Fuzzy logic, capital budgeting and,
185–187, 196–197

G

Gable, A.R., 192, 292
Gatian, A.W., 187, 290
GATT, 15–16
Gavin, J.G., 294
General Motors, 24, 281
standards for environmental reports, 125
waste management, 43–44
George, S., 290
Gibby, D.J., 153, 294
Giuntini, R., 303
Global Environmental Management
Initiative (GEMI), 66
Goals, 7–8
performance evaluation systems,
217–218
sustainable development, 8–9
Goldman, L., 291
Goldstein, J., 302
Government partnerships, environmental
strategy and, 17–20
Graedel, T.E. 294
Graham, J., 294
Graham, J.D., 294
Gray, G.M., 195, 294
Gray, R.H., 295
Greenberg, R.S., 295
Green Lights Program (EPA), 19, 21
Greeno, J.L., 101, 103, 295

Guide to Effective Environmental Auditing, 102

H

Hahn, R., 180, 295
Hahn, W., 303
Harmon, M., 129, 295
Harrison, L.L., 295
Hawken, P., 295
Hayes, D.J., 295
Hector, Gary, 295
Hedonic-pricing method, 190
Hedstrom, G.S., 295
Hellman, Thomas M., 20, 37–38
Henn, C.L., 295, 304
Herman Miller, 281
    waste management, 45
Hetland, J.L., 296
Himelstein, L., 296
Hochman, M.N., 296, 302
Hochman, S.D., 296, 302
Hudson, S.P., 192, 292
Hyde Tools, 281
    cost management and, 156–157

I

IBM, 125, 281
    external audits of external environ-
        mental reports, 135–136
    information systems, environmental, 84
    take-back programs, 33
    waste management, 44, 46
ICI, 281
    disclosures, financial, 119
    performance evaluation systems, 229
Identifying and tracking, costs, 149–153
Individuals, performance appraisals and;
        See Performance evaluation
        systems
Information systems, environmental, 73,
    75–87
    accounting and reporting systems,
        78–82
    links with other systems, 86–87

Information systems *(continued)*
    management accounting and financial
        reporting, 84–86
    management decisions and, 75–77
    other systems, 83–84
    for waste management, 76–79
Innovation
    balanced scorecard and, 73
    environmental strategy and, 14
Institute of Management Accountants
        (IMA), 9
    social accounting studies, 276–278
The Interior, U.S. Department of, 192
Internal environmental auditing systems,
        88–105
    acquisitions/divestments and, 93–96
    assurance letters and, 93
    audits, types of, 89–92
    broader audits, 100–102
    compliance audits, 89–90
    defined, 88–89
    departments for, 94
    due diligence audits, 90
    eco-auditing, 99
    environmental liability accrual audit, 91
    environmental management system
        audits, 90
    external reporting and; *see* External
        environmental reports
    pollution prevention audit, 91
    practices and programs, 96–97
    product audit, 92–94
    self-audits, importance of, 93
    standard for; *see* Standards
    treatment, storage, and disposal facility
        audit, 90–91
International Chamber of Commerce
        (ICC), 88, 120–121
International companies, EH&S organiza-
        tional structure, 60–62
ISO 9000/14000 standards, 128–129

J

Jaffe, A.B., 15, 18, 296
Jain, R.K., 296

Japan, Law for Promotion of Utilization of
Recyclable Resources, 32
Johnson, F.R., 261, 292
Johnson, L.T., 251n, 257, 296

K

Kansas City Division, AlliedSignal,
213–216
Kaplan, J.M., 276
Kaplan, Robert S., 72–74, 290, 291, 296
Karch, K., 296
Kenworth, L., 303
Kinder, P., 296
Kindler, Hans, 17
Kinzer, S., 32, 296
Kleiner, A., 296
Kleiner, B.M., 297
Koechlin, D., 195, 297
Koellner, M.S., 290
Kolluru, R.V., 297, 306
Kozmetsky, G., 291
KPMG Peat Marwick, 263
Kreuze, J., 297
Krutilla, J.V., 297
Kula, E., 193, 297

L

Landekich, S., 291
Law for Promotion of Utilization of
Recyclable Resources, Japan, 32
Lawrence, C.A., 185, 297
Lawrence, C.M., 297
Laws, environmental performance and,
5–7; *see also* Regulations
Leamer, E.E., 289
Ledgerwood, G., 297
Legacy costing, 162
Lent, T., 25, 297
Liabilities
accrual audits, 91
under CERCLA, 255–256
criminal, 5–6
estimated, capital budgeting and,
196–197

Liabilities *(continued)*
financial condition and, 4–5
Life cycle assessments (LCAs), 34–43,
155–156
ESI (environmental strategy imple-
mentation) and, 51–52
Life cycle costing, 35–36, 154–156
Lind, R.C., 297
Links, data, 86–87
Linowes, D.F., 268, 297
Lorensen, L., 297
Lucas, A., 298
Lutz, R., 291
Lydenberg, S.D., 296

M

Maastricht Treaty, 16
McCommons, J., 298
Macdonald, K. Linn, 106
McDonald's, 281
take-back programs, 32
TQEM (total quality environmental
management) and, 66
waste management, 45
waste reduction, 46–47
McDonough, J.J., 293
McGovern, L., 300
Mackenzie, J.C., 46, 290
McLaren Hart (engineering firm),
137–138
McLean, R.A.N., 300
McNichols, M., 290
Macve, R., 298
Maisel, L.S., 291
Makower, J., 22, 298
Malcolm Baldrige National Quality
Award, 70
Management, of costs, 156–157
Management accounting, 248–249
and financial reporting systems, 84–86
Managers
commitment of, to environmental issues,
7–8, 26–27
decisions by, information systems and,
75–77

Managers *(continued)*
  guidelines, corporate strategy imple-
    mentation, 245–248
  performance evaluation systems,
    225
  senior, performance evaluation and, 217
Manufacturing facilities, age of, 17
Marburg, S., 291
Marchant, G.E., 298
Marcil, A., 298
Market-price method, 190
Martin, Dale, 170, 172, 298
Maunders, K., 295
MD&A section, 260–261
Meade, N.F., 192, 291
Merchant, K.A., 298
MERIT (measured equity return incentive
    term) awards, 215–216
Meyer, Stephen, 15, 298
Mezzo, L., 298
Miakisz, J., 215, 298
Migros Cooperatives, 281
  life cycle assessment (LCA) and, 41
Miller, C.G., 86n, 292, 300
Miller, G., 300
Minnesota Mining & Manufacturing (3M);
    see 3M
Mishan, E.J., 275, 298
Mission statements, 7–8
  corporate strategy and, 27–28
  performance evaluation systems, 219
Mitchell, R.C., 192, 298
Mobil Corp., 281
  organizational structure, 53
Monsanto, 281
  disclosures, financial, 112–114
  organizational structure, 53–55
Monte Carlo simulation, 188
Montreal Protocol, 16
Morrissey, E., 291
Morton, M.S. Scott, 290
Motorola, 281
  waste management, 44
Moulden, J., 291
Muir, W.R., 86n, 292, 300
Muller, K., 195, 287

Mullins, M.L., 298
Multinational corporations, regulations
    and, 15–17
Murphy, M., 251n, 300

N

NAFTA, 15–16, 17
Naimon, J.S., 99, 298
Natural resource damage assessment
    (NRDA), 192, 254
Neidermeyer, A., 299
Nelson, J., 301
Newell, G.E., 297
Newton, Phyllis J., 310
New York State Electric and Gas Corp.,
    193
Niagara Mohawk Power Co. (NMPC), 282
  capital budgeting and, 181–187
  monetizing environmental externalities,
    190–191
  performance evaluation and, 215–216
Nikolai, A., 276, 299
Noranda Forest, 106, 282
  external audits of external environ-
    mental reports, 137
Northern Telecom Ltd., 22, 282
  life cycle assessment (LCA) and, 41–42
Norton, David P., 72–74, 296
NPL (National Priorities List), 4
NPV, 187, 190

O

Occidental Petroleum, 103
O'Connell, P.A., 296, 302
Odegard, B., 302
Oehm, R.M., 291
Oil Pollution Act of 1990, 192
Omer, K., 305
Ontario Hydro, 282
  disclosures, financial, 118
  full-cost accounting and, 160
  monetizing environmental externalities,
    197–200
  and waste taxes, internal, 230

Operations
 effectiveness of, balanced scorecard
  and, 73
 waste reduction through, 46–48
Option assessment, and screening, capital
  budgeting and, 150–189
Option pricing theory, capital budgeting
  and, 195
Organizational structure, EH&S departments; see EH&S departments
Otis Elevator division, information
  systems, 83
Owen, D., 295, 299

P

Pacific Gas & Electric, 27, 282
 environmental audits and, 97
Palmides, J.H., 291
Pariser, D.B., 299
Patella, R., 153, 294
Pava, M.L., 259, 293, 299
Performance evaluation systems, 212–231
 for corporations, 213–216
  scoring, 234–238
 for facilities, 213–216
 for individuals, 225–236
  ABB (Asea Brown Boveri Ltd.),
   227–229
  Alcan Aluminum, 228
  Amoco, 229
  awards and, 229
  Awareness Compliance Tools (ACT)
   for Environmental Responsibility,
   220
  Browning-Ferris Industries (BFI),
   219–226
  Chevron, 217, 228, 230
  Ciba-Geigy, 237
  DuPont, 226–227
  employee involvement and, 218
  environmental multipliers and, 219–226
  goals and, 217–218
  ICI, 229
  mission statements and, 219
  Polaroid, 227

Performance evaluation systems (cont'd)
 senior management, 217
 Sun Co., 227
 MERIT (measured equity return incen-
  tive term) award, 213–216
 for strategic business units, 222–225
 and waste taxes, internal, 230
PERI (Public Environmental Reporting
  Initiative), 125–26
Peterson, S.R., 296
Phillips, T.J., 303
Phillips Metallurgical, Inc., 271
Phillips Screw Co., 271
Pojasek, R., 301
Polaroid, 125, 282
 accounting and reporting system, 78–82
 performance evaluation systems, 227
Pollution prevention
 audit, 91
 Environment 2000 and, 39
Popoff, Frank, 17–18, 159, 299
Porter, Michael E., 13–14, 299
Portney, P.R., 289, 295
Post, James, 270
Post, J.F., 299
President's Commission on Environmental
  Quality (PCEQ), 67
Price Waterhouse, 96–97, 154
 external environmental reports
  external audits of, 136
 surveys of, 262–263
Pricing, full-cost, 158–160
Probabilities, Monte Carlo simulation and,
  188
Procter & Gamble, 282
 environmental audits and, 97
 TQEM (total quality environmental
  management) and, 66, 68
Product audits, 91–92
Profitability
 balanced scorecard and, 73
 environmental responsibility and, 5
Prosecution, criminal, 6
Protzman, F., 299
Purchasing
 checklist, corporate strategy implementation, 246

Purchasing *(continued)*
  waste reduction through, 46–48
Pyburn, P.J., 292

R

Rabinowitz, D.L., 251n, 300
Radner, R., 289
Randall, A., 193, 300
Rappaport, A., 20n, 300
RCRA (Resource Conservation and
  Recovery Act), 4, 91, 253
Recycling
  and the take-back principle, 32–34
  Vehicle Recycling Partnership, 43–44
Redesign, product and process, for waste
  reduction, 43–46
Reeve, J.M., 187, 290
Regan, M.B., 296
Regulations, 251–265
  accounting, 256–260
    FIN 14, 257–258
    MD&A, 260–261
    SEC regulation SK, 259–260
    SEC SAB 92, 259
    SFAS 5, 256–257
  CERCLA (Comprehensive
    Environmental Response,
    Compensation, and Liability Act),
    90, 192, 254–255
  Clean Air Act (CAA), 252–253
  Clean Water Act (CWA), 253
  and competitiveness, international,
    14–15
  international, multinational corporations
    and, 15–17
  RCRA (Resource Conservation and
    Recovery Act of 1976), 4, 91,
    253
  SARA; *see* SARA (Superfund Amend-
    ment and Reauthorization Act)
Research
  corporate environmental performance
    study/report, 9–13
  surprises, corporate strategy imple-
    mentation, 238–243

Resource Planning Associates, Inc., 271
Responsible care initiative, 66, 127–128
Rice, F., 300
Rice, V.R., 300
Riordan, D.E., 300
Risk assessment, capital budgeting and,
  193–194
Robertaccio, F.L., 301
Roberts, M., 298
Roberts, R.Y., 259, 261–262, 300
Robins, N., 292
Robinson, S.N., 16–17, 295, 300
Rockwell International, 21, 282
  EH&S organization, 55–56
Rohm and Haas, 282
  disclosures, financial, 118–119
Rouse, R.W., 291
Roussey, R.S., 300
Rubenstein, D.B., 300
Ruckelshaus, William, 109–111
Russell, M., 300
Russell, W.G., 300

S

SARA (Superfund Amendment and
  Reauthorization Act), 21, 114,
  254–255
  claims, 6–7
  costs and, 146
  innocent landowner defense, 104
  program sites, 4
Sarokin, D.J., 300
Saunders, Tedd, 47, 300
Savage, D., 178, 302
Schmidheiny, Stephan, 15, 23–24, 300
Schot, J., 294
Schuman, H., 289
Scorecard, corporate environmental
  performance, 235
Scovill Manufacturing Co., 271, 272
SEC
  disclosures, financial, 108–109
  EPA, coordination with, 261–262
  and MD&A section, financial reports,
    260–261

SEC *(continued)*
  regulation SK, 259–260
  SAB 92 regulation, 259
SEDUE (Mexican Department of Urban
      Development and Ecology), 22
Self-audits, internal environmental
      auditing systems, 93
Selling, T.I., 309
Senior management, performance
      evaluation systems, 217
SEPs (supplemental environmental
      projects), 22
SFAS 5, 256–257
Shank, J.K., 158, 301
Shanker, H.M., 94, 301
Shareholders, 64
Shell Cast Corp., 271
Siegel, P.H., 305
Silverstein, M., 301
Singh, D.K., 290
Skalak, S.L., 300
Smart, B., 301
Smith, J.K., 303
Smith, V.K., 192, 291
Smolin, M.R., 296
Social accounting
  cost-benefit analyses and, 271–276
  environmental economics and, 271–276
  failure of, 2–5, 278
  previous studies, Institute of
      Management Accountants (IMA),
      276–278
  social audits and, 270–271
  system, 269–270
Social audits
  social accounting and, 270–271
  social responsibility and, 267–270
Social responsibility, 267–270
Society of Environmental Toxicology and
      Chemistry (SETAC), 36
Solow, R., 289
Southern Co., 282
  disclosures, financial, 114–118
  environmental audits and, 97, 98
Sperber, S.R., 300
Spitzer, M.A., 301
Stacey, G.S., 296

Staff support, EH&S department, 59
Stagliano, A.J., 294
Stakeholders
  identified, 64
  total stakeholder analysis (TSA); *see*
      Total stakeholder analysis (TSA)
Standards
  for external environmental reports; *see*
      External environmental reports
  internal environmental auditing systems,
      lack of, 102–104
Stark, Richard D., 76n, 290
Stavins, R.N., 296
Strategic advantages, of environmental
      management, 6
Strategic Advisory Group on the
      Environment (SAGE), 100
Strategic business units, performance eval-
      uation systems for, 213–216
Strategic cost management (SCM), 158
Street, E., 297
Sun Co., 7, 58, 282
  acquisition and divestments, 94
  centralized vs. decentralized EH&S
      management, 59–60
  disclosures, financial, 112
  EH&S committee, 55
  external environmental reports, 130
  external audits of, 134–136
  performance evaluation systems, 227
  standards for environmental reports,
      124
Suppliers, 64
Supreme Court, 18
Surma, J.P., 291, 301
Sustainable development, 8–9, 15, 16, 19
  environmental strategy and, 22–25
  U.N. Business Council for, 100

                         T

Take-back principle, recycling and, 32–34
Tellus Institute, 177,178
Therivel, R., 297
33/50 program (EPA), 20–21
Thomas, L., 301

Thornton, Grant, 22, 153, 302
3M, 281
    life cycle assessment (LCA) and, 42
    organizational structure, 53, 54
    TQEM (total quality environmental
        management) and, 66
    waste management information systems,
        76–78
3Rs, for minimizing environmental
    impacts, 31
Tooker, Gary, 44
Tools for analysis, corporate environmen-
    tal impacts; *see* Corporate envi-
    ronmental impacts
Top management, commitment to environ-
    mental issues, 7–8, 26–27
Toshiba Corp., 63
Total cost assessment (TCA), 174–179
Total quality management (TQM), 44, 57,
    69
Total stakeholder analysis (TSA), 36, 48,
    62–66
    capital budgeting and, 172–173
    community interests and, 64, 66
    costs and, 148–149
    full-cost accounting and, 161–163
Toxic Release Inventory (TRI), 119
TQEM (total quality environmental
    management), 15, 66–69
Travel-cost method, 190
Treatment, storage, and disposal facility
    audit, 90–91
Tschritter, K., 302
Tuppen, C., 48, 301

U

U.N. Business Council for sustainable
    development, 100
Unger, C.A., 295
Union Carbide, 58, 283
    capital budgeting EH&S checklist,
        199–211
    capital expenditure approval process,
        167, 168, 169
    costs and, 153–154

Union Carbide *(continued)*
    disclosures, financial, 108–109
    environmental audits and, 97–98
    external environmental reports, 130
    performance evaluation systems,
        230–231
    responsible care initiative, 129
Union Electric, 194
U.S. Department of Defense (DOD), life
    cycle costing and, 35–36
U.S. Department of Energy, performance
    evaluation and, 213–215
U.S. Department of the Interior, 192
U.S. Sentencing Commission, 5–6
United States v. Fleet Factors Corp., 94
United Technologies, 283
    disclosures, financial, 112
    information systems, environmental, 83
Unocal, 285
    take-back programs, 32–33
Urban, L.V., 296
UST (underground storage tanks)
    program, 4

V

Valdez Principles, 121; *see also* CERES
    (Coalition for Environmentally
    Responsible Economies)
van der Linde, Claas, 13–14, 299
Van Wassenhove, L.N., 84, 292
Virginia, Commonwealth of
    partnership programs and, 22
    sustainable development and, 8
Vondra, A.A., 301

W

Wagner, M.J., 294
Wald, M.L., 302
Walker, K. Grahame, 7–8
Walker, K.D., 294
Walley, N., 302
Walters, D., 295
Wapman, K., 294
Warren, J.L., 303

Waste
  management of
    Dow Chemical, 31
    information systems and, 76–79
  reduction of
    through operations and purchasing,
      46–48
    product and process redesign for,
      43–46
    Waste Reduction Always Pays
      (WRAP), 31
  taxes, internal, 230
Weil, R.L., 294
Weiss, E., 193, 267n, 293
Weitz, K.A., 155, 302
Wells, R.P., 25, 296, 297, 302
Weyerhaeuser Co., 283
  disclosures, financial, 112, 122
  take-back programs, 33
White, A.L., 178, 302
White, T.M., 302
Whitehead, B.W., 290, 302
Willborg, B.M., 290
Williams, G., 257, 303

Willig, J.T., 303
Willits, S.D., 311
Winsemius, P., 180, 303
Wise, M., 2, 303
WMX Technologies, 283
  external audits of external environ-
    mental reports, 137, 138
Wolfe, J., 128, 311
Woolard, Ed, 17, 169
World Commission on Environment and
  Development, 1–2, 7

X

Xerox, 283
  take-back programs, 33–34
  TQEM (total quality environmental
    management) and, 66
  waste management, 45–46

Y

Young, S.M., 290

The IMA Foundation for Applied Research, Inc.
Trustees, 1994–95

Foundation Officers

President
Robert C. Miller
The Boeing Company
Seattle, Washington

Treasurer
Joseph G. Harris
IMA Vice President of
Finance
The Upjohn Company
Kalamazoo, Michigan

Secretary
Gary M. Scopes, CAE
IMA Executive Director
Institute of Management
Accountants
Montvale, New Jersey

Trustees by Virtue of the Bylaws

Keith Bryant, Jr., CMA
IMA President
University of Alabama at Birmingham
Birmingham, Alabama

Joseph G. Harris
IMA Vice President of Finance
The Upjohn Company
Kalamazoo, Michigan

William J. Ihlanfeldt, CPA
IMA President-Elect
Formerly with Shell Oil Company
Houston, Texas

Leo M. Loiselle, CPA
IMA Chair
Loiselle & Beatham, CPAs
Bangor, Maine

Gary M. Scopes, CAE
IMA Executive Director
Institute of Management Accountants
Montvale, New Jersey

Robert G. Weiss, CPA
IMA Vice President of Professional
Relations
Formerly with Schering-Plough Corporation
Palm Beach Gardens, Florida

Appointed Trustees

Victor Brown, CPA
George Mason University
Fairfax, Virginia

Paul P. Danesi, Jr.
Texas Instruments, Inc.
Attleboro, Massachusetts

Henry J. Davis, CMA, CPA
Reliance Electric Company
Greenville, South Carolina

Lou Jones
Caterpillar Company
Peoria, Illinois

Robert J. Melby
Defense Contract Audit Agency
Smyrna, Georgia

Kenneth A. Merchant, CPA
University of Southern California
Los Angeles, California

Robert C. Miller
The Boeing Company
Seattle, Washington

Robert C. Young
Digital Equipment Corporation
Nashua, New Hampshire

Institute of Management Accountants
Committee on Research 1993–94

Dennis L. Neider, CMA
Chairman
Price Waterhouse
New York, New York

Jack C. Bailes
Oregon State University
Corvallis, Oregon

Yolanda L. Clem, CMA
Phillips Petroleum Company
Bellaire, Texas

Frederick M. Cole
University of North Florida
Jacksonville, Florida

James P. Conley
Ernst & Young
Atlanta, Georgia

Paul P. Danesi, Jr.
Worldwide Products
Texas Instruments, Inc.
Attleboro, Massachusetts

Henry J. Davis, CMA
Reliance Electric Company
Greenville, South Carolina

Leslie A. Karnauskas, CMA
Ohmeda
Louisville, Colorado

Otto B. Martinson, CMA
Old Dominion University
Norfolk, Virginia

Charles D. Mecimore
University of North Carolina
Greensboro, North Carolina

Robert J. Melby
Defense Contract Audit Agency
Memphis, Tennessee

Kenneth A. Merchant
University of Southern California
Los Angeles, California

Robert C. Miller
The Boeing Company
Seattle, Washington

Wayne J. Morse
Clarkson University
Potsdam, New York

W. Ron Ragland
Martin Marietta Energy Systems, Inc.
Oak Ridge, Tennessee

Michael Robinson
Baylor University
Waco, Texas

Harold P. Roth, CMA
University of Tennessee
Knoxville, Tennessee

Arjan T. Sadhwani
University of Akron
Akron, Ohio

Richard B. Troxel, CMA
Capital Accounting
Washington, D.C.

Ray Vander Weele, CMA
Merrill Lynch
Grand Rapids, Michigan

Anthony A. Varricchio, Jr., CMA
Dexter Nonwovens
Windsor Locks, Connecticut

Robert C. Young
Digital Equipment Corp.
Nashua, New Hampshire